COUNTER INTELLIGENCE

COUNTER INTELLIGENCE

WHERE TO EAT IN

THE REAL

LOS ANGELES

JONATHAN GOLD

 An LA Weekly Book for St. Martin's Press ≋ New York

LA Weekly Books is a trademark of LA Weekly Media, Inc.

www.stmartins.com

Book design by Michelle McMillian

Library of Congress Cataloging-in-Publication Data

Gold, Jonathan.
    Counter intelligence : where to eat in the real Los Angeles / Jonathan Gold.
    p. cm.
    ISBN: 978-0-312-26723-0 ISBN: 0-312-26723-1
    1. Restaurants—California—Los Angeles—Guidebooks.   I. Title.

TX907.3.C2 L673 2000
647.95794'94—dc21
                                                                    00-034521

P 1

INTRODUCTION

For a while in my early twenties, my only clearly articulated ambition was to eat at least once at every restaurant on Pico Boulevard, starting with the fried *yuca* dish served at a *pupuseria* near where the street began in downtown Los Angeles, and working methodically westward toward the chili fries at Tom's #5 near the beach. It seemed a reasonable enough alternative to graduate school at the time.

After I'd finished work each day proofreading galleys at a legal newspaper near city hall, I would walk to the next restaurant on Pico for dinner. Then I would buy an orange from a street vendor and catch a bus the rest of the way home—I lived on Pico too, over a kosher butcher shop near Robertson. When the enormity of the adventure seemed overwhelming, I might buy a taco at one restaurant, a hamburger at the next and a bowl of *chilate y nuegado* at a third. I ate my way almost to Century City that year, from the El Salvador Cafe all the way to the old Roxbury Pharmacy grill.

I discovered the Persian-Jewish neighborhood around Beverly, the remarkable strip of soul food restaurants between La Brea and Fairfax, the pan-ethnic zone around Westwood. I ate at Pico restaurants—Mr. Coleslaw Burger, the *carnitas* place on the corner of Vermont with old boxing snapshots on the walls, Nu-Way, Chicken Georgia, Ben's Place, Kong Joo Goat Soup, Carl's Barbecue,—that have since vanished, leaving no traces more obvious than a shiny patch of sidewalk or the ghost of a painted sign. I especially liked the neighborhood, mostly Central American, that had sprung up between Vermont and the Harbor Freeway, thousands upon thousands of Guatemalans and Salvadorans who crowded Pico until dark, choosing toys from big displays set up in grocery-store parking lots, buying mayonnaise-smeared ears of corn from streetcorner pushcarts. The restaurants in that neighborhood were good too, and I learned to eat everything from marinated octopus—at El Pulpo Loco—to the griddle-baked Salvadoran corn-cakes called *pupusas*, from El Parian's Jalisco-style goat stew to El Nica's giant Nicaraguan tamales, from Cuban fried rice to Guatemalan *pepían* to the Ecuadoran mashed potato fritters called *llapingachos*. Pico, in a certain sense, was where I learned to eat.

I have spent the years since then working my way through the trenches of ethnic cooking in Los Angeles, hitting the first tentative cafés of Thais and Oaxacans and Laotians as they made their way into the country and tracking the increasingly complex restaurant cultures that resulted as well as documenting the vast profusion of Mexican restaurants in East Los Angeles and the extraordinary torrent of Chinese cooking into the San Gabriel Valley, which is now among the most remarkable restaurant communities in the world. It means something, I think, when Thai people learn how to cook Vietnamese noodles for Hong Kong–born teenagers, and as big a fan as I am of authenticity, it probably means something good.

If you live in Los Angeles, you become used to having your city explained to you by others, most frequently by others who jet in for a week or two and report on the world that they find within a few miles of their Beverly Hills hotel suites. Los Angeles is a city of nets, we are told, or a city of angles, the capital of the third world or a universe captured wholly within the whirring, oversize Rolodexes maintained by Jeffrey Katzenberg. Sometimes visitors will stumble across, say, a Cambodian neighborhood large and self-sustaining enough for a person with modest needs to spend his entire life speaking nothing but Khmer, and naïvely assume that nobody on the Westside or in Pasadena has experienced such a thing. But we have. And I have been lucky enough to have been able to write about Los Angeles cooking as an Angeleno.

Metropolitan Los Angeles can be an overwhelming place, endless and illogical, stretching for a hundred miles on some axes until the city grid melts into desert, high mountains, or the sea. A hundred different languages are spoken in the hallways of the city's high schools. Do you crave Chinese food? The local Chinese Yellow Pages weighs in at close to 2,500 pages. Have you a taste for Central American cooking? There may be as many as 500 Salvadoran restaurants in central Los Angeles, and at least half of them are pretty good. Los Angeles is the best place in the country to eat the cooking of Thailand and Burma, Guatemala and Ethiopia, Taiwan and any of a dozen states of Mexico.

While sometimes it seems as if the rest of the country still struggles to redefine the modern American chophouse, Los Angeles is a city where a great meal is as likely to come from Koreatown or the three-million-strong Mexican community as it is from Beverly Hills, a city where where inspiration is often as close as the cold case of the local Vietnamese deli.

What I'm trying to say, I think, is that the most authentic Los Angeles experiences tend to involve a mild sense of dislocation, of tripping into a rabbit hole and popping up in some wholly unxpected location. The greatest Los Angeles cooking, real Los Angeles cooking, has first a sense of wonder about it, and only then a sense of place, because the place it has a sense of is likely to be somewhere else entirely. Los Angeles is, after all, where certain parts of town have stood in for Connecticut or Indiana so often on TV that they look more authentic than the real thing; where neighborhoods are called Little India, Little Tokyo, Little Central America and Koreatown; where a typical residential block might include a couple of Spanish haciendas, a Tudor mansion, two thatched Cotswald cottages, a Palladian villa and a creampuff of an imitation Loire chateau.

As people here like to say, often when contemplating a piece of Peruvian-style sushi or one of the Teriyaki Donut stands that have popped up in Quentin Tarantino flicks: *only in L.A.*

Each of the restaurants in this book was visited anonymously and repeatedly, and each of them serves at least one dish that is the best of its kind in the city. Still: cooks and restaurant owners lead rich, chaotic lives, and any of the information in this book is liable to change for no apparent reason; usually on the day you've driven 35 miles to taste the crawfish etouffée.

COUNTER INTELLIGENCE

A

AGUNG

3909 BEVERLY BLVD., LOS ANGELES; (323) 660-2113. MON.–SAT., NOON–9P.M.

The overeducated misfits who frequent East Hollywood's ethnic restaurants have their well-known favorites: Zankou for chicken; Sanamluang for Thai noodles; Marouch for hummus, grilled quail, and *fattouch*. For *café con leche*, there's Tropical; for weissbeer and wurst, the Red Lion. And Agung near downtown has become the one place to go when you want avocado in your coffee.

Agung is a tidy, cinder-block Indonesian restaurant in an untidy neighborhood, a soothing world of spicy curries and continuous soft hits squeezed between a medical building and a lube pit a block or two south of the Hollywood Freeway. It's a tiny, family-run place, decorated with travel posters and batik. The customers seem to be mostly Indonesian students from USC and Indonesian-speaking Dutch guys involved in international trade. They always have avocado in their coffee.

Iced coffee and the creamy fruit go pretty well together, especially when blended with milk and ice into the fluffy consistency of a malted—coffee brings out a sweet richness in the avocado that isn't apparent in guacamole. If Tuscan peasants had stumbled across this combination, *es alpukat*, people would be lining up outside Melrose coffeehouses to drink the stuff from little cups. Agung is famous for its other beverages too, a Bordeaux-colored drink called *es cincau* that tastes a little like jellied Robitussin and a rosewater-scented drink called *es kelapa mundi* that's spiked with gelatinous shreds of baby coconut. Everybody seems to like a sweet, cool drink that's made with coconut, jackfruit, and avocado, which tastes a little like a malted from Mars.

Agung is probably the best place in California to try Padang-style cooking, the fiery, complex cooking of central Sumatra, but you'll find pretty good versions

1

of the dishes that would be standard eating if Indonesian food were as common as Thai—clumpy fried rice with scallions and ham; delicious fried *bakmi* noodles with dark soy, shrimp, and plenty of cabbage; the chicken soup *soto ayam*, thick with fresh vegetables and fragrant with spice. The crisp lettuce salad called *gado-gado* is dressed with chile-spiked peanut butter and sprinkled with crushed shrimp chips. There's decent *satay*, sweeter than the Thai kind, skewers of grilled chicken, pork or lamb, and an unusual, Sumatra-style tongue *satay* served with a pasty Indonesian velouté. The turmeric-stained lamb stew is fine, if a little ordinary.

And the Sumatran dishes shine. *Empek-empek* may sound like a noise made by a small Sumatran lizard, but is essentially a crusty turnover of house-pounded fish cake stuffed with egg, steamed, and fried. It comes cut into peppery, rubbery chunks, served in a bowl with glass noodles and diced cucumber floating in a soy broth. It's the sort of thing Japanese *kaiseki* restaurants are always trying to do but never quite get right. Or try *lontong*, loosely packed rice cakes cooked with mixed meats in a coconut broth, or *telur belado*, a big tofu patty that's been battered, fried, and doused with sweet, dark soy.

The best way to eat at Agung may be to order several items from the section of the menu called "rice table combination," tapas-size portions of crispy fried chicken in a vivid fresh chile sauce, curried beef, chilied hard-boiled egg, or Sumatra-style curry-roasted beef—served with a big plate of rice—that cost about a buck and a half apiece.

Don't miss the smoky *dendeng belado*, slices of beef fried until they attain the size, shape and crunchiness of Pringles.

ALADDIN FALAFEL

2180 S.WESTWOOD BLVD., LOS ANGELES; (310) 446-1174. MON.–SAT., 11A.M.–11P.M.; SUN., NOON–10P.M.

Consider the falafel, the Middle East's favorite grease bomb, a drippy, screaming-orange postcard from culinary cultures that would really rather be remembered for kebabs, seasoned rice, and sheep's brains garnished with sautéed pine nuts. Most food from Arabic-speaking countries is healthy, sparkling fresh, breathing the vitality of the earth. But a falafel sandwich is an oozing, stinking mess of fried chickpea batter and garlicky sesame goo that may have more calories per ounce than pure hog lard.

Still, as with cheeseburgers and sex, even bad falafel can be pretty good. I grew up craving the industrial-grade falafel from the cafeteria next to the molecular biology building at UCLA, and I still sneak down there once or twice a year for a hit of the sloppy, odiferous stuff. I am no stranger to the oil-soaked pleasures of Falafel King, whose vat of boiling orange grease has been bubbling in its

Westwood window for generations, or to the reasonably austere sandwiches served at Fairfax-area stands like Eat-a-Pita. Falafel usually finds its way onto the table at the Armenian-Lebanese restaurants Marouch, Caroussel, and Carnival. I even have a certain fondness for the hard, Sahara-dry falafel reluctantly served at Zankou Chicken, a dish that I have never seen anybody else actually buy. The best falafel place in Los Angeles County is Golden Dome, a Palestinian-owned restaurant in Bellflower, but lately, I have been going to Aladdin Falafel so often that my truck practically guides itself into the restaurant's tiny parking lot. In contrast to the other falafel stands in town, which are mostly Israeli owned, Aladdin Falafel is run by Palestinian-Americans, and the flavor is subtly different, smokier, tinged with cool. A sign posted in the window announces *halal* (Islamic kosher) meat, and a framed prayer is mounted high on a wall. The air is perfumed with cumin, garlic, clean oil. Classic Arabic riffage wails from the restaurant's stereo—a small, Tom Schnabel–ish selection of Middle Eastern CDs rests in a spinning case near the cash register—and even the Formica of the main counter is inlaid with blocky Islamic designs.

If you have been to a Middle Eastern restaurant lately, you can probably recite Aladdin's menu by heart: lamb kebab plates, rotisserie chicken, sour grape leaves stuffed with rice and vegetables. The *shwarma* is fine, thin, garlicky shavings of extremely well-done meat, flavored with cinnamon and cloves and sliced off a rotating spit; three plump, little grilled lamb chops, slightly grainy, are not precisely what you'd find at a grand restaurant like Campanile, but are a good value for eight bucks. The *tabbouleh* salad is fresh and tart, with parsley enough to deodorize a dozen people were the dish not so laden with garlic; the *baba ghanoush* is smooth, fresh, and cool. With every dinner comes a bowl of terrific cumin-laced lentil soup, yellow as a school bus, mellowed with a squirt of citrus.

But you've come for the falafel. It is a small miracle, an oblate Ping-Pong ball of ground chickpeas whose thick, tawny crust gives way to a dense interior, mildly spiced, barely greasy, tinted green with puréed herbs. Without the benefit of tahini, most falafel collapses into dry powder under the teeth; this one is moister, a little more resilient, almost chewy, and you may go through an entire plate of the stuff (it is also available dressed as a sandwich) before realizing you have forgotten to dampen the patties with sauce. On a plate with hummus, peppers, salad, and tart pickled turnips, Aladdin's falafel is a satisfying lunch whether you roll it into a pita or not.

ALAMEDA SWAP MEET

ALAMEDA AVE. AT 45TH ST. MON., WED.–FRI., 10A.M.–7P.M., SAT. AND SUN., 8A.M.–7P.M. MANY OF THE FOOD STALLS ARE OPEN WEEKENDS ONLY.

The Alameda Swap Meet may be the most overwhelming place you can visit on a Sunday afternoon, an immense converted factory complex south of downtown swarming with people, stuffed with hundreds of stalls selling everything from sea-turtle extract to straw ranchero hats, fluffy white first-communion dresses to the latest in pinstriped gangsta wear, and alive with the racket of two dozen pumped CD players blasting trumpet-bright *norteño* hits. You are reminded that the Mexican population of Los Angeles is second only to that of Mexico City itself.

The crush to get into the parking lot can sometimes back up Alameda for as much as a mile, and the streets teem with trucks selling tacos, or fresh mackerel, or bootleg rap cassettes, or a queer, sweet cactus drink called *lechugilla* that is sold in plastic packets that resemble silicon implants.

Outside at the swap meet, in a vast sort of asphalt plaza that separates the two main buildings, the fences are decorated with Mexican flags and portraits of Mexican revolutionaries. Small children totter about clutching cotton candy and ears of roasted corn. Sometimes a DJ presides over hundreds of couples executing complicated two-steps. It's a vast fiesta every weekend of the year. Around the perimeter of the plaza and stretching back along an arcade to the southernmost parking lot is a bewildering succession of food stalls that perfume the air with grilled meat and sputtering oil, and a certain high note of stickiness—every kind of Mexican food you could possibly walk around with, and a few that are destined to land straight on your shoes.

The big food stall under the awning closest to the main building is a full-on Mexican restaurant without the walls, featuring grilled chicken, *carne asada* and pretty good steam-table dishes: *chile verde*, chicken *mole*, and a really good, spicy goat-meat stew the color of fresh blood. The big awning at the other end shades a Salvadoran stall where a woman pats *pupusas* one after the other, frying them hard and stacking them up in front of her. The *pupusas* are fantastic, if not the subtlest version of the cheese-stuffed corn patties, ready to be mounded with the spicy cabbage slaw called *curtido* and moistened with a fiery, brick-red smoked-chile sauce. Around toward the south parking lot, marinated flank steak sizzles on steel-drum grills until it's tough enough to go into tacos. Across a walkway, at a stall named Tejuno, there are tostadas smeared with beans, garnished with lettuce and ripe tomato, and topped with slices of tart pickled pigskin or tasty roast pork. Outside the El Texanito ice cream shop, a stand specializes in *huaraches*, which are tasty sandal-shaped patties of *masa* mounded with diced *nopales* (cactus), sour cream, and peppery, crisp bits of extremely well-done meat.

The Alameda Swap Meet is the land of chile and lime, which are dribbled on freshly fried potato chips, sprinkled on popcorn, daubed on sliced mangos, squirted on the delicious *ceviche*, and splashed onto marinated-shrimp tostadas served at El Bucanero seafood, a concession hard by the main building's entrance. (As far as I know, there is no chile in any of the sweet, hospital-green limeade the vendors ladle out from iced glass demijohns, nor in the orangeade, nor in the canteloupe drink.)

One popular dish here, served in several different places, involves chile, lime, mayonnaise, kernels of fresh corn, and a generous squirt of Liquid Parkay, all mixed up in a cardboard bowl. It's obliquely delicious in its way, although not the sort of thing you'd smear on a slab of La Brea Bakery bread. You can also get corn that has been barbecued in steel drums until it becomes corn-on-the-cob jerky, chewy enough to chomp on for the duration of a really long drive.

And you can always perform a scientific assessment of the state of *flautas*, those deep-fried rolled-tortilla things that Jack-in-the-Box calls "taquitos," by rigorously testing each of the dozen or so varieties available: fat or thin; topped with sour cream or drenched in guacamole; brittle throughout or kind of bendy in the middle; but especially the meaty ones in the far southeast corner. That's my idea of pure empirical research.

ALEGRIA

3510 SUNSET BLVD., SILVER LAKE; (323) 913-1422. MON.-THURS., 10A.M.-10P.M., FRI. AND SAT., 10A.M.-11P.M.

Alegria is everything you could want in a neighborhood Mexican restaurant, with cool Day of the Dead stuff on the walls, fish tacos on the menu, and a motherly chef-owner, Nadine Trujillo, who may scold you for filling up on chips before dinner. There's no beer, but a waitress will whip up a strawberry-papaya shake for you if somebody's remembered to buy the fruit; if not, the homemade lemon *agua fresca* may be the best lemonade in town. The secret house salsa, made with puréed chipotle chiles and enough garlic to knock an owl out of its tree, is pretty great too.

The restaurant's clientele is the essence of groovy, post-boho Silver Lake—Latino families, spooning gay and lesbian couples, Spaceland regulars, a scattering of coffeehouse guys—searching for satori in pocketbook-size veggie burritos. On Saturday mornings the crowd includes most of the people you used to see in Silver Lake half a dozen years ago, only with one-year-olds instead of Guatemalan friendship bracelets wrapped around their arms. Like the Farmers Market, the bleachers at Dodger Stadium, and the Aztec playground outside Plaza de la Raza, Alegria feels like L.A.

The original Alegria was a grimy taqueria in the parking lot behind the Burrito King in Echo Park, known for its excellent *carne asada* but sparse in its amenities. The newer place, stuffed into a Silver Lake mini-mall space formerly occupied by the great Yucatecan joint Don Luis, is a sweet, family place in an area dominated by squalid taco dives and sterile margarita mills. Trujillo's food is sometimes regional, sometimes not, sometimes chefly, and always intensely personal. The cooking here is both blessed and marred with quirks, the lovable eccentricities you'd expect of food in a Mexican home.

Carne asada, which here means slabs of lime-marinated, grilled skirt steak instead of the usual forty-five grams of grayish beef byproduct, is stuffed into tacos or folded with beans, salsa, and herbs into one of the rare burritos in this world that might actually be worth five clams. When the *carne asada* is crusted with melted cheese, garnished with grilled poblano chiles, and flanked with rolled enchiladas in a sharply delicious roasted tomatillo sauce, it becomes part of a classic Tampiqueña plate.

Soft, salty *carnitas* may lack the garlicky presence and the crackly crunch you look for in lard-braised pork, but the flesh has the sweet, subtle presence of suckling pig. *Tortitas*, egg pancakes studded with aromatic vegetables and flakes of fresh crab, are misshapen, heavy masses, a little oversalted with an elaborate, almost Creole-like seasoning that makes them somehow compelling, even on the odd nights when they are made with artificial crab. *Tacos a la crema*, like deep-fried, potato-stuffed *taquitos* daubed with chunky guacamole and chipotle sauce, are almost up there with the legendary *flautas* at Ciro's.

But sometimes the cooking at Alegria is a little too close to the food at Mom's house. *Chilaquiles*, soggy things not up to the strict standard set by Toribrio Prado at Cha Cha Cha, are overwhelmed by the sharp, green flavor of unripe tomatoes. Something called *budín Moctezuma*, a casserole of tortillas, cheese, and vegetables, tastes a little like something your culinarily challenged aunt Armida might bring to a potluck family picnic.

The best food at Alegria may revolve around Trujillo's extraordinary *mole* sauce: sharp, thick, sweetly complex, with topnotes of smoke, clove, and citrus, lashed with dried-chile heat, black enough to darken the brightest Pepsodent smile. *Enmoladas* are corn tortillas folded around melted cheese and moistened with *mole; chilapitas* are sort of chicken *sopes* doused with the stuff. There is chicken *mole*, and sometimes a Oaxacan-style special of chicken, pork, and plantains cooked in *mole*. You can get a side of *mole* sauce to put on your burrito.

But sometimes you can't get *mole* at all. "The *mole* isn't ready yet," the waitress confessed one time. "It takes three days to make, a million steps, and has something like twenty ingredients. And if you'd been cooking as much as Nadine has been lately, you'd be in a bad mood too."

AL-NOOR

15112 INGLEWOOD AVE., LAWNDALE; (310) 675-4700. TUES.–SUN., 11 A.M.

As much as I like the more refined sort of Indian cuisine, I often find myself drawn to the brute glory of Pakistani cooking instead. Where some Indian curries can be as delicate as butterfly wings, Pakistani curries practically scream with flavor, not just of chiles but big handfuls of cloves, cardamom, and enough cumin to flavor your breath for days.

Southern Indian cooking features rice-flour pancakes as thin and crisp as the burnt sugar on a crème brûlée; Pakistani cuisine has whole-wheat *parathas* so thick and saturated with butter that they could probably stop bullets. The Indian diet is largely vegetarian; I sometimes get the feeling that some Pakistanis would be happy if they could figure out a way to fashion rice, bread, and carrots out of meat, so that they'd never have to put anything in their mouths that wasn't made out of cow, chicken, or goat.

Among the best Pakistani Muslim restaurants in town is the strictly *halal* (the Islamic equivalent of Kosher) Al-Noor, a busy storefront in a Lawndale strip mall, a quick five minutes south of the airport and a straight shot from the 405. Like most Islamic restaurants, Al-Noor is fairly spare, decorated chiefly with great swaths of Arabic script and a travel poster or two, but there are tablecloths, soft lighting, and silk roses encrusted with tears of plastic dew. Al-Noor is a nice place.

It is in a fairly rich restaurant neighborhood, across the street from a Sao Paulo–style fish restaurant located in a former hamburger stand (if you must eat *moqueca* in the South Bay, this is your place), a few blocks down from a pretty good teriyaki hut and a decent Madras-style Indian chicken restaurant, a five-minute drive from the Peruvian restaurants of Lawndale. At noon, the crowd eating lunch can be as varied as any in the South Bay: Pakistani businessmen, Spanish-speaking mechanics and *lassi*-swilling white guys in carpenter's overalls, a tableful of chador-cloaked women nibbling on grilled kebabs a few feet away from a table of fish-eating surfer dudes—all brought together by smoky, garlicky tandoor-barbecued chicken and great slabs of hot bread, a combination that seems to override every ethnic boundary in the world.

The chef once cooked at Bundoo Khan, a Pakistani restaurant in a Koreatown mini-mall around the corner from an apartment I lived in for years, and where I probably stopped in once a week for kebabs and Islamic "hamburgers" before it burned down in the '92 riots, but the menu at Al-Noor is more classically Pakistani, a short document of stews, vegetables, and tandoor-cooked meats.

The restaurant is locally famous for its version of *nehari*, which is more or less the Pakistani national dish, an intense, mahogany concoction of lamb shanks flavored with garlic, chiles, and an immoderate amount of shredded fresh ginger, along with what seems like half the contents of a spice cabinet. *Nehari* can sometimes be a little thin, as genteel as a country French ragout, but the *nehari* here is cooked down to a steaming, creamy mass with the density of a dwarf star, bubbling and glistening with red-tinted oil, a stew substantial enough to fortify three hungry men after a day of hard farm labor or a stringent religious fast.

The other stews at Al-Noor are wonderful too—the brightly flavored brains simmered with curry, and the *haleem*, a deeply flavored beef stew thickened with grain. But what draws the crowds—which often snake out the door on busy weekends— are the tandoor-cooked meats, boneless chunks of chicken *tikka* or hanks of ground beef roasted over super-hot mesquite coals, bits of shaved meat in a powerfully sour marinade, chunks of lamb kebab served on sputtering-hot steel platters with blackened onions, and fresh-baked, if slightly clumsy, garlic *naan*.

For a Pakistani dinner, Al-Noor is just about perfect. Unfortunately, it is just down the street from its only conceivable rival, the wonderful Al-Watan. The friendly rivalry between partisans of the two restaurants may be as pronounced as the one between Woody's followers and Phillips fans in the Crenshaw-district barbecue stakes: Al-Watan is where you'd take your best friend; Al-Noor is where you'd bring your mom.

AL-WATAN

13619 INGLEWOOD AVE., HAWTHORNE; (310) 644-6395. DAILY, 11A.M.– 10P.M.

In an area of Hawthorne dominated by plumbing wholesalers and auto-body shops, Al-Watan is a small, bare restaurant attached to the largest Pakistani market in California (which is not so large). Its dingy vinyl wallpaper is unbesmirched by so much as a calender or travel poster; its plain tile floor is burnished to a shine. The door to the bathroom is permanently open to the dining room, which is disconcerting until you realize that the tiny chamber contains nothing more than a sink. (Most of the regular customers eat in the traditional way, with their fingers, and wash their hands before, after, and several times during a meal.)

On weekend afternoons, you sometimes see big families here, but usually the restaurant is dominated by Pakistani businessmen in blue dress shirts, Sansabelt slacks, and shiny patent-leather shoes.

8

The businessmen seem almost to live at Al-Watan, dropping in a couple of times an afternoon, ordering big plates of lamb and rice, negotiating in Urdu on flip phones while they wait for the *biryani* to arrive.

Al-Watan's regulars seem to observe a protocol that involves strolls into the kitchen, fevered consultations with one or more of the cooks, and perhaps a trip to the butcher's counter in the store next door to take a look at the meat. The waiter may be slightly puzzled if you ask to see a menu but will eventually bring a computer printout of the takeout menu, which tends to be somewhat theoretical—only about half of the dishes listed will be available—and it is hard to escape the feeling that there are things at Al-Watan you will never get to taste.

Like any serious Pakistani restaurant, Al-Watan ostensibly specializes in the complicated offal dishes that make up the heart of Muslim Pakistani soul food. On weekends you'll find *magaz masala*, a ragout of chopped goat's brains cooked in a bright red spice paste; *khatakhat*, a stew of liver and stomach; and *paya*, a mildly spicy dish of beef shank.

First among the stews here is *haleem*, which is beef braised with something like shredded wheat until it breaks down into a thick, meaty gravy with the flavor of well-browned roast-beef drippings and the meat no longer discernable from grain. *Haleem* is absolutely spectacular scooped up with a bit of Al-Watan's buttery whole-wheat *chapati* bread. (There will always be a bit more oil than you might prefer oozing out of authentic dishes from India and Pakistan; abundant oil is a sign of generosity in that part of the world.) *Nehari* is a beef curry strongly flavored with fresh ginger; *magaz-nehari* is a creamy, unctuous beef curry plumped out, I think, with ground nuts.

There is even stuff for a vegetarian to eat in this land of abundant meat. *Navratan korma*, a mixture of cauliflower, green beans, and carrots stir-fried with chile and plenty of spices, is like a wonderful Muslim ratatouille, the flavors of each vegetable fresh and distinct while contributing to the cumulative effect of the cumin-scented whole. *Chana masala*, spiced chickpeas, is essentially the same stuff you'd find at a good Punjabi restaurant; *palak alu*, spinach cooked down with plenty of fresh ginger, is at least as tasty in its vegetarian incarnation, stewed with cubed potato, as it is in the lamb stew called *saag*. The breads—especially the *parathas* and the crisp garlic *naan* paved with bits of cilantro leaf—are superb.

But the essential reason to drive down to Al-Watan is what may be among the best tandoor-cooked meats in the United States—juicy, deeply spiced, and smacked with the resinous flavor of woodsmoke from the mesquite Al-Watan uses to fire the clay oven. There's smoky boneless chicken squirted with citrus and tossed with slivered onion, tandoori chicken with a strong family resemblance to great barbecue, and cubed lamb with the smoky chewiness you might associate with the best Texas pits. Even mediocre tandoor-cooked meats tend to be pretty good, but this stuff! If you lived close enough to Al-Watan, you might begin to bear a passing resemblance to the late, great, extra large Sufi singer Nusrat Ali Fateh Khan.

ANTOJITOS DENISE'S

4060 E. OLYMPIC BLVD., LOS ANGELES; (323) 264-8199. MON.-SUN. 8A.M.-6:30P.M. $7. ALSO 4930 HOLLYWOOD BLVD., HOLLYWOOD; (323) 661-8230. MON.-SAT., 8:30 A.M.-8P.M.

Meet *lonja*. *Lonja* is a slab of pigskin the size and heft of a Snickers bar, fried with a good half-inch of meat still adhering to it, and padded with enough insulating fat to power a team of sled dogs halfway across Saskatchewan. *Lonja* is fairly alarming as foodstuffs go—salty, chewy, breathtakingly high in cholesterol, and possessed of an extreme, tooth-cracking crunchiness that is probably responsible for half the bridgework in Sonora. What we're talking about is essentially a chunk of deep-fried lard sandwiched between leathery flesh and steel-hard skin, a chaw primitive enough to make a Slim Jim seem like a shining example of modern meat-processing technology. *Lonja*, the most radical form of Mexican *chicharrones*, may be the monster-truck pull of the salty snack planet.

I have personally seen a man go through two pounds of *lonja* so quickly that it looked like bits of pig were leaping into his mouth by themselves, and he would have eaten two more pounds, dredged in fiery chipotle-chile salsa, if they had been there for him to eat. I have heard that celery requires more calories to digest than it gives back to the body in fuel, but *lonja* is far more physically exhausting: eat a few pieces of the stuff, and you'll pant as if you've just finished a 10K run. Eat *more* than a few pieces of the stuff, and you'll feel like Shelley Winters in *Who Slew Auntie Roo?*

In Los Angeles, as far as I know, *lonja* is available more or less exclusively at Antojitos Denise's, a taco stand down on East Olympic known for a certain finesse with pig. Denise's is locally famous for its *chicharrones*, crunchy, airy sheets of fried pigskin that are as big around as tablecloths, and for its *cueritos*: cool, pickled bits of pigskin sharp with vinegar and spice that are perfect in a summertime taco. The stand serves tacos stuffed with something like a definitive version of *chicharrones* stewed in tomato sauce—slithery, numbingly rich squares of pigskin that acquire a squidlike texture and the haunting pig sweetness of good Carolina barbecue. You will find all the usual pig parts here, and some you'd never expect to see outside a charnel house. If it once oinked, Denise's has probably cornered the market in the stuff.

If you have been hearing about the magnificence of Denise's for a while, it can be kind of a shock to see the extreme informality of the actual restaurant, a tiny, walk up taco shack that seems to be patronized largely by the people who wait at the bus stop a few yards from the takeout window. On top of the building, the restaurant's sign features a caricature of Denise herself, all ponytail and Keene-painting eyes, looking about as jaunty as could reasonably be expected from a young woman whose job must largely consist of supervising boiling vats of lard. There is a small outside dining room—just a couple of picnic tables under a fiberglass awning, really, with Spanish-language admonitions on the wall saying stuff like, "Remember your culture and your education—throw away your trash."

Studded with restaurants steeped in pork-frying traditions from all over Mexico, Los Angeles is something of a wonderland for fans of the braised-pork dish *carnitas*, but even here, Denise's *carnitas* stand out: soft, long-simmered pillows of concentrated pig flavor, the sweet gaminess of the meat brought out, an occasional crisp edge but tending toward a rich, almost puddinglike texture. Denise's *carnitas* are great in the restaurant's tacos, folded into warm tortillas, sprinkled with onion and cilantro, and drizzled with the smoky salsa—though I have to admit I like the *carnitas* even better when I purchase a pound to go and fry them crisp at home.

Oddly, despite all the wonderful food on hand, it's easy enough to eat badly at Denise's. The fried *masa* saucers called *sopes* are hard and unfulfilling; the *taquitos*, quite ordinary; the soupy beans—and the burritos—generally bland. Though the well-garlicked chipotle salsa is mind-blowing, the tomato salsa, especially in February, can be watery. This is probably not the place to order seafood or grilled beef, because Denise's is where you go to eat, like, a pig.

THE APPLE PAN

10801 W. PICO BLVD., WEST LOS ANGELES; (310) 475-3585. TUES.–SUN., 11 A.M.–MIDNIGHT; FRI. AND SAT. TO 1 A.M.

Across the street from the vast Westside Pavilion and down the street from the computer stores of Pico stands the Apple Pan, the U-shaped lunch counter that has been feeding West Los Angeles since the first Truman administration. This crowded, genteel hamburger shack figures in every Westsider's dreams.

My family has been Apple Pan regulars at least since Lew Alcindor played freshman ball, and when my brother and his wife stayed home with their newborn, my mother and I independently had the same idea of what food might be appropriate to the occasion. My brother's refrigerator bulged with Hickory Burgers and pie.

It's a specialized operation, this place, with one grill dedicated to crisping hamburger buns and another to cooking the patties, a pie bakery in the rear, and

11

a man whose special skill is pulling leaves from heads of iceberg lettuce and riffling them into perfect sheaves like a riverboat gambler shuffling a deck of cards. Here are the worn wooden walls, the homey plaid wallpaper, and the clean, warm funk of frying meat. Here is Coca-Cola poured into paper cones snug in plastic holders. Here are long, thick French fries, unusually golden, that are customarily served with a separate cardboard plate for the catsup. No matter how many waiting people may be crowded in behind you, no matter how hungrily they stare at your pie, the countermen will always draw you another cup of coffee from the gas-fired urn and furnish you another dram of fresh, heavy cream.

It is no coincidence that when nostalgia-mongering restaurateurs attempt to duplicate the Los Angeles hamburger experience, it is to the Apple Pan hamburger that they turn. The top and bottom buns of an Apple Pan hamburger are both crisped and slightly oily, crunchy at the edges, working toward a near-complete softness at the middle; the pickles are resilient dill chips; the sheaf of fresh iceberg lettuce is a dozen-layered crispness at the core. The beef, generally cooked to a perfect, pink-centered medium, is juicy and full-flavored; the cheese, half-melted to a kind of sharp graininess, is good Tillamook cheddar. If you order a Steak Burger, it will be dabbed with a sweet chile relish; a Hickory Burger comes with sweet, slightly noxious barbecue sauce instead. Hamburgers are what they do here. I am partial to the sandwiches made with smoky, thinly sliced Virginia ham, but I suspect that I will never actually order one for myself.

ASANEBO

11941 VENTURA BLVD., STUDIO CITY; (818) 760-3348. SUN., TUES.-THURS., 5:30-10:30P.M. FRI. AND SAT., 5:30-11:30P.M.

French chefs in Los Angeles, most of them anyway, are resigned to nourishing their best customers on custom-ordered egg-white omelets, sauceless chicken, and swordfish broiled dry. The Zone diet forced the city's Italian chefs to devise *carpaccios* instead of pastas; New American chefs have redefined home cooking as spa cuisine. But for a sushi chef, Los Angeles is the Promised Land, a city of unlimited appetite and infinite malleability, of open minds and good cheer, which has long served as a crucible of sushi experimentation on a scale unknown anywhere else on Earth. Build it and they shall come, even if you fling your sushi onto conveyer belts, season it with garlic, or pepper it with loud reggae.

Sizzling olive oil over sashimi? Sure. Cream cheese on a salmon roll? Why not? Salsa with oysters? Fried *uni* with scallops? Avocado with crabmeat? Hey. Go right ahead. The customers who think nothing of lecturing Michelin-starred chefs on exactly what might go into an acceptable plate of *coquilles St. Jacques* are the same people who enjoy visiting sushi bars with signs on the wall that say SPECIAL

OF THE DAY: CHEF'S CHOICE. They accept—even embrace—sushi bars whose chefs will toss them out on their ear if they dare to ask for the yellowtail before they have finished eating their halibut.

In the middle of the Studio City sushi district, a bit past the Coldwater Curve, Asanebo occupies a small storefront tucked into a mini-mall, lighted with neon and surrounded by double-parked BMWs. Hairy music-industry guys sit at the sushi bar, trading quips in Japanese with Tetsuya, the primary chef. At the bar, a big Japanese guy—a local high school football coach who practically lives in this restaurant—holds an impromptu seminar on the Purdue secondary. Visiting tourists from Osaka clutch packs of Silk Cuts in sweating fists, not quite able to believe that the state of California will not allow them to smoke in restaurants.

For a while, Asanebo was famous as the "No-Sushi Bar," an establishment that served only sashimi and tiny portions of proto-Japanese cooked foods; grilled salmon with mashed potatoes and salmon eggs, fried squid with asparagus, steamed catfish with miso and ginger. All Hollywood seemed to flock to the place, eager to visit a restaurant that had come up with an entirely new way to deny satisfaction to its customers. "California roll? Sorry, can't help you." "Spicy tuna roll? Never heard of it." "*Maguro* sushi? Sorry, no rice today."

Asanebo achieved a small reputation as the poor man's Matsuhisa, although its food is actually a little closer to classic Japanese pub cooking than to Matsuhisa's Latinate take on the genre, and the cost, which can reach well upward of $75 a person with tax, tip, and a bamboo split of chilled sake, is not precisely a bargain.

Still, it is a pleasure to pull up a stool to the bar, to utter the magic word *omakase*—"Feed me until I burst!"—and to sit back and wait for the food to arrive. Perhaps there will be albacore sashimi, seared at the sides just until the flesh tightens up a little, served with a drizzle of citrus and the thinnest shavings of raw garlic, and funky slivers of Spanish mackerel sprinkled with salt and minced scallions, and fresh halibut walloped with spice. Soft, oily salmon, mounded in a bowl, is garnished with caviar; fillets of *kanpache*, a tiny coldwater tuna imported from Japan, are arranged into a little fishy Stonehenge. The *ankimo*, cylinders of molded monkfish liver in a sharp *ponzu* sauce, is fine.

Then come the cooked dishes: perhaps some steamed baby abalone in a thin, pungent broth made with wild mushrooms; almost certainly a nicely crisp version of the grilled, miso-marinated cod that has become as ubiquitous as tuna rolls in local Japanese restaurants. The bouncy spring roll stuffed with overemulsified fish cake does little for me, and I wasn't crazy about the steak, but the fried, *shiso*-wrapped *uni*, a crunchy little bundle of brine, can be mind-bending. You may not even miss the sushi. And if you do, Tetsuya may just condescend to make you the salmon-skin hand roll that you crave. Asanebo's more relaxed about that stuff these days.

13

ASHOKA THE GREAT

18614 S. PIONEER BLVD., ARTESIA; (562) 809-4229. DAILY, 11A.M.–2P.M., 5P.M.–10P.M.

The handful of regional Indian restaurants in Artesia's Little India are authentic by definition—if you're serving, say, the only Gujarati-style dishes in an area populated by Gujaratis, you may as well remind your customers of home. But even on Artesia's Pioneer Boulevard, perhaps the one street in America where nobody looks twice at a mustachioed man in a flaming-red turban, most restaurants try to span all of India in one menu, with a rather heavy emphasis on Punjabi-style tandoori cooking. I like to call it Subcontinental Cuisine.

Ashoka the Great, in the heart of Little India, has the same Punjabi-inflected menu as almost every other Indian restaurant in California: tandoori chicken and garlic *naan*, curried cauliflower, the spinach dish *saag paneer*. But unlike most other tandoori restaurants, Ashoka seems to deliver the goods.

Perhaps authenticity requires the freedom to use as much of the powerfully stinky spice *asafetida* as the cook thinks a dish needs, to go a little heavy on the *ghee*, to use only as much sweetening as is strictly necessary. At Ashoka, even the delicate taco-size crackers called *pappadum* are laced with seeds and aromatics, and the cool Indian yogurt *raita* is so strongly flavored with exotic spice that at first encounter somebody not accustomed to the stuff might think it was spoiled, although it's actually delicious. The bright red pickled carrot sticks are almost crunchy with pungent black mustard seed.

You might want to skip most of the appetizers here, grizzled little fritters of onion, cauliflower, or chicken that all seem to taste the same. The *masala dosa*, a crisp pancake as thin as parchment, rolled around a filling of curried potatoes and served with a lentil stew, is fine, though you'll find a half-dozen tastier versions within a few blocks' walk.

This is where to come for tandoori dishes: garlicky *naan* and potato-stuffed *paratha*, sure, but mostly the skinless chicken legs and fish kebabs and minced-lamb sausages marinated in yogurt and spices, flash-cooked in an ultrahot clay oven and served sizzling on a bed of onions on a heated steel platter. Ashoka's brand of tandoori chicken is wonderful, crisped at the edges and fragrant with spice, smoky, slightly tart, dyed the peculiar hue Frank Lloyd Wright used to call Cherokee Red. The curries are what you expect, more or less: ferocious, vinegary *vindaloos* of chicken and lamb; the soothing, creamy chicken dish *murg korma*, with cashews; shrimp *saag* in a creamy purée of spinach. *Karachi* chicken has the focused, gingery spice of a Muslim curry.

You'll find all the usual vegetable dishes done well: the locally famous curried okra dish *bhindi masala*, stewed with tomatoes and chiles; an excellent version of Punjabi *matar paneer*, homemade cheese sautéed with peas; and a nice take on *navratan korma*, cauliflower and potatoes and such cooked with spices and cream, that is a bit leaner, less luxurious than other versions but supremely well balanced.

Ashoka the Great has the usual sort of syruped boiled milk whatevers and puddingy things for dessert, but you may as well do as the Indians do after dinner and stroll up the block to Standard Sweets for a piece of the shop's splendid silver-gilded carrot *halvah* and a cup of masala tea.

ATLACATL

301 N. BERENDO STREET, LOS ANGELES; (323) 663-1404. MON.-THURS., 11A.M.-10P.M. FRI.-SUN., 10A.M.-11P.M.

Atlacatl is a handsome Salvadoran family restaurant on that midtown stretch of Beverly Boulevard dominated by ethnic markets and the kind of bikini bars whose names resonate through tough-guy novels. Where most Salvadoran restaurants are sort of tatty dives—tatty dives with some very good food—Atlacatl is a Nice Place to Go for decent *carne asada*, sweet-and-sour chicken with sautéed onions, or Salvadoran-style *chiles rellenos* stuffed with meat.

In an earlier incarnation, Atlacatl was the Beverly Gardens, a go-go bar that was locally famous for flat beer, brazen hostesses, and the wild tangle of grasses and untrimmed banana trees that surrounded the joint. Atlacatl's flora is impeccable now, like something neatly pruned around an expensive jungle retreat. There are tables and plush carpets where the boom-boom stage had been before. Silk flowers bloom on tabletops and everything is clean.

The first time I set foot in Atlacatl, I had just passed into the restaurant when I heard a dull thud. One of my friends, who is very tall, had knocked his forehead squarely on the top of the door frame, and I turned in time to see him crumple slowly to the ground as if he had been shot. He lay still, unmoving. Two cooks peered out of the kitchen to see what was going on. The waitresses giggled quietly into their hands. Three or four guys who had sidled to the front of the restaurant, pretending to check out the new selections on the CD jukebox, took in the scene out of the corners of their eyes. My friend rubbed his temples and groggily got to his feet.

"Are you OK, my friend?" somebody, apparently an owner, asked. "Come, get something to eat."

If Frank Sinatra himself had walked into the restaurant just then, accompanied by Joey Bishop, Charo, and the two sisters from Heart, he couldn't have upstaged my friend. I was dining with a celebrity.

Most Salvadoran restaurants specialize in *antojitos*—apart from its *antojitos*, or snacks, Salvadoran food is fairly indistinguishable from every other Central American cuisine—and it seemed like we got one of everything that afternoon. There were *pastelitos*, little fried turnovers stuffed with a savory mixture of spiced ground beef; dryish sweet-corn *tamales*; plantains fried to a crusty black, caramel-sweet, with thick Salvadoran sour cream and salty, puréed black beans; and *casamiento*, beans and rice fried to a mush in an impossible amount of lard and served with Salvadoran *crema* and a brick of crumbly cheese.

We had thick logs of the tuber *yuca*, deep-fried until crusty and served with sour cabbage slaw and big chunks of fried pork. We tried *shuco*, which is a thin corn gruel, slightly sweet, with a few black beans lurking at the bottom of the bowl. (The waitress beamed sweetly when we asked what it was, but *shuco* might be a little spartan for anybody not directly nostalgic for this kind of poverty stew.) We were pretty full.

If you know even a little about Salvadoran *antojitos*, you've probably heard of the *pupusa*, a 45-rpm-size discus of *masa* shaped around a filling of cheese or meat and baked to order on a griddle. It's more or less the Salvadoran national snack. I used to think all good *pupusas* were about the same: crisp *masa*, melted cheese, and hot grease tempered by the cool acidity of the cabbage slaw *curtido* that you pile on from a giant crock. Atlacatl's cheese *pupusas* are even better than that: chewy as well as crisp, cheese more pully than runny, spiked with pungent chunks of the Salvadoran vegetable *loroco*. The spicy, tart *curtido* is pretty great too. Two or three *pupusas* make a fine light lunch, maybe sloshed down with a bottle of Salvadoran Pilsener beer.

And if the food doesn't knock you off your feet, you can always forget to duck.

B

BAHOOKA

4501 N. ROSEMEAD BLVD., ROSEMEAD; (626) 285-1241. MON.-THURS.,
11A.M.-9:30P.M., FRI., 11A.M.-10:30P.M.; SAT., 12-10:30P.M.; SUN.,
12-9:30P.M.

Polynesian cuisine as most people know it has less to do with *lau lau* than with plastic parrots glowing in the dim light of a hundred hurricane lanterns, less to do with *poi* or *lomi lomi* salmon than the reeling sensation brought on by too many Flaming *Puku-Puku* Bowls. Polynesia means *rumaki* and flagstone waterfalls, fried shrimp and bamboo. If you grew up on virgin Zombies and candy-sweet spareribs, you know what I mean.

Forty years ago, every Los Angeles neighborhood had at least one tiki bar, built to slake the tropical thirsts of men who had served in the far-Pacific theaters of World War II. James Michener and Thor Heyerdahl cashed in on '50s tiki-mania; so did Trader Vic and Don the Beachcomber. The most elaborate bars featured hula shows or giant volcanoes that erupted every hour or so; the food, when it existed, tended toward coco shrimp and pu pu platters. Lengthy drink menus described in florid pre-twelve-step prose exactly how a Suffering Bastard or a Head Shrinker would anesthetize your date, and the drinks in question were invariably garnished with two straws, a parasol, and a flaming crouton.

But like drive-ins and Art Deco office buildings, most local tiki bars were demolished or retooled in the '70s and '80s, followed too late by hipster nostalgia. (If everybody I knew who collected Martin Denny records and Hawaiian shirts had gone out for a Missionaries' Downfall every so often, more of the places may have survived.) Branches of Kelbo's and Don the Beachcomber closed, one after the other: The Torches was razed for condos; the Islander became the briefly tony 385 North; and the Luau on Rodeo Drive, where three generations of Beverly Hills High School students purchased their first illicit drink, was replaced by the world's most expensive mini-mall. Even Trader Vic had its funky soul remodeled right out of it. Bahooka hangs on.

Bahooka is the kind of place you'd expect to find near a scruffy tropical seaport—all rusted nautical gear, stolen street signs, and scarred dark wood, lit like a navy-base bar and with more bobbing tropical fish than you'd find in a Jacques Cousteau special. Lifeboats hang out back—after the bar closes on a weekend night, you'll always find a giggling kid or two waving from inside of one. There are fish in the foyer, fish tanks surrounding three sides of each booth, and fish swimming inside the glass-topped bar, but not much fish on the menu, unless you count some cod that seems to have swum all the way from Iceland through a sea of old oil. Fish puffs go with a Monsoon or a Jet Pilot or a Flaming Honey Bowl better than you might think, though the leaden deep-fried balls of food aren't anything you'd want to look at by the light of day. There is no *rumaki*. Sorry.

When the steel-guitar lowings on the P.A. start to sound good, it's time for a Shark's Tooth or a Cobra's Strike. Halfway into one of those, a sticky order of Exotic Ribs may seem like just the thing, because the ribs are moist, soak up a lot of alcohol, and come with fries, sweet baked yams, or *cobbettes*. The *cobbettes*, definitely the *cobbettes*. You can also get teriyaki chicken breast, ham with sweet-and-sour sauce, roast beef, or fried golf balls of shrimp, but you won't. What will happen is that your date will suck up the last of his or her Jolly Roger Bowl and carve your initials in the booth. Don't worry, it's happened before.

BA LE AND BUU-DIEN

BA LE, 18625 SHERMAN WAY, RESEDA; (818) 342-9380. MON.-FRI., 8A.M.-7:30P.M.; SAT. AND SUN., 8A.M.-7P.M. ALSO IN WESTMINSTER, MONTEREY PARK, AND OTHER LOCATIONS.
BUU-DIEN, 542 N. BROADWAY, NO. 5, CHINATOWN; (213) 617-8355. DAILY, 8A.M.-6:30P.M.

By now, almost everybody knows about *pho*, the beef-noodle soup that seems to pop up wherever Vietnamese people live. If you frequent Orange County or the San Gabriel Valley, you have probably also run across Vietnamese juice bars, Vietnamese bakeries, and Vietnamese seafood joints.

Less explored is the phenomenon of *banh mi* shops, which are more or less the Vietnamese equivalent of delis. You might stop to buy a pound of pâté or a can of pennyworth juice at a *banh mi* shop, a glass of strong, iced filter coffee or a meat-filled *risole* that is about the size and weight of an Olympic discus. There will usually be bags of peanuts freshly boiled in their shells, plastic-wrapped packages of meat-stuffed rice noodles or bits of fish over rice, baroquely gelatinous desserts, and sliced deli meats of a sort you will never see at Canter's.

A good *banh mi* shop might have fresh-squeezed sugar-cane juice for sale, or shredded green-papaya salad garnished with bright red strips of Vietnamese beef jerky. But mostly, of course, a *banh mi* shop will have *banh mi*—French sandwich, it is usually translated—stuffed with Vietnamese charcuterie.

Banh mi are more or less Vietnamese hoagies, meat and vegetables daubed with mayonnaise, crammed into lightly toasted French rolls and wrapped in neatly folded sheets of butcher's tissue. You can usually get a meatball sandwich at a *banh mi* place, though the meatballs in question will be the grilled, garlicky Southeast Asian kind rather than red-sauced Italian lumps. *Banh mi* are often filled with chicken, grilled pork, or tasty (if gristly) mounds of the stewed pigskin called *bi*.

The king of *banh mi*, though, is the combination sandwich usually referred to as *banh mi dac biet* (house-special *banh mi*), which sounds complicated but is little more than a French-style, best-of-pig sandwich—ham, headcheese, liver pâté, and sometimes a sort of sour ham, a fillet of fresh cucumber, pickled slivers of vegetables, sliced chiles, and a handful of cilantro—with a distinctively Vietnamese taste.

Banh mi dac biet is always an inexpensive proposition—usually less than $2 per sandwich, which means you can have a splendid lunch for less than you'd pay for a Big Mac—and at peak hours, when the sandwiches are toasted, filled, and stacked behind the counter like cordwood, they can be even faster than McDonald's. Like cheeseburgers or tuna melts, versions of *banh mi dac biet* tend to be pretty much the same, but the sandwiches harbor a universe of subtle differences beneath their crusty rolls.

The standard in Southern California is probably the *banh mi* served at one of the several shops called Ba Le, a chain with constant commercials on Vietnamese television and lines that snake out the door at lunchtime. Ba Le's *banh mi* come on French rolls that are a couple of degrees softer and wider than the rolls at other *banh mi* stores, the pickles are crunchy, and the meat is arranged so that you get a taste of everything in each bite—it's a spectacular construction. The even-textured, mayonnaise-rich sandwich may be closer to a standard deli-counter sub than other *banh mi*—a little milder, a *banh mi* with training wheels.

However, the sandwich from Buu-Dien, a shiny place tucked into a Chinatown mini-mall, is clearly the best of any I've tasted—and I've tasted dozens. Buu-Dien's *banh mi* may occasionally be a little on the dry side, but it is otherwise almost a chef's sandwich of ham, headcheese, and two different kinds of pâté; a super-fresh, highly spiced sandwich slathered with liver paste almost as a condiment and spiked with chopped bits of pig's-ear cartilage for a surreal crunch. The chiles ease into mild glow midpalate, then ease out again into exotic, sweet spice. Buu-Dien's *banh mi* is powerful stuff.

BATAVIA CAFE

970 N. BROADWAY, CHINATOWN; (213) 626-6738. FRI., 11A.M.–2A.M.; SAT., 12P.M.–4A.M.; SUN., 11P.M.

You could program it into your laptop: the better the cooking at a Los Angeles Asian restaurant, the worse the music you may have to endure. The lousiest Indian restaurants in the United States have ragas on their sound systems, but the great ones have the sort of Bollywood soundtracks that make you long for Mariah Carey. The sushi bars that blast Augustus Pablo and Yellowman are universally less fine than the ones nurtured instead by Kenny G. Three or four of my favorite Thai restaurants feature earsplitting, live renditions of prom ballads as dinner serenade.

If you want to eat well in Los Angeles, you'd better be prepared to endure a lot of Kenny Loggins and Dan Hill, Olivia Newton-John and Air Supply. (If you have been lucky enough to forget about Dan Hill, you obviously haven't eaten a decent plate of *nasi lemak* in years.) And if bad music is a reliable sign of good food, Batavia Cafe would have to be among the best restaurants in the world. Whether the restaurant is full or empty, whether at 11:30 in the morning or 8:00 at night, the laser-disc karaoke machine at the sleek palace of Indonesian cooking cranks out soft hits by the yard. Sometimes you'll hear Indonesian translations of the Whitney Houston songbook, and sometimes "Feelings," the theme song from *Grease*, or the greatest hits of Dan Fogelburg. The restaurant is rather prettily decorated with batik tablecloths and ceremonial Indonesian umbrellas, wood-carvings, and masks, but you cannot avoid the mammoth Sony screen on which beautiful young Asian women moon into sunsets or mope past pagodas; cannot escape the giant speakers that reproduce every low-rent synthesizer sound in excruciating detail.

But even if Michael Bolton imitators make you break out in hives, you could do a lot worse than dinner at Batavia, where the iced coffee is good, the chicken *satay* is richly sauced with spiced peanut butter and garlic, and the traditional steamed-vegetable salad *gado-gado* is garnished with fried tofu, tempeh fritters, and half a dozen shrimp chips—silly-looking things that jut from the top of the salad like varicolored jibs.

Like most local Indonesian places, Batavia serves dishes from all over the Indonesian archipelago, sometimes sauced with the fiery chile sauces of coastal Sumatra: any dish (stir-fried tofu; crisply fried pompano) with the word *belado* in its name will be blanketed with a sweet-sour chop of chiles and red sweet peppers. Other food is glazed with the sweet soy concoctions endemic in central Java. Here you'll find the best *murtabak* in town, layers of crisp phyllo-like pastry encapsulating a sort of meaty Indonesian omelet. Fried noodles, *bakmi goreng*, have the firm, delicate texture of good pasta and the sweet smokiness that comes only from an extremely hot wok. *Kangkong*, the hollow-stemmed vegetable sometimes called *ong choy* or water spinach, is sautéed with shrimp paste, tomatoes, and mountains of garlic into a mess that tastes better than any mere vegetable ought to.

The essential dish here is probably the fried game hen, a stupendously good bird as good as anything from Zankou, with the brittle, spun-sugar crunchiness only Indonesian cooks seem to be able to coax out of chicken skin, the kind of skin you suspect would shatter if you dropped a thigh, but also sweet, juicy flesh laced with garlic and spice. The only shrimp preparation on the menu is a stinky affair, sautéed with the infamously pungent *pete* bean and walloped with a mega dose of fermented shrimp paste that you can smell across the room, although the taste is mild enough almost to accentuate the perfumey quality of Indonesian rice.

Desserts, as at so many Indonesian cafes, are mostly exotic sweet ices served in malted glasses: the mellow brown-sugar drink *es cendol*, shot through with translucent green mung-bean squiggles that look a little like dried Prell; various ices scented with rosewater; and *es teler*, a vanilla-flavored ice with young coconut, puréed avocado, and an eye-watering bit of durian, the smelliest fruit in the world.

BATTAMBANG

648 NEW HIGH ST., CHINATOWN; (213) 620-9015. DAILY, 7:30A.M.–6:30P.M.

If you didn't recognize Battambang from its original incarnation in Long Beach's Little Phnom Penh, it probably wouldn't occur to you that it served Cambodian food. There may be a smattering of Khmer script on the sign outside, which is not unusual in this part of Chinatown, but it seems somehow subsidiary to the English, Chinese and Vietnamese; the official name of the place is actually Battambang Chinese Restaurant. The menu, which is heavy on fish balls, stir-fries and the sort of rice-noodle soups you might associate with Saigon-style breakfast joints, suggests a Chiu Chow noodleshop like one of the Kim Tar chain (which is also, I think, run by Cambodians). The menu lists things like Mandarin garlic chicken among the restaurant's specialties.

But an illustrated card on each table lists mostly Khmer dishes (though not in English), and a long insert in the menu includes photographs of some of the other Khmer dishes (though it doesn't indicate which ones they are). If you ask nicely, the waiters will point out Khmer dishes too, although their English is sometimes not quite up to explaining precisely what might be in them.

Cambodian cooking is some of the most exotic in the world, sharing some techniques and ingredients with the cooking of Vietnam and northern Thailand but with a flavor unmistakably its own: clear, clean, and slightly bitter; inflected by fish sauce, coconut milk, fresh herbs, Chinese technique and a spice cabinet that leans slightly toward India. A typical mouthful of Cambodian food might include three or four different kinds of fresh mint, something fishy and slightly rank, and a jolt of garlic powerful enough to lift you out of your chair.

Great Cambodian cooking is not subtle, and the salads are some of the least subtle salads you will ever taste, arranged like Isaan-style Thai salads—vast heaps of vegetables tossed with citrus juice, meat and chiles—but with three times the herbs and half the heat. At Battambang, there is an acerbic beef salad whose herb content is pedal-to-the-metal, and a minty salad garnished with chewy, cool poached duck webs where you would expect the croutons in a spinach salad. One unusual salad involves leathery, parchment-thin strips of smoked, dried fish tossed with various mints and lettuces, and great lashings of a medicine-bitter vegetable—*sadao*—that looks like rapini punctuated with hundreds of bright-yellow flower buds that are no bigger than the head of a pin.

One dish, ground fish and pork simmered together in coconut milk (called curry fish on the menu and closely related to the northern Thai dish *nam prik oong*), comes with a vegetable plate as big as a salad in its own right—tiny Asian eggplants the size of Ping-Pong balls, long beans, cabbage—with which you are meant to scoop up the delicious red mass.

The soups might also be recognizable to anyone who's eaten a lot of Thai food, but stand in relation to the average *tom kha kai* as the Emerson String Quartet does to the ELO. Bubbling chimney-pots full of sour fish soup are flavored with pineapple and spears of fresh cucumber, broth slightly muddied by the wild flavor of the fresh, though decidedly not farm-raised slices of catfish cosseted in its depths. Powerfully sour, chile-red beef soup is thick with bits of herbs, Chinese long beans, and purely ornamental chunks of cow that have clearly given their all to the broth.

Amok—"steamed curry fish filet" on the menu—may be the most famous Cambodian dish, fish steamed tamale-style in a banana-leaf with coconut milk almost until the flesh collapses, and Battambang's version is pretty good, almost the texture of a fluffy coconut mousse, mellowness underlaid with a buzzy fresh-chile heat. The frog stir-fried with curry may be just okay, and the kitchen always seems to be out of eel, but Battambang also does a great version of beef sate, lengths of flank steak soaked in a fruity marinade that is the intense red of Hawaiian Punch concentrate, then threaded on skewers and charcoal-grilled to a

sweet, blackened, crusty medium rare, the sort of thing you may have always
wanted from a teriyaki stick.

Welcome to the jungle, baby.

BAY CITIES IMPORTING

1517 LINCOLN BLVD., SANTA MONICA; (310) 395-8279. MON.–SAT., 7A.M.–
7P.M., SUN., 7A.M.–6P.M. TAKE OUT ONLY.

Bay Cities is a bustling Italian deli near downtown Santa Monica, a supermarket-
size delicatessen that was slinging fresh pasta and roasted peppers thirty years
before the average Santa Monican could tell you the difference between porcini
and sun-dried tomatoes. If you grew up in the area, Bay Cities was where your
parents shopped for manicotti shells and provolone, for eggplant caponata and
super-peppery Toscano salami, but was mostly where you hoped they'd pick up
a few subs on their way home from work.

Everybody's got a personal pantheon of Italian sandwiches: *muffulettas* from
New Orleans's Central Grocery, heavy with cold cuts and garlicky olive salad; a
Trastevere sandwich of drippy *bufala* mozzarella and gamy wisps of Fruilian proscuitto; a simple train-station lunch of roast pork and a slab of that peculiar saltless
Tuscan bread that tastes like fresh cheese. Perhaps you have gotten lost in a
residential neighborhood in Milan, picking your way toward the famous sandwich
shop called Bar Quadronno. Decked out with bristly animal heads, frequented
by scooter kids in Armani jackets, Bar Quadronno serves as many flavors of panini
as Baskin-Robbins does ice cream, and the speciality is a sandwich of *bresaola*
and cured tuna roe that oozes sweetened mayonnaise, the richness and intensity
of flavor almost perfectly offset by the weightless crackle of the bread.

Bay Cities is no Bar Quadronno, but at lunchtime the crowd around the deli
counter is four deep, the smell of garlic is maddening, and people jostle hard in
their haste to take a number from the machine. The countermen spend most of
their time huddled over the long sandwich-making table, huddled over their he-
roes as seriously as white-coated surgeons over a kidney transplant.

Bay Cities makes a decent turkey sandwich, a loud, greasy meatball sandwich,
and a very respectable hero with Parma proscuitto, ripe tomatoes, and cheese, but
the sandwich of choice here is the Godmother, which includes a slice of every
Italian cold cut you've ever head of and a couple that might be new to you:
salami, mortadella, proscuitto, cappicola, ham, proscuitto, provolone cheese, all
on a foot-long, properly chewy Italian loaf.

Fully dressed, the Godmother includes lettuce, tomato, mayonnaise, mustard,
and a few squirts from unmarked squeeze bottles that probably add up to a

garlicky vinaigrette. Fully dressed, a Godmother feeds a couple of people at least, and the guys behind the counter will look at you quizzically if they suspect you're planning to eat a large Godmother yourself. When you eat a Godmother, even a half-Godmother, it is best to roll your sleeves up to the elbows.

BENITA'S FRITES

UNIVERSAL CITY WALK, UNIVERSAL CITY. (818) 505-8834. SUN.–THURS., 11:30A.M.–11P.M.; FRI.–SAT., 11:30A.M.–MIDNIGHT. 1433 THIRD ST., PROMENADE, SANTA MONICA. NO PHONE.

In the great march of world civilization, every country has done its part. The Germans contributed the symphony; the French, symbolist poetry; the Irish, William Butler Yeats. The Dutch chimed in with mannerist painting; the Nigerians with the great sculptures of Benin. And the Belgians? French fries . . . French fries and a funny kind of beer that tastes like cherries. Monks make it, I think. The Belgian fries, sometimes called *frites*, are a sort of medium thickness, and are served in big paper cones or with heaps of mussels, sometimes called *moules*. *Saveur* editor Colman Andrews once told me the best ones were supposed to have been cooked in rendered horsemeat fat, though he didn't think anybody does that anymore. There's always fresh mayonnaise around to dip the *frites* into in Belgium. As far as I know, catsup does not exist there.

You can find paper cones of the Belgian fries, though not the beer, on the Universal Citywalk, that terrifying security-state vision of urban Los Angeles parked just uphill from Lankershim. Benita's, a takeout stand in the true American tradition of overspecialization, serves Belgian fries and *only* Belgian fries— no mussels, no burgers, no shakes. The founder spent some time in Belgium, and as other expatriates may have had their lives transformed by the Altarpiece of Ghent or the NATO high command, his was transformed by *frites*.

Benita's fries to order: so the *frites* are always crisp and hot, but the potatoes take a while to cook. It is not fast food. You'll find more things here to put on fries than you can imagine, and you'll have time to consider them all: malt vinegar, red wine vinegar, white wine vinegar, salt, pepper, cayenne, seasoned salt, mustard, and even catsup. For an extra few cents, you can get a remoulade sauce spiked with tarragon, a creamy Dijon mustard dip, or a thick garlic mayonnaise that will later announce your presence in a room thirty seconds before you open the door. Something called a "sauce Andalouse," which no Spaniard would recognize, is basically the garlic mayonnaise tinted pink with peppers. There's chili that tastes like the orange stuff you get on hamburgers at the lesser-known stands—Tammy's, Timmy's, Tommy's—which is to say, in fact, pretty good. And the *frites* themselves are really good, clean-tasting, thumb-wide things cut from fresh potatoes.

Benita's fries them twice, the first time in coolish oil that cooks them through, the second in hotter oil that sizzles the fries to a fine golden-brown. They're not especially greasy, though you'll certainly feel a large order with garlic mayo rolling around in your belly for at least the duration of a Claude Chabrol film, and the oil they're fried in is super-polyunsaturated 98 percent cholesterol-free something or other.

Personally, I prefer the (breathtakingly expensive) fries served at Michael's in Santa Monica, which have a pronounced pan-dripping meatiness because they're cooked in pure suet. Beef fat may not be what the doctor ordered, but it makes French fries go pretty well with a bottle of '87 Ridge Montebello Cabernet. Benita's fries are up there with those, though.

And some days, it seems like everybody who sets foot in Benita's has a suggestion or two for the place.

"You know what you need, young man, is a larger menu," said a Beverly Hills type in an appliquéd denim jacket. "I think people would like some fish. Like fish and chips?"

"How about mussels?" a cosmopolite asked.

"Tartar sauce," somebody else said.

"Tabasco," said a third.

Of course, I had a suggestion, too.

"Lard," I said. "Pure lard. It's more authentic. Unless you have a line on some rendered horsemeat fat."

BEVERLY SOONTOFU RESTAURANT

2717 W. OLYMPIC BLVD. #108, LOS ANGELES: (213) 380-1113. DAILY, 9:30A.M.–10:30P.M.

What you eat in a Korean tofu restaurant: tofu. Also rice and a couple of different kinds of *kimchi*. At Beverly you get a simple water *kimchi* of white radish and a spicy red kimchi of white radish. All the menus are short, but Beverly's is the shortest of all, listing only three items, each of them a minor variation on the theme of tofu casserole. The thing to drink here is chilled barley tea served in soup bowls, which is very refreshing and is included in the price of the lunch.

The tofu casserole, *soontofu*, comes bubbling and sputtering, splattering the paper placemat with a fine red mist, forming a burnt crust on the rim of the red-hot cast-iron bowls in which it is served. Until it cools down a bit, *soontofu* looks more like a scene from the "Rite of Spring" sequence of *Fantasia* than it does like actual food. If you like, the waitress will break an egg over the seething, volcanic mass. The white of the egg sets at once, while the yolk remains pleasantly viscous, a nice, subtle contrast to the velvety smoothness of the thumb-size chunks of tofu and the thick broth. ("The tofu is made fresh every day—even on a holiday," the proprietress says to anybody who will listen.)

Soontofu here is available spiked with oysters, meat, and *kimchi* with oysters, meat, and small clams; or with sheets of toasted seaweed that you crumble into the stew yourself. There is no appreciable difference between the briny, savory tang of the three, though the tiny oysters are a nice touch and the one with the seaweed alone is marginally lower in calories than the rest. (You could probably have a filling bowl of each variety and still come out better than you would with a single Big Mac and fries.) Gradations of possible spiciness range from milky white (no chile) to a nostril-searing brick red, and you are allowed to decide.

Dessert, as it is at most Korean restaurants, is a stick of chewing gum.

BIRRIERIA BALDOMERO

3104 S. MAPLE AVE., LOS ANGELES; (323) 231-1682. MON.-FRI., 8A.M.-5P.M.; SAT. AND SUN., 6A.M.-5P.M.

In any Los Angeles neighborhood with more than half a dozen Mexican bars, there will be at least one *birrieria* ready to soak up the beer. *Birria*, the famous goat dish from the area around Guadalajara—banners for the soccer team Guadalajara Chivos are common at *birria* joints—may not be normally the first food you think of at breakfast time, but it can be as palliative as it is delicious, especially on a queasy stomach.

Birrieria Baldomero #2, in an old neighborhood south of downtown, looks almost like what you'd imagine a Depression-era restaurant to be, if Depression-era restaurants also featured orange Formica benches and soccer-blaring televisions. The vast, high-ceilinged dining hall is the size of a high school cafeteria, with steam tables at one end, a picture of Guadalajara's central square toward the other, acres of wood-grain Formica, and dozens of empty beer bottles crowding the tables.

There may be more than *birria* or weekend *menudo* on offer here, but it would be hard to tell by looking at the plates of the men around you, at the signboards above the steam table, or at the menu, even if there were a menu. Whether you ask for it or not, a counterperson thrusts a plastic bowl of goatmeat in a rich pan-dripping broth at you, accompanied by a dish of cilantro and another of finely chopped onion, a half lime, and a bowl of searingly hot chile salsa to mix in to taste. Some restaurants serve *birria* in plates so brimming with soup you wonder how the waiter makes it from the kitchen without spilling; other places roast the meat to a frizzly crunchiness or season the stew with strong doses of mint. This is plain-wrap *birria*, good and strong, tasting mostly of goat, the meat itself stewy and soft as a long-cooked lamb shank, generous in bones and cartilage and secret bits of flesh.

If you're thirsty, grab your own Bohemia or apple-flavored Sidral soda from one of the wooden glass-front iceboxes that look as if they have been around since Repeal. If you want your *birria* to go, head down the block to Birriera Baldomero #1, which is a little, goat-centered takeout stand on the corner. On Saturdays and Sundays, the hangover-friendly restaurant opens at 6:00 A.M.

BIRRIERIA CHALIO

3580 E. 1ST ST., EAST LOS ANGELES; (213) 268-5349. ALSO AT 2104
CESAR CHAVEZ AVE., EAST LOS ANGELES; (213) 261-0017; 11300
WASHINGTON BLVD., SANTA FE SPRINGS; (562) 692-6118. DAILY,
7A.M.–9P.M.

Chalio has sat forever on the stretch of East First Street sometimes called Calle Primero, amid a row of burger stands and dime stores, in one of the few bits of the Eastside that still has an old-fashioned city flair. Inside, you'll find the happy buzz, the three-generation families, the elaborate Christmas decorations, the wait for a table that lets you know you've stumbled into one of the best restaurants in the neighborhood.

Imagine a big plate of roast kid crudely chopped into wallet-size chunks, the snips of cartilage, the crunchy burned rib ends, the sweet little wisps of flesh that attach themselves to membrane or hide between slivers of bone; the muscly, fist-size knots of pure meat. *Birria*—chile-sluiced goat—might be the most primal dish of Mexican cuisine.

It's possible to order dishes like *carne asada* or *cocido* without imagining anything more vivid than poly-wrapped supermarket chuck, you can eat mild *tacos de tripas* without thinking of the calf intestines on your plate, but with goat, there is no getting away from the funky animal reality of the thing. Chalio occupies a tall room, with goats' heads and stags' heads high on the walls, a *norteño*-stocked jukebox in one corner, and on each table a squeeze bottle of sauce that seems hot enough to set off a fusion reaction in your silver fillings. As soon as you sit down, a waiter brings over a plate of chopped onion, shredded cilantro, halved limes, and a small plastic *molcajete* filled with fresh salsa. Vendors wander through selling flowers and bargain *banda* cassettes.

You've been to the Eastside restaurants where roving bands of mariachis dispense tunage to anybody with a couple of bucks for a song; musicians come through here too, but they're just as likely to set their accordions down on the floor and eat lunch as they are to play.

Chalio has creditable bowls of *menudo* and the hominy stew *posole*, saucy enchiladas, giant tacos made with hand-patted tortillas and what seems like a full quarter-pound of grilled beef, but *birria* is the most popular dish to the extent that you may not realize Chalio even has a menu—the waiters don't ask you what you're going to have, they ask you what you're going to drink with it.

Where the waiters at many birrierias periodically come by to top off the tomato-laced broth, consommé, on your plate, at Chalio a few dollars gets you all the goat you can eat—just as you finish one plate, sop up the superb *consommé* with a tortilla, pick up a rib to gnaw off an overlooked scrap of flesh, the waiter comes by to see if you'd like another. On weekends, it's not unusual to see guys plow through three or four plates of *birria*, and as many baskets of tortillas and cans of Modelo beer.

The *birria* here is flavored with a strong hit of a mint-like herb, which may be a trademark of the Zacatecas-style *birria* Chalio serves (most restaurants advertise *birria* made in the style of neighboring Jalisco state) or may be an interesting quirk in the family recipe. Corn tortillas are big, stretchy, unusually tan, handmade in-house, except on Sundays, when you'll have to make do with factory tortillas.

Once you've been coming here a while, you learn to specify the cut of goat you want—the crisp, oily rib section, teeming with little bones; straight boneless goatmeat cut from the flank or the leg; lean loin of goat—but until then, you'll get a combo platter with a little bit of each.

BOCA DEL RIO

3706 E. WHITTIER BLVD., EAST LOS ANGELES; (213) 268-9339. DAILY, 11A.M.–11P.M.

In East Los Angeles, there may be as many places to eat seafood as there are fast-food chains: fancy places that specialize in big-bucks lobster *parrilladas* and converted burger shacks that serve octopus cocktails; places with octopus ceviche and others with Baja-style fish tacos; representatives of the coastal states Colima, Nayarit, Sinaloa, even Ensenada. When a *mariscos* joint is jumping, there is no better way to spend an afternoon than laying waste to piles of garlic shrimp and oceans of cold beer.

Still, although its food is underrepresented in Los Angeles, the East Coast seaport Veracruz is the true center of seafood cooking in Mexico, and red snapper Veracruz-style is thought to be Mexico's greatest seafood dish. In Veracruz itself, you find sweet freshwater shrimp from the vast network of rivers in the region, crabs and lobsters from the bays, and fresh warm-water fish—snapper, sierra, pompano—from the gulf. There are as many seafood dishes in the state as there are villages to cook them.

Just down the street from the Eastside's main shopping drag and a couple of blocks from Ruben Salazar Park, Boca del Rio is named for a Veracruz suburb that, like Puerto Nuevo in Baja, is more a cluster of seafood restaurants than an actual place to live, a town where you go to eat lobster and stare at the sea. East L.A.'s Boca del Rio is pretty close to a perfect family Mexican seafood restaurant: a few tables, a bar, a jukebox, thickly stuccoed walls that almost gleam in their whiteness, and the clean, briny smell of fresh fish. Boca del Rio may lack the elaborate *chilpacholes*, the exotic jungly stews, the strange licoricelike herbs you might find in Veracruz, but mostly it delivers the goods: fluffy, garlicky rice; pungent fresh salsa; grilled lobster; stuffed crab; and the best shrimp *al mojo de ajo* imaginable—split down the middle, frosted with garlic, and grilled until fragrant and crisp. Shrimp Cancun, broiled inside thick flak-jackets of bacon and ham, then blanketed with melted cheese, may seem ghastly in concept but actually sort of works, like an hors d'oeuvre bombarded with mutant radiation in a '50s monster flick.

You'll find the usual seafood cocktails here—the deluxe version, no more exciting than the others, is called *vuelve a la vida*, a cocktail to "wake up the dead"—which are basically defrosted shrimp, octopus, and canned abalone drenched in brine and served in fluted sundae cups. There are perfectly adequate, if bland, bowls of shrimp soup, the customary enchilada specials, and grilled steaks. Boca del Rio specializes in crisp-edged griddled red snapper, which you can have marinated with garlic and dried chiles, and finished with browned bits of chopped garlic; or cooked in a dry egg batter, in which state it resembles the treatment fish is given in Korean pubs. Best of all is a classic *huachinango a la Veracruzana*, braised in tomato sauce and sharply flavored with capers and olives, which is as complexly seasoned as anything you might order at, say, l'Orangerie.

BORDER GRILL

1445 4TH ST., SANTA MONICA; (310) 451-1655. MON., 5P.M.–10P.M.; TUES.–THURS., 11:30–10P.M., FRI. AND SAT., 11:30A.M.–1A.M. (UNTIL MIDNIGHT, SUMMER ONLY); SUN., 11:30A.M.–10P.M.

It would be tough, I think, to imagine restaurateurs more of their time and place than Mary Sue Milliken and Susan Feniger in mid-'80s Los Angeles. Their City Restaurant pulled in Beemers and Turbo Saabs to an old carpet showroom on a previously uncolonized corner of La Brea; all the pretty people nibbled on the pair's chrysanthemum leaves and fried parsnips and creamed brussels sprouts with Parmesan. At their original Border Grill, a tiny, crowded place in the heart of

Melrose, they proselytized for their rather authentic versions of *posole*, Mexican tongue stew, and godhead green-corn tamales. They were first out of the gate on the high-end tequila thing, and the first to show surveillance-camera footage of the kitchen instead of the Lakers game on the bar's TV. Even their coifs, knocked off by TV hairdressers everywhere, said "chef."

The second Border Grill, a splashy cantina in a yawning Santa Monica storefront the two took over from a brew pub, looked as if it would become the hottest place of all. The long, black dining room, delineated by an abstracted safety-orange corral fence, given weight by its crazily skewed ceiling painted with rocket ships and wrestling-masked batmen, looks even better now than it did when the place first opened. The basic margarita-and-chips fare—grilled-beef tacos, guacamole mashed to order, limeade spiked with the slippery seeds that provide the greenery for Chia Pets, and the black-bean nachos called Eulalia's chips—was always first-rate. Melrose hip, though, is quite different from Santa Monica hip: as a phenomonon, Border Grill II didn't quite catch on, and the Milliken-Feniger empire began to fade.

The original Border Grill became a Melrose jeans boutique, and City Restaurant, despite the best vegetarian plates in town and interesting sallies into the unexplored terrain of low-fat, ethnic grain cookery, shut down, a victim of its graying demographic and declining chic. The Border Grill in Santa Monica, which had always been a little poppier than the original, declined into something not very different from a slightly more bohemian El Torito Grill.

But one of the advantages of living in Los Angeles is the constant possibility of reinventing yourself. People here do it all the time: from honors student to gangsta rapper, from toilet-paper saleswoman to studio chief, from carpenter to movie star. And finally, Milliken and Feniger reinvented themselves in the most Los Angeles way imaginable: they became the chef-queens of all media, the Keith and Mick of Mexican food.

First, I think, came the cookbook *Mesa Mexicana*, which to locals seemed like a nostalgic relic from a fading restaurant, but which won the two a certain following among the cardiologists' wives of the American heartland. They released a CD of dinner music. They began a radio food show in which they discussed things like hip fishmongers and the possibilities of preparing fourteen-course vegetarian banquets to take on camping trips. They were possibly the first serious restaurant with a full-on site on the World Wide Web.

Most of all, there was their TV show, *Too Hot Tamales*, which was by far the best thing to watch on the Food Network. Like Julia Child on PBS twenty-five years ago, Milliken and Feniger seemed to understand the voyeuristic nature of the medium, and they almost specialized in the tongue stews and pig's-foot tacos that they don't really serve in their restaurant anymore but which give so much squeamish pleasure on the tube. If your local cable system carried the Food Network, you used to be able to watch Mary Sue and Susan four times a day, every day, to the point where they became mythic figures whose banter become more familiar than that of your spouse.

And suddenly, Santa Monica Border Grill had the noise, the decent food, the buzz of a hot restaurant, the tourists from Ohio who penciled in Border Grill right after Disneyland on their must-see list, the foodies who long ago abandoned Border Grill for Melisse or the Buffalo Club. And, especially if you haven't been here in a while, Border Grill may be something close to great. In the way that a brilliant chef like Campanile's Mark Peel can, with superb ingredients and classical technique, make something as basic as a tuna salad or a BLT into something wholly his own, Milliken and Feniger transform the taco, the tostada, the homely *chile relleno*—here a freshly roasted poblano crammed with Mexican cheese and fried in an egg batter crisp and lacy as the coating on tempura shrimp—into creatures almost unrecognizable from their El Coyote equivalents. They don't redefine Mexican food; they just prepare it well.

Border Grill, for example, is the rare mainstream restaurant whose tacos don't make you yearn for a truck parked by an auto-parts junkyard somewhere in East L.A. There are rich tacos here stuffed with sautéed potatoes and the creamy roasted-pepper glop called *rajas*, and tacos whose salsa of ripe, minted mango mellows the fattiness of roast duck. Tacos come stuffed with crisp bits of grilled pork and a fresh tomato salsa, or with gamy shreds of long-roasted lamb splashed with pungently spicy dried-chile salsa. Cool tacos, which lack a little of the hot-corn savor that makes a fresh taco so delicious, might be wrapped around a uncommonly juicy mélange of cactus, diced tomato, and a little chile, the sort of taco recipe a Mexican grandmother might take with her to her grave.

The Yucatán-style bean-stuffed tortillas called *panuchos* may not be nearly so greasy as the classic versions you find down in Merida, but seem to capture the flavor essence of the dish, the round meatiness of well-done roast pork against the slight creaminess of puréed black beans, sparked with tart pickled onions dyed scarlet with beets.

Seafood *escabeche*, a frequent special, is less the sort of overvinegared raw sea-bass that usually goes by that name than something you might expect to find at a two-star restaurant in Perpignan: ultrafresh white Mexican shrimp, clams, tiny shelled mussels, and roasted red peppers slicked with olive oil, touched with an unconventional bit of roasted garlic, tossed with a little chile and slivered kalamata olives, and served on a bed of watercress whose slight bitterness etches the lush freshness of the seafood into sharp relief. At most of the good Mexican restaurants in Los Angeles, even the ones famous for their fish, freshness can be an issue; the seafood here is never less than impeccable: sweet rock shrimp sautéed to the subtly crunchy stage with garlic and pungent, leathery shreds of griddled ancho chiles; probably the best sea bass Veracruzano in town, baked with tomatoes, capers, and olives; lime-marinated baby octopus with carrots and sweet peppers.

Ropa vieja, which translates as "old clothes," is pure comfort food—a giant bowl of grilled beef, soupy beans, and shards of pork that comes closer to a chefly version of the homestyle Mexican dish called *carne en su jugo* than to the Cuban dish called *ropa vieja.* Grilled pork chops may have the sweet smokiness of commercial barbecued ribs but have a juiciness, a snap, all their own. Skirt steak, dusted with cumin and served with black-bean fried rice and chunks of unusually ripe plum tomatoes, is what a fajitas platter might taste like in the afterlife.

And the dessert menu includes both Los Angeles's definitive key-lime pie and autographed copies of *Mesa Mexicana.* High-cholestorol sweets and media overload: shake hands with the first restaurant of the *fin de siècle.*

BRUDDAH'S

1033 W. GARDENA BLVD., GARDENA; (310) 323-9112. TUES.–THURS., 8A.M.–8P.M., FRI. AND SAT., 7P.M.–9P.M., SUN., 7A.M.–8P.M. (SUMMER UNTIL 9P.M.).

If you're looking for the latest combination of diced papaya and unpronounceable Big Island fish, you might visit the Maui Beach Cafe. If you want to see what kind of Chinese dishes Japanese chefs might cook up for Californians in a restaurant owned by an Austrian famous for his French food, try Chinois.

But to taste the original pan-Pacific cuisine in Los Angeles, you have to travel to the South Bay, to a city-park cultural festival, a hula competition or one of the few dozen cafes that cater to the region's huge (and often overlooked) Hawaiian and Pacific Islander community. In Hawaiian cooking, Chinese, Japanese, Polynesian, Korean, and American cuisines come together as seamlessly as rice and beans.

If you are lucky enough to attend a serious luau on a Big Island farm, the pit-cooked pig, the local cockles, the salsalike *lomi lomi* salmon and the pastramiesque peppered beef called *pipikaula*—not to mention the mussels in a fragrant taro-leaf purée, the pickled raw crab, and the brothy glass noodles called "long rice"— show traditional Hawaiian cooking to be as rich in potential as any other Asian cuisine.

But the street-level version of Hawaiian cooking can be good too. Bruddah's is among the most "authentic" of California's island restaurants. A Gardena storefront on a block of dusty thrift stores crammed with bamboo-appliquéd furniture that started its life in Honolulu living rooms, kitty-corner from a '40s department store crammed with more Dickies and Carhartt jackets than you'll see in a lifetime of rap videos, the cafe looks like every greasy spoon in downtown Hilo. The long, spare room is decorated with vintage rice sacks and autographed pictures of island musicians; handbills advertising hula contests and Tahitian cultural festivals are tacked to a bulletin board. The day's specials—fried *ahi*, sweet-and-sour spareribs, *lau lau*—are inked on a board above the rear counter.

Bruddah's may be the plate-lunch capital of the South Bay, home to that uniquely Hawaiian marriage of Japanese *bento*-box formality and American abundance: austere combination plates blown up into heroic, multipound lunch-wagon platters big enough to nourish sumo wrestlers or NFL blocking backs. A plate lunch typically includes two ice-cream scoops of sticky rice and one of macaroni salad—Bruddah's mac salad, made with short segments of spaghetti and a sesame-inflected dressing dyed a deep yellow with puréed egg yolks, is excellent—as well as whatever pickles, noodles, or vegetables the proprietor decides to toss in. (At Bruddah's, usually none.) Where an order of *kalbi* at a teriyaki stand or an Asian lunch counter might comprise a skein or two of the thinly sliced Korean-style short ribs, Bruddah's serves a full half-dozen slabs of meat—crisp, well-marinated things, charred to a pleasing resinous blackness over the grill, fragrant with garlic, sweet but not sticky. Bruddah's *kalbi* is the mother of all teriyaki.

Sweet-and-sour spareribs taste like the stuff every Polynesian restaurant in the world tries to imitate, lightly vinegared and not too sweet, practically leaping from the bone at the touch of a fork. Short-rib stew, a soothing Hawaiian standard that appears most days as a special, is soft and rich and made faintly sweet with carrots: a faded souvenir of '30s American cooking that somehow springs to life with a few drops of Bruddah's chile-pepper water, a home-brewed Hawaiian hot sauce that at its best (and bottles here vary) has all the taste of fermented hot peppers without the searing heat.

There is a slight Filipino influence too: You will find pork *adobo* and *inihaw baboy* on the menu, and both the long rice and the thick *chow fun* are seasoned an awful lot like the Filipino noodles called *pancit*. Bruddah's is not a bad place to try traditional Hawaiian food, such as *lomi lomi* salmon, *lau lau*—fatty pork steamed in taro leaves—and smoky, extra-salty *kalua* pig mixed with cabbage. You can even get *poi* instead of rice for an extra dollar or two if you are so inclined.

The Hawaiian aesthetic of Pacific Rim cuisine contrasts fairly radically with Wolfgang Puck's, especially at breakfast time. There are banana pancakes and French toast made with thick slices of Hawaiian bread at Bruddah's, but you can also get Dinty Moore corned beef hash or fried bologna with your eggs in the morning instead of bacon or Portuguese sausage. Giant omelets wrap around fillings of Vienna sausage or Barbie-box-pink slices of Japanese fish cake.

Bruddah's even does an exemplary version of the notorious *loco moco*: an enormous plateau of rice topped with two well-done hamburger patties, which are in turn topped with two fried eggs and then drenched in a thick, viscous, dark-brown goo that tastes a lot like canned mushroom gravy. Looked at objectively, of course, a *loco moco* is a culinary Chernobyl, but there is a certain stark beauty in the composition, and in Bruddah's *loco moco* the patties of meat are extra-crisp and extra-oniony . . . really good, in fact, once you scrape off most of the sauce.

BURRITO KING

2109 E. SUNSET BLVD., LOS ANGELES; (213) 413-9444. ALSO AT 2823 HYPERION AVE., SILVER LAKE. DAILY, BREAKFAST, LUNCH, AND DINNER.

Like the Cornish pasty and the Korean sushi roll, the burrito started its life as brown-bag food, a ladleful of last night's dinner reheated and encased in an edible container that kept it warm all the way to lunch. The best burritos are based on hearty, steamy stews of meat and vegetables, stews that not only hold but improve with a couple of hours on the steam table: burritos keep. Even a bad lunch-wagon burrito is pretty good.

But like sushi, the burrito has a classic model, and while variations from it may be tasty, they violate the basic formal principles that make a burrito what it is: stew, providing the basic flavor, and beans, stretching the expensive meat, adding bulk, texture, and a nonassertive flavor. In a burrito, the beans serve the same function as rice does in a sushi roll or mashed potatoes do in a shepherd's pie. Rice in a burrito is distracting; dollops of sour cream or guacamole or cheese in a meat-based burrito are plainly wrong.

The original Burrito King is Los Angeles's classic burrito stand, a brightly lit takeout counter, decorated with prancing cartoon burros, jammed into a lozenge-shaped mini-mall a few steps from a liquor store well stocked with Mexican beer. Fifteen or twenty years ago, Burrito King was considered as worthy of a 2:00 A.M. pilgrimage as Tommy's or Pink's, and Angelenos who had moved to New York or Paris openly pined for Burrito King's *chile verde* burritos the way expatriate Chicagoans pine for Vienna hot dogs. In most of my friends' refrigerators you could find little plastic containers of *encurtido,* Burrito King's crisp little garnish of spicy pickled carrots and onions.

But Burrito King's stature declined somewhere in the early '80s. The chain slumped to just two restaurants, and it became hipper to go to the car-wash taco stand across the street instead of the mothership: the spicing was sharper, the formulas more Mexican than Mexican-American. The customers at the car wash blast *conjunto* music, and Burrito King customers Cypress Hill; the car-wash place caters to a crowd largely made up of recent immigrants, and Burrito King to their Americanized children. The car wash is where you might go after dancing all night to salsa at Nayarit; Burrito King is where you stop off after a Dodger game.

Regional Mexican food almost always rocks harder than Americanized hybrid cooking, but there are hundreds of stands like the car-wash place in Los Angeles, and many of them are actually better. Still, Burrito King, along with a few traditional compatriots like Lupe's Burritos in East Los Angeles, is in a league of its own. If your idea of a perfect burrito involves liquidy beans, oozing brains, or pig's stomach, I suppose the car-wash place is still the obvious choice. For the rest of us, there is Burrito King.

Burrito King's burritos are substantial but not grotesque, stuffed with mild red chile, beans, and cheese, or with a bland, sweet meat stew called *machaca*. The *chile relleno* burritos are renowned; spicy fresh poblanos dipped in batter and fried, served still a little crisp, plumped with orange cheese and surrounded with beans, sometimes including the seedpod of the chile, with a searing heat that benumbs the lips and gladdens the soul.

There are burritos that act like tacos here, stuffed with grilled beef or chicken, doused with chunky salsa, slicked with just enough beans to give a presence to the whole, and some of these are even really good, though they miss the point. The *carnitas* burrito may not be as good as the one you can get across from the dog track in Tijuana, but the clear, musky sweetness of crisply fried meat overlaid with the slightly scorched flavor of overheated oil is not to be despised. The green-chile burrito may be the *sine qua non* of Los Angeles burritos, spicy, though not as hot as I thought it was when I was in high school, and bright, with the fresh, almost citrusy taste of green chiles against the rounder sweetness of the pork and the grainy, almost fermented quality of the smooth beans (just enough of them left intact to give the rest texture) that cement together the whole. As a bonus, this burrito is so well engineered you can eat almost the entire thing in the car before the chile drools onto your lap.

BU SAN

201 N. WESTERN AVE., LOS ANGELES; (323) 871-0703. MON.-SAT., 11A.M.- 1P.M., 5P.M.-11P.M.

Bu San, a sushi bar on a seedy strip of Western dominated by carpet wholesalers and used-furniture stores, looks not unlike every other mini-mall sushi bar in Los Angeles. There are woodcuts on the wall either real or simulated, sushi identification crib sheets on the tables, and a poster above the sink extolling the virtues of New Jersey seafood. Chefs behind the long sushi bar deftly dissect fat blocks of tuna into sashimi, slip eel filets into toaster ovens, and roll up *futomaki* on bamboo mats. You could, if you were in the mood, order your meal in Japanese.

But Bu San, along with several other places in the neighborhood, is a Korean-style sushi bar: staffed by Korean sushi chefs and catering to an almost exclusively

Korean clientele, it serves a brand of raw-fish preparation that is different enough from the original almost to constitute a separate cuisine.

Where a Japanese sushi meal, a classic one anyway, tends to speak in delicate nuances, Korean sushi is bigger than life, meaty, full of the sort of strong flavors that sensitive sushi chefs wouldn't allow in the same mini-mall with their *maguro* sashimi. Japanese sushi is modestly proportioned; Korean sushi is served in generous, truck-driver slabs. Japanese sushi bars typically give you a bit of delicately simmered yellowtail collar to get your palate moving in the right direction; Korean sushi bars start you off with a chile-soaked dish of fermented cabbage you can smell across the room.

When you land a sushi bar seat at Bu San, the chef lays down a board laden with the usual ginger and wasabi, but also a few lengths of pungent *gobo* root, and knobs of pickled scallion that would go really well in a Gibson. Two small bowls contain a mild cabbage *kimchi* and slices of daikon pungently marinated with garlic and sliced jalapeño peppers. The chef will ask whether you trust him to choose the sushi. Say yes.

You will probably start with tuna sashimi, three hulking slabs of the stuff, then cured salmon, in sheets as big as entrée portions at Jozu.

As Korean sushi bars tend to, Bu San has tanks of live seafood behind the counter, teeming with wriggling things. At the tables, Korean businessmen seal deals with gallons of beer and giant portions of halibut that was alive until a minute earlier. Even if you're not hungry enough to eat an entire raw halibut, there is halibut sushi—called "live white fish" on the printed sushi menu—from a fish that was still alive at the beginning of lunch service, two giant pieces per order.

The chefs are fond of fishing big prawns out of the tanks, letting them nip at your nose a bit, and then beheading them in front of you before taking them back into the kitchen. The prawns reappear as sushi on elaborately arranged platters, garnished with both flying fish eggs and shrimp roe, and surmounted with their own spiky heads, which have been deep-fried until they are as crunchy as potato chips.

If you are up for truly Korean raw fish, a squadron of bowls appear: squares of cooked spinach smeared with sweet bean sauce and served on a bed of shredded daikon; cooked bits of squid with another hot bean sauce; a vinegary salad of crunchy jellyfish and mock crab tossed with a puckeringly tart rice vinaigrette. Raw squid, luxuriously creamy, with a small bit of crunch at the center, tastes alive, almost alarmingly so.

Slivers of raw sea cucumber in a bean sauce, impossibly tough, monochromatic at first, then seem almost to pump out a sweet, fresh brininess that keeps going on for as long as you care to chew, which could be hours. I don't particularly care for cooked sea cucumber—to me, the sea slugs usually taste like a cross between a sneaker sole and an old can of sardines—but this stuff is extraordinary.

If you can keep going, the chef might slice chewy bits of flesh from the halibut collar into julienne strips, or plop down a fresh *kumamoto* oyster topped with a few smelt eggs. Sometimes there is a wonderful little salad of halibut, cut into thin strips, chilled until it has the consistency of a fish sorbet, and then tossed with sesame oil, shredded scallions, and white and black sesame seeds, the sort of thing you'd expect to pay $23 for at Spago.

And as you rise from the sushi bar after fifteen or so courses, grab a check from the waitress, and pay before you can be tempted by hand rolls, omelets, or giant crabs, the chef's cries follow you out the door: "Don't you at least want an orange?"

C

CAFE BRASIL

CAFE BRASIL, 10831 VENICE BLVD., LOS ANGELES; (310) 837-8957. DAILY, 11A.M.–10P.M.

Cafe Brasil is a happy place on a weekend afternoon, a sort of Los Angeles facsimile of the indoor-outdoor cafes you find on busy street corners in the Ipanema district of Rio de Janeiro. The music blares; the air is perfumed with internal-combustion fumes and garlic; a multiracial, multilingual crowd of expatriates lubricates conversation with oceans of fresh-squeezed juice and caffeine-rich *guárana* soda.

The dining room, converted from the takeout area of what used to be a burger shack, is rich in the kind of details that make it into magazines like *Elle Decor*: battered ewers, wire baskets filled with fresh lemons, picturesquely scarred old tables. A bulletin board bristles with Portuguese-language posters announcing dinner-dances and rooms to let; Brazilian weeklies are stacked by the door.

Cafe Brasil came into existence as a simpler place called Carioca, and around it grew up sort of a micro-Brazil with a couple of restaurants, a lawyer's office or two, and a Brazilian "supermarket" whose stock seems to consist of a few jars of *malagueta* chiles scattered among videotapes of telenovelas and tattered, month-old issues of *Veja*.

When the restaurant first opened there was always a grilled-meat dish on the menu and maybe a soup or two, but it seemed to concentrate mostly on the Brazilian snacks, the fried-beef turnovers called *risole*, the baked heart-of-palm turnovers called *pastis*, the shortening-rich chicken *empanadinhas* that are the sort of thing you can expect to find behind the glass counter in any truck stop on the highway going between Rio and São Paulo. Later, after one of the original owners decamped, the place became locally famous for the tropical breakfasts—

fresh-squeezed passion-fruit juice, fried plantains, eggs, baked cheese puffs called *pao de queijo*—that make up the Brazilian equivalent of bacon and eggs.

While you still have to stand in line to order, and still have to carry your own food to the table, Cafe Brasil is more or less a full-line restaurant now, twice the size, with any number of variations on chicken breast, big bowls of pasta, and French-bread sandwiches glued together with melted cheese. Mostly, though, you will find grilled animal at Cafe Brasil: pork chops, lamb chops, steak, shrimp, and fish, all profoundly salty and resonant with garlic, charred at the edges, fragrant with citrus, and a little overcooked. Even the vegetarian plate, which consists mostly of various slivered squashes sautéed with vast quantities of garlic, has some of the belly-filling qualities you might associate with Big Meat. (This is not uncharacteristic. Of the thirteen pages of restaurant ads in the Rio de Janeiro phone book the last time I was in Brazil, something like nine of them were devoted to steak restaurants.)

With the protein comes what seems like a truckload of rice glistening with oil, as well as a couple of sweet fried plantains, spicy black beans, and a bowl of "Cajun-spiced" bean soup that is not quite so far away from that bowl of spicy black beans as one might wish. A Cafe Brasil lunch is generally an uncomplicated meal.

Rio, the birthplace of the thong bikini, samba, and the phenomonon of seventy-year-old women in midriff-baring sarongs, is also home to the Saturday-afternoon *feijoada*, a pork-and-bean stew heavy enough to make Toulousian cassoulet seem like spa cuisine. There is slab bacon in a proper *feijoada*, hot sausage and smoked sausage, tails and feet, tongues and shanks, ribs, innards and dried beef, stewed overnight with black beans until they surrender their souls to the broth.

It is quite a spectacle in Rio to watch perhaps the lithest people in the world tucking into 4500 calories of hog fat after a morning of beach volleyball. And Cafe Brasil, it almost goes without saying, serves wonderful *feijoada*, less offal-intensive than some versions, perhaps, but meat-fragrant in the best possible way and served with the traditional garnishes of fried manioc flour, oranges, herbed salsa, and well-garlicked shreds of sautéed kale. All that's missing from the *feijoada* experience at Cafe Brasil is the sand, the tropical sun, and foaming gallons of cold Brahma beer.

CAFE TROPICAL

2900 SUNSET BLVD., SILVER LAKE; (323) 661-8391. MON.–SAT., 6A.M.–
10P.M.; SUN., 7A.M.–10P.M.

Perhaps the most popular of Cuban sandwiches is the *media noche*, the midnight sandwich: garlicky roast pork stuffed into a plump roll. I have eaten "Cuban" grilled tuna sandwiches at street stands in Miami and Cubanesque smoked turkey sandwiches in a fancy restaurant on Melrose. When referring to sandwiches, Mexicans sometimes use the term "Cuban" the way Americans do "Italian," as a loose modifier signifying something like "hugely overstuffed," though the kind of Cuban sandwich you'd get in Guadalajara bears no resemblance to the ones you'd find in Havana or Ybor City. But what most people mean by a Cuban sandwich, the sandwich you'd get at a Tampa lunch counter if you asked for "a Cuban," is one of the most astonishing creations on earth: a split length of buttered Cuban bread, stuffed with ham, roast pork, Swiss cheese, and pickle chips and grilled in a sandwich press until the filling has steamed, the pickle has warmed, the flavors have melded, and the outermost crust of the bread has annealed into something crisp and shiny and thin as a dime.

A great Cuban sandwich is more than the sum of its ingredients, but there are arguments as to just what makes a Cuban sandwich great. Some connoisseurs insist that the sandwich be made with a damp loaf, which may be the only bread capable of becoming crisp without drying out too much. Some people think the meat ought to be given a chance to be grilled a little bit; others countenance soft meat crisped just at the edges. Some people enjoy mustard on the sandwich; others consider it an abomination.

It is technically possible to eat a good Cuban sandwich in a regular sit-down Cuban restaurant, though many of the places that list them on their menus are not actually prepared to serve you one. Like the burrito and the chili dog, a Cuban sandwich is ultimately fast food, mostly served at bakeries, better served in a red plastic basket than on porcelain, best eaten straight from the griddle, washed down with a *guanabana* shake or the sticky Cuban soft drink called *malta*.

Although the sandwiches are served all over Los Angeles, the best are still probably at Cafe Tropical, the famous Silver Lake coffeehouse famous for the cheapest espresso in town. When the right guy's behind the counter, Tropical makes close to a perfect Cuban, pressed flat as a waffle, the bread tender, a little soft but cracklingly crisp, moistened with a squirt of a mysterious but garlicky substance from a squeeze bottle. The meat is griddled and browned, not just steamed by the warmth of the sandwich. The intensely smoky ham is sliced thin; the fat pork dissolves into sweet juice. The cheese in the sandwich is more a faint presence than a dairy product. Even experts are unable to agree whether the Swiss cheese should have an integrity of its own or should just melt and add an anonymous richness to the meat, like the American cheese on a cheeseburger.

Tropical has never really felt the same since it was remodeled. Screenwriters and scenics largely replaced the old-time Cuban clientele; the music on the stereo modulated into the kind of stuff David Byrne might dig. But the Cubans are undeniable. Get one to go.

CAIOTI PIZZA CAFE

4346 TUJUNGA AVE., STUDIO CITY; (818) 761-3588. MON.-THURS., 11A.M.-3P.M., 5P.M.-10P.M.; FRI. AND SAT., 9A.M.-3P.M., 5P.M.-11P.M.; SUN., 10A.M.-3P.M., 4P.M.-10P.M.

When the secret history of California pizza is finally written, a greasy volume inscribed in arugula, white truffle oil, and ripe goat cheese, the name popping up like a hard-boiled egg inadvertently stirred into a tomato sauce will probably be that of Ed LaDou, Hollywood's oddball genius of dough.

When LaDou auditioned for Wolfgang Puck eighteen years ago, he reportedly prepared a pâté-and-mustard pizza so bizarre that the chef almost threw him out of his restaurant, but he was hired anyway as the first pizza chef at Spago—where his woodfire-cooked concoctions of goat cheese, duck sausage, broccoli, and Louisiana shrimp radically revitalized the form. After two years, LaDou left to consult for the company that became California Pizza Kitchen, and his inventions for the chain—barbecue chicken pizza, BLT pizza, Peking duck pizza—reworked the elite Spago style to popular taste. If a pizza in Dayton, Ohio, has smoked Gouda and pine nuts on it, if goat cheese pizza with sun-dried tomatoes has spread to Singapore and Guam, it is in no small part due to LaDou's influence.

The baroque LaDou style probably reached its greatest heights at the now-defunct Caioti Cafe, his very own dark, hippie-ish restaurant in the heart of Laurel Canyon, where Dylan or Cat Stevens was always on the tape deck, the salads were often composed from young weeds picked from the local hillsides, and the rantings of the canyon's homeless were often a part of the evening's entertainment. Mexican cactus pizza was born at Caioti, and smoked rabbit pizza, and foie gras calzone.

LaDou is back again, at the Caioti Pizza Cafe, a small, crowded pizzeria tucked into a charming street of coffeehouses and storefront theater companies, walls decorated with menus from long-defunct Los Angeles restaurants, the CD player still stocked with Dylan. Meals here still start with little knots of baked pizza dough slicked with oil and handfuls of garlic. The California pizza is first-rate: slightly sweet, gently risen, a chewy, unobtrusive platform for some of the most exotic ingredients in the world. Here is a wonderful version of Spago's Jewish

41

pizza, an ultrathin, cracker-crisp crust thickly laden with crème fraîche, smoked salmon, and peppery nasturtium blossoms, and a more substantial Cajun pizza topped with sliced andouille sausage, okra, and a weirdly tart sprinkling of file powder. (Pizza Rockefeller, with oysters, anise-flavored spinach, and toasted bread crumbs, is just weird.) The smoked chicken pizza is exactly the sort of thing that has made California Pizza Kitchen so popular, a sharply flavored arrangement lightened with goat cheese and peppers, and the spare, intense pizza with grilled eggplant and crumbles of lamb sausage may be the best of all.

The barbecue chicken pizza, with slivered red onion, smoked Gouda, and barbecue sauce instead of tomato, is definitive. It's almost an exercise in nostalgia, a dinner at Caioti, a taste of multiculti post-Olympics Los Angeles . . . with a hunk of Sweet Baby Jane's gooey chocolate raspberry cake for dessert.

CALI VIEJO

7363 VAN NUYS BLVD., VAN NUYS; (818) 994-2930. SUN.–THURS., 10A.M.–9P.M., FRI. AND SAT., 10A.M.–10P.M.

As the Chinese restaurant revolves around the stir-fry and the old-line French place rests on its heavy sauces, South American restaurant meals are, to many, almost synonymous with humongous platters of beef. In most of the Argentine, Chilean, and Bolivian places in California, the basic unit of currency is the giant mixed grill, the *parillada,* a megaton of charred protein that often comes unadorned by so much as a sprig of parsley or a french fry. Among the hillocks of grilled spinal cord, the mountains of blood sausage, the garlic-reeking Alps of short ribs to be found in Los Angeles, none is quite so majestic as the *picada* combination plate served at the restaurant Cali Viejo.

Cali Viejo is a smart, dim-lit red-leather booth place just down from the shuttered General Motors plant, specializing in the cooking of the warm Andean valley around the Colombian city of Cali. A television in the restaurant blasts Spanish-language news to the carnivores, except when there are merengue videos that look like something MTV might have shown in 1984.

Big Colombian tamales are steamed in banana leaves here, stuffed with potatoes and pork, spiced in a manner that might remind you of an extremely good tamale pie; flank steak is braised in a tomato-onion Creole sauce for the tough *sobrebarriga.* There is a ground beef dish that is something like a highly spiced Colombian *salpicon,* almost as dry and fine as powder, and pork chops fried in a spicy crust. *Bandejas* are the traditional combination plates of the Colombian mountain regions: massive amounts of rice served with fried eggs, underseasoned beans, plantains, and a small steak.

But you've come for the *picada.* Come hungry: The *picada*—"¡mira ve! . . .

picada," it says on the unbashful menu—is an oval ceramic platter heaped with grilled lengths of thumb-width Colombian chorizo, peppery nubs of grilled beef, pungent blood sausage, crisp chunks of spare rib, and a few chunks of peculiar though typical Colombian *chicharrones* that are more or less grids of crisply fried pork-fat anchored to sweet, ultrachewy pigskin.

Garnishing the meat are green plantains that have been pounded down to approximately the size and thickness of a three-by-five card and fried to a shattering crunch, lengths of slightly riper fried plaintain, a few slices of tomato, and chunks of fried cassava good enough to make you remember why *yuca* fries were so popular a few years ago. The hot salsa served on the side, *aji*, made from fresh chiles and chopped scallions, has an odd astringency that cuts through the garlicky richness of the meat. There are a couple of *arepas*, hockey pucks of barely cooked cornmeal encased in a sort of a cooked-corn leather, often dead-cold in the center, that are pretty much inedible—though oddly enough the fresh cheese *arepas* served as an appetizer are crisp and delicious. And though the *picada* is ostensibly served for one, the platter will probably serve three, perhaps augmented by an order of the wonderful corn-crusted *empanadas* or a batter-fried plaintain stuffed with cheese. The *picada* is a formidable plate of food.

CANARY HOUSE OF SANDWICHES

1942 WESTWOOD BLVD., WESTWOOD; (310) 470-1312. MON.–THURS., 11A.M.–12A.M.; FRI. AND SAT., 11A.M.–4A.M., SUN., 9A.M.–9P.M.

"So how do you eat this?" Margaret said, pointing at her very first serving of the Iranian stew *dizie*, a complicated concoction involving little bowls of soup, mashed stew, powerfully sour pickled vegetables, and fresh herbs.

"You tear up pieces of this bread," said the waiter.

"Yes . . ." said Margaret.

"And you put them in the bowl . . ."

"Okay . . ." said Margaret.

"And you take this spoon . . ."

"And . . ." said Margaret.

"And then you eat it. It's soup!"

Canary is an Iranian sandwich shop on Westwood's Iranian strip. The restaurant's facade is yellow—canary yellow—and daubed with cheerful admonitions in Farsi. Inside, there is a bright mural of flowers on one wall, and several dozen giant glass apothecary jars, arrayed on every horizontal surface, filled with gallons of pickling garlic. As W. C. Fields once said of the garlic packing town of Gilroy, you could marinate a steak just by hanging it on a clothesline here. If it is your first time at Canary, you will undoubtedly be steered to one of the kebab plates, skewers of grilled lamb or chicken served with the usual Iranian accouterments of saffron-gilded rice, grilled tomatoes, and a small green salad of exceptional freshness, dressed simply with citrus juice and a little oil. You may be able to talk the guy behind the counter into a small Styrofoam container of thick yogurt laced with quantities of fresh garlic sufficient to make your eyes water, like a great Greek *tsatsiki* overbuilt to military specifications, or possibly a little dish of Canary's *torshi*, made with herbs and lots of that vinegared garlic you see curing all around you. I am a fan of the homemade sour yogurt drink, *dough*—pronounced "doog"—which is garnished with crumbled mint.

If you pay attention, however, you may notice that most of the people in the restaurant are lunching not on kebabs but on something that you later come to recognize as an Iranian-style sandwich made with a split and grilled Hebrew National frank, a hollowed-out length of toasted French bread, and condiments similar to those you might expect to find on a Chicago-style hot dog. The sensation of that hot dog is a strange cross between Jewish excess, Middle Eastern flavor, and Cuban-sandwich crispness, like something you might hope to find in a cross-cultural corner restaurant somewhere in Miami Beach. These sandwiches, also available with grilled lamb's tongue, grilled chicken, or grilled beef, come garnished with a fistful of freshly made potato chips.

Canary, though, is obviously more than a kebab or sandwich place, and a couple of visits later, I traced a finger down the entire Farsi-only, right-hand side of the menu, making a guy behind the counter translate every dish. This did not make him happy.

"The first one," he said, "is lamb-and-lentil stew that we pound after we cook it, and you drink the juice as soup." "Like *dizi*?" I asked, remembering a long-gone restaurant in Glendale that used to specialize in the dish. "Of course, *dizi*," he said with a dismissive nod, as if he was wondering why I bothered to ask. "The next one you don't want, because it is made with the tongue of the lamb. The third one is meat with grain; we call it *haleem*. Then is heart, kidney, liver, things like that."

I always thought I liked *haleem*, at least the thick, stewy Syrian version of the dish, and I like the beefy, ultraspicy pastes of meat and shredded wheat you find under that name in Pakistani cafes even more. Canary's *haleem*, though, is one of the strangest dishes I've ever come across, essentially a bowl of Cream of Wheat spiked with shreds of cooked turkey and paved with a quarter-inch layer of ground cinnamon.

"Here," the waiter said, and plunked down a canister by my plate. "Add sugar. That way it is slightly less bland."

We ordered a sandwich to go, made with a fried vegetable patty, *kotlet*, that was remarkably similar to decent falafel, and we had a picnic lunch in the car.

CARIBBEAN TREEHOUSE

1226 CENTINELA AVE., INGLEWOOD; (310) 330-1170. TUES.-THURS.,
11A.M.-8P.M.; FRI., 11A.M.-11P.M.; SAT., 11A.M.-9P.M.; SUN., 12-8P.M.

On a green stretch of Centinela not far from the lush lawns of Ladera Heights, Caribbean Treehouse is perhaps the only local restaurant that currently serves the spicy food of Trinidad and Tobago—all thatch, travel posters, and exotic soda pop. Toward the rear of the restaurant, a giant palm tree grows straight out of the dining room floor, thrusting through the ceiling and topping out a good thirty feet above the restaurant's roof. On a good night, a Trinidadian video might blare from the television set high in a corner, perhaps a souvenir tape of Carnival or a shaky hand-held-camera document of a steel-band competition held in Port-of-Spain.

Service is casual to the extreme—if you want another bottle of pop, you walk over to the cooler and take one out yourself. Try the sorrel, which is similar to— but better than—the Mexican flower-petal drink *jamaica,* or a bottle of the thick (really thick) peanut-butter beverage called peanut punch.

The restaurant is often out of pretty much everything, which means that out of the three or four appetizers listed you would be lucky to find even one— perhaps the tasty pea-flour fritters called *polouris. Roti* are usually on hand, burrito-looking things made out of griddled Trinidadian flatbread wrapped around chicken-potato stew or a handful of curried beef flavored with the restaurant's fiery habañero pepper sauce. The curried shrimp, sweet little things stained yellow with annatto, are very nice. There are different kinds of *pelau,* variations on the West African rice dish, cooked with pigeon peas or earthy, delicious black-eyed peas, served with heaps of curried meat. Sometimes there is a Trinidadian version of jerk chicken, all backyard-barbecue smokiness and sweet, peppery sauce. And on Saturdays, there is the Sparrow Special, an enormous plate of food that involves jerkylike strips of salt cod, boiled cassava, sautéed onion, tomato, and a certain quantity of dense, chewy dumplings that seem rooted less in the Caribbean than in Mitteleuropa and balance out the pungency of the cod perhaps more effectively than one might expect. If you've ever wondered what a New England boiled dinner might taste like in the tropics, the Sparrow Special might be for you.

CARLITOS GARDEL'S

7963 MELROSE AVE., LOS ANGELES; (323) 655-0891. MON.–FRI., 11:30A.M.–2:30P.M., 6P.M.–11P.M., SAT., 6–10P.M.; SUN., 5–10P.M.

With a Gaucho Grill in practically every neighborhood affluent enough to support a Starbucks, *empanada* joints and Buenos Aires–style pasta parlors almost as ubiquitous as burger stands in certain areas of the Westside, Argentine cooking is probably the most popular new cuisine in Los Angeles since Thai food caught on a couple of decades ago. At its most basic, Argentine food is easy to like: grilled animal parts soaked in garlic, served with fries and a parsleyed garlic sauce called *chimichurri,* sluiced down with vast quantities of red wine or beer. It is masculine stuff, simple as burgers and fries.

Gardel's, on the eastern end of the Melrose antique district, has always been the most sophisticated Argentine restaurant in Los Angeles, a long, narrow dining room illuminated with thousands of tiny white lights and bathed in the bathetic tangoisms of a rather overamplified violin-and-piano duo that plays toward the rear. Napkins are folded with military precision; the stemware actually shines. Waiters wear tuxedos and conduct themselves with that peculiar professional aloofness you see everywhere in Europe, but almost never in restaurants staffed by moonlighting actors. Gardel's is a serious place.

Though I went a lot to Regina's, the sleek Western Avenue Argentine restaurant that moved west at the beginning of the '80s to become Gardel's, it took me a while to get around to Gardel's proper. When the restaurant first opened—when it introduced Los Angeles to the sensuous pleasure of squeezing an entire head of baked garlic until the soft, fragrant flesh oozed onto a crusty slab of Italian bread—Gardel's was too expensive to manage on my part-time salary. By the time I could afford to eat there once in a while, I was already on to Cantonese seafood and Taylor's steaks instead, and the first-wave Argentine places like Don Felipe on Western somehow seemed more soulful than I imagined Gardel's to be; realer, less expensive. Also, undeniably, not quite as good. Gardel's is still masculine, but not quite so butch as Don Felipe or the Gaucho Grill, significantly more refined, almost chefly. There is melted provolone cheese, laced with tomatoes and pungent Mexican oregano, to eat with the Vermont-style Argentine crackers in the bread baskets, and an appetizer of butter-smooth roasted red peppers just brushed with garlic and oil. The fried squid are the tender, delicate kind, hardly crunchy, tasting more of the sea than of oil. French fries, the skinny, crisp kind, come tossed with a double handful of minced raw garlic and parsley—an order of fries that could take on the offensive line of the Steelers with its sheer, brutal force. The most famous dish at Gardel's is probably still the baked garlic appetizer, a naked halved bulb on a plate, ready to pulp onto the house's quite decent bread. This stuff must have seemed revolutionary before the late-'80s wave of Urban Rustic Cuisine saw chefs tossing cloves of roasted garlic into everything but ice cream, and it is still good now, if a bit plain: mild, sweet, tender, but lacking the essential Major Protein—a roast chicken, say, or a Hunanese braised catfish—that might put the garlic into context.

At lunchtime there are sandwiches on crusty French rolls, stuffed with lettuce, ripe tomatoes, and things like spicy Argentine sausage; *milanesa*, a paper-thin sheet of breaded beef fried Italian-style to a sort of chewy crispness; or *matambre*, the classic Argentine roulade of cold flank steak rolled around roasted red peppers and chopped boiled eggs. You will find the usual heavyish Argentine pastas—two-thirds of the people in Argentina are of Italian ancestry—plumped out with cream; also the occasional grilled chicken breast or fish.

Gardel's, like almost any Argentine restaurant, seems proudest of its *parrillada*, a cavalcade of well-garlicked meats—sweetbreads, blood sausage, skirt steak, short ribs, Italian sausage—served on a smoking iron grill and accompanied only by a small bowl of *chimichurri* and a large plate of mashed potatoes. The meat is fine at Gardel's, juicer than you would ever expect such well-done meat to be, full of flavor and overwhelming in its variety. You could get a New York steak or a flank steak instead of the *parrillada*, but you would only feel deprived.

CAROUSSEL RESTAURANT

5112 HOLLYWOOD BLVD., HOLLYWOOD; (323) 660-8060. TUES.-SUN., 12-9P.M.

At the Hye Plaza in East Hollywood, you can book a trip to Yerevan, replace your contact lenses, or insure your Saab, all without speaking anything but Armenian. If you're in a mood for music, you might stop by Pe-Ko, where you can buy Lebanese disco records or tapes by Harut, the soulful, hairy Palm Springs resident who is more or less the Rod Stewart of Armenia.

Whether you ask for the tip or not, the guys behind the Pe-Ko counter, who know from Armenian food, will suggest that you check out Caroussel Restaurant next door, where the air conditioning is good and the kebabs are tasty. They eat there almost every day themselves.

Caroussel is a large, airy rec room of a restaurant, a basic place with a mirrored ball on the ceiling for communion parties and tables long enough to accommodate either large families or several pairs of hungry strangers. Crooned Armenian pop, the kind that sounds rather like Julio Iglesias, drones away. It's pretty wholesome—nothing stronger than the sour yogurt drink *tun* is served—and also very friendly, a great place for a party. (A larger, fancier, version of Caroussel in Glendale does serve Lebanese liquor, elaborate prepared dishes and outstanding grilled quail, but somehow feels less festive than the original Hollywood restaurant.)

The first thing you should order, especially on a hot afternoon, is the cool, Syrian-style dip *muhammara*, an extraordinary brick-red paste made from red peppers and ground walnuts that packs a cumin wallop and is complex as wine. It tastes something like a more delicate Mexican chorizo, but without the 1300 calories of hog grease. You can scoop it up with pita or daub it on everything in sight; it goes especially well with kebabs. Hummos is the usual stuff, smooth and rich, seasoned with an extra dose of sesame, best when spiked with chunks of the sweet, coarsely ground Armenian sausage called *sujuk*. *Mutabal* is hummos enriched with smoky eggplant; *labni* is a less than exciting bowl of homemade Armenian sour cream.

On a hot day, try another paste, *chi kofta*, a dish of finely ground bulgur wheat and raw lamb that's sort of the Armenian steak tartare, clean-tasting and subtly spiced, garnished with spears of raw onion. You can also get *kofta* fried into little wheaty capsules. *Maani* are small, soft links of sausage, strongly spiced with cinnamon and very good. *Arayes* seems the Armenian equivalent of the sloppy joe, a savory ground-meat and tomato mixture sandwiched in pita—a dollop of *muhammara*, if you happen to have one, sends it over the top. Eggplant salad is extremely simple—chopped with onion, tomato, and green pepper, doused with lemon, garlic, and olive oil—but delicious, the sort of earthy dish you might expect to be served in a country restaurant somewhere in Eastern Europe. Tabbouleh, chopped parsley salad brightly flavored with mint, tastes as green as it looks; artichoke salad, what seems to be storebought artichoke hearts pepped up with spices and canned mushrooms, is less successful.

Almost everybody seems to order one of the kebab platters, big piles of grilled, marinated pork or lamb or chicken or liver that come with roasted peppers, a grilled tomato and a good green salad. Each kebab is served with a stack of hot pita bread that has been smeared with a spicy tomato sauce.

"You must be at least half-Armenian by now," the waitress said the last time I came in. "You explain this food to your friends."

CASA BIANCA PIZZA PIE

1650 COLORADO BLVD., EAGLE ROCK; (323) 256-9617. TUES.–THURS., 4A.M.–12A.M.; FRI. AND SAT., 4P.M.–1A.M.

Of all the neighborhood pizza parlors that claim to serve the greatest pizza in Los Angeles, one of them has to be telling the truth. And after chomping my way through half the pies in California, I'm pretty sure that place is Casa Bianca Pizza

Pie. I realized I was on the right track when my friend Bob, who is usually fond of exchanging restaurant gossip, turned suddenly ugly.

"You realize that if you write about Casa Bianca," he said, "I'm going to have to kill you. Slowly. After I break both your legs. It's hard enough to get in on a Saturday night as it is."

Casa Bianca is located on a lonely stretch of Colorado Boulevard dominated by small apartment buildings and Rose Bowl motels, somewhere between Highland Park and Eagle Rock and usually a long block from a parking space. Its classic neon sign, a massive old thing, glows PIZZA PIE in nursery pink and blue. From the outside, it sometimes looks all misty and gloomy, like something evocative and late-'40s out of an arty new-wave gangster film.

When you step into the foyer, you're whomped with the smell of garlic and the roar of many, many people being happy. The walls of the waiting area are plastered with autographed celebrity photos—Ernest Borgnine, a young and cute Ed Asner—and a Perma-Plaqued 1973 interview with the owner from what looks like a produce-company journal. Sam and Jenny Martorana have been running the place since early in the first Eisenhower administration.

Tables are covered with red-checkered tablecloths; there are a zillion Moretti beer signs on the walls; red pepper flakes and grated cheese are there right next to the salt and pepper shakers; the wine selection is limited to pink, white, and red. If you listen hard, you can hear big-band music from the speakers overhead. This is the pizza parlor all Americans have been conditioned to look for since early childhood.

The salad to get is something called Quarter Head of Lettuce, which is a big crisp wedge frosted with anchovy filets, drizzled with Italian dressing, and surrounded with big heaps of chopped black olives, hot peppers, and ripe red tomatoes, like something you might expect to have found at a Chicago steakhouse in the '50s.

Pastas, most of them, are just okay: lasagna, linguine, and clams, spaghetti with marinara sauce, *mostaccioli* with sausage bathed in industrial-strength tomato sauce.

And the pizza—well, the pizza is just the best, especially the sausage pizza: speckled with sweetly spiced homemade sausage, dotted with mellow cloves of roasted garlic if you order them, and topped with plenty of the kind of mozzarella cheese that stretches half the way to Newark.

Tomato sauce is sparingly applied—a bit of tartness to cut through the richness of the cheese and the sausage (the eggplant topping, lightly breaded, is pretty good too); the cheese and sauce reach nearly to the edge of the crust, which lets you avoid the touchy problem of what to do with all those leftover pizza edges. The crust is chewy, yet crisp enough to maintain rigidity while you maneuver it toward your mouth; thin, yet thick enough to give the sensation of real, developed wheat flavor, and with enough carbony, bubbly burnt bits to make each bite slightly different from the last. And any leftovers taste superb with your morning coffee.

In other words, Casa Bianca makes a pizza worth driving across town for. But leave Saturday nights around seven for Bob. He has a family to feed.

CASSELL'S

3300 WEST SIXTH ST., LOS ANGELES; (213) 480-8668. MON.-SAT., 10:30A.M.-4P.M.

Though Tommy's and The Apple Pan may figure more prominently in the consciousness of most Angelenos, people who know generally consider Cassell's hamburgers to be among the very best in the country. The freshly ground softballs of USDA prime beef weigh a full two-thirds of a pound, are broiled in a massive grill of Cassell's own design, and are served naked on a toasted bun. Unless your mother was the sort of woman who liked to mix Lipton's soup mix into ground meat, this is the utopian version of the hamburger you probably grew up on.

Calvin Trillin once wrote that Cassell's burger was probably the best available in Los Angeles. Jane and Michael Stern have praised Cassell's burger as the best in America, and Cassell's itself as the number-one people's-food destination in Los Angeles. Cassell's generally wins hamburger surveys in magazines and restaurant guides. Even at times when the restaurant is crowded with besuited insurance guys gobbling a quick hamburger lunch, there are usually at least a few foodie tourists at Cassell's, nibbling on the mustard-tinged potato salad and having a Culinary Experience.

You stand in line, you put your cutlery on a cafeteria tray, you order your burger by number and degree of doneness: 32, medium. (The counterman will make fun of you if you order yours rare, but your hamburger will come out nicely crusted and bursting with juice.) You push your tray down a kind of buffet line, where you can load your burger with lettuce, sliced onion, ripe beefsteak tomato, homemade mayonnaise, catsup, mustard, and perhaps the gamy house-made Roquefort dressing. You grab a glassful of lemonade and pay at a register at the end of the buffet.

If Cassell's has a flaw, it is that the meat is too good, the preparation is too careful—so that, for instance, when you eat a cheeseburger you are perfectly aware of the awfulness of the processed American cheese, and when you splash your burger with catsup, every gram of Heinz-borne sugar makes itself known. Hamburgers buns are supposed to be crummy, but here the crumminess is unhidden by grease; iceberg lettuce is never all that flavorful, but seems even less so when contrasted with cleanly grilled beef.

Cassell's hamburgers stand out not because they are typical of the Southland—which after all did unleash the chiliburger, the Thousand Islanded multideck Big Boy burger, the Woody's Smorgasburger, and even McDonald's onto the world—but because they are apart from it, the sort of hamburgers you might expect at a quality obsessed diner somewhere in deepest Iowa, a spartan, antiexuberant hamburger qua hamburger in which each element tastes only of itself.

CEMITAS POBLANAS

5834 DENVER AVE., LOS ANGELES; (323) 759-8047. DAILY, LUNCH AND DINNER.

Perhaps the greatest of Mexico's many sandwiches, the *cemita* is the classic street food of Puebla, a crunchy sort of grinder as ubiquitous in that central Mexican town as fish tacos in Ensenada or burritos in Boyle Heights. A *cemita* looks superficially like a Big Mac—both sandwiches are multilayered concoctions on oversize, sesame-seeded buns—but the seeded roll of a *cemita* is actually closer to a dense, hard-grilled brioche than it is to spongy McDonald's product, and a *cemita*'s fearsome, if optional, chile heat will never be confused with any product of a multinational corporation. *Cemitas* vary in content, but rarely in form. The roll is griddle-toasted to a fine crunchiness and then crammed with onion, squeaky *panela* cheese, and slices of avocado ripe enough to constitute a condiment rather than a vegetable. Weighting down the cheese is a stratum of chiles, either sliced, pickled jalapenos or hot, whole chipotle *chiles en adobo*, which give the sandwich the intensity of good Texas barbecue.

There is a layer of meat over the chiles—pork loaf, perhaps, or the slippery pickled pigskin called *cueritos*, or chicken, or long-stewed Puebla-style *carnitas*. But most probably it will be a parchment-thin sheet of breaded, fried beef—the familiar pan–Latin American meat *milanesa*, named after the famous Milanese way of cooking veal—that has burnished to a bronzed crispness in a vat of hot, clean oil, and ties the elements of a *cemita* together better than any other meat. You can even get a vegetarian *cemita*, padded out with truly fearsome amounts of avocado.

Cemitas Poblanas, perhaps the first *cemita* specialist in Los Angeles, is a tiny family-owned storefront in South L.A. Mom and an auntie or two are likely hanging out in front of the restaurant; a daughter, almost hidden behind a mountain of *cemita* rolls, is at the cash register; her brother watches over a pot of meat and bubbling oil at the stove. If you come here on a Sunday night, Cemitas Poblanas is jammed with Poblano families watching the game, toasting each other with bottles of Fanta and Orange Crush, eating the house's inevitable speciality—

cemitas stuffed with *milanesa* so thin and so wide that you could probably fold it like a paper airplane and sail it across the room.

When you order a *cemita* here, the cook cuts a roll in half, tears out a little of the bread's interior to leave more room for stuff, and then presses it down on the iron griddle with a device that looks like a cross between a plunger and a giant potato masher, so that the edges crisp up correctly, then assembles the sandwich with the elaborate care of an ordinarily crooked contractor who suddenly finds himself working on a construction project for the mob. It is everything you could want from a sandwich—an essay in contrasts between the heat of the *milanesa* and the soothing coolness of cheese; the searing heat of the chipotle chiles against the bland smoothness of avocado; the solidity of the roll against the fragility of the meat.

Hats off! There's a new sandwich in town.

CHABELITA'S TACOS

2001 S. WESTERN AVE., LOS ANGELES; (323) 734-0211. DAILY, 24 HOURS.

If you were going to construct a typical L.A. burrito stand, it might look a lot like Chabelita's: a tight complex, all stucco and wrought iron, dominated by industrial-grade steel picnic tables and the bleatings of the NeoGeo machine. The customers range from truckers to cops, hood rats to priests, and a huge contingent of little kids, many of whom end up taking turns wearing the security guard's hat. You bark your order through one grated window and pick up your order to your left. While you wait, you will have plenty of time to admire the paintings airbrushed, onto the plaster, of a beautiful young Latina woman—Chabelita herself?—posed with burritos, tacos, and a watermelon-size triple-decker cheeseburger that threatens to drip onto her blouse. My favorite painting, on a truck usually parked across the street, is of Chabelita rising from the churning blue waves like a Venus of the Mariscos, beatifically bestowing octopus tostadas on us all.

Chabelita's, I think, exemplifies a particular style of Los Angeles burrito—thick layers of finely chopped grilled beef, roast pork, or stewed tongue, ballasted with a bulletproof paste of refried beans, weighted at one end with a scoop of well-seasoned Mexican rice and shot through with a thick vein of melted orange cheese. The salsa is of the juicy-tomato school, though not the kind that drips down your elbows at the earliest opportunity; the *encurtido*, lavishly served in a Baggies sandwich bag, includes plenty of crisp, freshly pickled carrots and onions alongside the usual bottled jalapenos. A Chabelita burrito seems designed to be eaten in a car, and you can finish, say, a chile-spiked burrito *al pastor* driplessly in just the time it takes to drive to the airport. What could be more Angeleno than that?

CHA CHA CHICKEN GOURMET TO GO

1906 OCEAN AVE, SANTA MONICA; (310) 581-1684. MON.–FRI., 11A.M.–10P.M., SAT. AND SUN., 10:30A.M.–10P.M.

Toribio Prado, a Mexican-American chef who likes to cook Cuban, has been the undisputed baron of upscale Caribbean cooking in Los Angeles since he cooked at the Ivy in his teens. Czar of the Cha Cha Cha restaurant empire, founder of the nuevo-continental Prado on Larchmont, mastermind of the Latin-inflected tapas bar Cava, Toribio Prado may be to black beans in California what Wolfgang Puck is to pizza.

Cha Cha Chicken Gourmet To Go may be the funkiest thing he's taken on since the original Cha Cha Cha. As Cha Cha Cha was sculpted out of a gritty East Hollywood *pupusería*, Cha Cha Chicken is a renovation not of a civic landmark or pricey fish house, but of a scuzzball hamburger stand at Pico Boulevard's western end. You—and the neighborhood dudes wandering around with their dogs—may remember this place as Tom's #5, a place that served truly crummy chili fries to street people, skate punks, and the twelve-year-olds just learning how to surf at the profoundly polluted Bay Street beach. Although Cha Cha Chicken seems to function mostly as a takeout stand, the patio off to the side is a pleasant place on a hot night, dotted with thatched *palapas*, enhanced by flowers growing out of old tomato-juice cans, ocean breezes, the milder sort of reggae music, and colored Malibu lights that cast a dim, jungly glow . . . everything for the tropical vibe but sweaty bottles of Red Stripe beer and machete-wielding dudes selling chilled drinking coconuts. There are bottles of spicy Jamaican ginger beer and imported Mexican Coke—the good stuff—which come with swap-meet tumblers of crushed ice garnished with spears of fresh sugar cane and sprigs of fresh mint. The house salad glistens under crunchy discs of fried plantains, and the cabbage slaw is dressed with a tincture of Mexican oregano that vibrates on your tongue like a mouthful of Pop Rocks. This is nothing like Kenny Rogers Roasters.

Where most of the other legendary chicken places in Los Angeles specialize in basic, garlic-zapped roast birds, Cha Cha Chicken's paradigm is Jamaican jerk chicken, the gnarled, allspice-encrusted chicken that inhabits at least one Jamaican-beach dream out of three. I like Cha Cha's jerk bird, but it is not much like the great stuff they used to serve at the old Ja'net's down by the Southwest police station, which was so densely seasoned with allspice that some people figured they knew what it was like to bite into a mahogany log.

Actually, a Cha Cha chicken is less classic Jamaican jerk chicken than it is

Cuban poultry with attitude: a luscious, crisp-skinned, Versailles-style chicken gritty with spices and painted with dense, black sauce. Cha Cha chicken is slightly sweet and intricately spiced . . . and the pepper heat starts burning about midway across your palate and works its way to the back of your throat, where it smolders for about the length of time it takes to gulp down a tall glass of lemonade and a spoonful or two of what Prado calls "dirty rice"—the beans-and-rice dish Cubans call Moors and Christians.

"I tell people this chicken is Hell hot," Prado warns a customer on one of the rare days he mans the counter himself. "The chicken is very tasty, but it is meant to hurt."

Mulato Cubano, Cha Cha's all-fowl version of the pig-intensive Cuban sandwich called *media noche*, is everything you could want in a pressed sandwich: violently spicy chicken, melted cheese, a pickle chip or two, and a French roll that has been folded, spindled, and mutilated in the maws of a sandwich press until the soft insides have the sort of steady, core heat that could probably stoke a geothermal power plant, and the outside has a sort of blistered, charred crunchiness to it that is fairly irresistible. The *mulato Cubano* is less a sandwich than a funky manifesto: it tastes great, it's less filling, and you could dance to it all night.

CHAMELI

8752 VALLEY BLVD., ROSEMEAD; (626) 280-1947. MON., WED.–FRI., 11A.M.–2:30P.M., 5–10P.M.; SAT. AND SUN., 11:30A.M.–3P.M., 5–10P.M.

Ever since the Northern Indian restaurant Chameli opened in Rosemead, the place has been sort of an open secret among vegetarians. Come on a Friday evening and you'll see Chinese Buddhist vegetarians from the neighborhood, Muslims of every stripe, the Hollywood hip crowd, and a strong cross-section of the local Indian community at what might be the fanciest meatless restaurant this side of San Francisco's Greens.

Chameli is a marble palace with brass fountains and elegant banquettes, big art on the walls, and sinuous sitar music on the sound system. (When Indians open restaurants strictly for themselves, they'll usually pop brassy Indian film music into the CD player instead.)

The front room at Chameli functions as an Indian cultural center, with a wall of Indian-themed novels and sociology tracts, a small selection of music cassettes, and a dozen racksful of gauzy saris, embroidered purses, and bright, watered-silk pajamas that look something like what you might hope to find at a high-end duty-free shop in the Bombay airport. A glass deli counter holds a modest assortment of fried Indian sweets and carrot fudge.

Where most Indian vegetarian restaurants are modest places with hand-scrawled specials on the walls, Chameli strives to be nothing less than an institution, and if you haven't been here in a while it is easy to forget how inexpensive, and accessible this place really is. The menu, mostly North Indian–style, is neither large or exotic at Chameli. It is, in fact, basically the left-hand side of the one at your local tandoori joint, the page without the meat dishes, but the usual dishes are done with unusual care. Even a basic dish like *matar paneer*, puréed peas with freshly made cheese, is likely to be the beneficiary of intricate spicing, the kind where you suspect a dish is seasoned with cardamom, fenugreek, and *asafetida* but all you can experience is multiple waves of flavor in your mouth.

You might as well start with some bread: tandoori-baked *naan*, singed from the intense heat of the clay oven, flecked with garlic, fresh cheese, or finely minced ginger; the whole-wheat flatbread *paratha* stuffed with curried potatoes or an unusual Kashmir-style filling of chopped nuts and maraschino cherries; and chewy, deep-fried puffs of the yogurt-laced *bhatura* that taste like Navaho fry bread.

You'll find the usual masses of curried lentils, the spinach-spiked fritters *pakora*, unspectacular potato *samosas*, and an ordinary rendition of the creamy mixed vegetable dish *navratan*. The chef here, though, seems unafraid of letting his vegetables taste like vegetables. The natural sweetness of pumpkin, *petha*, is brought out with a buttery, slightly tart tomato sauce; bell peppers, *bhara mirchi*, are simply baked with a mild stuffing of potatoes and peas; and puréed baked eggplant, *bhartha*, has a subtle, appealing bitterness under its blanket of tomatoes and herbs, making it almost closer to an appealing Indian inflection on the Sicilian antipasto standard *caponata* than like the stuff you find at your neighborhood curry shop.

Curried okra is spectacular here—smoky from a dollop of charred tomatoes, tinted with ground pomegranate, firm as stir-fried asparagus and as pungently green, the vegetable's natural sliminess is tamed into something of a sauce thickener. *Shahi paneer*, which tastes a little like loose ricotta curds stewed with a mild, sweet tomato sauce, may be the one Punjabi dish the late cottage-cheese-and-catsup lover Richard Nixon might conceivably have enjoyed. Chameli's mustard-green version of *saag*, a stew that calls for great, khaki glops of creamed spinach in most northern Indian restaurants, is as vivid, as intensely flavored as any Deep South dish of boiled collards. And, as in Alabama, the classic accompaniment to the greens is cornbread, in this case a flat, chewy disk of coarsely ground corn called *makki roti*. The combination is real Punjabi soul food.

CHAMIKA SRI LANKAN RESTAURANT

1717 N. WILCOX AVE., HOLLYWOOD; (323) 466-8960. TUES.-FRI., 11:30A.M.-9P.M.; SAT. AND SUN., 12-9:30P.M.

For a while in the late '80s, all of Hollywood used to go to the Sri Lanka Curry House, a bright, fragrant restaurant that served what was probably the best South Asian food in this part of the country: fierce, complexly seasoned curries and exotic Sri Lankan starches nobody around here had ever seen before; lacy bowl-shaped pancakes called *appes;* steamed, coffee-can-size logs of rice and freshly scraped coconut known as *pittu;* loose-woven noodle nets called string hoppers; rounds of coconut-scented flatbread called *roti.* If you remembered to reserve it a day in advance, you could even have the festival dish *lampries,* which are elaborate basmati rice dumplings steamed in banana leaves and served with a four-meat stew.

Now there is Chamika Sri Lankan Restaurant, owned by a guy who used to cook at Sri Lankan Curry House and frequented by most of its old customers, in a building once occupied by a hot dog stand called Big Weenies Are Better. It's small, this place, three or four tables wedged into a room nearly as vast as the backseat of a Camry, with a tall bronze statue in one corner and a stack of Sri Lankan weeklies in another, lace curtains in the windows, and *fado*-influenced Sri Lankan ballads crackling from a tape player in the kitchen.

Meals start with a basket of Sri Lankan *pappadum,* delicate lentil-flour wafers seasoned lightly with the spice *asafetida* and served with both a green chile *sambal* and a chile sauce that tastes a little like amplified catsup. You might as well try a vaguely Dutch-influenced fritter from the Nick Nack page of the menu, too: a soft, rolled-pancake curry puff, perhaps, or the fried, cabbage-stuffed marbles called *cutlets.*

Even the beverages are a little exotic here: Sri Lankan iced coffee has the sweet intensity of the White Russians you probably used to drink freshman year; mango smoothies taste like the pungent essence of that fruit; banana smoothies seem to be—but aren't—flavored with a shot of dark rum.

You can order any number of curries with rice: a gentle coconut curry in which softened cashews appear almost as succulent vegetables, an incredibly rich pumpkin curry with the peculiar bite of mustard, an eggplant curry cooked down to an intense sort of jam.

But a Sri Lankan meal here usually starts with a choice of starches—an edible utensil you can scoop up sauced dishes with or even use as sort of a bowl. Chamika only makes *appes* on weekends, but you should try them if you get a chance, coffee-filter-shaped crepes that are crisp at the edges, sweetened with coconut, and taper down to a thick, sour pancakelike base on the bottom that may or may not have an egg fried into it, and which you can daub with pungent, cardamom-scented red chicken curry, a greenish lamb curry gritty with spice, or the legendary well-toasted black beef curry for which Sri Lankan chefs are famous.

String hoppers, which look a little like goldfish nets made out of pale, floppy rice noodles instead of wire, come ten to an order with the same choice of curries. *Pittu* are rich, steamed cylinders of coconut rice served with a little pitcher of coconut milk and the curries. *Rotis* are griddled *pupusa*-size rounds of bread, spiked with coconut; crisp skin giving way to a chewy, sweet interior porous enough to soak up a tablespoonful of sauce. If you're at all inclined toward South Asian food, this is the real stuff, and it's a lot closer than London or Colombo.

CHICKEN GARDEN

18406 COLIMA ROAD, ROWLAND HEIGHTS; (818) 913-0548. FRI.-WED., 10A.M.-10P.M.

In Rowland Heights, the newest and shiniest of the Southland's Asian shopping districts, is the land of chicken, a vale of poultry in the sort of multiethnic mall where "multiethnic" refers to different parts of China.

At one end of the mall, neon signs advertise *kung pao* chicken; nearby is the Taiwanese-style Chicken Garden. Down past the chicken-serving Chiu Chow noodle shop Good Time Cafe, is a Cantonese barbecue with chickens in the window. The oversize Hong Kong Supermarket, which anchors the mall, sells plump, tasty roasting chickens of enormous size, as well as black chickens, "old" chickens, and chicken feet.

Some people think the restaurant Hainan Chicken serves the best chicken in the mall, though the busy, cheery place functions basically as a Malaysian-Chinese fast-food dive. Almost everybody treats Hainan Chicken as a one-dish restaurant—the one dish, of course, being Hainanese chicken rice, which was invented on the Chinese island of Hainan, but shows up on the menus of practically every restaurant in Singapore and Malaysia. The chicken rice here is very fine: glossy stuff cooked in chicken stock, each grain separate, with a definite ginger tang and a nicely oily feel.

The fowl-intensive cooking at the Taiwanese restaurant Chicken Garden, a nearly elegant if fairly spartan cafe, is on another level altogether. The "house special" tofu may be the homestyle bean curd of your dreams: small cubes sautéed until slightly crunchy on the outside but still creamy within, in a light, sharp sauce fragrant with soy and garlic: a sleek version of tofu you are often served in Chinese homes but rarely in restaurants. There is a dish of eggs scrambled with shrimp (the crustaceans barely jelled from the heat of the wok) and also a dish that involves the tiniest imaginable deep-fried fish (they resemble wispy rice stick noodles) tossed with scallions, chile, and fried peanuts.

Chicken Garden specializes, of course, in chicken: pungent smoked chicken with skin brittle as spun sugar; cool, brined chicken served with an intense ginger-oil dip; chicken stir-fried with pickled cabbage. "Three-cup" chicken—a famous Taiwanese dish traditionally sizzled in a clay pot with a wineglass each of soy sauce, oil, and rice wine—is superb, powerfully flavored with ginger and what must be an entire head of garlic, slightly sweet and impossible to stop eating until each little nub of chicken has been gnawed to the bone.

Another chicken, this one simmered with black dates, comes to the table immersed in a chafing dish full of boiling broth that has the intriguing, peaty aroma of good single-malt Scotch whiskey and the haunting, complex, sweet-smoky taste you might associate with top-notch artisanal bacon. The chicken itself seems to have given its all to the broth—the little pieces are tough and overcooked—though the soup is so nice, it's hard to imagine that you'd care.

"Burning Wine Chicken," by far the most expensive item on the menu, could be the most spectacular chicken dish in existence—a winey, strongly scented soup heated in a chafing dish, then detonated with a very long match into a pillar of vibrant flame that rises a good foot and a half above the surface of the liquid and spatters half the room with small droplets of boiling broth. Burning-wine chicken could be the subject of its own *National Geographic* special.

You may expect the spectacle to last a few seconds, like steak Diane or an order of cherries jubilee, but two minutes, three minutes, five minutes later, the soup is still ablaze, and you shrink back against the wall, away from the terrible heat, until the flames finally die down. By then, the soup will have a weirdly medicinal taste and a reek like the Fourth of July. When that guy in *Apocalypse Now* talked about loving the smell of napalm in the morning, burning wine chicken was probably just the breakfast he had in mind.

CHILI JOHN'S

2018 W. BURBANK BLVD., BURBANK; (818) 846-3611. OPEN TUES.-FRI., 11A.M.-7P.M.; SAT. 11A.M.-4P.M. CLOSED AUGUST.

Chili on the menu of a white-tablecloth joint might be the equivalent of hand-tooled cowboy boots on the feet of a Texas millionaire, a sign that the owner is really a regular guy even if he does sling a whole lot of *raie en vinaigrette*. Chili has always been easy to find in Los Angeles.

But Chasen's famous product was distinguishable from a bowl of Dennison's only by a silver chafing dish and an 1800 percent price differential. "Uncle George's Chili" at Patrick Terrail's late Hollywood Diner tasted as if Uncle George had been employed by a junior high school cafeteria in the Midwest.

The "Kick-Ass Chili" at 72 Market Street went better with a bottle of Bandol Rouge than it did with a cold longneck Bud, if you know what I mean. And Ken Frank's chili at the old La Toque, though exquisitely spiced, was made with duck. Basically, if you want to taste real chili in Southern California, you're stuck with chili cookoffs, where you'll find that championship chili is more macho ritual than foodstuff, more about funny hats than about American cuisine, and made by men who are apt as not to toss in a handful of *kimchi* and a *soupçon* of possum liver just for fun. Or you could check out Chili John's on the sleepy end of Burbank, which has been the best place to go for chili in Los Angeles for more than fifty years, and whose parent restaurant has reportedly been the best place to go for chili in Green Bay, Wisconsin for forty or so years longer than that. Possum liver would never make it through the door here.

It still looks like 1945 at Chili John's, with neat gingham curtains, ancient Coca-Cola gear, and a sleek, curved dining room that looks as if the architect had caught the wispy tail-end of Streamline Moderne. Along the U-shaped counter there are cruets of Tabasco sauce and bowlsful of oyster crackers, pecks of pickled peppers and containers of freshly chopped onion. Covering one wall is an astonishing painted mural of what looks to be the lake country of the Canadian Rockies, all greenery, waterfalls, and soaring peaks, except that right in the center a tiny figure of a Mexican woman drives her burro along a mountain trail. A few decades of yellowing menus are posted on the other wall, differing from the current one mostly in price.

From a series of stainless-steel vats in the center of the room, the counterman scoops out pinkish beans, mounds them high in a yellow plastic bowl, and carefully spoons thick, brick-red chili over the beans until the bowl nearly brims over onto the counter. With a flourish, he tops off the chili with a splash of bean water. He cocks an eyebrow, which means, "Would you like an extra little drizzle of orange grease with that?" You nod. Halfway through the meal, he may spontaneously decide to top up your bowl, too.

It is wonderful chili, dense and comforting, lean and hearty, with a cumin wallop and a subtle, smoky heat that creeps up on you like the first day of a Santa Ana wind. It's the kind of stuff that stays with you for a while, flavoring your breath for half a day even if you don't pile on the onions. It also goes strangely well with a cold glass of buttermilk, which is good, because Chili John's serves nothing stronger than near beer.

The beans are nice, too, firm and smooth, with a rich, earthy bean taste clearly perceptible even through the pungency of the chili. You can get chili with beans and spaghetti, the Burbank version of Cincinnati's famous five-way chili, or beans and spaghetti alone: Tex-Mex pasta fazool.

Dessert is that Midwestern oddity, pineapple-cream pie; cool, smooth and sweetly delicious, with a dusting of graham cracker crumbs where you might expect a crust. Pick up a pie to go.

CHINA ISLAMIC

7727 E. GARVEY AVE., ROSEMEAD; (626) 288-4246. TUES.-THURS., 11A.M.-3P.M., 5-9:30P.M.

One strange thing about eating a lot of Chinese food in Los Angeles is that you become blasé about places that would be restaurant Meccas in Chicago or New York, oversaturated as we are with grand seafood palaces and joints serving exemplary New Wave Shanghainese cuisine. China Islamic is a small, sweet restaurant in a near corner of Rosemead, with the usual upscale-ish lime-green decor and faux marble, window cutouts that resemble minarets, and fish tanks whose inhabitants are not destined to be eaten. China Islamic may be only the second best Muslim Chinese restaurant in the area—Tung Lai Shun, in the great Chinese mall up the road, edges it out on points—but it can be almost better than anyplace else.

Where China Islamic restaurant is a stronghold of Muslim-style Chinese cooking, it also prepares many of the standard suburban Chinese dishes—egg rolls, sizzling-rice soup, *kung pao* shrimp—sort of lackadaisically, but according to the strict precepts of halal. China Islamic may be the only Chinese restaurant I've ever seen where Pakistani customers outnumber the East Asians.

Almost as soon as you walk into the restaurant, you are asked if you want sesame bread (you do), which is a thick disk of flatbread made to order, the size of a Chicago-style pizza, whose thin, crisp crust encloses a dozen layers of steamy, scallion-flecked bread. Most people seem to order sesame bread here instead of rice, making little pocket sandwiches, dragging the bread through sauces, daubing bits of it with vinegar and chile and eating it straight. Sesame bread, probably the spiritual descendent of the stone-baked flatbread of ancient nomads, is at the center of this cuisine.

There are a number of cold dishes that go very well stuffed into the bread, cool smoothness contrasting with the bread's crunchy heat: translucent slices of pressed beef tendon that start out the texture of hard rubber but melt into a rush of beef and garlic; "home-style" roast chicken, fragrant with spice, a little greasy, a little like perfect picnic chicken; strips of rich, tender beef tripe flavored with a tincture of chile and soy, mercifully ungamy—for the first time I can remember, a tripe dish was the first thing to disappear from the table. There is a swell ox-tripe salad, tossed with slivered cucumber, hot mustard, and a delicious, slippery flat noodle made from pulverized mung beans; the version of the salad made with slivered white-meat chicken instead of tripe is perhaps even a little better.

Like other Muslim restaurants, China Islamic has a minor specialty in lamb, sliced thinly and quickly fried with green onions, garlic, and crunchy bits of fresh ginger; fried with the thick, resilient homemade noodles called "dough slice chow mein"; or served in a sweet cloying *sa cha* sauce. Lamb stew warm pot is an enormous thing, a seething mass in a clay vessel the diameter of a basketball hoop: thick, murky broth, cellophane noodles, cabbage, and the most extraordinary lamb red-cooked on the bone, chopstick-tender and pungent with soy and star anise. The lamb pot is almost enough to serve a family of ten—which is to say four hungry Chinese.

CHRONI'S SANDWICHES

5825 E. WHITTIER BLVD., EAST L.A.; (323) 728-7806. MON.-SAT., 9A.M.- 8P.M.

Ponce de Leon had his fountain of youth, Ahab his whale, Columbus his islands of spice. Dr. Leakey spent half of his life looking for a bone or two. I once met a botanist who had searched the Andes foothills nearly fifty years for the mysterious plant that he knew to be the common ancestor of both the tomato and the potato. My quest may be more modest, but sometimes seems no less consuming: For the better part of a decade, I have been seeking a legendary East Los Angeles sandwich, a *torta* I suspect hides somewhere in the old Belvedere district, a venerable concoction beloved to the neighborhood yet invisible to casual passerby—a toasted, chile-fired, gravy-sopped Mexican meat sandwich that burns like a flame.

I first heard about this sandwich from my father-in-law, a son of East Los Angeles, who told me about a *torta* so good that truckers used to detour miles just to get a crack at it. The next clue was from a man who said that the mere memory of it helped get him through a rough tour of duty in Vietnam. My wife's late grandmother had tasted this sandwich too. And because nobody seemed to know where the sandwich shop had been located, much less if it was still around, I have scoured hundreds of blocks looking for this place, browsed through scores of old Yellow Pages in the library, stopped off in dozens of delis and *carnicerias*, talked to countless strangers. I've eaten some good sandwiches on the way, but as far as I know, I haven't tasted The Sandwich. Or even come close to it.

Which is why I was so excited when a colleague first told my wife about Chroni's Sandwiches, an Eastside place he had seen immortalized in the liner notes of a Los Lobos CD. The man just assumed Laurie would know the place— she grew up in Whittier, which is where most of Los Lobos has lived for years.

Laurie, meanwhile, assumed I'd already have run into Chroni's on the way to pick up a bag of *pan dulce* or a bowl of *cocido*, but she also half hoped that it might be the great sandwich shop I'd been seeking.

Chroni's turned out to be a place I'd passed a million times, a faded old stand halfway between the Whittier Boulevard redevelopment area and the car dealerships of Montebello, and the smell of frying beef could probably have guided me there from the freeway if I'd taken the trouble to sniff. In a lunchtime line that stretched nearly to the corner, shaved-head East L.A. roughnecks chatted easily with beehived women who might have been their grandmothers, while in the parking lot out back, $30,000 custom Silverados shared space with new minivans, rusting Monte Carlos, and tricked-out '60s Impalas that gleamed like gold teeth.

"I think this sandwich is going to come out all right, ma'am," the fry cook behind the counter assured a customer. "I've been making them here for thirty-seven years."

On the sun-bleached sign above the restaurant, a little dog sat upon a giant hamburger, all but bowing to the giant hot dog that towered above them both. Chroni's may not have been the Great Lost Tortas Shack of legend, but it did turn out to be the great burger stand I never knew existed in East L.A., home to steaming orders of chili fries dense and hot enough to melt plastic forks into Brancusi sculptures; wet, sloppy pastrami dips stuffed with chewy, tissue-thin slices of garlicky meat; taut boiled frankfurters that snapped like the lowest string of a *guitarron*. Hamburgers, painted with yellow mustard and sluiced with a meaty, emulsified chili that seemed a couple of degrees spicier than its equivalent at, say, Jay's Jayburger, were robust creations, tasting distinctly of the grill, piled high with ripe tomatoes (at least in September) and crisp sheaves of lettuce—one of the finest chiliburgers imaginable, even in this chiliburger-obsessed metropolis.

I walked to a pay phone and called my mother-in-law to tell her about this great Eastside equivalent of Tommy's.

"You called up to tell me about Chroni's?" she said. "I've been going there since high school."

CHU'S MANDARIN CUISINE

140 W. VALLEY BLVD., NO. 206, SAN GABRIEL; (626) 572-6574. DAILY, 11:30A.M.–3P.M., 4:30–10P.M.

Say hello to Mr. Chu. Mr. Chu has met Arnold Schwarzenegger, and he has photographs to prove it. A large souvenir of the encounter is displayed in the window of Mr. Chu's restaurant in Rowland Heights, and also in the window, on the wall, and on the menus of his San Gabriel restaurant, Chu's Mandarin

Cuisine. You see Arnold's face so frequently at Chu's Mandarin Cuisine that it sometimes seems as if you are pursuing him through a carnival hall of mirrors.

Arnold has one arm around Mr. Chu's shoulders in the picture, and one beefy hand upon a pillow of dough. His smile, at least from a distance, looks very much like that of a dolphin. He has presumably just watched Mr. Chu transform a similar pillow of dough into a thick coil of hand-pulled noodles. Mr. Chu is a very good noodle maker. If you were going to eat a bowlful of Mr. Chu's hand-pulled noodles, you would be smiling like a dolphin too.

Mr. Chu's new place is in the fantastic Chinese mall called San Gabriel Square, a gleaming, sweet-smelling Oz with Chinese restaurants of every description and acres of landscaped parking. On a warm night, the red and green restaurant signs seem to glow like the lights of ships in the harbor, and wide walkways fill with contented Chinese window shoppers who have just eaten well. Chu's Mandarin Cuisine is on the second level of the great mall. It is a crowded, pleasantly lighted place. When acknowledging the photographs, the waitresses call the famous man "Arnold Whatshisname."

Mr. Chu's hand-pulled noodles are long, spaghetti-shaped strands of varying diameter, as big around as golf pencils in the middle and tapering to angel-hair at the ends, bouncy, springy things with a full wheaty flavor and an extraordinary bite. The noodles are perfect vehicles for Mr. Chu's spicy, oily black-bean sauce. They are delicious cold, piled with bits of squid and jellyfish (and, disconcertingly, artificial crab), tossed with sesame and hot mustard. They are good in a chile-red seafood noodle soup. They are good served in a strong pork broth underneath a floating fried pork chop. One can hardly go wrong with Mr. Chu's noodles.

To start, try the combination cold plate, which is actually a strongly garlicked salad that is garnished with stewed eggs, pressed tofu, and crunchy little strips of marinated pig's ear; garlic chicken; or perhaps the cool, anise-scented sort of Chinese pork aspic that goes by the unwieldy name of "aromatic pork jelly." Steamed dumplings are a little doughy by, say, Mandarin Deli standards, but the herb-flecked fish mousse inside the fish dumplings and the pungent, glass-noodle-spiked mince in the vegetable dumplings are first-rate. The soup, served in individual, tiki-looking bamboo cups, is peppery, teeming with crisp bits of vegetable, and conceals a single large meat dumpling that is almost Hungarian in its cinematic scope.

And although Mr. Chu is skilled at preparing the noodles and dumplings and soups and cold dishes of Chinese "deli" cuisine, his stir-fries tend to be a little better than those at other Chinese delis: curls of fresh cuttlefish fried with crunchy stalks of Chinese celery that are no thicker than *haricots*; slices of gammon, as sweet and chewy as griddled country ham, that have been sautéed with mild, scallionlike garlic greens; the delicious vegetable *ong choy*, sometimes known as Chinese watercress, briefly fried with garlic.

CIRO'S

705 N. EVERGREEN ST., EAST L.A.; (323) 269-5104. TUES.–THURS. 7A.M.–8P.M., FRI. AND SAT. 7A.M.–9P.M.

Up a hill from the big cemetery, just down the street from the famous El Tepeyac burrito stand, Ciro's is an East L.A. institution, around as long as anyone can remember, beloved by local teenagers, families, and cops. WHY GO SOUTH OF THE BORDER IF YOU CAN GO TO EAST L.A.? ask the T-shirts worn by Ciro's cooks.

Ciro's faded sign and black-iron security doors look fairly intimidating from the street, but inside the stark dining rooms are actually sort of cheerful, done up in the fake brick-and-wood paneling of a suburban rec room circa 1972, decorated with maps of Mexico and calendars from meat-packing companies, and filled with small children running amok.

"Ciro's" is basically the answer to the perennial L.A. question "Where'dja go for *flautas*?"—as opposed to "where'dja go for tamales?" or "where'dja go for chili fries?"—and if you have trouble remembering what to order here, the menu lists "SABROSAS FLAUTAS" in type that is approximately the size of the rest of the entrées put together.

A *flauta* is a corn tortilla wrapped around a meat filling and fried. (The difference between a *flauta* and a *taquito* is essentially semantic.) Stylistically, *flautas* can range from the greasy tubes your college dorm may have blanketed with guacamole-in-a-drum to the tasteless baseball bats served by upscale Mexican chains.

Ciro's *flautas* are tiny things, piccolo *flautas*, that come six to an order, tightly rolled, and very crisp, sauced with thick, chunky, fresh guacamole and a dollop of tart Mexican cream. The shredded meat inside is usually frizzled to a chewy consistency almost like *carne seca*, and tends to be a little salty, with a smack of pure beef flavor that cuts through the strong tastes of corn and hot oil. A lot of restaurant *taquitos* taste like something that has been flash-frozen in a plant in central Iowa; to go to Ciro's is almost like visiting a friend's grandmother who just happens to have homemade *flautas* on hand.

As soon as you sit down, a waitress brings over a basket of warm chips and the small bowl of avocado salsa that is the other reason to come to Ciro's: juicy, moderately chile-hot, spiked with bits of fresh tomato and chunks of smooth, ripe avocado. The rice is fresh and sharply garlicked. The beer is icy cold.

But after the *flautas* and the salsa and the rice, things can be hit or miss at

Ciro's, just like the cooking at your friend's grandmother's house. I have had *carnitas* here that were all crunch, and I have had *carnitas* that were flabby and dull. The chicken soup is delicious if inelegant, the broth tasting more of tomato than of chicken. The pork in the *chile verde* is cooked forever, until it is hard and strong-tasting; a *chile verde* for a palate trained in the '30s.

I like the giant Fridays-only bowls of *albóndigas* soup, abob with Mexican meatballs the size of lemons. I also like the vast, slippery sheets of fried pigskin that have been stewed with chiles in the old-time Los Angeles Mexican-American manner. But I can't really see what difference any of this makes. You're standing in line for *flautas*.

COLE'S P.E. BUFFET

118 E. SIXTH ST., DOWNTOWN; (213) 622-4090. MON.–SAT., 9A.M.–7P.M.
(BAR UNTIL 11P.M.).

When you trip down out of the bright sunlight into the dim warren of Cole's, located below sidewalk level in the old Pacific Electric Terminal, you stumble into another era, with real Tiffany lamps, sawdust on the floors, and a couple of pickle-nosed guys at the bar who look like they haven't budged from their stools since 1946. (Until pretty recently, the restaurant had a man on its staff who had been tending bar here since before Repeal.) On the wall opposite the bar, a large, framed photograph of the 1906 postquake ruins of San Francisco is a gleeful souvenir of a time when the L.A.-S.F. rivalry mattered to Angelenos. Three men in Sta-Prest short-sleeved white shirts, like office extras from a Doris Day movie, discuss a fourth man's affair with his secretary. There's horseradish and hot mustard on the tables, darts in back rooms and dark Ritterbrau on tap; a sort of romantic, Chandleresque dinginess you won't find anywhere else in town. This is the land of blood, sweat, and beers, the oldest restaurant in Los Angeles.

As you stand in line at the buffet, tray in hand, you might think that Cole's would be a nice place to try meat loaf, or knockwurst and beans, or corned beef and cabbage, or stuffed peppers. It's not, unless your particular nostalgia extends to the flavor of wet cardboard. Macaroni and cheese is utterly bland; barbecued lamb ribs, sweet and insipid. Little cafeteria dishes of salad, from cole slaw and potato salad to pale discs of something green, are uniformly dull.

In fact, if nothing but the steam-table food were available, you'd do just do as well eating at one of the fast-food places in the former Greyhound terminal across the street. But Cole's, where French-dipping was reputedly invented, serves huge, glorious sandwiches, and you'll lunch as well here as at any counter in town. Philippe's French-dip sandwiches are wonderful; Cole's are even better.

When it's finally your turn, a man in a white apron and a tall white cap takes your order, and dissects a pastrami deftly as a surgeon, flipping the fat to one side and piling lean, sinewy meat onto a French roll. He sogs the top half of the roll in a salty broth, and voilà, French dip, soft and crisp, rich and meaty, right there on your tray. Sandwiches are also made with freshly roasted turkey, meltingly delicious brisket, and good roast beef and pork. Skip the desserts, which tend to be variations on a theme of Jell-O. And get your beer from the bar rather than from the buffet line, unless you'd really rather have Budweiser than Ritterbrau.

COLEY'S KITCHEN

4335 CRENSHAW BLVD.; (323) 290-4010. DAILY, 7:30A.M.–10P.M.

As you power down Crenshaw, past the auto dealerships, past the Japanese restaurant in the bowling alley, past the Baldwin Hills mall, Leimert Park is just around the biggest curve, on an intimate sort of neighborhood business strip more familiar from old photographs than from actual experience.

Leimert Park is the intellectual center of African-American life in Los Angeles, with jazz clubs, coffeehouses, bookstores, and galleries of African-American art; a cultural center in a fine old movie palace; and African-American restaurants that draw people from all over town. Neatly suited Muslims stand on the streetcorners, offering newsletters and bean pies for sale. Reggae blasts from the record shops. Hip-hop blasts from the cars.

And in the center of it all, under a huge painted billboard, is the Jamaican restaurant Coley's Kitchen, which may be the single best Caribbean restaurant in the city of L.A. It's groovy in here, pulsing with the beat of dancehall reggae, great hats all over the place, African-American art on the walls, young guys handsome enough to make women stare. Sometimes you'll see an entire family stately in richly ornamented African robes; sometimes tablesful of black-college fraternity brothers; sometimes groups of women who look as if they've stepped straight from the pages of *Elle*.

Curried goat is hotly spiced, luscious, with the tender sweetness of really good lamb; slices of "Kingstonian beefsteak" are braised like pot roast, still a little chewy, blanketed in a dark-brown gravy. Jerk chicken is closer to a good braised bird than to the properly crisp, spice-rubbed chicken you find in Jamaica, but is redolent of pepper and allspice. Braised oxtails are spectacular, subtly gelatinous, profoundly beefy, with sauce reduced to a deep glaze. Almost all the sauces and gravies seem spiced with more ingredients than appear in the average Schillings display.

This is what you get on a plate with your entrée at Coley's Kitchen: a subtly sweet mound of rice cooked with red beans; a small heap of steamed cabbage; a fried slice of plaintain; an egg-size capsule of festival bread that will remind you of a buttermilk doughnut. Before this massive plate of food arrives, there might be a cup of thick, curried chicken soup, or spicy cow's-foot soup—or, on Mondays, incredible, intricately spiced red-bean soup, which tastes like the greatest pea soup of your life. You might want one of the hot, flaky Jamaican turnovers called "patties," filled with savory pastes of spiced beef, ground chicken, or stewed greens. You will want a tall glass of the restaurant's spicy, home-brewed ginger beer.

"*Akee*, rice, salt fish are nice," Harry Belafonte used to sing, and in fact *akee* and salt fish are quite nice here, fried together with a fragrant tangle of peppers and onions. The Caribbean vegetable *akee* looks and tastes not unlike pillowy scrambled eggs when cooked, and is so rich that a food editor I know got excited about its potential in low-cal cooking when I brought some back to the office. (It didn't pan out. *Akee* turns out to be higher in fat than practically anything this side of bacon.) The steamy richness of akee mellows the cod's pungent muskiness; the caramelized onions lend the strong fish an irresistable sweetness, like the dried cuttlefish you can snack on in Japanese movie theaters. A dash or two of the house's hot sauce, sort of a pink-hued pepper vinegar with the blistering smack of scotch-bonnet chile heat, puts a Carville-quality spin on this weird yet delicious plate of food.

COLIMA

1465 W. THIRD ST.; (323) 482-4152. DAILY, 11:30A.M.–9P.M.

What do we mean when we talk about restaurant minimalism? Do we mean the carpet showroom high-gloss-enameled into a chic cafe, or the artfully arranged snippet of chive that speaks volumes about its arranger's taste and refinement? Do we mean the small trapezoid of poached cod posed with three daikon sprouts in the middle of a vast Swid Powell plate? Or do we mean the old secret restaurant above Malibu that would serve you anything you wanted, as long as what you wanted was steak and clams?

Just west of downtown, the *ostioneria* Colima is as minimal as they come, with a menu nobody's ever consulted, an interior nobody's designed, and a building that barely exists. Colima's "dining room" consists of a sort of lean-to behind the kitchen, made out of a sheet of corrugated plastic, bamboo curtains, and some poles, like a makeshift *palapa* you might find sheltering a family at Eastertime on some deserted Yucatán beach. A faded lobster is painted on one wall, a marlin on another. When it rains, you get wet. When you slip into Colima from the parking lot, you seat yourself at one of half a dozen picnic tables, positioning yourself closer to either a speaker blasting Mexican disco near the front or the thrumming racket of a massive condenser motor, depending on your musical preference. It's a perfect spot to kill a hot Saturday afternoon, slurping Mexican oysters and drinking cold cans of Tecate imported from the supermarket next door.

Everybody in the place will be eating *cocteles*, big goblets of shrimp, octopus, or (canned) abalone marinating in the traditional, though ghastly, sauce of catsup, water, and chopped onion. A waiter will bring crackers and show you how to dose your *coctele* with lime and still more catsup, and demonstrate his special fluttery technique for speeding the flow from a Heinz bottle. Chase your beer instead with *tostadas de ceviche*, thick, fried corn tortillas spread with a chopped salad of marinated raw fish, onion, and shredded carrot, sharp with the tang of vinegar, mellow with toasted corn, sweetly fishy and dusted with fresh cilantro. Ceviche goes with Tecate the way foie gras goes with Sauternes.

If you order a half-lobster, a waiter will lean over and whisper confidentially, "You know, it will take twenty minutes, this lobster." What he doesn't tell you is that it will be frying all that time. When it finally arrives, it is like lobster jerky, permanently welded to its shell, as tough as a rawhide chew toy—which, if my experiences in the lobster houses of Puerto Nuevo can be viewed as typical, is undoubtedly authentic. Still, the lobster is sweet and briny, and comes with a dip that resembles what gets squirted on your popcorn in second-run movie houses. You'll probably hate it; I kind of dug the thing. And the curry-yellow rice and soupy stewed beans that come along with entrées here are not so bad.

Shrimp soup and fish soup are just okay, heavy with the potatoey taste of overcooked vegetables. Order instead *camarones rancheros*, the best entrée, and you'll get a dozen meaty shrimp sautéed with crisp green peppers, swimming in a light, buttery tomato sauce touched with garlic. The dish is a little rustic, folk-arty, a version of the kind of thing Angeli's Evan Kleiman might scour fishing villages for if she specialized in Mexico instead of Italy. The only beverages available are Coke, 7UP, and a sickly yellow fluid the counter guy called, appropriately, "pineapple water." BYOB.

CSARDAS HUNGARIAN RESTAURANT

5820 MELROSE AVE.; (323) 962-6434. DAILY, 11:30A.M.–10P.M.

Csardas is the strangest place on Melrose, a twinkling fairyland just past the point where the traffic narrows to a single lane near Vine, a Hungarian country inn in a former taco stand on the edge of a neighborhood that seems less Hungarian and less rustic than perhaps anywhere on earth. Skeins of tiny Christmas bulbs flash on and off outside the restaurant; a powerful green strobe light pulses; a waterfall pounds into a serene concrete pool. The L-shaped parking lot, newly paved with brick, seems especially designed to accommodate as few cars as possible. An enormous American Colonial bug zapper glows silently purple in the insect-free autumn dark.

Inside the restaurant, past the display of Hungarian crockery and the flyers advertising bargain flights to Budapest, past the clean, rich aroma of freshly made pastry cream, the dining room is long and narrow as a plush railroad car, rows of small booths on either side. Hungarian travel posters (the Nine Holed Bridge of Hortobagy), more Christmas lights, and backlit "stained glass" line the walls. Beer used to be served in Montreal Expos souvenir glasses. The most popular appetizer is an orange cheese ball.

And in the back of the place, behind a console of electric keyboards, a bearded organist plays sad Hungarian songs and Broadway kitsch, "Sunrise, Sunset" backed with strumming banjos as if it were by Stephen Foster, "The Blue Danube" coming in and out of focus like some dimly remembered Angelo Badalamente score, and always Liszt's greatest hits, at least the parts before the tricky runs come in. "Tell me, tell me," he says. "What would you like to hear most?" "Umm," says my friend, "I love cabaret music."

The organist scratches his head, hums a little to himself, sits suddenly upright as if a brilliant idea has come into his head, and with a crash and a flourish, he launches into the theme song from the musical *Cabaret*, beaming as furiously as if he'd made it up himself.

It is often said that Hungarian food has little to do with goulash, that a truly cosmopolitan Budapest guy has probably never seen the dish outside the context of a country inn. But though the restaurant may well specialize in dense, intensely garlicky roast pork, crisply fried Wiener schnitzel or crisp, though dry, roast duck, Csardas (which in fact is a Hungarian word associated with country inns) serves loads of the stuff: savory veal goulash stewed with peppers and onions, Transylvanian veal goulash with stewed cabbage, pork goulash.

Goulashes are served with the tiny Hungarian dumplings called *csipetki*, the traditional accompaniment, and like good home cooking, they lack the gut-busting heaviness you might associate with Southland Hungarian food. Most of the goulashes here may technically be *"porkolts,"* which is to say more like stews than soup, but the goulash soup, a hearty, tomato-based beef *potage* served in a burnished, table-size kettle that swings on a wrought-iron stand, is both delicious and authentic. Chicken *paprikas* is a tender half-bird in a ruddy, sour cream–thickened sauce; *bakonyi szelet* is two rather toughened fried pork chops blanketed in forty-weight mushroom gravy. *Vadas*, which is sort of the Hungarian equivalent of the sweet-sour German pot roast Sauerbraten, revolves around dryish slabs of meat, but it includes a delicious, pumpkin-colored sauce and three delicious, fluffy bread dumplings flecked with fresh herbs. The farmer's plate might be as close as it is possible to come in America to a Hungarian rustic feast: grilled garlic

69

sausage, Hungarian roast pork, and a great heap of crusty sautéed potatoes, sup-plemented with a kettle of the goulash soup, a perfect Hungarian country meal for two.

Desserts include rich *dobos tortes*, bready plum dumplings, and an ultra-chocolate thing called *somloi galuska*, which you may safely ignore in favor of the Hungarian dessert crepe, *palacsinta*, wrapped around a filling of candied walnuts or sweet farmer's cheese.

CUPID'S

VICTORY BOULEVARD AT TYRONE STREET, VAN NUYS; ALSO AT 20030 VANOWEN BLVD., CANOGA PARK AND SEVERAL OTHER LOCATIONS. MON.-THURS., 11A.M.-8P.M.; FRI. AND SAT., 11A.M.-9P.M.

If you grew up eating hot dogs in the swinging San Fernando Valley '70s, your family probably had allegiances to the Hot Dog Show or Flooky's or the Wiener Factory, which were as inarguable, as inevitable, as the question of Orthodox, Conservative, or Reform. My family was big into Flooky's, which prepared a creditable version of a Maxwell Street–style Chicago hot dog, so I didn't set foot in the Wiener Factory until my twenties; a friend who grew up going to the Hot Dog Show doesn't remember ever tasting a Flooky's dog.

But the biggest frankfurter cult of all was probably that belonging to Cupid's, a tiny Van Nuys chilidog stand that exuded a bravado, an allure, perhaps sur-passed only by the impossible glamour of the far-off Tommy's. (It was only recently that Cupid's added bags of chips to its one-item menu.) Flooky's may have been where your father took you for lunch on Sunday afternoons; Cupid's was where you headed yourself as soon as you were old enough to drive. If you head to Cupid's today, either the stand on Victory near Van Nuys or the satellites in Tarzana or the Simi Valley, you'll see as diverse a crowd as may exist in this part of the world: Chicano families dining on the tailgates of their Suburbans, Harley-riding nomads with bedrolls strapped to their handlebars, surfers whose hair is still crusted with salt, Mercedes drivers, and thirty-five-year-olds on BMK bikes.

The last time I went to Cupid's, the counterman appeared like an apparition out of a cloud of warm, hot-dog-scented steam that made the glass-enclosed kitchen look like the inside of a bong.

It is a beautiful thing to see a Cupid's dog assembled, to observe the counter-man aligning buns four, five, six at a time in a special ridged tray, to witness the quick flick of his wrists as he lays in the hot dogs, smears each with yellow mustard, sprinkles them with chopped onions, then sluices them with a precise amount of chili, enough to flavor every bite—to soak into the top few millimeters of the steamed bun without necessarily dripping onto your shoes—before twisting the dogs like anniversary presents into layers of soft, white tissue. If you order the dogs with cheese, a soft flurry of a grated orange substance is showered onto the hot dogs right over the onions, dissolving almost immediately into the chili. I'm not sure I even like Cupid's dogs all that much—give me Pink's tough-skinned Hoffys every time—but the Cupid's dog is undeniable, an object manufactured with the sole intent of sliding uninterrupted down a customer's throat.

It would be possible, I think, to unravel the formula of Cupid's chili, the exact dose of cumin, the provenance of the chili powder, the molecular density of the emulsifiers, the source of the starchy viscosity. If you poked around boxes in the dumpster, you could probably discover the source of the hot dogs themselves; the baker of the buns, the brand of mustard.

But a Cupid's dog is more than the sum of its parts. With its well-steamed bun, its saucelike chili, the puddingish softness of its skinless frank, a Cupid's hot dog is a chilidog evolved to a perfect state of being, chilidog satori, no unwarranted intrusions of texture or of bold flavor, no rough edges, no beans. A Cupid's dog is a puffy, oozing cloud of gravy and meat, soft and comforting enough that consumption continues as if in a dream. The path of least resistance often involves having a third.

CURRY HOUSE

163 N. LA CIENEGA BLVD., BEVERLY HILLS; (310) 854-4959. SUN.–THURS. NOON–10P.M.; FRI.–SAT., NOON–10:30P.M. ALSO AT 123 S. ASTRONAUT ELLISON P. ONIZUKA ST., LITTLE TOKYO.

Japan may be home to the most sophisticated food culture in the world, one where even schoolchildren can discern the subtle differences among a dozen different kinds of seaweed, where fish are expected to taste of themselves, and where delicacy is a virtue that ranks behind only absolute freshness. Japanese cooking is more seasonal than anything Alice Waters has ever dreamed of—some prized mushrooms measure their seasons in weeks, some herbs in days. Some *kaiseki* dinners cost a thousand dollars a head, and may actually be worth it.

Still, Japanese are as likely to sit through a four-hour *kaiseki* on any given day as you are to eat at l'Orangerie tonight—most Japanese live on noodles, and rice omelets, and bits of simmered fish. Consider a plate of Japanese curry, one of the most popular everyday foods in Japan, a giant slick of tan glop, uniform in texture, that wells up toward high drifts of sticky Japanese rice, laps at the base of fried pork cutlets, and fills Japanese bellies in a way that two hundred bowls of exquisite *sunomono* could not be expected to do.

Los Angeles has always been home to a number of Japanese curry restaurants,

71

and the sleekest is the Beverly Hills branch of Curry House, a big Japanese chain. The Curry House is a slick, highly designed restaurant in the building that briefly housed Robert Gadsby's Pyramid (and before that, Bar-B-Q Heaven, which was where Beverly Hills went for ribs in the '60s and '70s), a soaring space with acres of blond wood and bright paintings on the walls. At noontime, the Curry House seems to serve as a commissary for the Japanese employees of the Hotel Nikko across the street; later on, the restaurant fills up with hip professionals, bearded entertainment guys, and the Japanese hotel guests themselves, who can be spotted by Tokyo haircuts and Chanel purses so new that they squeak.

In Japan, curry is the rough equivalent of the American tuna-fish casserole—thrown together in minutes, easily reheated, and still edible when a family member comes home four hours late from the office. There are probably as many curry jokes in Japanese popular culture as there are meat loaf jokes in ours. If the Honeymooners were set in Osaka instead of Brooklyn, Ralph would eat a lot of curry.

Vermont House curry is the most popular packaged curry in Japan, a product as ubiquitous in Japanese pantries as Heinz catsup is in ours. The Curry House chain is run by an arm of the company that makes Vermont House curry, and while the Curry House product is both fresher and more complex than the powder that comes in those stiff foil envelopes, it is obviously a result of the same aesthetic.

It's decent stuff, the Curry House curry, a sticky, dense, vegetarian goo, dark as a Louisiana roux, copious enough in quantity to ease down several pounds of rice. You can order it at several levels of spiciness, ranging from super-mild to 'cue-sauce hot, have it garnished with breaded, fried cutlets of beef, pork, or chicken, or have it bathing seafood or vegetables. One variation includes fried shrimp that are more batter than seafood, and a mound of turmeric-yellow rice encased in a paper-thin omelet. The wiener and spinach curry—I've never tried it—is actually one of the most expensive things on the menu. And the seared hamburger, a high-tech version of the patty your Aunt Doris may have made with beef and Lipton soup mix, is not so bad.

A blurb on the back of the menu at Curry House credits the English with introducing curry to Japan a century ago. A more likely scenario points to the Portuguese, who were the first Westerners to trade with the Japanese, and whose dishes inspired tempura, tonkatsu, and various meat stews. Japanese curry, in fact, tastes more like the sort of "African" gravies you find in the Portuguese colony Macao than it does like anything you might run across in Britain, or for that matter India, but is characteristically Japanese: sweet, thick, homogenized, and powered by a multilayered pepper heat that somehow comes together as a single note.

D

THE DERBY

233 E. HUNTINGTON DRIVE, ARCADIA; (626) 997-2430. MON.-THUR.,
11A.M.-10P.M., FRI., 11A.M.-11P.M.; SAT., 4-11P.M., SUN. 4-10P.M.

The Derby is a splendid place, an old racetrack restaurant a few furlongs east of Santa Anita, hard by chain restaurants and coffeeshops and bars with fragrant names like "100–1" and "Drinkers' Hall of Fame." The sign is a violent burst of neon in the warm San Gabriel Valley night. There are a lot of horsey restaurants in the Southland, in the South Bay and down on old Route 19, but the Derby might be the horsiest, crowded with well-fed men, many of them pretty obviously ex-jockeys, women customers gone prematurely blonde, pinky rings, pearls, and rakish sportscoats.

Waitresses wear tight riding silks, kid around with each other, and serve you flaming baked Alaska on your birthday. The Derby is dedicated to the memory of George Woolf, a jockey who ran the restaurant until he was thrown from a horse and killed in 1946, and the restaurant is something of a dark-wood racetrack museum, with track souvenirs, racetrack murals, and portraits of the great horse Sea Biscuit, Woolf's favorite mount.

Old racing columns ("Rube Barbs!") mentioning Woolf are printed on the backs of the menus and autographed jockey pictures line whatever wall space Sea Biscuit has left them.

The first time I went to the Derby, after winning the price of a steak dinner on a turf race down the street, I almost believed, at least for a minute, that I had stumbled into the single best restaurant in the world.

"A rye Old Fashioned?" the waitress asked. "Will that be regular or would you like to make that a Daily Double?"

A minute later, she delivered a tumbler of rye, big enough to intoxicate all of Vermont.

"We serve a good drink here at the Derby," she said.

At the Derby, you will find stuffed mushroom caps, Cobb salads, and good shrimp cocktails that sit on a bed of what could be interpreted as celery remoulade. There is a respectable assortment of luxury fish and "scampi"; also grilled chicken-breast dishes for those who have wandered into here by mistake.

With your meal, you have a choice of gooey, cheesy onion soup, kind of bogus but also kind of delicious, or a salad tossed at table. (The croutons are tasty, the greens crisp and fresh, but the house dressing the waitress describes as "sort of like a Caesar" is more like an oversweet vinaigrette: go for the blue cheese instead.) There is garlic-cheese toast, the powerful, soggy kind that is in theory mildly detestable but in practice everyone demands more of—"I feel embarrassed that I have to serve you this terrible stuff," the waitress said, winking as she set down a basketful, "but it seems to be company procedure."

Something called "Brasholi" is a variant of the Italian-American classic *braccioli:* charred steak rolled around a herbed cheese filling and sauced with an old-fashioned marinara that tastes overwhelmingly of tomato paste. It should by all rights be dreadful, but somehow ends up as something wonderful, a crisp, pungent epitome of '50s dinner-party food.

Mostly, of course, as at all track-oriented restaurants, the specialties involve giant hunks of cow: great slabs of prime rib with horseradish-reinforced whipped cream, rare grilled strip steaks encrusted with peppercorns, Brobdingnadian hamburger steaks with brown mushroom gravy on the side. Rare filet mignon wrapped with bacon—"Odds-On Favorite," says the menu—is a ruddy disc of meat, so soft it seems a little like meat-flavored butter, the best thing in the house. Chateaubriand for two is the size of Arnold Schwarzenegger's forearm, a tremendous, tender piece of meat rimmed in black char, served with a sauceboat of Béarnaise sauce and carved tableside with great ceremony.

If you are for some reason not sated, there is smooth, cool cheesecake, not too sweet, or one of the Derby's special coffee drinks.

"Our cappuccino is made with five different liquors, which I cannot tell you what they are," the waitress said. She put a finger to her lips and cocked her head.

"It's a Derby secret."

DUMPLING HOUSE

5612 ROSEMEAD BLVD., TEMPLE CITY; (626) 309-9918. DAILY 11A.M.–9P.M.

Factory-made Chinese noodles have a certain jazzy sleekness to them. Knife-cut Chinese noodles are dense and thick, weighty enough for any sauce. The greatest of all Chinese noodles, though, are the hand-pulled noodles of northern China.

Hand-pulled noodles, elastic and pleasant to the bite, have a million little irregularities for sauce to adhere to, and they absorb flavors like nothing this side of a block of tofu.

Hand-pulled noodles are also notoriously hard to make. If you've ever seen the noodle guy onstage at a Chinese street fair, doubling and redoubling a massy glob of dough until it transforms into a gossamer web of angel hair, you know the degree of dexterity involved: throwing Chinese noodles is to Italian pasta-making approximately what a double backward somersault with three and a half twists is to a simple swan dive.

Dumpling House is hand-pulled-noodle paradise, a northern-style noodle shop in a Temple City mini-mall with a fish pond, a lot of marble, and giant, neon noodle bowls on the walls that glow black-light purple. The parking lot is clotted with Mercedeses—northern Temple City is an affluent corner of the Chinese diaspora—and there can be a wait for tables on weekend afternoons.

Hand-pulled noodles, at least in California, are usually found in Chinese noodle shops catering to the Korean trade—between the depredations of Tojo and those of Mao, a lot of Chinese wound up in Korea in the '30s and '40s—and Dumpling House does attract a certain Korean clientele: The menu is translated into Hangul, dumplings are deep-fried in the Korean manner rather than pan-fried, and as soon as you sit down, you are brought a dish of cool, marinated cabbage, slightly sweet, tinted pink with chile—in other words, a sort of northern Chinese *kimchi*.

The hand-pulled noodles here aren't quite as slithery as the ones at Mandarin House in Koreatown; the fried dumplings aren't as crisp as the pan-fried dumplings at Mandarin Deli downtown; the steamed dumplings are less juicy than their counterparts at San Gabriel's Dumpling Master. But Dumpling House may be the best place to get both hand-pulled noodles and dumplings. This may not seem like an earth-shattering distinction, but believe me: It is enough.

Here are the Southland's definitive onion pancakes, translucent crepes, very thin and very crisp, that shatter into a thousand layers under your teeth, exploding with flavors of scallions and hot oil. Steamed dumplings are also among the city's best—thin-walled, pleated capsules stuffed with vegetables and pork. Steamed vegetable dumplings are wonderful, bursting with a strong, vivid mince of a half dozen Chinese vegetables you couldn't pronounce if you tried; boiled fish dumplings, flavored with some of the same vegetables, collapse into luscious whitefish purée in your mouth. The kelp salad can be powerfully good, iodine-rich and flavored with enough chopped garlic to stun a moose. The cold hacked chicken with cucumber is fine.

Still, everybody comes here for the hand-pulled noodles, resilient, wheaty things that are thick in the middle and taper off toward the ends, except when they assume woozy, squiggly shapes not often seen outside the context of claymation. You can have noodles in soup, or in a rich, tarlike gravy of onions, pork, and black beans—*chachiang mein*—that will permanently stain your tie. A dish of the noodles in a deep-red broth of chiles and various tentacles tastes less like a classic *chow-ma mein* than it does like some marvelous version of a Mexican *sopa de siete mares* that just happens to be filled out with noodles.

Maybe the best way to eat Dumpling House's noodles is stir-fried with shreds of pork, tree-ear fungus, and bits of musky preserved vegetable, a sharp, complex dish with all the best flavors of northern cooking and a haunting, sweetish smokiness that comes only from a blazing hot wok.

DUMPLING MASTER

423 N. ATLANTIC BLVD., MONTEREY PARK; (626) 458-8689. SUN.–THURS., 11A.M.–9P.M.; FRI. AND SAT., 11A.M.–9:30P.M. (CLOSED WED., 3–5P.M.).

The coolest thing about the Monterey Park Chinese restaurant Dumpling Master is probably its name, which sounds like the title of a '60s martial arts movie where the hero regretfully lays down his skeins of noodle dough in order to avenge the death of his sister. I like to imagine the chef as an elderly man, beard down to his chest, rolling out dough while a strummed *p'i p'a* traces a contemplative melody, stuffing crunchy bits of shrimp into delicate pasta sheets with the practiced long fingers of a *tai chi* wizard. If the chef is a twenty-three-year-old heavy-metal fan who likes to watch Oprah as she works, I don't want to know about it.

Dumpling Master, located in a strip mall behind the supermarket Shun Fat, is an L-shaped San Gabriel Valley dining room with Formica and greenish fluorescent light, one glass-front icebox filled with cold soda and another with chilled tofu and smoked pig's-ear salads, a couple of wall banners listing the day's specials, a dozen or so tables set with bowls and spoons and jars of the house's sneaky-hot chile oil with black beans. A basic Taiwanese deli of the type made popular by the Mandarin Deli chain, the restaurant buzzes with customers slurping down giant bowls of beef noodles, platters of bean curd with minced pork and chile, and hubcapsful of the restaurant's well-known creamy corn soup, which tastes remarkably like something your Aunt Fanny may have made for lunch back in Iowa.

A specialty of the place is deep-fried pork chops, brown and crunchy, slightly sweet where the pork's juices have caramelized and coated with a salt crust just spicy enough to tingle. "Potherb," house-preserved mustard greens, can be had stir-fried with shredded bits of pork . . . or better, with fresh, sweet soybeans, in a dish that suggests more subtleties of green than a Jennifer Bartlett painting.

Gently smoked chicken legs are fine, slightly oily; salt-cured duck legs are sharp and firm.

If you remember to ask for handmade noodles, you'll get thick, wheaty, dense things the thickness of fan belts, fresh enough to soak up sauce yet developed enough to retain texture, the kind of noodle that would seem to have everything going against it except that it tastes so good. The handmade noodles come in an intense pork broth garnished with a salt-fried pork chop, in a powerfully gamy beef stew, with fried pork and potherb, in a thick, eggy broth—the "special combination" noodle soup—with the flavor of a really fine hot-and-sour soup.

But essentially—this being Dumpling Master and everything—you might as well have some dumplings, doughy boiled pork dumplings, boiled shrimp dumplings with pork and a clear seafood taste, thin-skinned pan-fried dumplings, crisp on the outside, spurtingly juicy within, that are in their way as good as the famous ones at Mandarin Deli. And don't leave without at least one order of scallion pancakes. Like a bad Elmore Leonard novel, a bad scallion pancake, even the doughy ones they sell in the frozen-food aisles of Chinese supermarkets, which you heat in your toaster like a Pop Tart, is still pretty hard to resist. Dumpling Master's scallion pies—crisp wheat pancakes studded with chopped green onion, thin and crackly as sheets of vellum—are the perfect vehicle for sopping up chile oil.

888

8450 VALLEY BLVD., ROSEMEAD; (626) 573-1888. DAILY, 9A.M.–10P.M.

888 is a terrifically elegant Chiu Chow–style Chinese seafood restaurant in a Rosemead mall, with a dining room the size of a hockey rink, multiple chandeliers and fish tanks, and more wedding parties than you can shake a bouquet at. Squadrons of tuxedoed captains roam the floor, troops of waiters, legions of busmen. On weekends, the crowd for dim sum is so vast that it actually seems to recede into the horizon.

Alone of L.A.'s biggest Chinese restaurants, 888 specializes in Chiu Chow seafood, the cooking of the ethnic Chinese who migrated from China to Southeast Asia dozens of generations ago. There are dozens of Chiu Chow noodle shops in the Southland, and a few slightly fancier places, but 888 at dinnertime (lunches are good, if fairly standard Cantonese dim sum) is the only place to check out the formal cuisine.

Chiu Chow cooking is clean and straightforward: sour flavors, strongly salted foods, clear broths and fresh seafood unmasked by complex sauces. My first meal at 888, which included a sort of sharply garlicky terrine of beef shank, crunchy, tofu skin–wrapped dumplings of fresh crabmeat and taro ("crab balls"), a soft, anise-scented lamb stew, and sugar snap peas sautéed simply with oil and a touch of salt, seemed almost country-French in nature.

Beyond the crab balls, the shrimp balls, and the minnows—"silver fish"—crisply fried whole in a coating of spicy salt, the Chiu Chow cold plate is a good place to start: symmetrically arranged slices of tender steamed geoduck clam, aspic-rimmed pork terrine, crunchy strands of jellyfish, and cold shrimp slicked with a sweet, citrus-based sauce. Fish noodles—chewy, lumpish strands of homemade chewy linguine with leeks and slivers of fish—are tossed in a very hot wok, so the dish is smoky, sweet, a little salty, with a subtle flavor of very fresh fish.

One soup, served in a bubbling chafing dish, holds a whole perch gently poached in the heat of broth, sharp with the flavor of Chinese celery and herbs, made complexly tart with sour plum. A thick, peppery shredded-duck soup has almost the flavor of a classic hot-and-sour soup but made vivid with the occasional blast of muskiness from dried orange peel; duck and sour plum soup has a slightly high, slightly sweet poultry/fruit taste that is almost like a blast from a Thanksgiving dinner.

888 has a splendid menu of Chinese-style barbecued poultry: roast chicken whose skin is brittle as spun glass, served with a sour plum/fermented tofu dip the pale rose color of a nineteenth-century Japanese print; another roast chicken that had been rubbed with five-spice powder; extremely good roast duck. There is an astonishing dish of Chiu Chow–style braised goose, a specialty of the restaurant: neat slices of white and dark meat arranged in a heap, garnished with strips of fried bean curd served with a dipping sauce somewhat like a fruity Chinese vinaigrette, and worth every dime of the fortune it costs.

Desserts, if you remember to ask for them, can be pretty wonderful here: various sweet red bean soups, richly flavored hot taro puddings and cool mango gelatins that are perfectly refreshing after a multi-course Chiu Chow meal.

EL AMANECER

3059 W. EIGHTH ST., KOREATOWN; (213) 382-2591. MON.–THURS., 9A.M.– 10:30P.M.; FRI. AND SAT., 9A.M.–MIDNIGHT; SUN., 9A.M.–11P.M.

Amanecer is Spanish for "sunrise" and the restaurant's logo, a stork silhouetted against the rising sun, seems to be on almost everything here but the actual food. Chicken tamales are wet, almost puddinglike, steamed in banana leaves and delicately herbal in flavor, stuffed with cassava root and slivers of meat; sweet-corn tamales are plump but a little dry, with the nearly vanilla aroma of roasted corn and a puddle of tart Salvadoran cream alongside. I like the *yuca con chicharrones*, the profoundly crunchy crust of fried cassava fingers giving way to a moist, steamy interior as compelling as that of the best steak fries, served with the traditionally tart cabbage salad and a few chunks of fried pork skin that are almost numbing in their richness.

Somebody here has an addiction to (Spanish-language) signs. THANK$ ARE NOT ENOUGH, one notice translates roughly, admonishing the patrons to tip. Other signs warn that vandalism is a crime, that a maximum of three beers will be served with dinner, and that children mustn't be allowed to play on the stairs.

Someone here also has a sense of humor: the lunch special one day was CALDO DE POLLO Y UNO BUD.

Main dishes are served with rice, puréed beans, and thumb-thick tortillas that are close to Colombian *arepas*: one stewed chicken served with sweet, sautéed onions, and another, *pollo guisado*, in a smooth tomato sauce. Little balls of grilled Salvadoran chorizo tied with bits of corn husk, hotly spiced and intensely herbal, are terrific, among the best chorizos in town. *Carne deshebrada*, dried, shredded beef sautéed with onions and peppers and egg, is something very like a good Mexican *machaca*.

Of course, a Salvadoran restaurant lives or dies with its *pupusas*, the griddled cornmeal cakes that seem to be the combined hamburger, hot dog, and pizza of Salvadoran snack cuisine, and El Amanecer's made-to-order *pupusas* are swell, if a tad more elegant than the usual crunchy, oily variety: soft in texture, with a clear corn flavor, filled with salty melted cheese and either roast pork or minced bits of the pungent Salvadoran flower bud *loroco*. You garnish *pupusas* with a few forksful of the spicy cabbage slaw *curtido* taken from a big jar, and splash them with El Amanecer's splendid housemade tomato sauce. One *pupusa* makes an appetizer; two, a filling lunch.

EL CHAMIZAL

7111 PACIFIC BLVD., HUNTINGTON PARK; (323) 583-3251. DAILY, 8A.M.– 2A.M.

Pacific may be the grooviest street in southeast Los Angeles, a mile or so of wide boulevard lined with Mexican boutiques, faux gaslights, antique towers, and pretty two-story buildings, Spanish-language movie theaters and a jillion stores selling wedding cakes as elaborate as, well, wedding cakes. People walk here in Huntington Park as they do hardly anywhere else in Southern California, stopping one place for a *gordita*, another for a glass of fresh-pressed tropical juice, maybe sitting for a while in a sidewalk cafe. It's a little like Broadway downtown without the grime; a little like a Mexican-American take on Main Street, USA. Ranchera bleats split the air.

And toward the bottom of the boulevard, across from El Gallo Giro and just down the block from a popular *quebradita* club, is El Chamizal, the Mexican steakhouse that is the swankest restaurant on the strip, a sprawling place with a velvet rope, a million kinds of margaritas, and some of the best Mexican cooking on the southside. On weekends, you get a decent salsa band doing *cumbias, charangas*, and the like for the sharply dressed couples on the dance floor; toward the beginning of the week, you get a one-man band slaughtering "Feelings" *en español*. Sit down, in the front near the music or in back where you can talk, and the parade of vendors begins: some children selling chocolate bars for their schools, and others selling little bundles of Chiclets; mariachi bands eager to serenade you and photographers ready to capture the moment for posterity; women selling flowers and hats and giant stuffed bears. The beer is cold; the salsa, hot. Guacamole, mashed tableside in a big, stone mortar, is stunning: creamy, and rich, sharp with the flavor of fresh chiles. Caesar salad, not made tableside—whatever it may say on the menu—is a weird, sweet thing that tastes mostly like bacon.

The essential tool at El Chamizal is the *parrillada*, a squat, iron brazier shimmering from the heat of the charcoal within, brought to table piled high with thin grilled steaks, pork chops marinated in chile, hunks of chorizo sausage, fried bananas, whole jalapeño peppers burnt black, little ramekins of melted cheese, and scallions bronzed and wilted to a superb sweetness. The meat is terrific, well marinated, rich with crunchy carbonized bits—rather overrich in them if you leave the stuff on the grill too long—very nice folded into a little taco with the house's fine smoked tomato sauce and a spoonful of the smoky bacon-stewed beans. Some of the *parrillada* combinations include crispy, well-done *tripitas*, the goop-filled small intestine of a milk-fed calf; grilled chicken breast; the spicy pork stew *cochinita pibil* (pretty good, if not up to the stuff at Yucatecan places), or half a grilled lobster (luxurious, if dry). The baby lamb chops, like the burn-your-fingers chops that you find in small restaurants in Rome, are crisp, spicy, and full of juice.

You can get enchiladas, and you can get fried fish, *mole*, or chicken breast, but basically, El Chamizal is a palace of grilled meat.

EL CHORI

5147 GAGE AVE., BELL; (213) 773-3011. SUN.–THURS. 11A.M.–8P.M.: FRI. AND SAT., 11A.M.–9:30P.M.

El Chori is the sweetest place, a tablecloth Cuban restaurant in a far corner of Bell: Families eat at tables for ten, a Sunday harpist strums in front of a ceiling-height mural of palm trees, and there is the clean scent of frying onions that is a reliable signal of the very best Latin American food. Posters for *charanga* shows dot the walls. An espresso machine hisses behind the cashier's desk. Children plow through platters of caramelly fried bananas; their parents tuck into the peppery creole vegetable stew *ajiaco*.

A few of the waitresses speak no English, but are extremely patient with whatever halting Spanish you might be able to muster, sometimes patting their tummies and whispering *rico* when they feel you have ordered something particularly good.

Some people mistake El Chori for a Spanish restaurant, but most of the strictly European items on the tapas section of the menu—fried hunks of dense chorizo sausage, slices of cured pork loin, superb salt-cod fritters, *jamon serrano* with imported Manchego cheese—owe more to the proximity of the excellent Spanish delis in the South Bay than to any affinity with Spain. Try the excellent pickled tongue, thinly sliced, drenched in good olive oil.

Tasajo, a dense stew of onions, sweet peppers, and chewy bits of shredded salt-dried beef, splashed with sherry, slightly spicy, is not unlike a Cuban version of a properly made Mexican *machaca*. (Cuban friends assure me *tasajo* is most authentically made with horsemeat.) *Boliche asado*, which seems more like a hearty German tavern dish than something you might eat on a hot day in the tropics, involves thick, soft slices of pot-roasted beef, flavored with smoky ham, tinged with bitter orange, and served lukewarm in a thick, brown gravy. A dish with the intriguing name of *rabo encindido*, which roughly translates as "tail in flames," is a spicy, melting oxtail stew stained with tomato.

On Sundays, El Chori serves a creole lamb stew; on Fridays, salt-cod; on Saturdays, giant lamb-shanks that sing with garlic. There are *chicharrones de pollo*, which are crunchy, thumb-size pieces of chicken thigh garnished with a sort of spicy Cuban piccalilli, and delicious *steak a la cazuela* braised in tomato sauce, and chunks of fat pork that have been marinated in garlic and orange and deep-fried to a numbingly rich crispness. Only the sautéed chicken dishes, which tend all to be reheated and rubbery, have been less than very good. It is much easier to leave El Chori happy than hungry.

EL COLMAO

2328 W. PICO BLVD.; (218) 386-6131. MON., WED., FRI., 10A.M.–8:30P.M.; TUES., 10A.M.–5P.M.; SAT. AND SUN., 12P.M.–8:30P.M.

For a while I went every Sunday afternoon to El Colmao, a thriving big-city Cuban restaurant set among the bodegas and Spanish-language record stores of the Pico-Union district, and I listened to the *cumbias* that blared from the big jukebox, and I got pleasantly drunk on half-liters of cold, red wine. El Colmao is to Los Angeles Cubans what Ratner's on New York's Lower East Side is to Long Island Jews: a good old place in the old neighborhood frequented mostly by suburban people who want to feel ethnic once in a while.

My girlfriend at the time, who was in fact Cuban, had an interesting sense of humor. She goaded me to order meals for the two of us in sputtering menu Spanish, which she then mocked to the waitress. She once taught me to ask for the bill by saying. "El check-o, por favor," which amused everybody in the dining room but me, and she'd comment loudly on each woman who came into the restaurant in a way that implied she was responding to something I'd said. I was young enough to be a good sport about it all, and after we broke up, she got to keep my World War II officer's cape and I got the Sundays at El Colmao.

Each time I went to the restaurant I ordered the same things, and after a while, the waitresses would just recite my regular order to save me the embarrassment of mispronouncing *aguacate* once again. It was a huge, greasy, splendid lunch.

There was always an avocado salad to start, cool, ripe chunks garnished with thin slices of raw onion, dressed with splashes of vinegar and torrents of good Spanish olive oil; then a heaping plateful of thin, pounded circles of unripe plantains, fried crisp as potato chips and dusted with salt. Sometimes I ordered a cup of *caldo Gallego*, a thick, Galician-style white-bean soup spiked with shredded collard greens and smoky chunks of ham and sausage, that made even the dry, puffy Cuban rolls taste good.

And then the real food would come: Play-Doh-textured boiled *yuca*, the color of a legal pad, sauced with oil, lemon and a truly astounding quantity of garlic; a big plateful of *moros y cristianos* (Moors and Christians), which is a tasty miscegenation of black beans and rice fried with garlic and gobbets of fat pork; piles of crisply fried sliced pork leg topped with an immoderate portion of caramelized onions, all washed down with cold red wine served in those flared jugs pizzerias use for Almaden. (The house wine at El Colmao is pretty bad, but anything subtler would probably be lost amid the garlic.) For dessert there was good flan, torpor, and cups of strong Cuban espresso to snap us awake for the short ride home.

Even now, thinking about those meals makes me want to reach for a breath mint and a pillow.

Since then, though I've cut back to about one El Colmao meal a month, and I still order the same thing every time. I've managed to try most of the things I'd only seen sail by before. Various fried steaks and chops are garlicky and fine, if a little dry sometimes. The *arroz con pollo* is wonderful, a big, fragrant bowl of rice, stained Easter-chick yellow with *achiote*, studded with pimientos and the meat of at least a quarter-chicken. You can get chicken or fish sautéed with garlic and tomatoes, or sautéed and glazed with an intense sauce of sherry and fried onions. There's a good version of the shredded-beef stew called *ropa vieja* and a delicious smoked pork chop served only at weekday lunch. There's real, fizzy Asturian cider served in champagne glasses.

And as it turns out, almost everybody in the restaurant speaks good English.

"I was wondering when you were going to figure that out," my favorite waitress finally said.

EL COYOTE SPANISH RESTAURANT

7312 BEVERLY BLVD.; (323) 939-2255. SUN.–THURS., 11A.M.–10P.M.; FRI. AND SAT., 11A.M.–11P.M.

One sign of a native Angeleno, I think, is a relationship with the restaurant El Coyote, a relationship that often begins just a few weeks after birth. Half the kids in Los Angeles grew up coveting the tacky toys and souvenirs displayed in a locked glass case in the lobby, craving the warm sweetness of corn tortillas thickly spread with butter and sprinkled with salt.

When you began going there as a young teenager, it may have been your first time in a restaurant without your parents. You went because it was, as it still is, the cheapest respectable restaurant in Hollywood and because you could order the No. 2 dinner without fear of mispronouncing anything or using the wrong fork.

Slightly later in life, the Angeleno learns that El Coyote's margaritas, though next to impossible to obtain if you happen to be underage—not only have these guys seen many generations of fake IDs, but they also have seen you come in since you were a baby—are among the quickest and cheapest ways to nirvana, especially if the way down is lubricated with a nachoesque "Mexican pizza" or two. By the time you reach your mid-twenties, you have learned to point out the booth in the back where Sharon Tate ate her last meal, discuss the evolution of the El Coyote waitress petticoats, and discern the possible ingredients of those margaritas. (A reliable source, who was a bartender at El Coyote for a couple of years, swears that the ingredient that makes El Coyote margaritas taste different from everyone else's is a healthy slug of pineapple juice.) El Coyote is in its eighth decade, and if the two-hour lines on weeknights are any indication, it will be around for eight decades more.

I haven't been a regular at El Coyote for a long time, but I have eaten more meals there than at any restaurant on earth. When I was growing up, my family used to go to El Coyote every week or so, partly, I suspect, because it was one of the few places on the Westside where family of five could eat out and get change back from a ten, and my mother was fond of the *enchiladas rancheras* blanketed in sour cream. The furtive, salty sips of margaritas briefly filched from across the table were probably the first liquor my brothers and I tasted.

My wife, who grew up on the Eastside, has never really gotten the point of El Coyote; guys from out of town point out that Mexica, across the street, is better, which may technically be true but is beside the point.

You don't even really have to like the watery soft *chiles rellenos*, dominated by the thick egg batter, to be an El Coyote fan, or the sugary green-corn tamales vaguely flavored with the mildest chiles, or the fried tacos, crisp at the edges and pleasantly toughened where the tortilla bulged out with meat, or the giant tostadas that seemed to contain an entire No. 8 can of peas.

El Coyote food has a specific taste, a gestalt that transcends cuisine: the slightly acrid pungency of chopped green onion tops and the milky funk of inexpensive cheese broiled until most of the fat has separated out; grainy enchilada fillings and the not-unpleasant reek of overheated beans; an abundance of sour cream where it doesn't really belong; chile salsa mild as Cocoa Puffs; guacamole that coats the chips a little too smoothly. You could probably turn an enchilada combo upside down without incident, because almost everything on it is welded to the plate with great leathery straps of molten cheese. Many restaurants vaguely resemble this place, from the cheap margaritas to the walls decorated with broken mirrors, from the guacamole dinners to the ersatz tostadas, but I could pick an El Coyote combination plate blindfolded out of a hundred others, and most of the regular customers could too. This isn't really Mexican food—or, heaven forbid, the "Spanish" food alluded to in the restaurant's name. It's El Coyote food, as cheerfully inauthentic as the Laguna Beach Pageant of the Masters, "Ramona," or the thousands of tiny tile-roofed bungalows that line the streets of the restaurant's neighborhood. The city is unimaginable without it.

EL GALLO GIRO

7148 PACIFIC BLVD., HUNTINGTON PARK; (323) 585-4433. ALSO AT 8309 VAN NUYS BLVD., PANORAMA CITY; (818) 891-5533 AND FOUR OTHER LOCATIONS.

On a crucial bit of sidewalk in Huntington Park, at the core of Los Angeles' Mexican-American suburbia, El Gallo Giro is as chaotic as any giant fast-food complex ought to be: walls of blasting music and smoking copper cauldrons, dozens of surging queues, framed paintings of cockfighters, sweet oceans of *agua fresca* and steaming hillocks of meat.

You can sit at a table or eke out shoulder room, poke your elbows into your neighbor's *salsa verde*, eat burritos the size of your head. The normal reaction upon entering El Gallo Giro for the first time is panic mixed with awe, which may be the only sensible reaction when you are faced with a crowd, a foreign language, a squadron of food stations and a pounding marimba-orchestra version of "Jesu, Joy of Man's Desiring."

The secret is to position yourself in front of the counter that serves the sort of food you're interested in, bark out an order, and somehow worm your way to the nearest cash register to pick it up. If you want a beverage, say, a milky banana drink, the process is reversed: pay first or you will be sent to the back of a very long line. He who hesitates is lost. The countermen at El Gallo Giro are relentless, especially if you try to order a quesadilla from the taco line.

Order a quesadilla in the proper line, though, and you'll get a thick corn turnover, more like a rustic empanada really, deep-fried to order and oozing with melted cheese, served under a blanket of salsa and tart *crema Mexicana*. You can also get the quesadilla split, and stuffed with a ladleful of pungent sauteed mushrooms, or *longaniza* sausage cooked with potatoes, or a dollop of the smoky beef-chipotle glop *tinga* that tastes like a sophisticated version of Brunswick stew, only better and without the squirrel.

Also at that station there are *sopes*, thick deep-fried saucers of cornmeal topped the same way, chewy and delicious and absolutely impossible to eat with a flimsy plastic fork and knife; and *gorditas*, thick deep-fried discuses of cornmeal stuffed with spicy, stewed pigskin; and fat *taquitos* filled with a chicken-tinged potato mixture that is flavored with sort of a Mexican curry.

The tamales can be fluffy but sawdusty: don't bother, unless you're chasing a sweet tamale with a glass of thick, chocolatey *champurrado* at breakfast. Tacos are fine, of the overpacked and pricey school. The hominy stew *pozole* is bland and uninteresting, the *birria* fatty and mild.

But El Gallo Giro *tortas* share more than a little in common with great Philly cheesesteaks, mostly in that the individual ingredients are a little disgusting when considered individually—sliced jalapeños, fried beans, a shmear of avocado, a sweet, soft roll, a slab of rubbery *panela* cheese—but are delicious when slapped into a sandwich with meat: a paper-thin sheet of batter-fried steak, roast chicken, greasy nubs of *carnitas*, or slices of rich roast pork. Though the *torta* can seem dry and disappointing at first, the three or four middle bites, where all the ingredients coincide, are superb. Share the ends of your sandwich if you must, but save the middle for yourself.

EL GALLO PINTO

5559 N. AZUSA AVE., AZUSA; (626) 815-9907. TUES.–SUN., 11A.M.–9P.M.

In the early '80s, when Angelenos were just beginning to venture beyond the enchilada plate, everybody went to eat at La Plancha, a little Koreatown restaurant that was Milton Molina's shrine to Managua-style cuisine. Nicaraguan cooking was even slightly chic then, given the grooviness of the Sandinista revolution, and Molina's fantastically three-dimensional creations of meat and tubers, named after volcanoes and served with great slabs of fried cheese, were probably more famous than any Central American food will ever be again in Los Angeles.

But after the restaurant closed, and people sought out Nicaraguan food at such fly-specked dives as El Nica and El Rincon Nicaraguense, it turned out that La Plancha's food was less classically Nicaraguan than classically Milton Molina—and despite a brief revival of La Plancha in a Highland Park coffee shop, most people forgot Nicaraguan food even existed. The quasi-Argentine Gaucho Grill chain, which provides a reasonably accurate facsimile of the Latin American meat experience, was not only closer to home, but took American Express.

In the last few years, though, the number of local Nicaraguan restaurants has actually swollen. And now there is El Gallo Pinto, which not only has the best Nicaraguan food in town, but also its own cult of personality—in this case around its owner, former real estate agent Jose (Chepe) Cabrales.

"There is no other Nicaraguan restaurant in Los Angeles," Cabrales says, idly munching on a fried plantain.

El Gallo Pinto, named after the classic Nicaraguan preparation of rice fried with beans, is a smallish place a few blocks south of the 210, tucked in among the usual 7-Elevens and video stores. The dining room, which looks as if it might have started life as a steak house, is lined with booths, decorated with brightly colored Nicaraguan folk art, and on weekends resounds with the music of a singing organist. The restaurant may not seem like much, but some Nicaraguans drive a hundred miles on weekends for the plain beef-and-tuber stew called *baho de res*.

"This food is not fancy," Cabrales says, "but we Nicaraguans feel it in our bones."

There is an okay version of *yoltamales*, a dryish sort of sweet tamale you probably have to be born in Managua to appreciate; a decent if unexciting version of *vigorón*, a Nicaraguan dish of boiled *yuca*, cabbage slaw, and pork rinds; the usual fried cuts of beef and pork; and a very nice *nacatamal*—a giant, wet Nicaraguan tamale steamed in a banana leaf and stuffed with olives, chicken, and half the produce of a Managua garden.

Veal tongue, somewhat overcooked, comes in the caper-enriched tomato sauce that seems common to prettified ethnic cooking from Tunis to Brazil. The dry, sandy *salpicon*—chopped roast-beef salad, easily the most disappointing dish in the house—has almost no flavor until you mix it with the house condiment of onion minced with chiles.

But *chancho frito*, chunks of pork marinated in something like Worcestershire sauce and fried, is soft and luscious here, in contrast to the crisp-edged, hard-fried, thin kind you may have tasted elsewhere, and a bright-yellow beef stew called *Indio Viejo* is a little rich yet undeniably exotic, the sort of stew you might use to fortify yourself on a cool mountain night.

El Gallo Pinto has a large array of cool Nicaraguan *refrescos*: an absolutely first-class version of *cacao*, which is an elegantly spiced sort of chocolate milk made with smashed cocoa beans; the vivid, pink-colored cactus-fruit cooler called *pitahaya*; tart tamarind water. *Chicha*, a shrimp-pink beverage made from crushed, partially fermented corn, is too weird to actually drink, with a powerful smell like artificial vanilla and an almost industrial grade of sour. There are pleasant

Nicaraguan desserts: little cheese fritters called *buñuelos* doused in a clove-scented syrup; well-made flan; cinnamon-saturated rice pudding.

Cabrales takes over the kitchen himself on Tuesdays, and his cooking is a little simpler than that of his chef, rougher around the edges, but possibly more delicious. His *churrasco*, a thin, broad slab of less-than-prime steak, grilled way too long and glazed with a pungent tincture of fresh oregano and garlic, is off-putting at first, but somehow gains funky soul with every bite.

"This steak—doesn't it taste like Nicaragua?"

EL GRAN BURRITO

4716 SANTA MONICA BLVD.; (323) 665-8720. DAILY, 6A.M.–3A.M.

You've seen the great brotherhood of taco eaters, huddled around trucks late at night, trying to maneuver seventeen grams of highly spiced cow's brains or whatever to their mouths without draining detergent-resistant chipotle sauce down the sleeve of their new Christmas jackets.

There's something about the smell of charring meat, the island of warmth and light in the cold dark, that can practically compel you to stand around, eat off soggy paper plates balanced on the roof of your car, and guzzle things like grape soda or the hibiscus-blossom infusion *jamaica* that you ordinarily wouldn't drink on a bet. You munch still-muddy radishes in a vain attempt to disguise the smell of cumin and raw onion that will crawl into bed with you like a faithful pet. You might actually strike up a conversation with your fellow devotees of the taco one of these days—it's easy to sense something in common with the rest of the midnight shift, though it's true that commonality often expresses itself in a certain furtiveness around the eyes—if not for the certainty that all that is beautiful and holy about the mess of corn and gristle in front of you would dissipate as soon as you said hello. If you've been there, you know: the *chi*, the elusive fire-energy of tacos, vanishes seconds after the tacos are served, and unless you're at a first-class place, you'll never experience it at all.

If you're into the taco thing, at one time or another you've probably noticed the leaping flames outside El Gran Burrito, a stand tucked next to a Metro Rail station in East Hollywood, protected with razor wire, at its most crowded after the bars close. Like most great Los Angeles taco places, El Gran Burrito is less notable for the food served inside the restaurant than for the food served out back on evenings and on weekends, when the big grill is set up under an awning, and the mingled aromas of wood smoke and charred beef permeate the air for blocks.

Like all great taco stands, El Gran Burrito can seem slightly sinister after midnight, not in a watch-your-wallet kind of way but with an atavistic dude vibe:

bits of meat roasted on the communal fire; the fire-lit black-hats-gnawing-flesh thing that seems to have figured in half the Westerns ever made.

What is on the menu at El Gran Burrito: *carne asada*, grilled beef snatched from a big fire, chopped—*thwack!*—into gristly nubs with a big cleaver, and swept into a gray pile of meat that glistens under the harsh artificial light. From the pile, still hissing, the grill man tips the meat onto a juxtaposition of two thick corn tortillas that have been briefly toasted with oil, splashes it with a bit of the stand's tart, green *tomatillo* salsa, dusts it with chopped onions and a little cilantro, and slides the taco—or four—onto a thin paper plate in less time than it takes you to fish a couple of dollars from your jeans. It is a grand taco, sizzling hot, oily, glowing with citrus and black pepper, the kind of taco that can for a fleeting instant seem like the best thing that ever happened to your life—until it's time to get the next one. A truly fine taco may be something like the crack cocaine of the food world.

There are things to eat inside El Gran Burrito that are not *carne asada* tacos—burritos stuffed with chicken, rice, and beans; the mild beef stew called *carne guisada*; pork rinds stewed in tomato sauce; *carnitas* sandwiches served on toasted white rolls—but I can see no reason why you'd bother.

EL INDIO

4579 S. CENTINELA AVE.; (310) 822-8456. DAILY FOR LUNCH AND DINNER.

Centinela Avenue, in that odd stretch just before it swings through Culver City, may be the oldest surviving melting pot on the Westside. It's an amiable polyglot of Japanese-American, Mexican-American, and Italian-American businesses that dates from right after World War II, when the future housing developments and strip-mall centers around here were still planted in vegetables, and this no-man's-land was as remote a part of Los Angeles as most people could imagine. If you squint a little, Centinela still has the dusty feel of the main street in a small farm town.

Surrounded by junk stores, announced by a long-faded sign, El Indio is the kind of storefront you could drive by for decades without noticing. A high school girlfriend lived a couple of blocks from here for a while, and the two of us must have walked past El Indio fifty times on our way to Paco's Tacos or Mago's, but I had no idea El Indio sold anything but tortillas. El Indio is a quintessential undiscovered Mexican dive, right down to the *Cinco de Mayo*-themed beer ads on the tables and the handwritten daily specials posted on the walls. The first time I wandered in here, the restaurant was practically empty, and the owner seemed taxed to the limit by the exertion of preparing a small lunch for two. The tortilla chips were wonderful, though, any fool could tell that right away: thick, irregular, tooth-breaking objects with the slightly high taste of fresh toasted corn. The salsa, made from canned tomatoes and lots of fresh chiles, intricately flavored with vinegar and cumin, was a little idiosyncratic but fine. The big tacos of fried *barbacoa* or gristly grilled beef weren't up to the best East L.A. standards, but they were overstuffed, made with good tortillas, and pleasantly oily.

The best things at El Indio are the dusky, spicy stews somewhat in the New Mexico manner: *chile colorado*, slightly bitter and sneakily hot, colored sunset orange with dried chiles; steak simmered with chopped onions and ultrahot fresh peppers; *carne adobada*, pork steak steeped in spices and vinegar, cooked to an almost spoonable softness.

"I cook whatever I feel like," says the owner, plonking down a bottle of pineapple pop. "Sometimes I use pork in a dish, sometimes beef . . . It's always different."

One day, the *chile verde* may be almost like a pork *machaca*—dry, chewy strips of meat fried hard with onions and shreds of chile, a dish that is all salt and smoke and intense chile heat. The next, it might be beef simmered with gentler chiles to a pillowy softness and served with a fiery, complex green-chile salsa that works its way into the stew like salve into a sore back. Sometimes the broth-steeped rice is fluffy and sharp with garlic; sometimes it's hard-fried and bland. There's just one guy at El Indio—he's cook, proprietor, waiter, and tortilla salesman—and his cooking probably varies as much as your own.

EL IZALQUEÑO

1830 W. PICO BLVD., LOS ANGELES; (213) 387-2467. SUN.–THURS., 10A.M.–10P.M.; FRI.–SAT., 10A.M.–11P.M.

Seen briefly through the windshield of a moving car, El Izalqueño has a certain film-set improbability about it: a vivid neon volcano silently erupting on a grimy stretch of Pico, a warm and friendly place glimpsed through the haze of gang graffiti on its windows, like some fake exterior plastered on a downtown place for an episode of *Law and Order*. Though the restaurant is around the corner from the genteel Victorian mansions of Alvarado Terrace, one of L.A.'s poshest residential streets in 1903, this is the sort of neighborhood where you're glad to find a guarded parking lot after dark.

With eighty-odd dishes on the menu, El Izalqueño is the most ambitious Salvadoran restaurant in an area that breeds Salvadoran restaurants the way Melrose does Italian joints. The menu itself is a fairly amazing document, thick as the September issue of *Vogue* and shaped like a volcano (Izalco is a volcano in central El Salvador), illustrated with scenes of village life and spiked with directives on what to eat as a hangover cure, as a restorative on a cold morning or as a macho tonic.

Most Salvadoran places serve *pupusas* made from corn and stuffed with meat or cheese, or sometimes with the mildly bitter flower buds called *loroco*. El Izalqueño has all of these, plus *pupusas* made from rice flour. Where you can find an *atol* or two anywhere else, El Izalqueño offers a half-dozen varieties of the warm gruel, including a delicious sweet one made with corn, pineapple, and cloves, and a fine version of the savory chocolate/black-bean/pumpkin-seed gruel *shuco* that is often thin and uninteresting elsewhere. *Atols* are served here in dried-out calabash halves that are kept from tipping over with little twine-wrapped rings.

You can get all your favorite Salvadoran innard dishes here as well, and a spicy, exemplary *sopa de pata*, calf's-foot-soup, which as the menu proudly points out is El Salvador's most famous dish. To start, you might try *pastelitos de carne*, delicious, crispy fried cornmeal turnovers stuffed with a savory mush of meat-and-veg, or what Salvadorans call *empanadas*, deep-fried banana bundles filled with a sort of sweet pudding. A *tostada de asada* is about what you'd expect—a fried tortilla topped with beans, lettuce, and peppery bits of well-done steak—but *tostada de platanos* is a plateful of thinly sliced green plantain chips with crumbles of aged Salvadoran cheese: not that interesting by themselves, but nice implements for scooping up salsa. What El Izalqueño calls Salvadoran guacamole is chunky, well-seasoned avocado dip with lots of chopped-up hard-boiled egg in it. Salvadoran tamales are the wet, tasty kind, steamed in banana leaves and stuffed with beef or chicken and vegetables.

One of the best appetizers—though the menu implies that it's an entrée—is the grilled chorizo sausage, three tiny balls to an order tied off with bits of corn husk, fragrant of black pepper and tart spice and char, and are served with the house's good refried beans and a sour lake of Salvadoran cream.

The oddest dish in the restaurant is the batter-fried *pacaya* flower, a really bitter thing filled with stamens that look like fat, white worms, and sort of too weird for many people to actually eat. *Arroz a la Valenciana*, a Salvadoran take on paella, includes chicken, tomatoes, capers, and little rounds of what appear to be sliced hot dogs. *Arroz con camarones*, rice with shrimp, is very nice, with a subtle marine flavor and a dose of garlic, and *tortas de carne de puerco*—chopped pork patties fried in an egg batter and doused with a sweet-and-sour tomato sauce—are tasty in a bogus, egg-*fu-yung* sort of way. And then there's *gallo en chicha*, which is rooster stewed in white wine with olives, capers, and tomatoes, given a haunting, Southwest France-style sweetness with prunes. *Gallo en chicha* is the cosmopolitan Salvadoran equivalent of *coq au vin*.

EL PARIAN

1528 W. PICO BLVD.; (213) 386-7361. DAILY, 8A.M.–11P.M.

The concept of the single-item restaurant is well known in Los Angeles: Lawry's for prime rib, Tommy's for hamburgers, Philippe's for French dip. If you want crab, you might head for the Crab Cooker; if chili, for Chili John's. And when you find yourself cruising the boulevards south of downtown, El Parian is destination number one when you're in the mood for a steaming bowl of goat.

The restaurant is located in the throbbing heart of the Pico-Union district, half a mile east of the *pupuserias* and ballrooms of Little Central America, just west of the Harbor Freeway. Here's the kind of vital street life everybody tells you doesn't exist in L.A. On the sidewalk in front of El Parian, babies scream and vendors sell battery-powered puppies and Los Tigres del Norte cassettes. For a dollar or two, you can buy a tamale, a hot ear of corn, or a sliced mango seasoned to order with chile and salt.

The market next door sells *masa* by the kilo and pigs' snouts by the pound, but the action is in El Parian's grease-stained picture window, through which you can see women stamping out tortillas and men with cleavers ripping into giant sides of roasted meat. You can look toward the rear of the crowded restaurant, down the length of the trompe l'oeil brick arcade, and everybody's digging into the same thing, *birria*, which is a portion of roast kid submerged in a thick, chilied goat broth. The sweet, mild meat has crispy parts and stewy parts, just like *carnitas*; it clings to the tiny goat ribs, which you suck and then spit back into the bowl. The broth, basically amplified pan drippings, is the rich essence of goat. (In my opinion, El Parian's *birria* is the best single Mexican dish in Los Angeles.) There's a thicket of cilantro to flavor the broth, a heap of chopped onion, limes to squeeze and dried oregano to crumble, and a fat radish to sweeten your breath. The thick, freshly made tortillas are warm and smell of fresh corn. The beer is very cold. *Birria* is supposed to be somewhat aphrodisiac and a palliative for hangovers too, which is a special bonus on a Sunday morning.

And goat's about all there is to El Parian, except for *carne asada*, grilled beef, which is on the menu for the same reason "Landlubber's De-Lite" might be at a seafood restaurant.

EL POLLO INKA

15400 HAWTHORNE BLVD., LAWNDALE; (310) 676-6665. 1425 W. ARTESIA
BLVD., GARDENA; (310) 516-7378. 23705 HAWTHORNE BLVD., TORRANCE;
(310) 373-0062. 11000 PACIFIC COAST HWY., HERMOSA BEACH; (310) 372-
1433. 11701 WILSHIRE BLVD., WEST LOS ANGELES; (310) 571-3334.
DAILY FOR LUNCH AND DINNER (SOME LOCATIONS CLOSE LATE ON FRI.
AND SAT.).

Not unlike Los Angeles, Lima is filled with grilled-chicken restaurants of every size and description, elegant chicken places in the tony Miraflores district and dumpy ones out by the airport, drive-through chicken and tuxedo-service chicken, even a chicken joint built for some reason in the shape of a giant cat. In Plaza San Martín, the traffic-choked square at the heart of downtown Lima, the most crowded restaurant used to revolve around a giant, circular fire pit, like an oversize Jacuzzi filled with coals, over which hundreds of chickens turned, skewered and spinning, crisping over the hardwood heat.

Peruvian poultry tends to be fed on fish meal, which lends a strange, fishy tartness to its flesh, so Peruvian-style chicken, even more than El Pollo Loco-type Mexican birds, is usually marinated with some fairly strong stuff—citrus, *ají*, spices—that drives out not only the fishy taste but the factory-farm insipidness of the meat. Peruvian chicken is pretty good in Peru; in Los Angeles, where chickens don't happen to taste like fish, it is even better.

The most famous of the Southland's Peruvian-chicken specialists are certainly the restaurants of the small El Pollo Inka chain. At the original Lawndale El Pollo Inka, there are crowds lined up to get in and live Peruvian music on weekends. The Gardena location has a llama-encrusted bas-relief of Machu Picchu that bursts out of the wall, and a vast, dark dining room painted with a vast wraparound black-light mural of Lima's Plaza de Armas. The Westside restaurant is a peculiar place, a kitschy Andean fantasy superimposed on a space that used to belong to a neo-'50s diner. Each restaurant resonates with all the usual Andean panpipe hits—if you have spent any time in Peru, even one playing of "El Condor Pasa" is one too many—but fortunately, they do not play them too loudly.

El Pollo Inka is definitely a big-city restaurant, its menu filled with the seafood dishes typical of Lima's industrial port suburb Callao, including the vaguely Chinese-influenced dishes of the area's many Peruvian-Chinese *chifa* joints, but minus both expense-account Lima's fancy Europeanized sauces and the spicy tuber-based stews of Peru's Andean plain.

Peru has as many kinds of tuber preparations as the United States does cable channels, and the restaurant does several of them well: potatoes *ocopa*, from the southern Peruvian Andes, slicked with a mixture of walnuts pounded with pungent dried shrimp; a rich though blandish version of potatoes *Huancaina*, in a dense, egg-enriched cheese sauce; and a splendid crackly-skinned potato, stuffed with a forcemeat of ground beef and raisins, garnished with a tart salad of thinly sliced red onions.

You will find big plates of *ceviche*, fresh, raw fish marinated in lime juice and hotly spiced with puréed chiles, served with the typical Limeño accompaniments of potato, sweet potato, and corn.

Under the best of circumstances, *parihuela*, a sort of highly flavored Peruvian bouillabaisse, can be the greatest fish stew of the Americas, but here, though seafood is fresh, the shrimp and fish and squid and clams aren't the same as the stuff Peruvians pull from the cold Magellan Current, and there's a weirdly starchy quality to whatever the restaurant uses to thicken its version. *Jalea* is a a big, expertly done Peruvian version of the Captain's Plate at Red Lobster, vast, breaded heaps of deep-fried seafood.

Ají de pollo is more like it, an oily, tan mash, vaguely scented with crushed walnuts, that has something of the texture of wet bread and the elusive spiciness of a TV-dinner enchilada. El Pollo Inka's *ají* may be one of those dishes some people push away after a bite or two but later realize is close to the godhead, a salty, softy-puffy thing as hard to stop shoveling down as a bowl of butterscotch pudding.

You will certainly order spit-roasted chicken the first time you visit El Pollo Inka, and the juicy, crisp-skinned bird is as good as it smells, good enough that you may decide to order another whole bird to go so that you can make another meal of it the next day. If you come to El Pollo Inka on a Saturday or a Sunday, do not neglect to order *picarones*, a dish of crunchy pumpkin fritters in a dark syrup that ranks among the most delicious Latin American desserts in town.

EL SAZON OAXAQUEÑO

12131 WASHINGTON PLACE; (310) 391-4721. DAILY FOR BREAKFAST, LUNCH, AND DINNER.

The Westside, or at least the Centinela corridor, has so many decent Oaxacan restaurants that the cuisine has become something of a Los Angeles tourist attraction, a new, clean, ineffably exotic kind of cooking that happens to have popped up in Studioland rather than somewhere down the 10, a cuisine unusual enough in the United States to have attracted national attention, yet centered five minutes from Brentwood.

But even in a neighborhood well-furnished with Oaxacan cafes, Oaxacan bakeries, and butcher shops that sell fairly specialized Oaxacan cuts of meat, El Sazon Oaxaqueño has become an institution in just a few years, a spare, tidy restaurant tucked in near a video store and a laundromat in a Westside mini-mall. The place is filled in the morning with locals scarfing coffee and sugar-crusted rolls before work, *enfrijoladas* and vast *empanadas* at lunch, and broad, sparsely garnished *clayudas*, Oaxacan pizzas, in the late afternoon. The kitchen hums under an elaborate tile hut built within the restaurant. A bakery area up front attracts a crowd of its own.

The restaurant is missing a few of the touches many of us have grown to expect from our local Oaxacan cafes: Chips are served with spicy tomato salsa instead of the small bowls of exotic *mole* you can find at some other restaurants, and the music that blares from the stereo includes more Ricky Martin songs than chipper festival music. Where some places serve a whole range of oozy, fermented homemade Oaxacan beverages, El Sazon has only the Oaxacan version of *horchata*, a smooth, cinnamon-scented rice drink garnished with chopped pecans and a scant ounce of red syrup. Chile-rubbed fried crickets are nowhere to be found. And of the seven classic *moles*, the elaborate, multispiced sauces that make up the soul of Oaxacan cuisine, here you will find only two.

Still, where many of the other Oaxacan places in town interpret *mole* as a mandate to serve fairly incidental segments of reheated chicken or boiled pork spine in great, sopping plates of sauce, the chicken at El Sazon is fresh, full of juice, tending toward old-bird chewiness rather than dissolving into mush under your fork, and the pork spine, which was nobody's favorite cut, is nowhere to be seen. Oaxaca's roster of *antojitos, masa*-based snacks, is unique in Mexico, I think, and El Sazon's are among the best in town: the sweet, soft *mole*-stuffed tamales steamed in banana leaves; the bean-smeared tortillas called *enfrijoladas*; even the crisp little chicken *taquitos*.

Memelas, often constituted as thick, bean-smeared tortillas, more closely resemble saucer-shaped *sopes* here, and are similarly filled with beans, cheese, and meat. First among these snacks is the *clayuda*, a sort of Oaxacan tostada dotted with lettuce; crumbles of fresh, wet cheese; what the menu accurately identifies as "pork-fat-flavored bean purée" and also a handful of meat, perhaps sweet, marble-size Oaxacan chorizo sausages or the pleasantly gamy house-dried beef known as *cecina*. *Clayudas* are enormous things, built up on griddle-baked tortillas as big as manhole covers, and are basically as hard to cut as rawhide. An Oaxacan Emily Post may well recommend eating *clayudas* with a knife and fork, but you will eventually tear the thing apart with your hands, roll the scraps into leathery tubes, and chaw. (*Empanadas*, filled with the restaurant's mild, cumin-scented *mole amarillo*—thickened with *masa*, which tastes like an Olympian version of the enchilada sauce you might find in a Swanson's Hungry Man dinner—are more or less *clayudas* folded into rough half-moon shapes.)

The best-known Oaxacan specialty is probably *mole negro*, as interpreted in half the Mexican restaurants in the world, and El Sazon's version of the famous sauce is impeccable, a thick, oily substance, almost blue-black in hue, slightly sweetened and vaguely hot, vibrating with drawerfuls of toasted spice. The ruddy, delicate broth that sauces the *barbacoa de chivo* is finer still, scented with the subtle licorice taste of toasted avocado leaves and the funky essence of stewed kid—this is as refined a goat dish as you are ever going to see in a Mexican restaurant. But it is the extravagantly hot *coloradito de pollo* that is El Sazon's best dish, a brick-red sauce that almost sings with roasted chiles, sautéed spices, and ground, charred bread. Glorious.

EL TAQUITO #2

467 N. FAIR OAKS AVE., PASADENA; (626) 577-3918. DAILY, 8A.M.–5P.M.

Old Town Pasadena may be the most gentrified downtown in America, a sort of mega-mall sprinkled like fairy dust through hundred-year-old office blocks and polished to a shine. In Old Town—which for some reason has been renamed Old Pasadena—you are never more than a few yards from a cashmere sweater or a nonfat latte. And if you are hungry, Old Town is well stocked with marketing consultants' conceptions of '40s Hoboken, '50s Los Angeles, and '70s frat-house Ohio, of ancient ports evoked through their respective cruise-ship cuisines, and the kind of chain restaurants that send their customers home with fourteen pounds of dripping foil swans.

But just a couple of blocks north, a bit past the freeway, there is El Taquito Mexicano #2, an utterly authentic lunch counter in as concentrated a Mexican neighborhood as exists in California—kitty-corner from a hardware store parking lot that serves as Pasadena's informal clearinghouse for day labor, anchoring a strip of bodegas, *taquerias* and piñata shops, booming polkas and games of street soccer that, but for the live oaks, might be in Boyle Heights. This neighborhood of Pasadena is only a five-minute walk from the shiny boutiques of Old Town, but it may as well be another world.

El Taquito Mexicano #2 (the first is in Highland Park) is a cheerful yellow storefront that looks no bigger than a bread box when you speed by it on the way to Altadena, a tiny taco stand that somehow opens up to a dining room almost as roomy as a tool shed, furnished with a few rough picnic tables and some wooden booths that look as if somebody fabricated them in a junior high school shop class. While the restaurant technically has an "inside," it is the kind of inside where the coffee-inhaling regulars usually don't bother to take off their cowboy hats. The short Spanish-language menu, mostly of burritos and soups, is painted on the wall; a shorter list of specials—*chilaquiles*, chorizo and eggs, stewed pork skin—is posted near the cash register.

Like many of Los Angeles's best small Mexican restaurants, El Taquito may function less as an institution unto itself than as a docking station for a fleet of taco trucks, which fan out from the restaurant every day at dusk. (The taco truck from rival La Estrella, which once parked each night just across the street, seemed from its hourlong lines on Saturday nights to be the local equivalent of Old Town's perpetually crowded Cheesecake Factory.)

But El Taquito is a genuine center of Mexican home cooking, a *loncheria* with an ever-changing menu and Styrofoam cups of the rice-pudding drink *horchata* as big around as swimming pools. This is almost as far as you can get from *taqueria* fast food: fresh-simmered rice; oily, homemade-tasting refried beans; *posole* that tastes like somebody's grandmother had a hand in it.

When you order a full lunch (as opposed to a burrito), a waitress brings over a huge bowl of freshly made chips, tooth-crackingly dense, usually served with a fresh salsa made from roasted green chiles or an intense chipotle dip. Some people are drawn here for the chips alone. As in most *loncherias*, the food varies from day to day, even hour to hour. Sometimes the *chiles rellenos* are crisp and oily, magnificent beasts sturdy enough to stand up to a thick blanket of tomato sauce, though at other times they can seem as pale and limp as a bad Jay Leno monologue.

I have eaten some of the best *carne asada* of my life at El Taquito, peppery, fragrant with citrus and garlic, charred black at the edges, but I have also had gray, steamy stuff that tasted mostly of overdone meat. Burritos can be tremendous—and are always huge—but once or twice have been the watery things I sometimes drive across town to avoid. The restaurant has a small specialty in pork skin, *chicharronnes*, cooked down to a luxurious softness, sometimes in red chile, sometimes green.

I love this place: It has a sense of neighborhood about it that no $2 million decorating budget would be able to replicate, and I have taken visitors to El Taquito who subsequently felt compelled to eat there every single day for the rest of their stay. Lunch at El Taquito is like lunch at your mom's house: If it's great, it couldn't be better; if it's mediocre, at least you're at home.

EL TAURINO

1104 S. HOOVER ST.; (213) 738-9197. MON.–THURS., 8 A.M.–2 A.M.; FRI. AND SAT., 24 HOURS; SUN., 6 A.M.–2 A.M.

In tacos as in sex, timing is everything. If you've ever eaten street food in Mexico, you'll know what I mean. On practically every corner in Mexican cities, you'll find a vendor grilling scraps of beef an ounce or two at a time over a dented charcoal brazier, then folding the meat with minced onion and fiery hot salsa onto tiny, freshly made corn tortillas. You gulp the taco seconds after the steak comes off the grill: desire and fulfillment are concomitant.

Even—especially—the busiest stands make each taco from scratch, though the operation is far too labor intensive to be replicated in a country where everybody reasonably expects to earn more than a couple bucks a shift. North of the border, tacos are as subject to the economies of scale as any other fast food, and even the smallest *taquerias* are likely to use preheated tortillas, prefab salsa, and precooked meat kept warm on a steam table.

Expensive places are hardly better. I'm as much a fan of Border Grill tacos as anyone, but by the time they've been assembled, made the rounds of the kitchen, and traveled the thirty-odd yards to the table, they've lost much of the elusive taco energy, the *chi,* that probably made them so damned good to begin with. Plus, you've got to eat them with a fork. The closest local approximation of the True Taco Experience, I think, is to be found at good taco trucks, where the ingredients are fresh because the turnover is awesome and there's little storage space, and where the time elapsed between taco assembly and taco consumption is essentially nil. One friend travels out to a certain East Los Angeles construction site every Wednesday for what he swears are the tastiest brain tacos in the world; another friend likes to report stories about mud wrestlers because she likes to eat *carne asada* tacos from the truck that parks across the street from the Hollywood nightclub where they perform.

My particular favorite tacos come from the truck that spends its weekends parked behind El Taurino, a taco stand on Hoover, a bit south of MacArthur Park. At 2:30 A.M. on a Saturday night, just as the last stragglers lurch out of the Seventh Street bars. the large El Taurino parking lot seethes with life. Competing accordion polkas blast from new 4x4s and old Camaros; a canary yellow car bounces as it exits the lot. Two giggling teenagers in matching dresses stop by the beverage cart for a tart *tamarindo,* then disappear in a whoosh of pink tulle. Piles of crumpled napkins and grease-stained paper plates look like snowdrifts in the harsh light.

You fight your way to the front of the throng and take a number from a deli-style dispenser attached to the truck. In less time than it takes the guy next to you to drunkenly croon the chorus of some long-forgotten ballad, you hear somebody call out *"cuaranta y seis."* You order in broken Spanish, specifying *con todo,* with everything. (Sometimes the counterman answers you in unaccented English, and you feel a little foolish.)

A gleaming column of marinated pork *al pastor* rotates before a simulated shepherd's fire, and bits of the outside layer of meat caramelize and drip juice. Somebody hacks off a few slivers, slivers you know are meant for your very taco, and rushes to anoint the pork with finely chopped onion, cilantro, and a stupendous, dusky hot sauce that perfectly accents the sweetness of the meat.

There is also decent stewed tongue, *carnitas*, and *carne asada*, which are as besides the point as the hot dogs are at Tommy's.

The tacos are all eaten before you even reach your car.

EL TEPEYAC

812 N. EVERGREEN AVE., EAST LOS ANGELES; (323) 267-8668. OPEN WED.-MON. FOR BREAKFAST, LUNCH AND DINNER.

El Tepeyac has become practically synonymous with the burrito in the Southland, the legendary East L.A. place with the eight-pound burritos, as popular with policemen as it is with the locals, and crowded with customers who have moved from small, tidy houses in the old neighborhood to Montebello and Whittier.

Like the giant bowls of oversauced pasta devised a century ago by immigrants translating Calabrian poverty-cooking into the language of new American prosperity, the burrito symbolizes a cuisine of a newly found abundance—the humble taco, in which cheap tortillas stretch a small amount of meat into a filling meal, transformed into a plump, overstuffed creation, where meat and beans overwhelm the flimsy tortilla in which they are wrapped.

"Eat!" the burrito says. "Eat until you are full and more."

At El Tepeyac, few people ever manage to finish the enormous burritos, some of which approach the size of lap dogs, and it is rare to see a party of four leave the restaurant without at least one parcel of leftovers. To-go orders are stacked in corrugated cardboard shipping cartons—paper bags would certainly collapse from the weight—and a simple $10 burrito order feels heavy as a load of bricks. You know you are at El Tepeyac when your friend's burrito is bigger than her purse.

The Hollenbeck, named after the local East L.A. police division, is more or less an old-line Mexican restaurant's entire No. 2 dinner wrapped into a tortilla the size of a pillowcase—rice, beans, stewed meat, guacamole—all garnished with tomato sauce, more meat, and something like a half pound of melted taco cheese.

Some of my wife's earliest food memories involve the Hollenbecks that her mother sometimes brought home after a night out on the town, nostalgia tempered by recollections of the inevitable fight with her sister when they both coveted the single glob of guacamole tucked into a corner of the burrito.

Manuel's Special is sort of like a Hollenbeck but three times the size—buy one and feed your family for a week—and an Oscar is a purist's burrito, all meat and red chile sauce. I am fond of the Okie burrito, which is more or less a Hollenbeck finished off like an enchilada, and the intense, spicy chorizo-and-egg burrito, and the salty *machaca* burrito made with onions, eggs, and sautéed shreds of beef. The crisp, fat *taquitos*, served with a vast wash of fresh guacamole, are pretty good, if not quite up to the standard of Ciro's, which is across the street. This may not be the most delicious Mexican food in town, but it is among the most evocative.

EL TEXATE

316 PICO BLVD., SANTA MONICA; (310) 399-1115. DAILY, 8:00A.M.–10:00P.M.

Near the beach in Santa Monica, on a stretch of surf shops and video stores, a few yards from a bowling alley, El Texate sits in one of the last places you'd expect to find a Oaxacan restaurant in Los Angeles. It looks like a surf-dude bar centered around a giant TV. Before you open a menu, unless you scope the plurality of tables that happen to be occupied by Mexican families, you might feel that *memelas* and *nicuatole* seem less likely here than tacos and Corona.

The bartender, in fact, does make pretty good margaritas. But El Texate is the real thing, maybe not the single best Oaxacan restaurant in town (that would be the original Guelaguetza in Koreatown), but authentic to the point that its menu owes almost nothing to standard Mexican-restaurant cuisine.

Enchiladas, for example, are the Oaxacan kind, tortillas dipped in *mole* and rolled, then garnished instead of stuffed with chicken and a few crumbles of salty, white cheese. *Clayudas*, more or less the Oaxacan equivalent of pizza, are plate-size dried tortillas, smeared with a black-bean purée and the signature crumbled cheese, garnished with a small piece of chile-impregnated *cecina*, beef jerky. *Memelas*, thick, fried cornmeal platforms, are also smeared with black beans and sprinkled with cheese.

Sometimes El Texate can be a little too authentic: No restaurant much north of Monte Alban may serve the dish called *igadito*, a sort of fuzzy, bland matzo ball made out of scrambled eggs and plopped into a mild chicken broth, but *igadito* is not going to be replacing the fajitas platter in Los Angeles anytime soon.

When you ask for *mole* here, the waitress patiently waits until you specify which kind of *mole* you'd like: *mole negro*, tar-black, sweet-bitter, with a specific gravity that lies somewhere near that of plutonium; oddly herbed *verde de pollo*; the bright red spice mixture that heats up the goat *barbacoa* to almost the point of incandescence.

The *mole* called *amarillo*, especially mild, with a clear chile flavor, a strong top note of cumin, and the sort of slightly oily texture of gravy in a chicken-dinner restaurant, seems almost like an ideal version of commercial enchilada sauce, but is somehow apt here in this stew of vegetables and odd cuts of beef. (Whenever I order *amarillo* here, I spend a few minutes trying to figure out the bowl-shaped pieces of beef in the stew. Cow kneecaps? Shoulder joints?)

It's the *mole coloradito* that's the best food in the house, brick-red, sharply spicy, a little smoky, with the roundness of toasted grain, more pungent than the *negro*, everything you're looking for when you order *mole* . . . with not a kneecap in sight.

EMPRESS PAVILION

988 N. HILL ST., CHINATOWN; (213) 617-9898. MON.–FRI., 9A.M.–10P.M.; SAT. AND SUN., 8A.M.–10P.M.

If you are like most of my friends, you are sick of hearing me talk about Empress Pavilion. It's true, there are other Cantonese restaurants, and some of them are even in Chinatown; most of them serve jellyfish salad and roast quail, and many of them even make decent fish-bladder soup. But Empress Pavilion's small menu of seasonal specialties—you often have to make a point of asking for a copy— always lists a few dozen things that you have probably never eaten before.

Los Angeles is a pretty good town for the swanker kind of restaurants, shiny places with famous chefs and great wine lists and the patronage of David Geffen. But no matter how hard you search, you will never find a better dish than the steamed Dungeness crab with garlic and flat noodles at Empress Pavilion, a restaurant you may have burned out on back in 1989, but which may still serve the very best Hong Kong–style food in Los Angeles. I have eaten this particular crab dozens of times since I first ran across it, and whenever I get a little down, I imagine a big bowl of it waiting just for me.

The meat of the crab has that high vanilla sweetness you hope to find in utterly fresh crustaceans, tending more toward underdone gelatinousness than toward technically correct dryness, and it is almost swollen with the taste of freshly chopped garlic—which blankets the dish in snowy-white drifts but also manages to work its way into the deepest recesses of the creature.

Live steamed crabs are generally pretty good, but this is a crab that practically compels you to spoon every drop of juice from the ruined carapace, excavate for milligrams of meat in the remains of once-chewed legs, harvest the dodgy bits of internal organ that you would leave untouched in nineteen crabs out of twenty, but which seem to carry the key to the pungent sea essence of the beast. When you get tired of gnawing at the crab, you can gnaw on the bed of chewy flat noodles it rests upon—homemade noodles as perfectly garlic-soaked as anything you are likely to come across this side of a late-night order of spaghetti *aglio e olio* in a stinky Trastevere cafe. Or you can just sip the garlic-enriched broth. If Crustacean, the puzzlingly popular Vietnamese crab place in Beverly Hills, served crab even half this good, the crush of customers might be great enough to influence the rotation of the earth.

Empress Pavilion, the grand marble-and-glass banquet hall at the top of Chinatown, has always been a dependable restaurant, but one that has been overlooked by a lot of people in the rush to the new Shanghainese, Islamic Chinese, and Chiu Chow restaurants in the San Gabriel Valley. It's hipper to patronize a place that wraps spicy chicken in mung-bean sheets than one that merely steams live prawns perfectly every time. Empress Pavilion has always been one of the best two or three places for dim sum in town, but a lot of people would rather schlep out to Monterey Park. And it's the more seafood-focused Cantonese restaurants that tend to get the critical recognition, though even the best of them are more or less the Gladstone's of Cantonese seafood restaurants in Southern California: immensely popular, reasonably priced, and reliable. Empress Pavilion (and maybe its sister Empress Harbor, too) is a vastly more ambitious restaurant, more like Patina or Campanile than like the Reel Inn, with a vast menu and an improvisational, ever-changing cuisine, sometimes showing influences from Japan—I will always remember a dish of sliced sea snail sautéed with smoky *gobo* root—as well as Hong Kong exotica such as peanut sauce on oysters. One meal included shiitake mushrooms braised with snow-pea leaves, a musky combination that somehow breathed summer; Chinese water spinach sautéed with blindingly pungent fermented soy; and a clay pot filled with something called "drunken inflamed chicken," which sounds like a Chinese name for a guy who likes to get into bar fights but was actually sheets of pounded poultry breast in a fragrant burnt-wine sauce as complex as anything you'd find at Lucques. Winters at Empress Pavilion are notable for little bamboo cups of yin-enhancing snake soup, hearty black-chicken casseroles, and fried frog.

A dish called something like pan-fried mashed bean curd, which I was expecting would resemble a stew, turned out to be the most delicious mixture of tofu and shrimp, patted into thick ovals and gently sautéed until they were golden and crisp, yet delicate inside as lightly scrambled eggs.

You will find most of the Cantonese classics here, most done extremely well: steamed rock cod drizzled with crackling oil, searing-hot clay pots of chicken with caramelized eggplant, Hong Kong–style shrimp with sweet mayonnaise and candied walnuts, shrimp-stuffed bean curd steamed to a puddingy softness. You will also find many of the usual stir-fried dishes—squid with spicy salt, clams in black-bean sauce, sautéed shrimp with garlic—which are made with impeccable ingredients, but suffer slightly from the vast distances they must cover en route from the kitchen to faraway tables.

5 C's

2329 W. 54TH ST.; (323) 298-9313. TUES.–THURS., 11A.M.–8P.M.; FRI.
AND SAT., 11A.M.–10P.M.

When you first step into 5 C's, a gated storefront that opens onto Fifty-fourth, you might think you've stumbled into the wrong restaurant. There's a big takeout counter right in front, a sizable group of people waiting for shrimp baskets, and a certain spareness of decor you might associate with any number of barbecue stands. Plus—you might as well get used to this—the funk of fried seafood hangs heavy in the air, so that after a minute or so you may feel a little like a fried piece of buffalo fish yourself.

Five C's is a swell place, an ancient bastion of New Orleans–style fried seafood in a neighborhood so densely populated with Southern-style fish mongers that it might as well be called the You Buy, We Fry district. If you've spent much time in New Orleans, you've probably stumbled across po' boy joints like 5 C's, attached to ancient taverns in obscure wards, whose sandwiches are good enough to make you weep. 5 C's is a shrine to that most hallowed of po' boys, the oyster loaf.

If you look confused enough, somebody will eventually point you toward a hall leading to the well-worn dining room in back, which seems secret as a speakeasy and twice as cool.

Scenes from the French Quarter are abstracted on one wall in a way that would have looked great on a '50s rayon shirt. A bayou sunset is daubed on another; an awesome, glitter-splashed mural of old King Neptune rising from the briny deep is on a third. The decor is otherwise dominated by chandeliers and posters and cunning little sconces that make the entire room look as if it has been sponsored by the Miller Brewing Co.

Five C's isn't much for appetizers, unless you include the good hush puppies:

103

dense, golden Ping-Pong balls of fried corn batter, flecked with black pepper and dried herbs. The restaurant adheres to rather a strict interpretation of a lettuce and tomato salad—shredded lettuce, a couple of tomato slices, a squeeze bottle of Italian dressing. The French fries register as homemade, but they are on the limp side.

These are merely waystations on the way to oyster-loaf ecstasy. The oyster loaf served here, as at old New Orleans joints like Eddie's, is essentially a loaf of bread neatly split in half, buttered and toasted, layered with chips of sour pickle, and filled with fried oysters. There are about a dozen oysters to a sandwich here, sandy-crusted, dense and gnarled, and the sandwich's snappy, buttery crunch gives way to fragrant mollusk chewiness and an explosion of their exotic, marine essence.

Some purists shudder at the idea of cooked oysters, even the curried oysters with cucumber sauce they used to serve at Chinois, but this is the wrong place to be a purist.

At 5 C's, you can also get sandwiches filled with fried trout, fried snapper, or crackly lengths of fried Louisiana sausage that sing with black pepper.

Mostly, though, there are fried catfish sandwiches, five or six crisp fillets to a buttered bun, with an undertext of the fluffy, steamy texture of properly cooked catfish but really 99 and 44/100 percent crunch—5 C's catfish sandwich is to other catfish sandwiches what a really fresh head of iceberg is to a limp head of Boston lettuce. And if you're really into crunch, you can always order the catfish sandwich unfilleted.

"Why would anybody want bones in their catfish sandwich?" I asked the waitress.

She looked at the ceiling and sighed.

FLOSSIE'S

3566 REDONDO BEACH BLVD., TORRANCE; (310) 352-4037. LUNCH AND DINNER DAILY.

On the eastern edge of Torrance, a couple of blocks from El Camino College and a two-minute drive from the sushi bars and poi-slingers of Gardena, Flossie's is a cheerful place in a corner mini-mall, a storefront shrine to sweet, heavy food and the Southern ideal of meat-and-threes. Flossie's may be the closest you can get in Los Angeles to Mississippi boarding-house cuisine. People waiting for their takeout order on a Saturday afternoon catch up on the local gossip, occasionally interrupted by the exclamations of a Trinidadian man working his way through a huge mound of pork ribs. "Mon, this stuff is good," he says to nobody in particular. "But oh, ho ho . . . those Friday beef ribs are even better." Flossie herself looks up from a tray of macaroni and cheese, and smiles.

What Flossie's serves is mostly daily specials, except for the perfect Southern fried chicken, which is always on hand. Regulars know that Monday is soft sweet mountains of meat loaf; Wednesday is long-smothered pork chops cooked so that they fall apart when you look at them; Thursday is chewy, crusty chicken-fried steak. One of Flossie's dinners feeds two with leftovers for breakfast. And your car smells like heaven, all the way home. What you want for the starch is the mac 'n' cheese, not the effete four-cheese kind at upscale restaurants but the tremendous, greasy American kind—crusted, curdled, buttery, at least one-third cheese by weight. The alternative is rice and gravy, in the classic, dull truck-stop version. Vegetables change with the season but usually include red beans, mixed in with rice and studded with chunks of hot sausage; delicious cabbage steamed to just this side of mush; and smoky black-eyed peas. Collard greens are the sugary type, spiked with chunks of yam and sweet as Frosted Flakes, even when you sprinkle them with pepper vinegar. If you can get the corn-and-okra glop, sort of a gooshy succotash, while the corn is still crisp, go for that—the flavors are fresh and clean. For an extra buck and a half, you can get firm, well-cooked yams, floating in a heavenly liquored sauce.

Desserts include crusty, sweet red pudding in incredibly sweet lemon sauce, good sweet potato pie, and hot peach cobbler in sugary syrup, sweet and simple as a valentine from a six-year-old.

And then there are the tamales, thin spicy tubes of *masa* lightly wrapped in corn husks, intensely fragrant of corn and served in a searingly hot chile gravy: real Delta food, great for parties. You can buy the tamales by the half-dozen . . . but you'd better get at least twice that if you want any left by the time you get home.

FURAIBO

368 E. SECOND ST., LITTLE TOKYO. LUNCH, MON.–FRI.; DINNER NIGHTLY. ALSO SAWTELLE BLVD., WEST LOS ANGELES; (310) 478-8979.

One of the cool things about small Japanese restaurants is the seemingly absurd level of specialization to which many aspire, focusing not just on Japanese noodles, say, but on cold buckwheat *soba*; not just in pork, but in a certain cut of pork loin fried in a very specific way. One restaurant may serve only sweet curries; another, just eels; a third, only such dishes as may be coaxed out of a freshly slaughtered sea turtle.

Little Tokyo is home to a branch of the restaurant Furaibo, part of a huge Japanese chain which is also represented by a fancy location in a Gardena mini-mall and another over on the Westside. Furaibo specializes not just in chicken but in *teba sake* chicken wings: spicy, funny-looking appendages that are to Buffalo wings what tempura is to the fried clams of HoJo's. A *teba sake* chicken wing is not precisely a chicken wing, including as it does neither meaty drummette nor vestigial tip, but is rather that spindly middle segment of the wing in which a couple of bones form sort of a frame protecting a sweet, if minuscule, oblate ellipse of meat. If hens flew like eagles, this hollow, thumb-size segment might provide a lot of the lift, keeping the wing rigid and extended as noble chickens soared upward into the cool autumn wind. As it is, the part is a chicken-eater's dream, seemingly custom-designed for deep-frying and deeply absorbent of Furaibo's tart, spicy marinade. A *teba sake* wing is greaseless, although it is practically all brittle, crunchy skin.

After the chef has dusted the wings with various white powders and heaped them on plates alongside scoops of shredded cabbage and mayonnaise-intensive chicken salad, you could gnaw through a million of them: sucking out the meat, seeking out the little hidden crunchy bits with your teeth.

A sign inside the door sometimes advertises what Furaibo calls its Happy Meal: chicken wings and Bud.

How could you go wrong?

FU-SHING

2960 E. COLORADO BLVD., PASADENA; (626) 792-8898. DAILY, 11:30A.M.–10P.M.

A few years ago, Fu-Shing was a divey restaurant in a converted San Gabriel pie shop, crowded and noisy, famous among local Chinese as the best Sichuan-style restaurant in town though in the straightforward Taiwanese style rather than in the sneakily numbing manner you might run across in Chengdu. If the wind was right, you could smell the garlic from three blocks away.

Then the restaurant moved uptown, to the part of eastern Pasadena you might think of as Greater Arcadia, into palatial, drapery-hung quarters that might remind you of certain swank restaurants in San Francisco's Chinatown.

The new Fu-Shing advertises widely, accepts American Express, and is perhaps the closest grand Chinese restaurant to San Marino and blue-blood Pasadena. Unlike other Southland Chinese restaurants of its authenticity and scale, Fu-Shing is as used to American customers as it is to the Chinese-wedding crowd, and you will always see a few tablesful of people who look as if they've escaped from a Ralph Lauren ad: It is practically two restaurants in one. If you happen to be an Anglo customer who does not have chicken chow mein on your table, three or four waiters may even come around to compliment you on your ordering. Fu-Shing sells a lot of sweet-and-sour pork.

Fortunately, there are other options. Sichuan cuisine is cold-climate cooking, dark and musky and sometimes numbingly hot, dominated by the flavor of chiles, garlic, and preserved vegetables, grounded in animal pungencies and the bite of Sichuan peppercorns.

Fu-Shing's spicy beef shank in fire pot is a quintessentially Sichuan dish, a chafing-dishful of tendons stewed with chiles, garlic, and a handful of Chinese spice, powerfully scented, astonishingly rich, and soft enough to collapse into just a rumor on your lips. A spoonful is adequate to flavor a bowl of rice; if you eat much more than that, garlic will exude from your pores for the next day or so.

Preserved pork homestyle, thin slices of house-cured gammon fried with hot chile and hanks of leek top, is salty and gamy and delicious; garlic eggplant is soft and spicy-sweet. Fu-Shing's *kung-pao* chicken, ferociously spiced, alive with the musky flavor of toasted, dried chiles, is so much better than anything else you may have had by that name that it almost deserves to belong to another species. A clear turnip soup, hot with white pepper, garnished with sliced pork, has all the soft sharpness of the boiled root vegetable but twice the pleasure.

Fu-Shing is also home to one of the spiciest dishes in California: a bright-red, brothy thing called Sichuan-style beef that is chokingly hot, searingly hot, hot enough to cause first-timers practically to go into cardiac arrest. Underneath the chile, the dish is stunningly complex, and even the heat is modulated, smoky and subtle before it expands into a white-hot glow, but there is no getting around the incendiary nature of the beef. Fu-Shing's Sichuan beef, it almost goes without saying, is one of my favorite things to eat on the planet.

It is, though, pretty easy to have a disappointing meal at Fu-Shing, particularly if you come with too few people—four or more would seem about right—and order the wrong sort of stuff. The cloying honey ham is done better at half a dozen other places; the braised fish with garlic sauce is dull and one-dimensional; the sticky stir-fries are done as well at every other Chinese restaurant in town.

Still, the Chinese vegetable *guy choy*, a cabbagey thing juicy as a ripe melon, is sautéed with crab roe, and the strong brininess brings out subtle sweetness of the vegetable. Ruddy, intensely smoky tea-smoked duck is hard to stop eating; snow-pea leaves, briefly fried with garlic, taste like the essence of spring. And the renowned cold plate—sweet jellyfish shreds, cold chicken in sesame sauce, aromatic sliced beef, smoky chunks of salted duck, sliced octopus, spiced shrimp and fantastic, garlicky tripe tender enough to persuade the staunchest *menudo*phobe—is good enough to repay the longest drive across town.

G

GADBERRY'S

5833 S. BROADWAY,; (323) 751-0753. TUES.–THURS., 11A.M.–12P.M.; FRI. AND SAT., 11A.M.–1A.M.

The front inside wall of Gadberry's is an amazing thing, a life-size, pale-green plaster frieze of a forest scene that includes finely wrought 3-D leaves, singing birds, and a textured brown tree trunk that extends down to include most of a door. The sylvan effect is almost enough to make you forget that you are in fact standing in a bare, harsh-lit lobby, the only furniture a couple of ashtrays, the tile floor scrubbed clean, in a part of town not known for trees. Gadberry's wall may be the Ghiberti doors of early-'50s barbecue kitsch. (The Bear Pit, a mediocre Ozark-style barbecue joint in Mission Hills, is barbecue's Sistine Chapel.)

Customers pace back and forth as if they were expectant fathers outside a maternity ward. Anticipation of great spareribs can make a person feel that way. Smack in the center of Gadberry's forest is the takeout window, through which you can see great expanses of black, galvanized steel—steel, white bread, and a guy hacking at spareribs with a big knife.

Barbecue stands have never been noted for the encyclopedic breadth of their menus, and Gadberry's takes minimalism to an extreme: meat, beans, and potato salad.

Pork spareribs are meaty, smoky, red right through to the bone as if they have been cured, and are as intensely flavored as a Virginia ham. Their texture, though not as crisp as some, is also not unlike that of a dense country ham, and they seem to be some of the leanest ribs around. Links are big, coarse-ground things, crisp on the outside and chewy within. Links are spiced heavily enough to leave the illusion of an almost chemical-pure aftertaste, the kind of thing you find sometimes in barbecued potato chips or huge, tannic young Napa Cabernets. Some people might find a Gadberry's link too powerful to eat, the same people who turn up their noses at properly pungent Thai *yen ta fo* or good runny sheep cheese from France. Barbecued beef might be the best food in the house, a profoundly smoky sliced brisket that's crusted with black, marbled with fat, moist and dripping with juice. It's the sort of Texas-style barbecue all those places in the Valley tell you they make, but don't.

Strictly speaking, Gadberry's meat needs no sauce. The sauce, though, is fine, faintly tart, not too sweet. The pepper heat comes on as a glow, works its way up to a slow burn and then gracefully diminishes—the time-tested art form that's found in both the best barbecue sauces and the best Brahms adagios. The sauce is almost too elegant for Gadberry's powerfully smoked meat. It is, however, the kind of sauce that will stain your fingernails for days, no matter how often you wash your hands.

GAGNIER'S CREOLE KITCHEN

1622 OCEAN PARK BLVD., SANTA MONICA; (310) 319-9981.

For most of its existence, Gagnier's was a white-tablecloth Creole restaurant in the Baldwin Hills/Crenshaw Plaza shopping center on Crenshaw, casual enough to stop into after a morning of shopping at Macy's, though still one of the fanciest places adjacent to the swank black communities of Baldwin Hills. The nearby Boulevard Cafe may have been groovier, Harold & Belle's more soulful, and Stevie's on the Strip possessed of better gumbo; Gagnier's was as current, as popular, as the latest Bebe Moore Campbell novel. Within a few months of its opening, it seemed to have assumed the status of a neighborhood institution, and its oyster loaves, its peppery fried chicken, became legend.

Then, a few years ago, developers ripped up the mall to put in the Magic Johnson Theaters, and a lot of people assumed that Gagnier's had closed, hidden as it was by the detritus of heavy construction. Many of its customers drifted away. Last year, when the developers ripped up the parking lot once again, to put in more theaters and more parking, Gagnier's closed its doors and decamped . . . to the scrubbed environs of Sunset Park. To a few of us, this seemed as unthinkable as Pink's relocating its chili dogs to Tarzana. But here they are again, Gagnier's catfish sandwiches and oyster loaves.

Gagnier's serves neither the corn muffins that were its signature at the Baldwin Hills restaurant—a sizable takeout order is likely to include half a dozen small loaves of buttered French bread instead—nor the fried chicken, but it is nevertheless a fairly orthodox Creole restaurant, which is to say plenty of roux-darkened stews, complex peppery seasoning, and lots of fried seafood. The restaurant's version of oyster loaf, the quintessential fried-seafood sandwich, leans toward austerity: a length of French bread is neatly split in half, buttered and toasted, layered with chips of sour pickle and a leaf or two of lettuce, and heaped with deep-fried oysters. You'll find a dozen or so oysters on a sandwich here, crusted with coarsely ground cornmeal, cooked to a gnarled crunch, briny juices concentrated to a single pop at each bivalve's center.

This may not be the best oyster loaf in creation—these days, I tend to day-dream about the spare, drippy oyster loaves from Domilise's in New Orleans—but this sandwich, especially sluiced with the Bajan *habañero* sauce Gagnier's keeps around, is plenty good enough. The fried shrimp and fried catfish po' boys, (but not the gummy crab-cake po' boy) are pretty good here too—get them with a side of smoky stewed greens. Gagnier's gumbo is thin and on the bland side, more like a sausage-spiked seafood chowder than like the dark, mysterious sub-stance you find locally at, say, Stevie's on the Strip. The pallid red beans and rice could have benefited from a lacing of Creole pickle meat, or at least a good ham bone, though confirmed vegetarians may be happy with the dish.

But I like the restaurant's chicken Creole, a spicy, long-cooked concoction imbued with the Creole trinity of onions, garlic, and sautéed bell peppers and dominated by the high, sweet note of tomatoes cooked down almost to caramel. "Barbecued" shrimp are in the style of—though not in the league of—the Italian shrimp at the Louisiana Creole-Italian restaurant Mosca's, drenched in an emul-sion of butter, olive oil, garlic, and enough rosemary to stun a mule. The jam-balaya, drier and better than most other jambalayas in town, is just moistened with tomato and shot through with chicken, smoked sausage, and shrimp. And the crawfish étouffée is wonderful, complexly seasoned, impeccably fresh, and glowing with peppery spice. Gagnier's usually serves only one dessert, but its warm, raisin-studded bread pudding with whiskey sauce may be all the dessert that any restaurant needs.

GALLO'S GRILL

4533 CESAR E. CHAVEZ AVE.; (323) 980-8669. MON.-FRI., 11A.M.-9A.M.; SAT. AND SUN., 8A.M.-9P.M.

Gallo's Grill is the kind of Mexican steak house we've all always dreamed of finding in East Los Angeles, a tiled patio furnished with oversize wooden tables, shaded from the sky by a canopy, and decorated with citrus trees and the sort of opera-set peeling brick that you find on turreted Hollywood apartment buildings. The illusion is of the kind of tiny courtyard restaurant that often has laundry hanging overhead and a fountain burbling just out of sight. Speakers hidden in fake rocks blast Mexican ballads; tiny children in first-communion dresses conduct screaming games of tag, or perch on stools and make faces at the cooks manning a big, oak-fired grill like the ones you see at the big steak restaurants in Santa Maria. Almost everybody from the neighborhood dresses up a little when they come here.

Fifty years ago, before most of the area was razed to make way for freeways and transit yards, the restaurant would have been at the heart of the Eastside's Belvedere district, which was in its era the most densely populated neighborhood in Southern California, and probably the biggest Mexican community in the United States. My wife's great-grandfather owned a blacksmith's shop a couple of blocks from here, and her family still gets its *pan dulce* around the corner from La Fama, the oldest—and best—Mexican bakery in this part of town. (Try the gingerbread pigs called *puerquitos.*)

Gallo's Grill may not be as grand as Arnie Morton's or the Palm, and the beef certainly isn't USDA prime, but it serves everybody's fantasy of a great Eastside meal: warm, thick corn tortillas (or paper-thin flour tortillas) patted to order, fresh salsas brought to the table perched on intricate wrought-iron stands, garlicky steaks served still sizzling, flanked by bushels of charred scallions on superheated platters. An order of *queso fundido* brings what seems like an entire pound of cheese crusted into a steel baking dish, smoking and sputtering, flavored with dry, spicy crumbles of sausage. There are big bowls of guacamole, decent if a little watery (the chef uses full-flavored Mexican avocados instead of the buttery, expensive Haas) and freshly fried chips to scoop it up with. The house beans come either creamily refried or *a la olla*, bathed in smoky broth.

Gallo's Grill prepares its beef in a specifically Mexican way: butterflied and rebutterflied and laid open like a scroll. The brick-size filet mignon that you might see on your plate at Taylor's or Dan Tana's is flayed and reconfigured into steak for the multitudes here, a broad, thin sheet of seared meat—*filete abierto*—with something like an acre and a half of surface area and the maximal ratio of brown, crusty outside to red, squishy inside, marinated deeply enough even to allow for a bit of juice. Gallo's Grill is Valhalla for fans of extremely well-done beef.

The stuffed fillet is opened up like a loaf of French bread; layered with ham, cheese, and sliced tomatoes; secured with half a box of toothpicks; and grilled until it resembles the sort of club sandwich that might be endorsed by Dr. Atkins. The grilled, air-dried beef called *cecina*—Yecapixtla-style, the menu says, after a town in central Mexico's Morelos state—is even thinner, pounded nearly to the transparency of parchment, and has something of the clean, milky tang of prosciutto, of meat transformed into something beyond meat.

The dining room here may host the highest concentration of nonlocals of any restaurant on this side of town, and the shirt-and-tie lunch crowd is likely to include fire inspectors, downtown office workers, groups of Asians from nearby

Monterey Park—and would undoubtedly be home to even more if it served beverages more potent than *pepino*, a sweet, oddly refreshing drink made from cucumbers. Bring your own beer.

GINZA SUSHIKO

TWO RODEO, BEVERLY HILLS; (310) 247-8939. LUNCH AND DINNER BY RESERVATION ONLY, MON.–SAT.

Masa Takayama may be doing nothing that generations of forebears haven't done in the luxury kitchens of Kyoto and Osaka; his ingredients, mostly imported from Japan, may be nothing more than any highly skilled sushi master might be able to pick up at Tokyo's Tsukiji fish market; but there is this: on a good day, his Ginza Sushiko, an eight-seat sushi bar in a Beverly Hills mall, may be the single best restaurant in the United States.

In fact, the experience of Sushiko, despite the exquisite blond wood, the elegantly kimonoed waitress, the cool, melon-scented sake poured out of the kind of Japanese glass kettles Andy Warhol would've given half of his cookie jars to own, is less like a sushi lunch than like a meal in a three-Michelin-star restaurant in which the chef cooks for you alone, making sauces as he goes along. Wasabi is ground to order. Ginger is freshly pickled. The springy disposable chopsticks are made from the wood of an endangered Japanese tree.

In season—Takayama keeps a ledger of your past meals at his restaurant, so you needn't fear ever eating the same dish twice—there might be Japanese sea bream in the lightest of white miso purées, flavored with a rare, citrus-scented frond, or neat slices of *hamo*, a meaty fish so hard to fillet that it requires a special knife. Sometimes there is *fugu*, the legendary blowfish of Japan, its flesh arranged into transparent petals, its skin slivered into a chewy, lip-tingling salad, its collar Southern fried and served on a checked napkin as if it were picnic chicken, just at the point when all the exquisiteness might have started to cloy. And the actual sushi served toward the end of the meal is so much better than anything you may have eaten by that name that it seems like another food entirely.

This all, of course, comes at a price—a price that usually adds up to several hundred dollars per person. Ginza Sushiko may be the best restaurant in the United States, but it is also the most expensive.

GOLDEN DELI

815 W. LAS TUNAS DRIVE, SAN GABRIEL; (626) 308-0803. THURS.-TUES., 9:30A.M.-9P.M. CLOSED AUGUST.

I am fairly obsessed with the spring rolls served at Golden Deli, which is a Vietnamese noodle shop in the depths of a multiethnic San Gabriel mini-mall. Every August, when the restaurant is closed, finds me pressing my nose against the window like a sad kitten whose family has neglected to tell Fluffy that it moved out of state. Golden Deli is like a great Vietnamese coffee shop, a Vietnamese equivalent of Ship's or The Apple Pan, pumping out a greatest-hits list of quick Vietnamese food to patrons who can tell one cup of java from the next. The restaurant is small, but the crowds are enormous—sometimes five-deep on the sidewalk—college kids and families and bands of young single dudes who wait patiently for a shot at Golden Deli's sandwiches and grilled meatballs and regional noodle soups, and strong filter coffee over ice.

Golden Deli's spring rolls, *cha gio*, are crusty, golden things, four inches long and as thick as a fat man's thumb, crudely rolled in a manner that suggests rustic abundance rather than clumsiness, and perfectly, profoundly crisp. You wrap leaves of romaine lettuce around them, forming bursting green tacos that you may stuff with fistfuls of mint, cilantro, opal basil, and *rau ram*, an odd, elongated herb with a powerful metallic taste. You may add a few shreds of marinated carrot and turnip, a slice of cucumber, and a squirt of hot chile paste. You dip the bundles into little bowls of *nuoc cham*, which is the thin, sweetish fish sauce that Vietnamese use as ubiquitously as Americans use catsup. Then you bite through the vegetable-crunchy herbs to the many-layered rice-paper crispness of the spring roll wrapper, hot oil, the garlicky, pepper-hot forcemeat of crab and minced pork inside. No two bites are alike. Golden Deli has a long and complicated menu, but it is difficult to contemplate a meal without at least one order of *cha gio*.

Hearty and gamy, chewy and saturated with sweet spice, Golden Deli's version of the famous Vietnamese beef soup *pho dac biet* is a little different from other *phos*: The broth is neither so concentrated as Pho 79's nor as spicy as Pho Hoa's; the garnishes of brisket, tendon, tripe, and rare beef seem rather less distinct from one another, and the noodles themselves are softer than most.

Bun bo hue, a beef noodle soup in the style of the Central Vietnamese city of Hue, is tart and hot, complexly herbal, stained brick-red with chile, with thick, dense noodles that feel almost alive under your teeth; *bun bo kho* features the same noodles in a delicious curry-scented beef pottage. The pungent, marine-tasting glass-noodle soup *hu tiu*, full of crab and shrimp, is the classic Saigon breakfast dish, and is done very well here.

Cha gio is availaible as an appetizer, but also served over rice, as a garnish for thickish rice noodles (*bun*) and atop soft mats of vermicelli-thin rice noodles (*banh hoi*) that you wrap into the lettuce bundles right along with the spring rolls and herbs. Along with the spring rolls, as part of a noodle or rice combination plate, you can mix and match bits of shrimp paste that are molded around a piece of sugar cane and grilled; slices of garlicky grilled beef or grilled pork; the crunchy barbecued meatballs called *nem nuong*; the shredded stewed pigskin *bi*, and the fluffy, spicy pork-egg mousse called *cha*. At Golden Deli, they do egg rolls any way you like 'em.

GOLDEN DOME FALAFEL

10316 ALONDRA BLVD., BELLFLOWER; (562) 925-6013. MON.–SAT., 10A.M.– 9:30P.M.; SUN., 10A.M.–8P.M.

As you pound down Alondra Boulevard toward Cerritos, Golden Dome Falafel seems almost a surrealist's apparition of a fast-food restaurant. Arabic script looms starkly against the landscape of Taco Bell signs and mortuary façades; the picture of the namesake dome, painted in the flat but searching manner of some sign-painter Giotto, transforms the old burger stand into something both familiar and ineffably exotic. Even if you're on your way to lunch somewhere else, it's hard to resist a double-take and a quick U-turn.

At the restaurant's outside tables, you'll usually see dining Middle Easterners and pickup-truck loads of blond, lunch-scarfing guys in painter's caps; you'll hear swift, melodic Arabic and the drawl of So-Cal dudes. In the dim dining room, posters offer immigration assistance and videotape conversion; a small hutch in a rear corner displays camels carved out of wood, and gilt souvenirs of the Dome.

The Jerusalem shrine from which the restaurant takes its name, also known as the Dome of the Rock, is one of the holiest places in Islam, the place from which Mohammed ascended to heaven. The very existence of Jerusalem's Golden Dome—it is built on the site of the Second Temple—is something of a sore spot with fringe ultra-Orthodox Jewish sects. One gathers that, unlike the many falafel stands in the Fairfax district, the Golden Dome does not cater primarily to an Israeli-emigrant trade.

You may consider ordering a *shwarma* or learnedly discuss the contents of a pita burger; here everybody gets the falafel, which is the stuff of every vegetarian's dream. First, consider falafel *qua* falafel: college town–style pellets of fried stuff stuffed into pocket bread with vegetables, doused with sour white sesame paste. Then consider Golden Dome's falafel, starting with the patties: crisp, gold-brown balls of spiced, ground garbanzos, thin crust giving way to a dense interior colored moss-green with herbs, exterior crunchiness giving way (just like a perfect bagel) to a slight but definite chewiness underneath.

The falafel balls are tucked into whole-wheat pitas with fresh cabbage, tomatoes, and slices of the beet-red house-pickled turnip. You slick it yourself with the house sesame sauce, light tan in color, a toasty intensity that is quite different from the blander tahini sauce you may be used to. You may add a dab of fiery-hot Arabic tomato sauce.

When you order falafel as part of a platter, it comes naked, four little balls afloat on a sea of smooth, cool hummus or a nicely textured, tahini-rich version of the eggplant dip *baba ganoush*. The chopped parsley salad tabbouleh is ultra-fresh, studded with chewy dots of soaked bulgur wheat, powerfully tart. You can get falafel balls on the side, sort of like fries, with sandwiches made with the loose, juicy, powerfully garlicked ground-beef sausage *kofta*, served with caramelized onions. But you will get falafel. Simply put, Golden Dome falafel is a superior product.

GOLDEN TRIANGLE RESTAURANT

7011 S. GREENLEAF AVE., WHITTIER; (562) 945-6778. MON.-SAT., 11A.M.-10P.M.; SUN., 11A.M.-9P.M.

Golden Triangle is in the genteel center of Uptown Whittier, cheek-by-jowl with the art galleries and the collectors' bookstores, five minutes from City Hall and a short walk from the Whittier College quad. M. F. K. Fisher grew up a few blocks from here. So did Pat Nixon. Uptown Whittier might be the last place you'd expect to find a place like Golden Triangle, whose name evokes inappropriate poppy-field hi-jinx, and which was probably the first restaurant in the Southland to specialize in the exotic cooking of Burma.

Burma itself is apparently not much of a culinary destination these days (unless tired roast beef and watery curries are what excite your palate), but it makes a certain amount of sense that the country, snuggled as it is between Thailand, Bangladesh, and China, would have some interesting cooking of its own. Burma is in the right neighborhood.

"The Burmese restaurants in San Francisco are all run by Chinese people," Golden Triangle's chef says with a dismissive snort. "This one is run by true Burmese."

The flavors at Golden Triangle are clear and focused, alive with citrus and ginger and the musk of fermented shrimp paste, nutty with roasted beans and toasted coconut, crunchy with peanuts and fried garlic. (The owners grow some otherwise unobtainable Burmese ingredients in their own backyards, notably the sour vegetable that is the star of the strong-tasting *chin baung kyaw*, the one dish here that might be too funky for sensitive American palates.)

Instead of the pages and pages of Chinese food that fill out Bay Area Burmese menus, Golden Triangle serves most of the old Thai standbys and a handful of

Laotian dishes. If you order a couple of Burmese things, somebody will probably come out of the kitchen and ask if you've ever been to Rangoon, then send a plate of fried red-bean/ginger patties out to the table, or suggest an order of delicious batter-fried squash. A photo supplement to the menu, showing most of the really good dishes, makes even something called *htaminh baungh* almost a tangible concept.

The national dish of Burma is a garbanzo-flour-thickened catfish chowder called *moh hin ga*, shot though with noodles and mellowed with coconut milk, and Golden Triangle does a fantastic version of the dish. *Lap pad thoke*, a salad made from Burmese tea leaves that have been soaked in a running stream, vibrates with the strong flavors of chewy dried shrimp, toasted beans, and the winy, pickled leaves, which have the consistency of stewed collard greens and the caffeinated kick of a double espresso. The salad *nga-phe thoke* combines sour tamarind, slivered onions, and shreds of house-made fishcake into a whole new groove.

Burma is not far from India, and some of the food at Golden Triangle is quite similar to what you might find at an Indian restaurant: fried turnovers, *somosas*, filled with curried potatoes and served with a sweet-and-sour Thai-influenced cucumber salad; split pea-onion fritters called *beya kyaw* that taste like a Gujarati snack; rich *parathas* served with fragrant chicken curry. At lunchtime, the restaurant serves a terrific sort of pilaf called *dun buk htamin*, cooked with cashews, raisins, vegetables, and spices, and topped with a quarter of a baked chicken.

But the best thing of all may be the Burmese ginger salad—biting shreds of the herb tossed with coconut, fried garlic, fried yellow peas, peanuts, and sesame seeds—whose fugal crunchiness is quite unlike anything you've ever tasted yet somehow familiar, like an ancient prototype of exotic cocktail-party snacks. If the world ever gave it a chance, ginger salad might be as popular as Big Macs.

GREAT TASTE PLACE

708 E. LAS TUNAS, SAN GABRIEL; (616) 286-6032. DAILY, LUNCH AND DINNER.

Consider the hundred-layer pancake, a lacy, golden disk of Chinese bread the size and shape of an upside-down skullcap, which pulls apart into strands as easily as a length of frayed rope. When the pancakes, the great specialty of the Hunanese restaurant Great Taste, first come to the table in their woven baskets, they are smoking hot, capable of doing serious damage to your fingertips, but are ultimately too delicious to resist. Each freshly baked skein of dough is supple yet crisp-edged, fragrant with heated oil, just right for swabbing a bit of pungent black-bean sauce from the bottom of an emptied service plate. As at Tung Lai

Shun or La Brea Bakery, at Great Taste you are perfectly capable of feeling that one can indeed live by bread alone.

The very modestly named Great Taste—which used to be called Wei Fun before the owner, but not the chef, split town—is a cool, dark place near the eastern edge of San Gabriel, another good mini-mall restaurant on a stretch of Las Tunas Drive that is home to perhaps more good mini-mall restaurants than any other street in California. The small dining room is pretty bare, decorated mostly with those hanging red banners that describe, in Chinese, seasonal menu specials that most of us will never decipher.

Great Taste may be the good Hunan-style restaurant that the world is looking for, with a chef who truly understands spicy bean curd, and the proclivities to satisfy the hot-pepper fixations a lot of us picked up in the '70s. Local chefs with actual Hunanese training are as rare as NFL quarterbacks from the Ivy League; Great Taste—though the cooking is closer to straightforward Taiwanese-style food than the smoky, subtle cooking at Monterey Park's superb Hunanese restaurant Shiang's Garden—has the goods.

Here are the spicy eggplant, the sweet-and-pungent fried chicken, the garlicky flash-fried beef-and-scallion dishes that are common in neighborhood restaurants but rarely prepared with this country-style intensity. Here too is sliced lamb in Hunan sauce, a spicy, garlicky, half-sweet stir-fry with a taste that unfolds layer after layer of complexity as you eat, almost definitive of what you may think of as Hunan food. At most Chinese restaurants, stir-fries are among the dullest items on the menu; at Great Taste, they shine: garlic sprouts with sweetly cured belly pork, chicken with dried chile, shredded pork with pickled vegetables, lamb with double handfuls of shredded scallions.

Of course, the menu doesn't end with stir-fries. The restaurant does a wonderful version of the standard Northern Chinese dish of braised duck with taro: meltingly tender strips of the bird arranged neatly over a dome of what tastes essentially like the best refried beans in the world. A small steamed sea bass in hot bean sauce, served sizzling on a Sterno-fired platter and topped with a salty crumble of fermented beans, is superb. If you look imploringly enough at the posted specials, a waitress might translate a couple of them for you, or suggest something like succulent sautéed Chinese squash as juicy as ripe melon, cuttlefish fried with shredded vegetables and spicy sauce, braised tofu skin stuffed with powerfully flavored Chinese mushrooms—or the best Hunan honey ham in town, profoundly smoky, steamed almost until it crumbles, then layered on a bed of water chestnuts and garnished with the inevitable accompaniment of steamed Wonder Bread.

GREEN FIELD

GREEN FIELD, 381 N. AZUSA AVE., WEST COVINA; (626) 966-2300. DAILY
11 A.M.–10 P.M.

Visitors to Rio de Janeiro who come to the city dreaming of the light, fruity, uncomplicated cooking found on fusiony pan-Latin menus are generally brought to earth within thirty seconds of browsing through the restaurant section of the Yellow Pages. There, they find half a dozen restaurants that specialize in the African-influenced seafood dishes of Bahía, another couple that prepare the jungly stews of Minas Gerais, some fancy European places in hotels, and eleven solid pages of *churrascerias*, restaurants specializing in Brazilian grilled meats. *Cariocas* know what they like, and it isn't pan-roasted Amazonian riverfish served with three-mango chutney and a minted cashew-fruit coulis.

The best and most expensive of the Rio *churrascerias*, like Marius and the superb Plataforma, are distinguishable from old-line American steakhouses mostly by the general level of garlic in the air and the availability of unusual cuts of beef. But restaurants at the level just below that, like the *futbol*-star hangout Porcao—sometimes called "*rodizio*-style," or all you can eat—are dripping carnivals of meat: belly-out, high-consumption mess halls lubricated with oceans of foaming Antartica beer and populated with tuxedoed waiters, wielding what appear to be dueling swords rammed through bits of animal flesh, who wander the dining rooms like dim-sum-cart jockeys.

On each table is a signaling device, a fancy coaster, which you turn green-side-up when you want the waiters to keep slicing meat off their swords onto your plate; red-side-up when you are full enough to burst. In the sleekest places, the swords fit into rotating slots above a special charcoal oven: The meat comes out charred on the outside like *souvlaki,* and when the waiter has cut off all of the burned part, the pink flesh is put back in the oven to blacken again. (*Rodizio*-style *churrasco* appeals most to fans of extreme well-doneness.) A gourmet will never leave a *rodizio*-style restaurant until he or she has had at least one portion of the grilled hump of a *cebu* ox.

The center of *rodizio* in the United States is probably Queens, New York, where there are four or five restaurants that specialize in Brazilian-style swordsmanship and flesh. The most popular restaurant among these (although by few accounts the best) is Green Field, a monster Korean-owned place whose decor is dominated by a wall-size waterfall. Some New York restaurant mavens are charmed by the Korean connection, happy about the availability of *kimchi* in the steaming theater of meat. Others are offended—*kalbi* is a wonderful grilled-meat tradition, but it is not, after all, *churrasco.*

Green Field's first California venture is a mammoth shopping-center *churrasceria*, across from a Black Angus in West Covina, that at three hundred seats is not just the biggest Brazilian restaurant in California but among the biggest Latin American restaurants of any kind. There is the rushing wall of water that is the Green Field trademark, and a yawning, light-filled interior space that may remind you of the lobby of a brand-new Caribbean hotel. The waiters and waitresses seem to be from everywhere but Brazil—I heard the Brazilian *cachaca* cocktail *caipirinha* pronounced about six different ways—and about half the tables fill up with Asians, who load up their barbecue with A-1 and Thai *sriracha* chile sauce.

The first thing you do at Green Field, as in Rio, is grab a plate and wander through the long buffet station, picking up pickled hearts of palm and fresh asparagus, while avoiding the artificial-crab salad and the dullish tuna salad. A few steps from the salad line is a hot-food buffet, the sort of thing you might see at a Brazilian wedding.

And then comes the meat. The second you turn the knob on the table green side up, well-done skirt steak, chicken, bacon-wrapped turkey, spare ribs, sweet Italian sausages, and tiny well-charred chicken hearts appear, slid by a procession of waiters from their swords onto your plates. The overcooked lamb seems practically radioactive with gaminess, but the bacon-wrapped rabbit parts are mild and juicy.

The earthiness of crisp-skinned duck, a flavor you might associate with wild game, is perhaps too strong, and seems, like the rest of the meats, unmitigated by even a sprinkling of salt and pepper. Other offerings, like the crunchy strip deftly carved off what looked like a tri-tip, fulfill the common culinary fantasy of cutting off and eating the salty, fatty crust from a roast beef and leaving the meat behind. The rib-eye, which a manager seemed to hoard as if it were a jar of triple-zero beluga, was meaty, rare, and wonderful. Green Field's batting average, about .340, may suit an All-Star shortstop better than it does a restaurant, but the sheer variety of the meal helps the good forkfuls cancel out the mediocre ones.

If you are entertaining thoughts of dessert, the flan is fine, the other desserts forgettable. "I'm not sure what kind of cake that is," our waitress said, pointing at something chocolate on the pastry platter. "Let me go look at the box."

THE GRILL

9560 DAYTON WAY, BEVERLY HILLS; (310) 276-0615. SUN.–FRI., 11:30A.M.– 11P.M.; SAT. 11:30–MIDNIGHT.

My favorite corned-beef hash in the world is served in this swank businessman's grill in Beverly Hills, sniffing distance from the Fred Hayman perfume outlet and around the corner from the weird, cobbled boutique mall that locals refer to as Eurotrash-Disney. The ceilings are high, the wood dark, the linen heavy, the martinis clear and cold and dry. The dining room is washed in a pale, masculine light that seems imported from some century-old restaurant in New Orleans, and the white-jacketed waiters call you *sir*, even if you are wearing sneakers. This is, in other words, a serious place to have lunch.

I manage to eat here every couple of months or so, usually in the late afternoon, usually alone, and the only time I remember looking at a menu was when a British friend asked me to translate some of the dishes for him from the American. I grew up not far from here, in that southeast corner of town they used to call Baja Beverly Hills, a neighborhood so alienated from the rest of the city that it didn't even make it into the 310 area code.

I am aware of the reputation of The Grill as the kind of place where the Beverly Hills Rotary might hold its meetings if the Rotary had a chapter for aspiring billionaires—I am always running into a pin-striped real-estate speculator my mom knew or a high-school classmate who is making a strong go of things at CAA—although I'm generally paying too much attention to the food to take much notice of the other customers. The hash, edged with deep brown, speckled with crunchy, carbonized bits, is a crisp, ruddy thing that is always delightful to behold. White guys in $2,200 suits all tend to look pretty much alike.

So the first time I walked up toward the maître d' station with my friend Angela, an editor who knows Hollywood the way Julia Child knows a rump roast, it was almost as if I had entered a different restaurant. She barely had time to register the dining room before she scurried into a far corner behind the bar. "Oh my God— everyone's here. Stand in front of me for a minute while I fix my makeup."

I did. I also didn't recognize a soul.

"In the back," she said, leaning on the bar, "that's Brandon Tartikoff, who used to be president of Paramount; there's Barry Hirsch, who is a really big lawyer for Streisand, Tom Cruise, people like that . . . and over there is Ovitz, meeting with Ron Perelman. I've got to start having lunch here more often."

I glanced at Michael Ovitz, whose face had the queer, moonish luminescence I usually associate with Japanese lanterns, and I noticed that people were approaching his table as reverently, as gingerly, as if it were a shrine.

"So is this Perelman the makeup guy?" I asked. Angela wrinkled her nose.

"Perelman owns, like, half of New York, my dear; Marvel Comics and real estate and God knows what else. Revlon is, I don't know, about two percent of what he does. Oh, and there's Ron Meyer—you know, he runs Universal."

An elaborately coiffed blond woman swept past on the way to the door and blew a kiss. "That's Nikki Haskell, who does . . . I'm not sure, but she's in Liz Smith's column a lot. I think the guy walking behind her is the one on the billboard for that diet pill she invented." I stared into my Gibson. Then Goldie Hawn got up and strode out of the restaurant, though all I saw of her was one tanned shoulder and the back of her head. My friend urged me to get up and follow Hawn so I could get a better view. I declined.

I felt like an entomologist who had spent so long inspecting the ant hills of the Serengeti that he'd never noticed the unusual number of lions and wildebeests strolling across the plain.

"Can you see that guy over there?" Angela asked. "He's a big lawyer, too. You've got to know Jake Bloom; he's the lawyer for Arnold, Sly, everybody. The guy he's with is his partner, Alan Hergott, who is brilliant."

I shrugged, underwhelmed. Angela rolled her eyes.

"Are you sure you grew up here?" she asked.

GUATEMALTECA BAKERY

4032 BEVERLY BLVD., LOS ANGELES; (213) 382-9451. DAILY, 5:30A.M.– 9:30P.M.

One of the most intriguingly mixed neighborhoods in Los Angeles is that bit of Beverly Boulevard stretching west a few blocks from Vermont, where Koreatown and the Filipino neighborhood to the east crash headlong into the giant Central American community that stretches up into Hollywood.

If you spend enough time around here, you are bound to discover the Guatemalteca Bakery, which is a locus of the large Guatemalan community in central Los Angeles. On the sidewalk in front, street vendors sell fuzzy stuffed apes and *banda* cassettes, homemade tamales and hot ears of corn. On Sundays and holidays, the line at Guatemalteca often twists through the bakery, out onto the sidewalk and most of the way down the block, because Guatemalteca's soft white roll, *perujo*, is the best Central American bread in Los Angeles. Even on a midweek afternoon, people line up for rolls and cakes and super-sweet custard-filled pastries; maybe a bottle of hot sauce or a pound of herbed Guatemalan *longanizas*.

My favorite thing to buy here is a sort of oblong, cream-cheese-enriched Guatemalan poundcake, *quesadilla*, which is sweet and impossibly rich, and even better when you take it home and toast it for breakfast. For a long time, Guatemalteca *quesadillas* were among my standard contributions to potluck dinners, and over the years I've experimented with *quesadilla* strawberry shortcake, toasted *quesadillas* with ice cream, and rum-soaked *quesadilla* bread pudding.

Next to the bakery, Guatemalteca runs a quick-service restaurant specializing in $4 steam-table lunches and the Guatemalan *antojito*-like snacks called *chapines*. The plate lunches here are delicious, if basic: the chunky, tart beef stew *carne guisada* and the tomato-laced shredded-beef stew *hilacha*, intensely flavored *longaniza* sausages in tomato sauce that are better the fresher they are from the grill, and the musky Guatemalan innard stew *revolcado*. Sometimes the terminology can be confusing: What the restaurant calls a tostada, you'll call a fried tortilla smeared with beans, and what you might recognize as a tostada—a crisp tortilla heaped with beans, cream, and a bright-purple mixture of beets and beet-stained cabbage—Guatemalans call an enchilada. Tamales are the soft, airy kind, steamed in banana leaves, fluffed out with lard, filled with chunks of chile-stewed pork, and the flavor is terrific, although the texture might be a bit off-putting if you're used to the firmer Mexican tamales.

The fairly bland steam-table food may sometimes remind you of what a Woolworth's lunch counter might serve in Guatemala City. But I fairly often find myself stopping in here for a quick bite: fried plantains with black beans and thick Guatemalan cream; a delicious, simple sandwich of black beans on a roll; *rellenitos*, which is essentially sweet fried plantains wrapped around salty black beans. They like black beans here, and they know how to use them.

GUELAGUETZA

3337½ W. EIGHTH ST.; (213) 427-0601. DAILY, 8A.M.–11P.M. ALSO 11127 PALMS BLVD., WEST LOS ANGELES; (318) 837-8600.

A dozen Oaxacan restaurants have come and gone over the last few years, and the food served at Oaxacan carnivals and soccer games in Los Angeles has long been legendary among advanced aficionados of local street food. And through it all, Guelaguetza, the Wilshire District restaurant named after Oaxaca's famous midsummer Zapotec festival, has been the obvious place to go for gourdfuls of the sweet summer-squash drink *chilcayote*, for marble-size Oaxacan chorizo sausages in tomato sauce, for giant, leathery *empanadas* plumped out with chicken and the mild Oaxacan chile sauce called *amarillo*.

There is a fairly large Oaxacan community in Los Angeles, big enough to have its own weekly newspaper and soccer leagues, big enough to have a major presence in the fancier Los Angeles restaurant kitchens, and sometimes it seemed as if most of them were in the original Guelaguetza at any one time, nibbling on the manhole-cover-size Oaxacan pizzas called *clayudas*, guzzling the peculiar Oaxacan grain beverage *texate* and watching sports on TV.

Now there is also a Guelaguetza on the Westside, squeezed into a former burrito place in a Lucky parking lot, a bare, safety-orange dining room broken up by a couple of fast-food arches, a few Oaxacan travel posters on the walls, and a sign advertising money transfers to Oaxaca. (The customer base seems as solidly Oaxaqueño as it is in the original restaurant.) The second Guelaguetza also throbs with Oaxacan music and the thick, sweet smell of a dozen Oaxacan stews, the rhythmic thunk of the *metate* and the giggles of a dozen children.

The second you sit down at either restaurant—there will be a wait for a table—a waiter brings over an oval plate of freshly fried tortilla chips and a little footed bowl of *mole* better than anything you've ever paid $12.50 for at a fancy Mexican restaurant. This is serious food.

Guelaguetza has all the Oaxacan appetizers you've read about in the travel magazines: handbag-size baked *empanadas* stuffed with bright-orange zucchini blossoms and pungent Mexican cheese; the fried cornmeal platforms called *memelas*, smeared with black beans and drizzled with the molten fat of roast pork; and just about the best chicken *taquitos* in Los Angeles. You will sometimes even find crunchy chile-fried grasshoppers.

The giant pizzalike *clayudas* are built on chewy corn tortillas the size of bed sheets, baked on a griddle, squirted with beans and smoky chile sauce, and sprinkled with salty crumbles of cheese. You'll find enchiladas dipped in *mole* and *enfrijoladas* dipped in a purée of black beans, the chile-saturated dried pork called *cecina* and the dried beef called *tasajo*. Guelaguetza's tamales are some of the best imaginable, banana-leaf packets that unfold to reveal thin, broad envelopes of wet cornmeal surrounding—and saturated by—a sticky, black *mole* sauce about a hundred times thicker than Thanksgiving gravy, which tingles like a nine-volt battery hot-wired to your tongue.

To drink, there is *tepache*, a drink made from brown sugar and fermented pineapple juice that closely approximates the taste of Worcestershire sauce, which sounds offputting but really cuts the richness of the cooking rather well. The Oaxacan version of the rice infusion *horchata*, garnished with cubes of melon and chopped nuts, is topped off with a half-inch of violently red syrup that has the high, sweet smell of the ice cream counter at Sav-On.

Of the classic seven *moles* of Oaxaca—dark, complex sauces flavored with seeds, nuts, herbs and chiles of every description—Guelaguetza usually has at least five or six: the *coloradito*, brick-red, elusively spicy, with a slightly tangy sweetness; the *amarillo*; sometimes even the dusky *chichilo*. *Verde de espinazo* is an astonishing *mole*-like stew, a thick, spicy broth enriched with puréed spinach, barely tart, exotically flavored with mint, that is quite unlike anything you've ever tasted. *Barbacoa de chivo*, intricately flavored, almost the essence of stewed goat, could pass as one of the better *birrias* in town, though the meat is less interesting than the broth.

Estofado, a sweet-sour yellow *mole* with a tang of sharp green olive, tastes like a cross between traditional black *mole* and the kind of tomato sauce you might encounter on a good fish *a la Veracruzana*. In addition to those, Guelaguetza uses a different *mole* to sauce the enchiladas, and still another to fill its tamales.

And the black *mole*, based on ingredients the restaurant specially imports from Oaxaca, is truly extraordinary: rich with musky undertones of chocolate and burnt grain, toasted chile, cinnamon and cloves, ripples of exotic spice. Guelaguetza's *mole* is as simple yet nuanced as a great Burgundy, and so much better than other *moles* you may have eaten that it is almost like seeing a Tamayo painting up close for the first time after a lifetime of peering at reproductions.

H

HAKONE

1555 W. SEPULVEDA BLVD., TORRANCE; (310) 539-9602. MON.-FRI., 8A.M.–2:15A.M.; SAT., 12P.M.–3:15A.M.

As it takes a hard left into Torrance, Sepulveda Boulevard runs through one of the major Japanese neighborhoods in the United States. Near the low-rise industrial parks that house the U.S. headquarters of the great Japanese companies, near the condo villages where their employees reside, the streets are lined with cafes and bookstores and supermarkets catering to the specific homesicknesses of expatriate Japanese. Torrance—some locals refer to it as "the Torrance prefecture"—may be the only place in the Los Angeles basin where a transplanted Osaka manufacturing executive can expect to lead a reasonable life without speaking a word of English.

In the late eighties, the Japanese area of Torrance formed a boom town within the aerospace-depressed South Bay. When the recession hit Japan in the early '90s, however, most of the local expats were sent home, leaving noodle shops half-empty and karaoke joints subdued.

In the relentless economic Darwinism of early-century America, Hakone has survived by inviting the custom of non-Japanese. It makes very fine Melrose-style salmon-skin hand rolls. The "spider rolls"—deep-fried soft-shell crabs tightly wrapped with rice, crunchy Japanese vegetables, and a healthy slug of dried *bonito* shavings in a sheet of dried seaweed—are actually sensational, small essays in saltiness and crunch.

But if you can ignore all the trendy specials, the loud wall posters, and the fry cook, you'll find within Hakone a superb traditional sushi bar: The fish is sparkling fresh; the chef's technique is close to impeccable.

A sashimi plate shines: tuna as red as a glass of Burgundy; *tai* (though perhaps really local snapper instead of the prized bream from Japan's Inland Sea) that is dense and impossibly rich; ultra-fresh salmon ribboned with white; mild slabs of yellowtail; tender, sea-sweet blanched octopus.

There is *ankimo*, the rich monkfish liver some people call the foie gras of the sea, sliced thin, fanned out on a small plate and simply dressed with a splash of citrusy *ponzu*. Red-clam sushi is almost ethereal; wisps of halibut taste only of the sea.

Kohada (sometimes translated, unappetizingly, as "gizzard shad") is one of the most beautiful fish on a sushi chef's palette, its pearlescent silver skin stippled with regular black spots; its sharp astringency contrasting with the hundred delicate subtleties of really fresh fish. *Kohada*, which needs to be steeped in rice vinegar to soften its flesh, is a notoriously difficult fish to serve. Overmarinated *kohada* can be stringy, tough, almost woody; undermarinated fish is overwhelmingly strong and booby-trapped with dozens of annoying pin bones. Japanese connoisseurs often judge a sushi chef by his skill in preparing *kohada*—it is infrequently served in U.S. sushi bars. Hakone's *kohada* is close to perfect: full-flavored, luxuriously soft, with a strong-fish pungency that comes through almost as a nuance.

There have been minor flaws: Once I found a shiso leaf garnishing a plate of sashimi to be slightly wilted; another time, a piece of salmon was a little dried out at the edges, as if it had been too loosely wrapped. These are small faults, perhaps, but in sushi, as in watercolor painting, the genius is often in the accumulation of details. Still, somebody here has obviously mastered the most important job: that of choosing the fish.

HAPPY VALLEY

407 BAMBOO LANE, CHINATOWN; (213) 617-3662. DAILY, NOON–3 A.M.

Happy Valley is pretty much everything a person could want in a Chinatown restaurant, two minutes from the Music Center, convenient both for an early jury duty lunch and 3:00 A.M. post-Spaceland suppers, mostly cheap enough for artistically inclined proofreaders yet with expensive live seafood among the finest in town. If you want, the waiters will even read through the seasonal wall signs for you, translating as they go: "Steamed live scallop . . . nope, we're out of it; tiny scallop, out; abalone, too expensive; crunchy bamboo-insides, you wouldn't like; pan-fried frog with pepper-salt, that's really good."

And because Happy Valley is tucked away in a fragrant Chinatown alley, your friends will think that you've stumbled onto a secret place. If you've ever been into a basic Chinese restaurant, you know what Happy Valley looks like, right down to the live-fish tanks and the plastic water glasses. If you've spent any time in Cantonese seafood joints, you can probably recite the menu before the waiter sets it down upon the table. It's all here, higher than the seafood-fresser's Mon Kee standard, clams in black bean sauce and crabs sauteed with ginger and garlic, steamed tilapia and fried rock-cod filets.

There is an incredible scallop and dried scallop soup, the marine sweetness of the one bouncing off the subtle smokiness of the other in a cornstarch-thickened base.

Casseroles are wonderful, sizzling things served in blackened clay pots, though they're listed on the menu only in Chinese for some reason: Ask for the hot-pot with roast pork and oysters, which are plump and fresh in a fine, briny gravy, or for the hot-pot with catfish and garlic. Vegetables include the usual bok choy and Chinese broccoli, as well as the harder to find snow-pea leaves. An incredible vegetable sautéed with crabmeat and egg, the imported pith from a certain kind of bamboo plant, is slippery and sharp-tasting, with an elusive crunch that makes it the rough textural equivalent of eating shark's fin and jellyfish at the same time. (It's too bad bamboo pith is so ferociously expensive.)

Shrimp with spicy salt are deep-fried to impeccable crispness, peppery enough to leave your lips tingling and as impossible to stop eating as great crinkle-cut fries set out on a delicatessen table. Every new-style Cantonese restaurant in town has this dish on the menu. Happy Valley's is somehow fresher, snappier, though not so tasty as the godhead version served at San Francisco's Yuet Lee restaurant. Happy Valley prepares frog the same way, a big, delicious platterful of amphibian crunchies—watch for the bones.

There are many varieties of squab, minced and served in lettuce cups, sautéed or roasted whole to a superb, glossy meatiness.

But, of course, no visit to a Chinese seafood house is complete without a visit to the live tanks, where the dearest and most delicious foods are to be found.

Exhibit A here is likely to be the Alaskan king crab, a gnarled old monster that looms over the lobsters in the tank as Gamera did over Tokyo. All evening long, people are ceremoniously ushered over to examine the beast, to pay homage to its massive shovelhead body and its sapling-thick arms. All evening long these potential executioners calculate the price of its head and back away from the tank with shrugs and regrets. A hundred and fifty clams is a lot to pay for a plate of crab.

Somewhat less expensive is the Maine lobster, a tender animal cooked just long enough to jell its sweet flesh and served, perhaps, in a fragrant garlic sauce. Giant oysters are briefly steamed and served on the half shell with a sprinkling of black beans and chopped scallion. A flounder is served "double-pleasure" style, its flesh briefly stir-fried with carrot and ginger, and its spine quickly deep-fried into crisp, battered slivers, to be dipped into pungent bean sauce and eaten like skeletal potato chips.

There's always one guy at every table who will play with his food, doing Shari Lewis routines with the fish heads and combining pigeon heads and shrimp antennae and lobster carapaces into hideous Frankensteinian creations.

HOT DOG ON A STICK

DAILY. AT VARIOUS FOOD COURT LOCATIONS INCLUDING SANTA MONICA PLACE, MUSCLE BEACH, GLENDALE GALLERIA, SHERMAN OAKS GALLERIA, AND THE WESTSIDE PAVILION.

New York has pushcart dogs and the garlic *knobelwurst* at Katz's deli. Chicago has Vienna franks. Rochester has its white-hots, Cincinnati its chili-sluiced coneys. Sheboygan is famous for grilled brats. Santa Monica . . . Santa Monica is the birthplace of Hot Dog on a Stick.

Frankly, as regional hot dog styles go, Hot Dog on a Stick may not rank with Nathan's Famous in Coney Island or the red-hots served outside Wrigley Field, but no other hot-dog stand in the world has a spectacle that comes close to the sight of a miniskirted Hot Dog on a Stick employee mixing a tankful of cool lemonade on a hot day. Hot Dog on a Stick is yet another gift Southern California has bestowed upon the world.

It would be hard to find a native Angeleno without primal memories of Hot Dog on a Stick: of cheese-on-a-stick dribbled on the midway at the long-gone Pacific Ocean Park, of the smell of clean oil that has emanated from the muddy-red outpost under the Santa Monica Pier for more than fifty years. A summer behind the fryers at Hot Dog on a Stick is almost the archetypal first teenage job, and the garishly costumed employees figure in local teenage iconography as surely as lifeguards or cheerleaders.

The high level of organization and the extremely limited menu—hot-dog-on-a-stick, cheese-on-a-stick, fries, lemonade—could almost have been custom designed for the valuable slivers of real estate in the food courts of shopping malls, and at the Westside Pavilion or the Glendale Galleria it sometimes seems as if the Hot Dog on a Stick franchises attract more customers than all of the quickie Chinese and falafel stands combined. One high school senior shimmies to Britney Spears and the Spice Girls as she burnishes the kiosk's metal to a high shine, and a second runs the cash register. A third twirls skewered frankfurters and cheese sticks through vats of pale corn batter, then plunges them into specially designed canisters of boiling canola oil.

Even within the skewed universe defined by Johnny Rockets and Tacones, Hot Dog on a Stick has always stood a little bit apart, bathed in the sort of unearthly glow that comes from underneath the lid of a Xerox machine. The high parabolic curve of the Hot Dog on a Stick cap may (or may not) allude to the elongated shape of the stand's principal product; the super-bright graphics may (or may not) derive from the cheerful color scheme of an old-fashioned beach ball.

"The hat seems sort of awkward at first," confesses a veteran Santa Monica dog dipper, "but you really do get used to it after a while."

You can find corn dogs at county fairs, junior high school cafeterias and in Oldsmobile-size boxes at the Price Club, but the model served at Hot Dog on a Stick would be instantly distinguishable in a blind taste test, even if you hadn't tried one since you were a teenager.

Institutional corn dogs tend to be on the wan side, but a hot-dog-on-a-stick is fried to a deep chestnut-brown that is several degrees past the doneness of its competitors—a full city roast, if you're into coffee metaphors—and the slight bitter tang of caramelization balances out the inherent high sweetness of toasted corn. The outer crust is smooth and crisp, more complexly flavored than you may remember, speckled with gritty bits of burnt grain that crunch under your teeth. The batter is slippery where it touches the hot dog, slightly rubbery, almost crepelike, resilient as the underskin of a really fresh bagel. The thick turkey hot dog inside seems quite bland, essentially a vehicle for garlic and juice.

This is rude food, resisting the attempts of civilizers far more strenuously than, say, the burrito or the triple-decker cheeseburger, though Vida's chef Fred Eric can sometimes be seen at chefs' events, meting out bite-size samples of corn dogs as if they were morsels of sautéed foie gras.

The hot-dog-on-a-stick we love is a space-age variation on the classic pig-in-a-blanket, Victorian-era American comfort food retooled to meet the demands of the California beach.

HONG KONG LOW DELI

408 BAMBOO LANE, CHINATOWN; (213) 680-9827. DAILY, 8A.M.–6:30P.M.

Not so long ago, Hong Kong Low, housed in a pagoda-eaved tower at the hub of New Chinatown, was one of the swankiest restaurants in the area, with lacquered ceilings and parasol-topped drinks and a piano bar crowded with World War II vets hungry for torch songs and mediocre Cantonese-American food.

It was a place where smaller Chinese Opera troupes gave recitals when they were in town, low-budget office parties were thrown, and Angelenos who hadn't caught on to the new Cantonese seafood thing hung out at Sunday dinner.

In the late '70s, the faded upstairs dining room became L.A.'s best punk-rock club, and on weekend evenings, chow mein noodles and spareribs in black-bean sauce gave way to only slightly less subtle entities like Black Flag and the Germs.

The place went Chiu Chow for a while, I think, around the time a lot of

Chinatown businesses moved east to the San Gabriel Valley and the piano-bar business drifted down the street. Not many people noticed when the restaurant closed its doors for more or less permanent "remodeling," and Hong Kong Low became the center of the local senior hot-lunch program.

But a small piece of Hong Kong Low survived or became reincarnated or something, and the little dim sum takeout place behind the restaurant is nothing less than a miracle. If you're the least bit nostalgic for the Chinatown that existed before the last wave of immigration, before anybody ate double-pleasure flounder or thought of driving to Monterey Park for anything but enchiladas or county offices—nostalgic for beef curry pies and sweet buns filled with coconut—Hong Kong Low Deli is about all that's left.

The deli sits in a back alley behind the restaurant, a couple of yards from the site of a spectacularly failed jewel heist, and is moody in an Alan Rudolph sort of way: Chinese characters scrawled on tattered scraps of colored paper, high ceilings, long lines, armies of women cooks, flaky chicken buns and squares of fried taro stacked on steam tables behind greasy panels of glass. The women behind the counter can be as brusque as those at Canter's. If you can't decide what you want within a few seconds, you may well be passed over for the next guy in line.

Open in time for early breakfast, Hong Kong Low Deli serves what dim sum used to be back when everybody called it "teacakes," dim sum without the par-boiled geoduck and jellyfish salad and mango mousse with a cherry on top: dumplings. Unfortunately, you have to get them to go, but the dumplings are impeccably fresh, pulled straight out of ovens or steamers and put straight into pink boxes without a fourteen-kilometer noontime ride in stainless-steel carts. Ten dollars' worth of shrimp dumplings and egg rolls will comfortably feed the UCLA starting five.

Baked *bao* (buns), browned and hot and brushed with sticky syrup, are spectacular, large as small throw pillows and filled with barbecued pork in a sweet and garlicky syrup. Fluffy steamed *bao* filled with chicken and black mushrooms are marked with little red dots to differentiate them from the *bao* stuffed with sweet barbecued pork. Turnoverlike pies are made of flaky pastry, egg-washed to a deep, burnished gold, and stuffed with a blandish chicken stew, barbecued pork, or a truly fine pungent mince of curried beef.

There are capsules of sticky rice flavored with a few bits of meat and vegetables, deep-fried to a wicked, oily crunch; dense fried sesame dumplings; savory turnip cakes; greasy, if delicious, squares of pan-fried taro; and fried *chow fun* noodles rolled out to truck-tire thickness. You'll usually find long buns filled with custard, freshly baked squares of yellow cake, and gorgeous egg-yolk custard tarts the vivid yellow of a five-year-old's painting of the sun.

I'm all for stately homes, but if hungry people had political clout, Hong Kong

Low Deli is the kind of thing the city's Cultural Heritage Commission might be dedicated to preserving instead of a bunch of old buildings that don't even have restaurants in them.

HEAVY NOODLING

153 E. GARVEY AVE., MONTEREY PARK; (626) 307-9533. MON.–THURS., 10A.M.–6P.M.; FRI. AND SAT., 10A.M.–7P.M.; SUN. 11A.M.–5P.M.

The Chinese ideal of noodle-making probably belongs to those guys who fling lumps of dough across the room, transforming balls of flour and water into skeins of wire-fine pasta deftly as street-corner scam artists hide peas under walnut shells. Heavy Noodling, a small Chinese deli in Monterey Park, specializes in the sort of noodle two hundred generations of Chinese chefs have probably regarded with horror—thick, clumsy noodles that run somewhere between spaetzle and *pappardelle*, self-consciously rustic things that taste of themselves whether fried with mixed seafood and lots of garlic or immersed with tendon in a deep, anise-scented beef broth, dipped in vinegar or painted with Heavy Noodling's smoky house chile-oil, topped with braised brisket or sautéed with fresh-tasting, authentic *moo shoo* pork.

The noodles, hand-cut in the style of Shanxi—a northern Chinese province sandwiched somewhere between Beijing and Inner Mongolia—are irregular and kind of lumpy, which makes them ugly but enhances their ability to pick up sauce. They have that good, dense pasta bite you find sometimes in farmhouses outside Modena but rarely in Chinese noodle houses—where noodles, after all, are basically conduits for vast quantities of sautéed pork or sesame, something to pick at after you've eaten all the pan-fried dumplings. And the noodles are delicious, so delicious you may catch yourself eating them plain out of the box if you take out out an order to go. (Heavy Noodling—the restaurant's odd name comes from the headline a copy editor gave a version of this review when it came out in the *Times*—sensibly packs the noodles separately from the soup so that they don't get soggy on the way home.)

Cold plates at Heavy Noodling, little appetizer dishes whose flavors are more focused than those at most other Chinese noodle shops, include a pungent salad of seaweed and shreds of pressed bean curd; crunchy bits of pig's ear doused with chile; crisp, thin slices of marinated cucumber; melting slabs of beef tendon that dissolve to soy and sweet anise on your tongue. There are peanuts boiled with anise until they resemble soft, bloated beans. There are tiny dried anchovies spiked with chewy shreds of meat and fresh, sliced chiles: spectacularly good.

In place of the usual scallion pancakes, there's "House Special Pie," a thin, fried wheat pancake, studded with vegetables, that starts out crisp as a potato chip before it slumps into an appealing, sweet chewiness. Where most Chinese delis feature pan-fried dumplings, you'll find steamed yellow-chive-and-pork dumplings here, wrapped in a lumpy sort of dough, which are great and juicy when hot but cool into something sort of leaden.

And then there are huge bowls of those noodles, dense and lumpy but undeniably rock 'n' roll. Heavy Noodling, indeed.

I

INDO CAFE

10428½ NATIONAL BLVD., PALMS; (310) 815-1290.

Indo Cafe is a tidy storefront restaurant in that part of the Palms district where the main streets twist in the most confusing way; it's next door to a Mexican joint that specializes in "Pregnant Burritos" and a toss of a betel nut from a decent pizza place, a bohemian-gourmet cafe, a rathskeller, and the best-known Sichuan restaurant in this part of town. The Indonesian cooking, sort of an intelligently gentrified, Muslim-accented greatest-hits version of pan-Indonesian cuisine, is hands down the best on the entire Westside, even if it may be modified a little too much to the Western taste.

Ayam belado, for example, a crisply fried chicken dish from central Sumatra, is served here under a mildly spiced red-bell-pepper purée where its traditional garnish is a blistering-hot purée of hot peppers; the *dengdeng belado,* a dish in which dried beef is often frizzled to something resembling a potato chip, is chewy and pleasant. Fried whole fish is seasoned with enough fermented shrimp paste to set off the flavor of the flesh, yet not enough to startle. The *sayur lodeh,* cabbage and long beans and such cooked down in turmeric-stained coconut milk, is as gentle a vegetable curry as you'll find. Indo Cafe is a user-friendly restaurant.

Tamarind soup is hotly spiced, tart and luscious, filled with bits of squash, Chinese long beans, and sliced corn cobs in an intricate bowl of broth; mellow Javanese-style chicken soup is slightly soured with lemongrass, thick with slippery glass noodles, garnished with handfuls of musky-tasting toasted betel-nut chips. *Martabak,* a scramble of meat, eggs, and herbs folded into something like filo dough and fried, is a terrific sort of Indonesian *borek,* an exotically spiced version of something you'd expect to find at a North African restaurant.

Indo Cafe may be the only Southland restaurant to serve the fried, stuffed mashed-potato fritter called *perkedel*, crisp-edged and fine, that is pretty good on its own, but which almost explodes with flavor when you daub it with a bit of one of Indo Cafe's fiery chile condiments: the standard chile-hot *sambal olek*, plus a dusky, pungent *sambal* made with fermented shrimp and an unusual *sambal* scented with rosewater. The beef-stuffed squid dish *cumi isi* is powerfully seasoned with fermented shrimp paste but is still oddly compelling. Occasionally there is coconut-rich yellow rice, like an Indian *biryani*, topped with *perkedel*; a piece of the chile-fried chicken; and a chunk of the coconut-stewed beef *rendang*: a delicious plate of food.

If the sautéed *bakmi* noodles are sometimes bland, the *gado gado* salad oversauced, the fruit salad *rojak* unavailable out of season, Indo Cafe, like Pasadena's Kuala Lumpur, is one of a very few Asian restaurants that manages to be accessible to Westerners while still delivering the goods.

INDRA

517 VERDUGO AVE., GLENDALE; (818) 247-3176. DAILY, 10A.M.–10P.M.

If you like to play with your food, you may as well try the seafood curry at Indra, a mini-mall Thai-Chinese restaurant a few blocks down from Glendale High.

The curry comes on a large, superheated terra-cotta platter, streaked with dun-colored sauce and decorated with an assortment of chessman-size clay fetishes that resemble primitive nuclear cooling towers. When a waitress first sets it down on the table, it is hard to know whether to hunt for the food or to figure out how to gamble with the thing—I instinctively looked for a pair of dice the first time I saw the plate. Eventually, you will discover that each cooling tower conceals a dimple on the platter, a half-golfball indentation, and in each dimple there is an extremely minimal, slightly overcooked portion of mixed shellfish—a shrimp, half a mussel, a scrap of squid—seething in a tiny puddle of coconut curry. You would probably find the sauce extremely spicy if you could manage to spoon out more than a few drops of it at a time.

Indra has pretty much everything you could ask of a neighborhood Thai restaurant, which is to say fairly good chicken-coconut soup, a few oddball regional dishes that will impress your friends, and an owner who looks the other way when you bring your own beer. The clientele seems to be about half Thai, half other (this eastern edge of Glendale is as rich in Armenians and Cubans as it is in youngish would-be Ozzies and Harriets), meaning that most of the cooking is not only authentic but accessible. There is a wide assortment of homemade Thai desserts, including both alarming-looking green coconut things and fresh Thai dessert crepes whenever somebody feels like making them. If you live in the area, Indra even delivers.

Green-papaya salad is spicy and fresh; Indian-curry noodles, rich; stuffed chicken wings, fried crisp in their coating of eggy batter. There is an intense, herbal smoked-pork-innard soup called "noodle sheet, browny soup," with rice-noodle sheets wrapped into tight candle shapes, that rivals the best Malaysian-Chinese noodle soups. There are crisp, luscious mussel omelets fried with taro and chile, and there are overcooked, stir-fried beef dishes of every description.

Essentially, though Indra, a clean, basic place decorated with travel posters and dominated by the glass-front hot-food counter that sits just inside the front door, functions as a Thai curry house, a steam-table takeout joint where for a few dollars you get a plate of rice and a stew or two to ladle over it. This style of restaurant is common in Bangkok, but fairly rare here—and Indra has the best Thai curry-house food I've had since Renoo's burned down in the '92 riots.

On the steam table you'll find chicken legs simmered in a thick peanut butter curry, fish balls in a yellow curry, slices of catfish fried with chile and Thai basil, crumbles of ground pork that have been fried crisp with chile. Sometimes there is *har mok*, coconut-moistened seafood steamed in a little bamboo basket, which may be prettier than it is delicious, but is worth getting anyway. The steam table food is clean, spicy, direct, the food Thais eat themselves. The menu, it seems, is mostly for show.

If strips of beef in a brick-colored coconut curry or chicken in a bamboo-shoot curry are tougher than usual, it is because they have given their all to the sauce, which after all has to flavor a vast quantity of rice. Sometimes it seems as if the curries act more as condiments here than as dishes in their own right. If you listen to the government guys who put together the food group pyramid, meat is supposed to be a condiment anyway.

ISOLA VERDE

6001 W. WASHINGTON BLVD., CULVER CITY; (310) 204-1250. DAILY, 10A.M.–11P.M.

Isola Verde is a curious place, one of those sweet corner restaurants that always seems oddly unpopulated, almost more a drop-in hang for the local Eritrean expatriates than a full-blown restaurant (although the food is very good), with a liquorless bar, a pool table and a jumble of Eritrean-liberation posters. It is a comfortable enough place to spend a rainy afternoon, reading magazines and drinking strong clove tea.

There is a corner stage for Sunday night dance bands and neat stacks of flyers in Amharic script and a cool wonders-of-nature photomural; a string of plastic used-car-lot flags is stapled high on the dining room wall. Strange and interesting music in the background plays, swirling guitars and organs, ululating voices, tricky trance rhythms that appear to have no beginning and no end. The music sometimes seems like a Philip Glass score heard from the bottom of a swimming pool.

Eritrea is a small country on the southern Red Sea coast, once a colony of Italy—thus the spaghetti and veal cutlet on Isola Verde's short menu—and recently freed from Ethiopian rule after a long and nasty war of liberation. (Isola Verde's owners, used to representing their business to new customers as an Ethiopian restaurant, may seem surprised and delighted when you ask about Eritrean dishes.) Isola Verde's cooking may be remarkably similar to basic Ethiopian food—rich with butter, hot with red pepper, and complexly spiced with cardamom, ginger, and clove—but it seems lighter somehow, almost a vegetable-intensive, Mediterranean-style version of Ethiopia's heavy, high-plains cuisine.

As at an Ethiopian restaurant, a meal at Isola Verde revolves around vast sheets of fresh *injera* bread, soft and faintly springy, strongly sour, pale, with a bubble-pitted surface that looks sort of what your Dad might have told you to look for at the moment you have to turn over a pancake. In *American Fried*, Calvin Trillin described *injera* as a product that looks like it has a hundred industrial uses, not including being used as food. The acidic tang of *injera* is as basic to Ethiopian cooking as the toasty flavor of tortillas is to Mexican cuisine.

Entrées are served family style, on *injera*-lined metal platters the size of bicycle wheels, and you tear off a piece of another sheet of *injera* to eat them with, sort of wrapping things up taco-style in lieu of using a fork or spoon. At Isola Verde, the selection isn't large—the meat dishes, for example, consist essentially of a spicy sauté of beef and onions called *tibs*, the lavishly buttered Ethiopian steak tartare *kifto*, and the only intermittently available lamb sauté *zigni*—but they can all be had as *fitfit*, tossed with still more *injera*, which can fill you up pretty fast. The thing to get at Isola Verde is the Eritrean vegetable combination plate: mounds of red-lentil stew, a sort of Eritrean ratatouille, spicy spinach, and cabbage and string beans dyed yellow with turmeric, which costs about five dollars, and which would comfortably feed two.

ITANA BAHIA

8711 SANTA MONICA BLVD., WEST HOLLYWOOD; (310) 657-6306. TUES.-SAT., NOON-11P.M.; SUN., NOON-10P.M.

Moqueca, a sort of spicy bouillabaisse from Brazil's Bahia state, may be the single greatest seafood dish of all South America, mellowed with coconut milk, made pungent with pounded dried shrimp, and flavored with a funky, scarlet splash of the palm oil known as *dende*. Like Brazil itself *moqueca* is a true marriage of African flavors, tropical American abundance, and European refinement.

If you poked your head into the kitchen of a fancy Salvadór restaurant specializing in Bahian cuisine, you might see an endless line of cooktops devoted to *moqueca,* two dozen clay pots fired over two dozen burners, two dozen portions of marinated seafood simmering in rich coconut milk, all of it reddened with *dende* and chopped tomato. *Moqueca* of crab, *moqueca* of shrimp, *moqueca* of fish, *moqueca* of lobster . . . it's all good, as Snoop Doggy Dogg might say.

Moqueca, especially in its authentic form, used to be rare as absinthe in Los Angeles, served halfheartedly in a Brazilian barbecue place or two, a Lawndale surfers' cafe, and sometimes in those after-midnight buffet lines in Brazilian-style nightclubs. I suppose I have ordered the dish a dozen times, and tried to cook it myself half a dozen times more. I was pretty sure that the next proper *moqueca* I tasted would be on my next trip to Brazil.

Then Itana Bahia opened, a sleek Bahian-style cafe that feels more West Village than West Hollywood. Oil paintings and African drums ride the walls; sweet Brazilian music drips from the speakers overhead. Images of *orixas*—Afro-Bahian deities—sit on each table in the sort of plastic holders that usually display drink specials. The owner, Bahia native Itana Dorea, presides graciously over the narrow dining room.

Bahia, particularly its capital, Salvadór, is the traditional center of black culture in Brazil, and—perhaps because Bahia lies in roughly the same agricultural zone as West Africa; perhaps because the population is so predominantly of direct African descent—it may be the only place in the Americas where African culture exists relatively unmediated, with African crops, polytheist African religion, and starchy African cuisine.

Itana Bahia may not quite mesh with your idea of what a Bahian restaurant should be. There are neither jars of *malagueta* peppers on the table nor platters of the distinctive black-eyed-pea fritters *acaraje* as appetizers; there is only one of the traditional four *molhos,* table salsas, and no cutesy diorama of village life. But the food itself is fairly Bahian.

You'll find a multitude of Africanesque fritters, shaped like chicken legs around little sticks. A salad of flaked salt-cod with onions, peppers, tomatoes, olives, and sliced hard-boiled eggs comes across as a vivid, Lenten dish. *Casquinha de siri,* crabmeat baked with *dende* and coconut, is a wonderful Bahian analog to Louisiana creole-style stuffed crab.

Itana Bahia, though, like most Bahian restaurants, is mostly a world of stews, smooth, highly spiced, explosively flavored concoctions, gentled with ground nuts, long-cooked vegetables, and coconut. There are *moquecas* here, of course, nearly great ones made either with lime-marinated whitefish or crunchy, big shrimp, as complex as the bouquet of an Oregon pinot noir, and tinted pink with a smaller than usual dollop of *dende* oil. Main dishes are served with soup or salad, mounds of garlicky boiled rice, and a schmear of the odd paste called *vatapa*, which is a sort of a Bahian version of Hawaiian poi, tempered with coconut milk and made positively stinky with dried shrimp.

Bobo de camarao, a shrimp stew in the *moqueca* family, may be even more African in concept, thickened with manioc flour and ground cashews, slightly sweet, and spiked with cubes of cooked manioc that act like the potatoes in a chicken potpie.

Ximxim de galinha, chicken cooked with dried shrimp, peanuts, and shrimp, can be a bit dry but is redolent of its citrus marinade. The stuffed pot roast of pork seems identical to the Cuban dish *boliche asado*, flavored with smoky ham and long-stewed vegetables. And on weekends, there's the black-bean stew *feijoada*, the traditional Saturday lunch in Rio and São Paulo, enriched with shreds of meat but without the chicken legs and hanks of sausage that make *feijoada* southern Brazil's answer to the cassoulet.

Desserts tend to be oddly dainty for such a hearty restaurant: delicate little flans, mousses, and upside-down cakes. But don't miss the dessert called *Romeu e Julieta*, a big wedge of guava paste garnished with two chunks of salty white cheese and a layer of thick cream that tastes closer to proper Devon clot than to anything from Brazil.

INDIA'S TANDOORI

5947 W. PICO BLVD., LOS ANGELES; (323) 936-2050. DAILY, 11:30A.M.–3:30P.M.; 5–10:30P.M. ALSO AT 11819 WILSHIRE BLVD., WEST LOS ANGELES; (310) 268-9100.

Indian pizza is not a euphemism like Armenian pizza or Japanese pizza, or Mexican pizza, but an actual sort of pizza-pizza, partially baked in a charcoal-fired tandoor, topped, and then finished in a conventional oven. (One suspects that the mozzarella cheese might char immediately in the tandoor's intense heat). It's no weirder really than the Peking-duck pizzas and Mexican cactus pizzas that you can find at any number of Southland chain restaurants and is far better done. The pizza is about the size of an old Blue Note 10-inch, lightly smoky, blistered at the edges and with a consistency that ranges from a brittle, cracker-like crunchiness to a crisp-edged chewiness, depending on the day and the chef.

If a Spago lamb-sausage pizza is like a Whitney Houston ballad, brassy, powerful and impeccably recorded, an India's Tandoori pizza with, say, tandoor-baked shrimp, bell pepper and tomato is lush and supple as late Marvin Gaye: maybe a little underproduced, but bursting with subtext. The pizza topped with tandoori chicken sings with the bittersweet spiciness of the tart chile *sambal* that appears where you might expect tomato sauce; the little cubes of chicken serve almost as comforting islets of blandness. All the pizzas, even the vegetarian one, are garnished with cute, little rounds of California black olives.

It's less surprising that an Indian restaurant would have great pizza—tandoor-baked flat breads have always been renowned—than that nobody had thought of it before . . . and the restaurant's idea of tandoori chicken pizza did indeed spread to the California Pizza Kitchens of the world.

It's also not surprising that the people at India's Tandoori would be a little embarrassed about the pizza, as if its existence were too undignified for a restaurant of this stature.

"Sorry the pizza is taking so long," a waiter apologized. "We had to go up the street and find an Italian guy."

JAVAN

11500 SANTA MONICA BLVD., WEST LOS ANGELES; (310) 207-5555. DAILY, 7:30A.M.–11P.M.

Javan may occupy the least subtle restaurant building on the Westside, a two-story complex emblazoned top to bottom with disembodied three-foot chef's heads. You used to see chef's heads—mustachioed, betoqued things smirking at the excellence of their own demiglaces—on matchbooks, billboards, and the signs of every restaurant in Los Angeles with pretentions to Continental Cuisine, but you've never seen chef's heads like these babies—the screaming skulls on the wall outside La Luz de Jesus seem practically restrained by comparison.

Javan's original location a block west was always the sort of place you wouldn't have minded taking your boss to dinner. The newer restaurant, which comes complete with underground parking and, doubtless, a banquet room or two, seems as luxe as anyplace this side of Valentino, all marble and wood, and packed with overdressed customers. While Sallar Brothers may have more immediately appealing kebab platters, and Sharzad Flame better bread, Javan is the best Iranian restaurant in Los Angeles, a sleekly bourgeois counterpart to the raffish kebab houses of Westwood Boulevard, a palace of grilled meat and refined Iranian stews.

Local Iranian menus tend to be mostly the same, a march through the dozen greatest hits of the cuisine. Javan's menu may not be so different, but the genius of Iranian cooking shines through, from the crunchy bits of crust pried from the bottom of the rice pots, *tah dig*, to the classic version of Oliveh salad, which in the hands of most chefs tastes like supermarket potato salad but at Javan tastes like something a two-star French chef might use to garnish lobster.

Usually the appetizers at an Iranian restaurant are something you power through on your way to the kebabs, but at Javan they can be almost the point of the meal. The house version of *torshi*, marinated raw garlic, has steeped in vinegar for seven years, becoming tart enough in the process to pucker an elephant. The marinated grape leaves, stuffed with a paste of meat and rice, have a sweet-sour piquancy that could send a scholar of Middle Eastern spices back to the reference books. The dolma of spinach-spiked yogurt is a 40-weight salad, thick enough to stanch the fieriest seasoning; the barley and spinach soup, *ash e jou*, tastes a little like a Tuscan *farro* potage drizzled with sour whey. The eggplant salad, cooked down to a tart, fragrant mash, glistens with herbed oil.

Javan is famous in the local Persian community for its stews—intricate, long-cooked things that form the basis of the cuisine in Iranian homes—although the stews are rarely at their best in restaurants. One stew of lentils, garlic, and shreds of lamb, *gehmeh*, resembles a French-fry-garnished Iranian cassoulet. Javan serves what is by far the best version in town of the Iranian chicken stew *fesenjan*, a thick, tan sauce that for once achieves some sort of balance between the sour-sweetness of reduced pomegranate juice and the mellow bitterness of ground walnuts.

Still, the heart of an Iranian meal is usually rice, extravagant drifts of the stuff, flavored with sour cherries, herbs, enough saffron to flavor six pans of paella, and—almost as an afterthought—grilled skewers of marinated chicken or beef.

Zereshk polo is an enormous saffron-yellow brick of rice frosted with a compote of the bittersweet Iranian fruit called barberries, split in half, and filled with bits of charcoal-grilled chicken. The taste, if you discount an exotic pungency or two, is not dissimilar to every course of a Thanksgiving dinner rolled into one dish. This presentation of *zereshk polo* may be absolutely traditional, but it seems pretty close to the prankish sort of culinary trick you might find at a restaurant like Boxer or Vida.

Baghali polo, a dillweed-laced pilaf studded with fava beans, comes with either grilled whitefish or what may be the best lamb shank in Los Angeles, a big, soft thing oozing lamb juices and garlic, served in a bowl of tomato-red lamb broth.

Meals at Javan, as at most Iranian restaurants, end with tall glasses of strong Iranian tea sweetened with little disks of homemade caramel. If you're up to it, Javan serves an exemplary version of *faludeh*, a sort of lemony sorbet spiked with little cornstarch noodles that go limp on your tongue, and scented with enough rosewater to perfume a thousand grandmothers. At Javan, less is never more.

JAY BHARAT RESTAURANT

18701 PIONEER BLVD., ARTESIA; (562) 924-3310. TUES.–SUN., LUNCH AND DINNER.

If you've hung around grad students much, you've probably eaten a lot of what passes for Indian vegetarian food: gloppy masses of peas and lentils, great handfuls

140

of exotic spice, loaves and casseroles and stinky clots of cauliflower. It's the kind of cooking groovy, planet-conscious guys invariably turn to as soon as they've mastered Rice-a-Roni and Kraft Dinner. You can throw together enough grub to feed a large dinner party for about $2.99, and you can always feed the leftovers to your cat.

The next step up on the food chain is the college-town Southern Indian vegetarian restaurant, where the emphasis changes from curried baked things to curried fried things: course after course of crisp little balls, tubes, and patties that seem always to be stuffed with turmeric-stained potatoes, served with a sweet mango dip, and accompanied by the drearier sort of North Indian music. The cuisine might be vegetarian, but you'd be hard put to find anything you could actually identify as a vegetable.

Better than those are sweet shops, found in Indian neighborhoods in Culver City, Artesia, and Reseda, which usually sell fresh, simple Indian vegetarian snacks along with their various halvahs and boiled-milk bonbons and milky spiced teas. Cooked to the Indian taste, the snacks are at least authentic, and are often delicious.

Jay Bharat Restaurant, one of the few local sweet shops specializing in the vegetarian cooking of the Indian region Gujarat, anchors the south end of Artesia's Little India.

Jay Bharat is about as unassuming as a restaurant can get, furnished with sticky tables and folding chairs, decorated with a few posters, centered around a glass counter filled with sweets. The menu, a couple-dozen-odd Indian phrases conspicuously without English explanation, is posted behind the cash register. I sometimes end up ordering randomly, hoping that I haven't gotten too many fried dough balls. And the funny thing is, no matter what you order, it all comes out kind of the same. Which is all right: Gujarat is as renowned for its vegetarian snacks as Toulouse is for cassoulet.

Bhel are thin-shelled, crunchy, hollow things, cradling a few beans and bits of potato, into which you spoon a spicy vegetable water the color of a pine forest; *pani wada*, soft biscuits that look not unlike White Castle burgers, are filled with an intensely garlicky vegetable purée. *Pettis*, fried balls stuffed with a coconut-chili mixture, look like but taste different from *kachori*, fried balls stuffed with spiced peas. By the time you get through a few of these, your table will be littered with little containers of sweet chutney, *dal*, and spicy, green coconut chutney, and you will be fuller than you've been since last Christmas.

Of the soups, *ragda pattis* is a masterpiece of texture, a thin yellow-pea stew topped with crunchy fried noodles, garnished with raw chopped onion, concealing pillows of soft potato and a bright cilantro purée.

And then there are the pancakes. *Masala dosai,* the famous South Indian crepe, is done very well here, huge and crispy, wrapped around the inevitable spiced potatoes, and served with coconut chutney and a little container of thin vegetable curry; *mesui masala*, a variation, is folded over spicier potatoes. *Uttupan*, great sourdough pancakes of approximately IHOP consistency, can be had stuffed with a thick, sweet layer of sautéed onions, or with spiced potatoes. Go for the onions. *Khandri* are rolled, room-temperature pancakes dusted with cilantro, shredded coconut, and spice.

The *thali*, which comes with *puri*, all of the sauces listed above, a stew or two, and some pungent Indian pickles, is a meal you won't forget. Especially at about 3:00 A.M. the next morning.

JAY'S JAYBURGER

4481 SANTA MONICA BLVD., LOS ANGELES; (323) 666-5024. SUN.–THURS., 6:30A.M.–11:30P.M., FRI.–SAT., 24 HOURS.

Jay's Jayburger is a small chunk of old Los Angeles entrenched at the corner of Santa Monica and Virgil, a hamburger shack with a half-dozen stools, a tiny counter, and a permanent cloud of White Owl smoke that almost overpowers the funk of frying meat. At one end of the counter, a chrome rack displays congealing slabs of pie as sleekly as if they were Claes Oldenberg constructions; toward the rear, a handlettered sign lists the cigars for sale. Like Irv's Burgers in West Hollywood, perhaps, or the old Pete's Grandburger downtown, Jay's anchors its neighborhood with a flourish and a paper cup of bad coffee.

The most distinctive thing at Jay's Jayburger is probably Jay, a longtime neighborhood guy with a scowl and a permanent tan who always dresses as if he were headed for a one o'clock tee time instead of the back door of a hamburger stand.

"When I get back from vacation," says Jay, "the first thing I do is go get a Jayburger. Sometimes, I drive down to the stand before I even take the suitcases out of the car."

The Jayburger, after all, enjoys a bit of renown. Ken Frank, who is one of the two or three best chefs working in the Napa Valley right now, comes to the stand a couple of times a month for his Jayburger fix, no doubt when his steady diet of foie gras and triple-zero caviar begins to pall. Fred Eric, the chef/owner of Vida down the street, is a regular too.

Jay is a defector from the Tommy's chiliburger empire, and in fact a Jayburger tastes the way a Tommyburger might if it were put together by a chef instead of a fry cook—a small essay in textural contrast that just happens to have a glob of chili at its core. Where a Tommyburger is soft and oozing, a gooey mass, a Jayburger is almost an elegant thing, a mutation of the chiliburger into a genteel, multilayered California-lunchroom sandwich, a chiliburger for the bourgeois.

Like a good lunchroom burger, the greatness of a Jayburger depends on its play of textures: the rough crispness of a toasted bun plays against the stereophonic crunch of fresh iceberg lettuce, the sulfurous snap of raw onion against the slightly luscious bite of tomato, the black crust of seared meat against the rubbery crunch of pickle chips.

Smeared on the top bun, almost subtle in its effect, is the chili, portioned no more lavishly than thousand-island dressing on a coffee-shop hamburger—a presence, a cumin-laced meatiness, but still only a condiment. You can have a Jayburger for lunch and go back to the office without offending.

"You know," Jay says, touching the side of his nose for emphasis, "I went to Chasen's once, bought some chili to take home—it was something like $22 for a quart, frozen—and I took it home to share with my wife. I'd always heard about that chili: Elizabeth Taylor supposedly had it sent to her wherever she went. Well, a couple of days later, I heated it up, and my wife and I, we tasted it. It was good chili, sure. But it was also about fifteen, twenty percent beans. I could never get away with trying to sell chili with beans in it! You know, I think I serve the best chili in town."

The preferred side dish at Jay's, as at Pink's and Tommy's, is a bag of potato chips—there may not be an open-air hamburger stand in Los Angeles that serves decent French fries—and the preferred beverage either freshly squeezed lemonade or Coke from a can.

"Sometimes I'll vary it, have a regular Jayburger one day," confesses Jay, "maybe have one without the chili the next day, the day after that maybe have a Jaydog. I don't know why, but I never get tired of this food."

JOE JOST'S

2803 E. ANAHEIM ST., LONG BEACH; (562) 439-5446. MON.–SAT., 10A.M.– 11P.M.; SUN., 11A.M.–7P.M.

As much as I like Khmer restaurants, as much time as I have spent stalking the aisles at Acres of Books or wincing through Iron Maiden shows at the arena, a visit to Long Beach sometimes seems like a thinly veiled excuse to swing by Joe Jost's, a fragrant corner of old Southern California complete with liverwurst sandwiches, mustaches worn without irony, and frothing mugs of beer. Like Cole's in downtown Los Angeles and the Berghoff in Chicago, Joe Jost's is a place that seems hardly to have budged since Repeal, a testament to the honest, hard-won pleasures of the American afternoon.

For generations of Long Beach men the phrase "schooner and a special," an enormous, overflowing glass of Pabst Blue Ribbon and a Polish sausage on rye, has been capable of inspiring a Pavlovian frenzy.

Jost's anchors a neat, working-class Long Beach neighborhood centered on

Anaheim Street, a straight shot from the massive aircraft plants and not far from the former naval yards, that has shifted from Iowa transplant to African American (Snoop Doggy Dogg and Warren G grew up a few blocks from here) to Cambodian, but though the soul clubs and Khmer-scripted billboards have lately been giving way to signs advertising *licores* and *zapatas,* Jost's still feels like a solid, friendly slice of Iowa-by-the-Sea.

In the back room, men play pool on tables that are older than your grandfather; high on the barroom wall, a baleful deer, wearing not one but two old Joe Jost's caps, stares down at the door. It wouldn't quite be correct to say that Christmas decorations are up all year, but then it wouldn't be correct to say that they are really all the way up even during the holiday season.

The bar actually has a decent selection of brew, including Guinness and Sierra Nevada Pale Ale on draft, but there is something about the tradition of the place, the battered wood and the parade of foaming schooners, that makes the default choice of Pabst Blue Ribbon almost automatic. Pickled eggs sit in a jar near the center of the bar, immersed in chile-pepper brine and practically glowing with neon-green radiance. (The egg jar is the holy of holies at Jost's—when a photographer recently asked to take some pictures of it, two bartenders hovered a couple of feet away, as if to protect the eggs from harm.) When you order an egg, it is served with a scattering of chile peppers on a bed of pretzel rods. Jost's claims to have served six million pickled eggs since it opened in 1924. Unshelled peanuts, roasted at Jost's each day and served in half-pound bags, are as fresh as you have ever tasted them, without the stinging rime of salt that coats ballpark nuts.

The liverwurst sandwich is probably not the most exquisite thing you have ever eaten, but it's a real bar sandwich, a solid two inches of pink, smoked liverwurst capped with a thick slice of red onion, smeared with strong mustard and clapped between two slices of sturdy rye bread—beer is to liverwurst what wine is to cheese. But it is the Special that is the basic unit of cooking at Joe Jost's, a steamed Polish sausage split down the middle, stuffed with a skinny pickle spear, then wrapped with onions, mustard, and cheese in a single slice of rye—a tear-inspiring vision of purest Dad Cuisine.

JOHN O'GROATS

10516 W. PICO BLVD., WEST LOS ANGELES; (310) 204-0692. DAILY; BREAKFAST AND LUNCH, WED.-SAT., DINNER.

The best cowboy breakfasts may be an hour's drive toward Pearblossom, and the best place for dim sum seems to change every week, but everybody seems to know the best breakfast place on the Westside, which is why on weekend mornings at John o'Groats the line spills out onto the pavement, fills the benches and even wanders over to check out the par-3 course at Rancho Park just down the block. Fresh-squeezed grapefruit juice, sourdough French toast with a side of Vermont syrup, crunchy pecan waffles: John o'Groats has it all. The place is rather genteel, really—patterned blue wallpaper like the kind your grandmother used to have, a mounted fish over the coffee machine, splendid, friendly waitresses. The U-shaped counter seems equally at home occupied by country-club women in tennis dresses and grotty UCLA film majors who look as if they haven't slept in a week.

There is a town called John O'Groats at the northernmost point of Scotland, a cod's toss from the Orkneys, but the menu here is pretty much all-American— no finnan haddie or haggis or anything like that, just bacon and eggs, fried ham and eggs, spicy turkey sausage and eggs, wonderful asparagus omelets. Also, there seem to be no actual groats around, which is kind of a relief. Instead, there are buckwheat pancakes dotted with fresh blueberries or with pecans, bowls of ripe bananas in heavy cream, and great servings of oatmeal—the imported steel-cut kind, served with cream and fruit and sugar. Egg dishes come with crisp home-fried potatoes. Fat smoked pork chops are ruddy to the bone, intensely smoky, salty as prosciutto; eggs Benedict, very fine, are made with profoundly smoky ham and a lemony hollandaise. But essentially, everybody comes for the buttermilk biscuits. High, vaguely beehive-shaped things, light and soft with a crunchy exterior, they easily split into four or five warm layers. They do have a slight, bitterish tang of baking powder that some people consider a fault, but it brings out the essential sweetness of the biscuits themselves—if you don't pile on too much marmalade.

Evenings and lunches there is a very nice version of fish and chips—moist, a little chewy, with a shatteringly crisp fried crust—and a good fried chicken recipe borrowed from the late '60s Westside mecca Bit o' Scotland, one kind of brawny dad food after another.

On the other hand, breakfast is served all day.

JOHNNY REB'S

4663 LONG BEACH BLVD., LONG BEACH; (562) 423-7327. SUN.-THURS., 7A.M.-9P.M.; FRI. AND SAT., 7A.M.-1P.M.

"Hey," says a waiter who looks like a lean version of Bill Clinton, "you've brought along another critter." The baby, cradled in her father's arms, positively beams.

Johnny Reb's is like an Alabama roadhouse somehow transported to the northern edge of Long Beach, a temple of boogie music, peanut shells, and worn plywood floors pickled in spilled Dixie beer. Though Southern culture is broad enough to embrace Eudora Welty, Craig Claiborne, and the Marshall Tucker Band, at Johnny Reb's, Southern culture fried stuff: fried chicken, fried hush puppies, fried pork chops, and fried catfish whose crispness potato-chip companies would do well to emulate.

Here, at least some of the time, are fried green tomatoes, firm, tart, slightly sweet slabs of green tomato, dipped in cornmeal and cooked in hot grease, topped with a fistful of crushed bacon. It's like some white-glove ladies' lunch dish hijacked by the Dukes of Hazzard. Hush puppies, round balls of corn batter deep-fried into a golden crunchiness, have all the terrific, trashy fried-onion flavor that most places try to civilize out of them.

Lavishly buttered bowls of grits appear at breakfast, served with hot cornbread, eggs any way you like them, and pungent, profoundly salty slabs of real country ham—the kind of breakfast that any sensible person would trade for the ability to squeeze into a pair of size-6 jeans.

Johnny Reb's prides itself on its barbecued ribs and links and pork—in the mornings, the restaurant even serves something called a barbecue omelette—which is fine in an authentically generic sort of way, but lacks the crispness, the smoky punch of first-rate pit work. So does the bland, chicken-based Brunswick stew served as an inevitable side dish in much of the South, though here you can coax it into life with a splash or two of Texas Pete hot sauce.

French fries are enormous, crisp logs of unpeeled potato; Cajun rice is the liver-rich dirty rice some of us have been missing ever since Carl's shut its doors a while back; pinto beans are sweet; collards are manly; mashed potatoes are smooth and gluey, but unmistakably real.

The main dishes can be spotty here: the gumbo dull, the chicken-fried steak soft, the barbecued-chicken sandwich dry as a wishbone. Johnny Reb's, in fact, is not the place to get fried chicken, either; the bird tends to be underseasoned and overcooked.

But the blackened prime rib—smoked first in the pit, coated with Prudhomm-esque seasonings, and charred—can be powerfully good, and the batter-fried pork chops are juicy and crisp. The curls of fried catfish, cornmeal-coated fillets that practically dissolve on your tongue, are all spice, juice, and crunch.

You will not be hungry after a Johnny Reb's meal, but at least one person at your table should order the pecan pie, which is rich and pully, full of nuts, and has the kind of perfectly crisp, ultrashort crust that falls to powder at the touch of your teeth. It is almost assuredly a rare, welcome visit from The Shortening That Dare Not Speak Its Name.

JOHNNY'S SHRIMP BOAT

2712 WHITTIER BLVD., EAST LOS ANGELES; (323) 262-8713. SUN.–THURS.,
10A.M.–10P.M.; FRI. AND SUN., 10A.M.–11P.M.

Before most of the businesses were turned into parking lots or government office buildings, before street people became feared as The Homeless, Los Angeles's Main Street was a seedy, good-natured strip of "art" movies, fried food, and beery, loud dive bars that were straight out of John Rechy's *City of Night*.

One theater near City Hall played the kind of cheeseball samurai movies that never quite made it to the more respectable Japanese theaters; one theater down toward Seventh, decorated with a grand mural rendered all but invisible with grime, functioned mostly as a flophouse but showed the bottom-bill AIP and Herschell Gordon Lewis stuff that was too weird for even the Hollywood Boulevard theaters. Sometimes on a summer Friday evening, Main could seem like a giant, vice-ridden block party.

And right in the middle of it, the fried-seafood stand Johnny's Shrimp Boat sold cheap coffee, ladled out chili and beans, and drew a crowd of late-model cars. It was the one place on that stretch of Main Street that anybody seemed to go to on purpose. Sometimes at Johnny's, amid the discarded wine bottles and the passersby pestering for quarters, the line stretched as long as the one at Tommy's or Pink's.

For forty-odd years until its closing, Johnny's made the fried shrimp that fed the Eastside: crisp golf balls of fried dough, deep golden and speckled with sandy brown, that tasted of clean oil and happened to have shrimp hidden inside them. They were kind of weird, these shrimp, and sometimes the batter stayed too liquid at the center, but they satisfied a primordial fried-shrimp need: bought by fours, sixes, or eights, swabbed with a dab or two of the Shrimp Boat's mild chile sauce. The shrimp were supposed to be Chinese, I think, though the owners were Korean and the customers mostly Spanish-speaking: The thick batter defied ethnicity.

Anyway, Johnny's reopened a while ago on the Eastside. The fried shrimp is pretty much the same as ever: fresh and hot, crisp and greasy, a little gooey. There are $2.99 lunch plates, which include a couple of the shrimp, a braised short rib or two, a mound of rice, a ladleful of plain pinto beans, and a wash of thick brown gravy: the kind of tasty, Spartan lunch you'd probably want if you had only $3 to your name. The chili fries aren't bad. You can even get a T-bone steak, though I've never actually seen anybody order one.

Sometimes, all it takes is a basket of shrimp and a Pepsi with ice for everything to be right with the world.

JUANITO'S TAMALES

4214 E. FLORAL DR., EAST LOS ANGELES; (213) 268-2365.

Holidays at my in-laws' house, the talk is always of the great tamales that some-body's mother at work made, or a great little tamale place in Montebello that got torn down, or the green-chile-cheese ones from the Christmas of '79. The first good tamales I ever had, I think, were from Cinco Puntos, a place in East L.A. where they also sell good *chicharrones,* and fresh hog's blood for sausages, and delicious hand-patted tortillas. I am fond of the tamales at La Indiana.

But the greatest tamales on the Eastside are without doubt to be found at Juanito's Tamales. The tamales are so good that friends regularly hand-carry stag-gering amounts of them back to New York.

Juanito's is a nice place, a cool, cavernous storefront on a residential street near East L.A. College, that sells nothing but tamales-to-go, but a lot of those. If you don't call first—two weeks in advance for holidays—Juanito's is likely to be out of the fine sweet tamales, or the delicious tamales stuffed with sautéed green chiles and cheese. Juanito's—whose tamales are steamed in stock instead of plain water—employs the two-cornhusk technique, in which thin sheets of masa adhere to the husks as you unroll them, becoming slightly chewy and sweetly fragrant of corn. The inside, the tamale itself, is thin-walled and tender, barely containing its savory payloads of pork and red-chile sauce, which engulfs the masa when a fork breaches the dough. It is a tamale to remember.

JULIENNE

2649 MISSION ST., SAN MARINO; (626) 441-2299. MON.–FRI., 7A.M.–
3:30P.M.; SAT., 8A.M.–4P.M.

Julienne may be the last restaurant of its type, a patio cafe in the heart of San Marino's small downtown that rolls the experiences of La Coupole, *Mayberry R. F. D.,* and the Bullocks Wilshire Tearoom all into one. Julienne is a white-glove lunchroom at the nexus of old society and new cuisine, and the provider of rosemary-raisin Parmesan crisps to half the parties in Pasadena. Julienne is as central to San Marino as Ciro's is to East L.A. or Nate 'n' Al's to Beverly Hills.

On a sunny day, the tables at Julienne are jammed with the genetically gifted whose perfect cheekbones, even teeth, and straight, blond hair seem to have been polished through several generations of careful breeding, a vivid cross-section of people who wouldn't have talked to you in high school. Half of the appeal of Julienne seems to be the intramural schmoozing that takes place in the half-hour or so between signing in with the hostess and finally landing a table. If you belong here, you will inevitably run into half a dozen people you know.

Each person is brought his or her own small plate containing two slices of the house soft rosemary-raisin bread and a tiny individual ramekin of butter; you need not fear your great aunt Dorothy contaminating a shared bread basket with her fingers.

You would expect a place like Julienne to serve genteel luncheon salads, and it does: a basil-and-spinach salad laden with roasted pine nuts; a "Southwestern" Caesar, zapped with smoky chile dressing and garnished with grilled beef fillet; a respectable, if sweet, Chinese chicken salad sprinkled with crunchy noodles. And every day sees a different quiche, a sleek, often broccoli-infused custard with a layer of wadded cooked spinach acting as the crust.

Most people seem to come to Julienne for the sandwiches—soft chicken-salad sandwiches of a sort many of us haven't tasted since the Bullocks Wilshire tearoom closed down, and super-sweet roast lamb on hard rolls—halved and served with a salad.

The Provençal-style ravioli, stuffed with whatever they happen to have on hand that day, is likable, decked out in minced tomatoes and a basil emulsion and garnished with crunchy toasted bread crumbs.

Julienne's food isn't necessarily low in calories. One sandwich involves two lengths of sliced baguette jutting heavenward like conning towers of a submarine, glued to the plate with melted Brie, and stuffed with more cheese, bits of bacon, and chicken. The hamburger is actually one of the very best in town—a big, lean patty on a seeded roll, decorated with sliced ripe tomato, sweet onion relish, mayonnaise, and about a dozen different kinds of baby lettuces. It's kind of twee for a hamburger—not even Pinot Bistro bothers to serve a mizunaburger—but the thing is drippy, bloody, rare, and served with a handful of crusty, skin-on french fries that most restaurants would consider a minor specialty.

Julienne is famous for its desserts, presented on a platter that also includes two orchids and enough exotic greenery to inspire three Henri Rousseau paintings: bread pudding; dense, cool lemon soufflé; cream puffs the size of your head. Still, two times out of three, your best choice might be a white-chocolate-chunk macadamia cookie from the takeout shop next door.

JUNIOR'S RESTAURANT

2379 WESTWOOD BLVD., WEST LOS ANGELES; (310) 475-5771. MON.-FRI., 6:30A.M.-10P.M.; SAT AND SUN., 7A.M.-11P.M.

Marvin Saul built his Junior's Delicatessen from a tacky Westwood storefront into a fortress of pastrami, with an oversized brick façade intimidating as a movie star's castle. Junior's is perennially among the highest-grossing restaurants in California. Generations of Westside Jewish kids grew up on Junior's cold cuts and blintzes. Junior's was also the favorite hangout of the Compton gangsta-rap posse N.W.A before they became famous, and where the late industrialist Armand Hammer used to go for chicken soup . . . and he sat at the counter.

Nate 'n' Al's, the Beverly Hills deli, gets away with a haimisch feel; because its largely Brooklyn-bred customers come to be reminded of home. The Santa Monica delis are more or less coffee shops that serve tongue sandwiches. Canter's on Fairfax has a lock on L.A.'s last major concentration of working-class Jews. But Junior's, like the Westside it serves, is an assimilated, hard-working sort of place, proud to be Jewish but even prouder of its position in the scheme of things. The advertising slogans have included both "The Rolls-Royce of Delicatessens" and "A Touch of Class." Since its last remodel, Junior's has been glitzy as a Cadillac showroom, but it still serves deli food, no surprises. Well, some. They've improved the chicken soup lately—put more chicken in it—and you get a dish of whole kosher dills free instead of the usual few spears. If the waitress likes you, your table may get a whole loaf of rye bread before dinner. Pastrami sandwiches and such are dependably good, among the best in town, though they lack the unctuous garlicky clout of Langer's. The specialty sandwiches, still named after classic cars instead of celebrities, are as thick as encyclopedias.

The waitresses are motherly:

"Did you like the egg cream?" the waitress asked.

"It was fine," I said.

"But was it good?"

"Sure," I said, unsure.

"You waited an extra-long time, so I made it with cream instead of milk. I wanted it to be nice for you."

Be nice, and they'll tell you the truth: "Ahhh, honey, don't get the brisket platter. It's so expensive, and what do you get more than with the brisket sandwich? I'll tell you. You get some vegetables. And believe me, for these vegetables it's not worth the money. You want a potato pancake? I'll give you a potato pancake with the sandwich, no charge."

And Junior's was one of the few places on earth where my old man could be persuaded to eat lunch.

"So, Pop, how was the Novy platter?" I once asked.

"It tasted very much like lox. You can quote me on that . . . but are you sure you can pay for this?" he said as I reached for the check.

"Here, let me buy you a salami."

J.Z.Y. CAFE

1039 E. VALLEY BLVD., SUITE 102C, SAN GABRIEL; (626) 288-0588. DAILY, LUNCH AND DINNER.

J.Z.Y. is fancier than the usual Chinese mini-mall restaurant: The walls glow in brilliant shades of vermilion and forest green, and a fountain burbles by the entrance. The plain wooden tables are surrounded with Eastlake chairs; a burnished bar at one side of the room looks like an import from a chic Taiwan coffeehouse. The soundtrack leans toward Simon & Garfunkel songs rearranged tastefully as Chinese folk tunes. Customers sport Dolce & Gabbana sweaters and Chanel handbags, Gucci pumps and chunks of jade as big as Mike Tyson's fists. At lunch time, J.Z.Y. can seem a little like a Chinese version of the Polo Lounge: Samo Hung, Jackie Chan, and Joan Chen have all been spotted here.

The restaurant, the first American satellite of a century-old Beijing shop that also has branches in Taiwan, is as much of a cultural center as it is a café, and the menu is a virtual encyclopedia of the kind of seasonal Beijing snacks and ultratraditional Beijing desserts that might once have been served to the Empress Dowager, re-created in painstaking detail. Even if you eat Chinese food every day of your life, you have probably never seen dishes like some of these: slices of cool, crunchy bean jelly tossed with julienned vegetables and a nostril-searing sauce of sesame and grated wasabi; "cherries" of pork stewed with cabbage; cold noodles tossed with fried pork and bean ketchup; a sweet porridge made with purple sticky rice.

Most of the customers check off their orders on little Chinese-language paper menus attached to clipboards on each table, but a cheat sheet is available, a thick volume that identifies each preparation with photographs, notes on ingredients, and a small essay on seasonal appropriateness. After a few meals here and a couple of passes through the menu, you could probably give your own lecture on Chinese foodways—or at least on the imperial love of haw cake.

Actually, though the menu may seem comprehensive, it is also fairly short: a few cold dishes, a few stews, a few kinds of noodles. The house cold plate is a compendium of the sorts of things you might order at a noodle shop, but raised to a higher level: boiled peanuts with the peculiar crispness of fresh celery; pressed tofu with the rich density of roast pork; delicate boiled seaweed; bouncy simmered egg. Cool slices of long-cooked pork "arm," arranged like the petals of a flower on the plate, exude levels of piggy complexity you may associate with great Italian prosciutto, though the flavor hints more at anise than at cheese.

In many Chinese restaurants soup can be an undifferentiated salty fluid, but J.Z.Y is as careful with its stocks as any French restaurants. *Hun tin*, floppy wonton stuffed with a rough paste of smashed pork, float among shredded scallions in a clear, delicate consommé, and spurt their own, meatier broth into your spoon when you bite into them: a superb contrast. Tofu, as soft and slithery as if it were homemade, drifts in a thickened stock inflected with the subtle sweetness of exotic fungus. Crunchy, melonlike slices of white gourd bob in a broth tightly poised between the pork richness and the salty funkiness of dried scallops. Even the soup for the noodles—a supergamy beef-organ soup for the ox-tendon noodles, a rich lamb broth for the lamb noodles—is fine. And this is one Chinese restaurant where you absolutely must try dessert: rich puddles of walnut purée or bitter-almond "tea"; fried, stuffed cakes shaped to resemble ears; elephant trunks and celebration cakes; *osmanthus*-scented "cool cake" and rice-flour balls shaped around sticky chopped nuts; the most extraordinary sliced lotus root stuffed with sticky rice and painted with an herbed syrup.

KAGAYA

418 E. SECOND ST., LITTLE TOKYO; (213) 617-1016. MON.–SAT., DINNER.

Most of us think of *shabu shabu* as a distinctly Japanese food, saturated with a dozen levels of ritual and a rigid politesse, sparely seasoned, emblematic of the Japanese habit of finding the greatest possible pleasure in a gram and a half of raw protein. Anyone who has ever seen a Japanese gourmet swoon at the sight of a microtomed sliver of bluefin tuna will understand. But to the Japanese, *shabu shabu* is only slightly less Western than a Big Mac. I might be imagining this, but the swagger of the chefs at the downtown restaurant Kagaya suggests, if not a Louis L'Amour scene transplanted to a Little Tokyo mini-mall, a dash of at least a cowboy-chic.

Water is heated in rugged, hammered-metal pots without handles and snatched off the flame with a battered pair of pliers. A branding iron glowing at the back of the stove seems a mystery until a cook applies it to the top of a crème brûlée, instantly caramelizing the sugar into something resembling thin glass and sending thick plumes of white, marshmallow-scented smoke into the restaurant. Chefs regularly reach into scalding stovetop steamers with their bare hands to pick up superheated appetizer plates.

This isn't to say Kagaya is rustic. Kagaya is sort of a fancy place, and the *shabu shabu* here is but the centerpiece of a multicourse meal. To start, perhaps there will be a slab of marinated halibut, then some miso soup with clams, and a steamed shiitake mushroom garnished with intensely fragrant grated radish. The cooks sear tiny scallops of *Kobe* beef as if they were sliced lobes of foie gras, and serve them with a reduction sauce and a flourish.

The routine of a *shabu shabu* meal is a well established, and if you have ever spent time around a fondue pot you will be at home here. A cook sets a basin of simmering broth, scented with a square of the Japanese seaweed *kombu*, onto an induction burner in front of you. Another cook slices raw beef—USDA prime rib—into transparent petals of meat; a third arranges vegetables (napa cabbage, fresh tofu, shiitake mushrooms, scallions, dark green chrysanthemum leaves). One man in the kitchen seems to do nothing but skim the protein scum from seething pots.

Basically, you swish a slice of the meat through the bubbling broth for a second or two, just until the vivid pink becomes frosted with white, and then dip it into one of the two sauces—a basic, citrusy *ponzu* or a thin, fragrant paste of fish stock and ground sesame—and then eat. If you've done it right, the texture is extraordinary, almost liquid, and the concentrated, sourish flavor of really good beef comes across as it does no other way. *Shabu shabu* can sometimes seem more like a haiku about meat than like meat itself—especially if your idea of beef is twenty-six ounces of bleeding steer—but there are times when all of us crave heightened essence rather than gross animal abundance.

KAMON

5185 HOLLYWOOD BLVD., HOLLYWOOD; (323) 667-2055. DAILY, 9A.M.– 10P.M.

To people not actually raised in Bangkok, Thai desserts may be as specialized a taste as oboe recitals or light bondage: gelatinous masses slicked with bland, fresh coconut cream and lashed with stinging doses of salt, inflected with the reptilian stinks of jackfruit or ripe durian, or garnished with any number of flavorful crispies—fried onions, hot chiles, dried shrimp—that you will never find on top of a Baskin-Robbins sundae. The most famous Thai dessert (or at least my favorite) involves great lumps of sticky black rice, a mango ripened almost to the point of deliquescence, and enough salted coconut milk to clog the arteries of an Ethiopian marathon runner.

In the midst of the densest Thai-restaurant neighborhood in America, next door to Sapp Coffee Shop, across the street from Sanamluang, and a block's walk from Vim, Krangtedd, Ruen Pair, and a dozen other places, Kamon may be the epicenter of Thai desserts.

There are fried bananas to nibble with your Thai tea, translucent gelatins the color of milky jade, warm peanuts boiled with spices, and tiny, exquisitely colored jelly fruits realistic enough to make a marzipan master sigh. You will find peculiar multicolored ropes, dried fruit with sugar-salt, vast expanses of sugared squid, and delicious Thai sticky-rice tamales filled with thick, sweet mashed taro, coconut, and red beans.

A lot of Thai restaurants prepare an off-menu takeout snack or two, a homemade sweet or a cellophane packet of garnished rice noodles that you'll find stacked up next to the cash register. The back room of Kamon is practically a library of these indie snacks from restaurants all over town, Technicolor jellies and salty beef sticks, coconut blobs and taro fritters, rice cakes, mango jerky and powdered shrimp, all tightly Saran-Wrapped and glistening in individual foam trays.

Behind a long glassed-in counter, half a dozen young women grill coconut pastries on hot irons, pop fritters into roiling seas of grease, and roll warm crepes into pastries as deftly as Martha Argerich plays Chopin. For a buck or two, you can taste these études in coconut, sugar, and wheat. Ping-Pong balls of fried dough, piled high in stainless-steel bins, are chewy, oily, unsweetened Thai dough-nut holes ready to be dunked in chile-heightened syrup. Tiny fried dumplings conceal thimble-size portions of ground nuts and honey. Hemispheres of slightly jellied coconut cream nestled in wisps of pastry—*knomkuk*, they're called—are displayed pressed together in pairs, batter flaring at the edges to make them resemble ringed planets.

The English legend on the restaurant's sign reads THAI DESSERT & VEGETAR-IAN FOOD, although the actual selection of non-dessert stuff here is severely lim-ited, and the senior woman behind the counter may actually yell at you when you try to negotiate a bowl of noodles. "No food!" she barks. "Go next door."

If you persist, she may point out a few savory items. They are not especially vegetarian: chicken pies called curry pups, which are a sort of Thai equivalent of Cornish pasties; golden-hued baked capsules shaped like computer mice, crisp as puff pastry, stuffed with a gently curried mash of chicken and tropical roots. And there are suave, floppy-skinned dumplings, ten or so to an order, sprinkled with toasted garlic and filled with diced radish, sautéed Thai greens, or a mysterious hamburger-textured substance that appears to be based on ground taro.

In the end, though, it always comes down to dessert.

"Have a Thai taco," a counter lady said one afternoon, feeling generous.

She handed me a tiny, crisp Thai crepe that looked like something Malibu Barbie might enjoy with a strawberry margarita, glazed with a quarter-inch layer of thickened coconut milk, folded in half, seasoned with cilantro and chile, and stuffed with deep orange Brillo-pad tangles of carrot.

A Thai taco may not have the stage presence of a crème brûlée or a slice of ricotta cheesecake with fresh mulberries, but after a Hollywood meal of Thai food, it seems just right.

KIM CHUY

727 N. BROADWAY, NO. 103, CHINATOWN; (323) 687-7215. DAILY, 8A.M.–
8P.M.

The best-known part of Chinatown might be the smartly pagodaed stretch of grand restaurants and back-scratcher emporia at the northern edge. But the heart of the area lies a few blocks south, in the great arcade at 727 Broadway that stretches between Broadway and Hill.

Here you'll find some of the better Chinese barbecue shops, the original Mandarin Deli and the best branch of Pho 79, as well as places to buy tea, medicinal herbs, and pink-tinted Vietnamese pork tartare. When fresh bamboo shoots or Shanghainese hairy crabs come into their brief seasons, they are sold out of boxes at the Broadway end of the arcade, and people cluster to buy them.

At the head of the arcade is the bustling noodle shop Kim Chuy, with a splendid motto painted on one window—KING OF CHIU CHOW WONTON—and a gallery of noodle photographs posted on the other. Kim Chuy specializes in the noodle dishes of the Chiu Chow people, the Chinese diaspora in Southeast Asia more or less, and the words Chiu Chow appear helpfully before nine-tenths of the items on the menu, just in case you happened to forget what kind of restaurant you were eating in. Elderly women totter out of the place clutching big bags of peppery fish balls to go.

The food crowd frequented Kim Chuy at the beginning of the first wave of authentic Chinese food in Los Angeles, raved about the jellyfish and the noodles with spicy beef, and then sort of forgot about the place, though the restaurant has never lacked for customers. I used to go to Kim Chuy a lot when I worked at an office downtown, and though I hadn't been back in a while, the proprietor still remembered my favorite order when I walked through the door for the first time in a decade. "Hey there," he said, beaming. "You're Mr. Leek Cake. It's been a long, long time."

Chiu Chow leek cakes are flying-saucer-shaped capsules of rice dough, filled with rather intense-tasting sautéed leeks and seared to an oily, crisp-edged chewiness.

On each table is an incredible array of condiments: soy sauce, fish sauce, two or three kinds of chile sauce, black vinegar, squeeze bottles of sweet bean paste, dried red-pepper flakes, and those pungent Thai pickled chiles. I miss the sugar bowls of crushed roasted peanuts that used to be my favorite garnish here. I am happy that they still serve the smoky imported *sriracha* chile sauce as well as the fruitier domestic brand.

Chiu Chow shrimp and crab balls involve shrimp, fake crab, and diced taro root, wrapped in a sheet of bean-curd skin and fried crisp. The appetizer is served with a sweet, gingery dipping sauce whose aftertaste may remind you of jellybeans you have known and loved. And although the crab and shrimp balls may seem at first glance to be something you would not eat on a dare, they are quite delicious.

The Chiu Chow fried fish cake is not unlike a heavy-ish Thai *tod mun*; the Chiu Chow cold jellyfish is properly crisp-tender, but drowning in an oversweet sauce. I'm fond of the Chiu Chow–style rice porridge with shrimp, brothy and sharp with fresh ginger.

The basic deal at a Chiu Chow noodle shop is, of course, Chiu Chow noodles, slippery rice noodles the width of your little finger and firmer, square-cut egg noodles that resemble bouncy linguine, submerged in broth, garnished with things like boiled duck legs and sliced pork. The Chiu Chow special noodles include duck, shrimp, squid, cuttlefish, and four kinds of fish cake—also floppy, herb-spiked wonton if you ordered it that way. The Chiu Chow beef stew noodles come with melting shanks of tendon and hunks of long-simmered chuck, and the broth has an interesting anise top note. Chiu Chow spiced beef noodles come in a gritty, spicy demicurry, almost crunchy with ground nuts—another missing link between Chiu Chow cooking and Thai.

Fried noodles—with chicken, beef, or mixed seafood—are passed through an ultrahot pan, smoky but still soft, served not ten seconds after they are cooked, and fully possessed of that elusive quality that Chinese call *wok chi*, a special wok energy that is possible only in restaurants as small and informal as Kim Chuy.

KOBAWOO

698 S. VERMONT AVE., LOS ANGELES; (215) 389-7300. LUNCH AND DINNER DAILY.

Barbecued short ribs are nice, but the Korean dish that all of us are looking for is the true mung-bean pancake, a crisp, golden creature flavored with shreds of leek. There are many ways to eat a mung bean, but only a couple that taste this good.

Kobawoo is an archetypal Korean greasy spoon, the kind of Koreatown mini-mall restaurant Korean friends will try to steer you away from, then admit that they sort of like themselves—sort of the way people who nosh at Canter's twice a week still tend to warn you off the place. Kobawoo is a stripped-down cafe, with worn tables, a pungent smack of *kimchi*, and strewn cardboard signs that advertise Korean rice wine. Kobawoo is widely reputed to serve the best mung-bean pancake in Los Angeles.

As soon as you wander into the cafe, you are led to a table and set up with cold barley tea and three kinds of *kimchi*: a crunchy radish pickle; a tart, fiery-red cabbage pickle; and a little bowlful of crisp water *kimchi* powerfully flavored with garlic. The waitresses are unused to non-Korean customers, but try to be as helpful as they can. Nobody will talk you out of ordering squiggly piles of steamed pig's feet if that is what you really want to eat.

Kobawoo's thick mung-bean pancakes come two to an order and are fragrant with the greasy tang of the griddle, brown at the edges, dotted with little nubs of pink meat. Beneath their thin veneer of crunch, the pancakes seem almost ethereal, melting away almost instantly in the mouth like an intriguingly flavored polenta. A soy-citrus dip cuts through the richness of the dish. A waitress, watching you struggle to tear the pancake apart with your chopsticks, may hurry over with a pair of sewing scissors and snip the pancake into bite-size pieces.

You will find the usual barbecued short ribs and flank steak at Kobawoo, bubbling iron cauldrons of bean curd cooked with *kimchi,* and thin omelets stuffed with different types of marine life. There is an intriguing dish of warm tofu cubes, sprinkled with sesame seeds and a Chinese-style chopped pickle, that you eat with the hot cabbage *kimchi* that is served on the side. Kimchi-fried rice is really good, another one of those cauldron things where the pot looks as if it's filled with white rice, but turns out to conceal a seething core of fermented-cabbage stew.

The Cornish-hen soup (which comes to the table unsalted) is delicious, with an intense broth that only comes with cooking a lot of bird in a very little water, flavored strongly with a huge knob of ginger and at least a dozen cloves of garlic, mellowed out with a handful of rice. It is among the best chicken soups in Los Angeles, richer than any delicatessen's—and just the thing to eat with a mung-bean pancake.

KOKEKOKKO

203 S. CENTRAL AVE., LOS ANGELES; (213) 687-0690. MON.–SAT., DINNER.

In one of the essays in *Blue Trout and Black Truffles,* Joseph Wechsberg wrote about a Viennese restaurant famous for its extremely specific cuts of boiled beef, a general who dined at the restaurant every day, and his refusal to settle for a slightly different cut of beef the afternoon the *tafelspitz* dissolved into the broth. As long as men refuse to compromise on matters of taste, Wechsberg seemed to imply, everything will be all right with the world.

I think of that story almost every time I walk into Kokekokko, a small yakitori restaurant in Little Tokyo that serves nothing but skewers of chicken parts grilled medium-rare. Kokekokko caters to a level of chicken connoisseurship most of us will probably never develop; an appreciation of the particular striations of one particular muscle in a chicken breast, the flavor of the right thigh over the left, an ability to identify feed, breed, and gender of a fowl with one small bite of a charcoal-broiled leg. This may be the only place in town that serves chicken-breast sashimi, a Japanese delicacy described in Shizuo Tsuji's famous *Japanese Cooking: A Simple Art.*

Kokekokko, named after the Japanese word for a rooster's crow, has the rustic look familiar to anyone who's seen an Ozu movie or two: walls of peeled logs, hollow stumps as stools, big sake bottles stacked and arranged artfully as a fancy supermarket display. The dining room, half counter seating, half not, is hazy with the smoke coming off the hardwood grills and crowded with everyone from elegantly dressed couples stopping in after an opera at the Music Center to guys who look a little like unemployed 7-Eleven clerks, and more than a few expatriate salarymen, several sakes into their evenings, whose loosened Windsor knots droop even with their sternums.

Until you've been in often enough to know to ask for a particular tendon or grilled pope's nose, the ritual at the restaurant is to order one of the set menus, either five or ten courses of grilled chicken and innards: loosely packed chicken meatballs, faintly scented with herbs; grilled chicken skin, pliable but just crisp, threaded onto the skewer in accordion pleats; marinated silvers of chicken thigh, grilled like shish kebabs separated from one another by bits of onion. Sometimes a pre-appetizer of warm, ground chicken salad seems almost to have the texture of a Thai *larb*, though the Japanese seasoning is considerably gentler.

At Kokekokko, you will inevitably start with something that tastes like the chicken-world equivalent of the seared albacore sashimi so popular at new-wave sushi bars: thick slabs of breast muscle that have the weight and the texture of good tuna sashimi, grilled just until the pink center begins to pale with opacity; each of the three pieces on a skewer brushed with lemon and wasabi. Grilled chicken hearts, skewered and served with a smear of hot Chinese mustard, are tough as chuck steak but are intensely chicken-flavored, in the way Peruvian chefs manage to make grilled heart taste better than any other part of the cow. Tiny, grilled hardboiled eggs could be the unborn chicken eggs beloved of Yiddish-speaking grandmothers, though they taste suspiciously similar to quail eggs.

Where you'd expect the bracingly pungent bowl of miso soup in the middle of a sushi meal, Kokekokko serves a bowl of clear, double-strength chicken consommé, flecked with a few bits of scallion top, which for all its elegance tastes like something straight out of Nate 'n' Al's.

Wisps of chicken breast stretched around okra and Japanese chile have the bite of hot chile, crunch and green flavor of okra and, only lastly, a smidgen of residual sliminess that works to intensify the texture of the chicken. Other bits of meat are wrapped around chunks of Japanese eggplant or firm, almost-sweet slabs of grilled zucchini. The last course is usually crunchy grilled chicken wings—the second joints of the wings, anyway, neatly threaded on skewers and almost too hot to eat.

Come early: If the kitchen runs out of livers and gizzards, you will become bored when the chefs begin to repeat themselves halfway through the ten-course dinner. At a certain point, no matter how much of a connoisseur you may fancy yourself to be, one piece of grilled chicken becomes very much like another.

KOTOHIRA RESTAURANT

1747 REDONDO BEACH BLVD., GARDENA; (310) 323-3966. WED.-MON., 11:30A.M.-9P.M.

Consider the unlovely *udon* noodle, that squirmy Japanese pasta, thick as a pencil and white as a grub, poor sister to the elegant buckwheat *soba*. *Udon* is generally pasty and lifeless, taking up space at the bottom of a bowl that might better be occupied by ramen or even seaweed. Many people eat *udon*, but few of them would mourn were *udon* to vanish from the earth.

Yet in the hands of an artist, there can be poetry even in *udon*; its slick paleness more reminiscent of shimmering moonlight than of slimy things, its flavor described as delicate, its texture described as firm. And when owned by such an artist, there can be poetry even in an *udon* restaurant, the kind of place where you can get anything you want, as long as what you want is *udon*.

Kotohira Restaurant hides in a corner of the bustling Tozai Plaza, a big Gardena shopping mall that is also home to Japanese travel agents, a Japanese video store, and at least half a dozen other restaurants. Masahiro Nogughi, Kotohira's *udon* master, is one of the few people in the United States who still make *udon* by hand, *udon* that are thick, white, and long, diminishing to squiggles at the ends, clean in flavor, with the bouncy resiliency of elastic ropes. The place Kotohira, a small town on Shikoku, hard by the Inland Sea, is famous within Japan for the chewiness of its local *udon*. The founder of this restaurant comes from a well-known Kotohira noodle family—he spent many years cooking in his uncle's restaurant—and the *udon* here may be the best in the United States.

Kotohira's combination dinners might include scrambled chicken and eggs over rice; oversweet sushi rice stuffed inside chilly cocoons of fried tofu; fried shrimp served on seasoned hot rice. The vegetable and shrimp tempura, offered in about half the combinations, is decent: crisp, light, and hot, the best nonnoodle dish in the house.

What you eat at an *udon* restaurant is, of course, *udon*, and at Kotohira you eat *udon* dunked in fish soup or anointed with curry, though it sometimes seems as if the chefs would prefer that you not besmirch the clean flavor of their noodles with anything so common as hot broth. The purist will eat his or her *udon* cold, the ends perhaps briefly dipped into a bowl of soy sauce seasoned with wasabi and chopped green onion. *Udon* may also be eaten hot, snatched from a tall bowl of plain hot water, drained and dipped, a noodle preparation austere as a woodcut.

Warm *udon* are served dry in a bowl, garnished with ginger, green onion, and wisps of freshly shaved *bonito*, with a tiny pitcher of soy alongside. Before you have a chance to dribble the black fluid onto your noodles, a chef is at your side. "A few drops only," he barks. "You can always put on more if you like, but you can not take it out again." You do not argue. The wheaty sweetness of the noodles, set off by the clean, smoky smack of the dried *bonito*, is among the most delicious things you have ever eaten.

KRUANG TEDD

5151 HOLLYWOOD BLVD., HOLLYWOOD; (323) 663-9988. DAILY, 11A.M.-2A.M.

Kruang Tedd is a dim, crowded room with the sharp, smoky light of noir films, a place that feels like midnight even at noon. Other Thai nightclubs in the area may be fancier or attract bigger-name acts; Kruang Tedd's crowd is younger, a little hipper, without even a trace of the usual mom-goes-to-karaoke-night vibe.

The menu recalls, in its own way, the kind of delicatessen menus that offer everything from pastrami sandwiches to *moo goo gai pan*, with a large emphasis on the Thai equivalent of the nachos and buffalo wings you might order with beer at a honky tonk: chile-fried peanuts, grilled Thai sausage pungent with lemon grass, curls of deep-fried chicken skin that taste a little like packaged pork rinds. The chef may be willing to improvise a dish of garlic-fried noodles for a vegetarian customer, and he may spend hours on elaborate presentations of taro-stuffed duck, but at Kruang Tedd, the bar snack is king.

There are tons of Thai salads, of course, dressed with lime, chile, and salt: glass-noodle salads garnished with fish maws that look a little like deep-fried Ping-Pong balls, grilled beef salad with raw garlic, squid salads and chicken salads, sausage salads and raw fish salads. The house version of the ground-pork salad *nam sod* is tossed with crunchy bits of chopped pig's ear, which either is your thing or isn't. (I like it a lot.) In Kruang Tedd's interpretation of crispy catfish salad, the fried ground fish swaps the usual Rice Krispies Marshmallow Treat texture for a strange, powdery, grainy feel something like crunchy fresh snow tossed with a few peanuts.

The essential snack here is the banana-leaf chicken: thumb-size bits of dark meat, marinated in something that must include mashed bananas, folded into banana leaves and then deep-fried. Unwrapped, the meat is marked with crusty black nubs and chewy parts, pockets of juice and caramelized patches, and a subtle banana sweetness that transforms the meat.

A southern Thai–style bamboo-shoot curry, blazing hot and incorporating more than a bit of fermented fish, has an intriguingly complex flavor if you can get past the overwhelming horse-barn bouquet that will let everyone on your end of the room know precisely what you ordered for dinner.

You'll find all the Thai standards here too—chicken-coconut soup; pork with string beans; *pad Thai* noodles; and an unusually good version of minty beef, notable for deep-fried leaves of Thai basil and a mellow, pervasive flavor of toasted garlic. Kruang Tedd is a perfect place to stop by for a beer, a plate of fried squid, and an hour or two of jangly Thai pop.

KUALA LUMPUR

69 W. GREEN ST., PASADENA; (626) 577-5175. LUNCH AND DINNER, TUES.-SUN.

Is there a better bowl of noodles anywhere than the curry *laksa* at the Kuala Lumpur restaurant in Old Town Pasadena, a big, soothing bowl of dense, coconut-infused broth, thick with rice vermicelli and turmeric-dyed a brilliant, Donna Karan yellow-brown? Ronnie Ng has always been the best Malaysian chef in town, obsessed with clean flavors and fresh produce, the balanced richness of coconut milk and ground nuts, the most fragrant *pandan* leaves, the subtle differences in the curries that bathe beef and the curries that glaze chicken. Most of the decent Malaysian restaurants in town have at least one Ng-trained chef in their kitchens—when he's on, Ng is a classicist master.

Kuala Lumpur is pretty sedate, and some Pasadenans who would never think of exploring the restaurants of the Asian neighborhoods just a few miles south of here have for several years been as conversant with *rojak*, beef *rendang*, and *assam laksa* as other people are with chicken-coconut soup in suburbs where Thai restaurants lie thick on the ground. Malaysian cooking, the original crazy-quilt Pacific Rim tradition, is one of the world's pleasantest, most accessible cuisines.

Ng is one of L.A.'s great obsessive chefs, tracking down and importing obscure Malaysian ingredients, hand-pounding curries anybody else would mount in a food processor. After starting Kuala Lumpur, Ng worked for a while at Yazmin in San Gabriel, but he has been back in Pasadena for years. Any restaurant where Ng is cooking is probably the best Malaysian restaurant in America.

Here you'll find a good "Indian" fish curry—fillets poached to a perfect underdoneness in a a mild, complex yellow sauce—which is perhaps not the fish-head curry, ubiquitous in South Asia, that the dish alludes to, but is subtler and more pleasant to behold. *Rojak* is the classic Malaysian salad of sliced cucumber and jicama and dead-ripe mango, spiked with crunchy bits of fried bean curd and tossed with a dark, syrupy dressing of black soy, vinegar, and the pungent dried-shrimp paste *belacan*—a fugue of sweetness, funk, and texture.

Nasi lemak, rice boiled with coconut milk and musky-smelling screw-pine leaves, is mounded in the middle of a platter and surrounded by little heaps of garnishes—spicy stewed squid, boiled egg, red beef curry and yellow chicken curry, tiny fish cooked with a tangle of sweet onions, fried peanuts—which you mix in to taste, sort of like a Malaysian variant of the Korean *bi bim bap* throbbing with the flavors of turmeric, chile, and dried fish.

Sambal shrimp, spicy and sweet, are sautéed with tamarind and a healthy, stinky wallop of the *belacan*; the coconut curries are delicious. Coriander chicken, simmered and grilled in that special South East Asian way that makes the skin improbably crisp, is coated with a spiced, pale-green cilantro-yogurt paste, and is spectacularly good.

Not everything works here: leek dumplings are flabby and dull; the fried noodle dishes can be oily and uninteresting. And when you're ordering for a crowd, the structure of the menu, set up in the American appetizer-entrée-dessert fashion, is incongruous with the way most people eat Asian food.

On a cold afternoon, though, there may be nothing more satisfying than that bowl of curry *laksa.* The surface of the broth shimmers through a thin, bright-orange scrim of chile oil, which adds a presence but not really a heat to the dish; cubes of fried tofu soak up the broth and make the flavors resonate in the way that subwoofers intensify the bass in your stereo system. Bits of chicken and a few large shrimp float just below the surface. One sector of the bowl hosts an ounce or so of lightly steamed Chinese broccoli, whose bitterness keeps the richness of the coconut in check.

On the side, almost tipping over into the saucer, is a dish containing a slender wedge of lime and a few grams of Kuala Lumpur's brilliant red fresh-chile *sambal,* which lend a certain brightness to the *laksa,* though neither is strictly necessary. The soft, slithery rice vermicelli seem less noodles in themselves than an instrument to give the broth texture, solidity, and weight. Ng's *laksa* has everything you could want in a bowl of soup.

LA ABEJA

3700 N. FIGUEROA ST., HIGHLAND PARK; (323) 221-0274. BREAKFAST AND LUNCH, WED.–MON.

I've been going to La Abeja for a long time now, long enough to see the owner's kids grow up and propel themselves into college, long enough to see the kids who come by the old-fashioned wooden cigar counter for candy and gum come back with children of their own. And I've gotten the *carne adobada*, marinated pork crisped on the griddle, every time. I ordered a *chile colorado* plate once back in 1993, and I've regretted it ever since.

La Abeja, a modest Mexican-American lunchroom near the Southwest Museum, is a real neighborhood institution, the one place in this part of town where you are likely to see bungalow dwellers eating in the same room as the mechanics who work on their cars, where Mount Washington families descend from the heights. All of Highland Park drifts by here on a warm afternoon—activists scarfing steaming bowls of *cocido*, artists and musicians drifting in for breakfast after 1:00 P.M., still shaking sleep out of their eyes.

When you find a seat, perhaps in one of the cracked, sunken banquettes in the backroom or around one of the sticky tables in the front, the owner ceremoniously hands you an old-fashioned printed menu, which is an oddly formal document, like something borrowed from an an Ensenada restaurant circa 1962. Everything is carefully set in antique Spanish type, then paraphrased in English on the facing page.

"*Tocino con huevos . . . tocino con huevos*—that sounds just so delicious," says my friend Michelle.

"That's just bacon and eggs," I say.

"Oh, you're right," she says. "But doesn't it sound good?"

Michelle settles for a *carnitas* plate, which tastes exactly like a *carnitas* plate, and sighs with happiness when the food finally arrives. Nobody cares if you order an expensive *carne asada* plate here or settle for a burrito; a big bowl of cabbagy beef soup or a couple of tacos. The *chile verde* is too soupy, too bland; the *carnitas* are often on the soft side. The *chiles rellenos* are pretty good, the kind somebody's grandmother would make, soft and puddinglike rather than crisp and fried, wetted with the house's *ranchero* sauce.

But La Abeja's glorious *carne adobada* is just magnificent, thin sheets of marinated pork dyed bright orange with chile paste, crisp as pastry and burnt black at the edges, meat juices concentrated, caramelized into a semigloss sheen that keeps the pork moist even as it kisses it with the vivid taste of the grill. Some *carne adobada* is wet and sloppy, more about the complexity of spicing than about the forceful flavor of meat. This *adobada* is primal stuff, cowboy food, almost too intense to eat without first folding it into a tortilla with a spoonful of beans.

Other restaurants may be more ambitious, but La Abeja, from its green-sauced enchilada plates to the soft tacos of stewed tongue, tastes like Los Angeles.

LA CABAÑITA

3447 VERDUGO RD., GLENDALE; (818) 957-2711. DAILY, 8A.M.–10P.M.

La Cabañita, on the mountainous edge of Glendale, is the clean, well-lighted place all suburban Mexican joints should aspire to be: basic, but never less than pleasant. The *tomatillo* salsa is fine. The dining room is decorated with woven wall-hangings that depict either flowers or red chiles. A photograph of Liz Taylor and Larry Fortensky is prominently displayed on a far wall, which may be the most impressive bit of celebrity you'll see this close to the city of Montrose.

The menu, vaguely Mexico City/cosmopolitan in flavor, is loaded with things like *entomatadas* and *mole de olla*, which turn out to be basically chicken enchiladas and a slightly spicy beef soup, respectively, but which sound ineffably chefly and exotic. The tacos, made with chewy, freshly made corn tortillas, are stuffed with a sweetly spiced beef *picadillo* studded with almonds and raisins, with dryish fried pork, or with chopped beef and melted cheese. The chips are terrific, though the *chiles rellenos* are not.

But even if there's little here to challenge the palate of Liz or Larry, La Cabañita does have some interesting food: a musky, complex green *mole*, alive with a dozen unfamiliar pounded barks and seeds; a soothing chicken soup; delicious long-cooked pork chops smothered soul-food-style in a smoky gravy made with *pasilla* chiles; roasted poblano chiles stuffed with a sweet, intricately spiced forcemeat. Somebody has obviously thought about this food.

LAGOS CAFÉ

1663 S. LA CIENEGA BLVD.; (310) 246-0973. MON.–SAT., NOON–10P.M.

When Lagos works, there's almost no restaurant where you'd rather be, old funk grooves popping from a tape player back in the kitchen, swaggering dudes lining up at a rear counter for big Styrofoam containers of Nigerian dinner to go, tables chaotic with Nigerian families wearing native dress. Lagos is a storefront Nigerian restaurant a mile south of Beverly Hills, sort of generically ethnic-looking—walls bare except maybe a Nigerian oil company calendar or two, an unused stage, glass-covered tablecloths.

From La Cienega, if you're hurrying past toward the freeway, Lagos can look a little like an abandoned restaurant, windows blacked out, graffiti scratched into surfaces, but inside, it couldn't be livelier.

"Hah, nice bay-bee!" shouts an extravagantly robed Nigerian man to a smiling infant across the room. "You are wearing the same hat as me!"

There is palm wine to drink here, the effects of which Nigerian novelist Amos Tutuola described with vividness sufficient to make it unnecessary to actually try the stuff. On the upside, there is also Star Beer, brewed in Nigeria, which has the apply, acidic edge of English cider, and which goes well with heavy, spicy Nigerian food.

The menu is long, essentially untranslated, and filled with exotic dishes you haven't seen before unless you're in the practice of eating *moin-moin* with your cornflakes for breakfast in the morning: *amala, akara,* beans and *dodo, palpe.* On the facing page, in French, daily Senegalese specials are listed, elaborate chicken stews and such, which the restaurant doesn't actually serve, but which are nice to dream about if you've ever eaten the great Senegalese food in Harlem.

At a Nigerian meal, like that of other West African countries, you essentially choose a starch—bland, pounded white yam or cassava root, steamed into a puddinglike consistency—and then get some highly-seasoned stuff to roll into a little ball with the starch with your fingers. Like Thai sticky rice or Liberian *fufu,* Nigerian pounded yam is fun to eat.

In practice, as a non-African, you'll probably be provided with forks and spoons, plus a large bowlful of pretty much everything on the steam tables that day, usually spicy black-eyed peas, the sweet fried plantains called *dodo,* and the spicy West African pilaf called *jollof* rice.

Moin-moin is often described as a Nigerian tamale, and the description is pretty close, a big, wet cylinder of steamed black-eyed-pea flour with the consistency of a Nicaraguan *nacatamal,* stuffed with egg and bits of meat, sliced into half-pucks of dough.

Efo riro, a mass of collard stewed with hot chile until it seems almost to form curds like cottage cheese, is one of the spiciest greens you'll encounter this side of Sichuan, drenched with palm oil, pungent enough to flavor something like 14 kilograms of cassava. And you must try *egusi* stew, pounded melon seeds cooked down with greens and palm oil into something that tastes a little like boiled chrysanthemum leaves, but with a sharp, nutty bite you'll encounter nowhere else.

Assorted meat is pretty much what it sounds like, various cattle parts simmered in a spicy tomato sauce and served in a big bowl. Sometimes the dish is delicious, folds of tripe softening under the sauce, garlicky chunks of canned corned beef becoming almost palatable with the chile heat; sometimes the meat is heinously overcooked.

It's sort of hard to know what to expect here on a weekend night, when what appears one minute to be a quietly dining couple turns out to host to a party of twelve, where waitresses either swarm or seem to vanish into a void, where a stew can be extremely delicious on one visit and inedible the next—a visit to Lagos can feel like being inside a magical realist novel that accepts credit cards.

LA FONDA ANTIOQUEÑA

4903 MELROSE AVE., LOS ANGELES; (323) 957-5164. DAILY, LUNCH AND DINNER.

La Fonda Antioquena is a clean, well-lighted place on the seedy end of Melrose, an oasis of track-lighting and pink tablecloths among bodegas and Thai video stores. The restaurant specializes in the cooking of the Colombian state of Antioquia—you may have heard of its capital, Medillín, in a context totally unrelated to food—and large, eerie oil paintings on the walls recall Botero. The customers tend to be either well-dressed Colombian couples or unreconstructed Anglo counterculture types. And Colombians steam steaks, which might be surreal enough all by itself.

I loved the food at La Fonda, but I rarely went into the place in its original location a mile east of here. The chalkboard menu was written in idiomatic Colombian Spanish, and nobody there ever seemed to be able to explain the concepts behind *bandeja* or *ave maria pues*. It was too easy to order a meal that turned out to be composed of all innards, or of six variations on the thick Colombian tortillas called *arepas*. I usually ordered grilled *morcilla*, a sweetly spiced Spanish blood sausage, because I had figured out what it was. But though the restaurant was literally around the corner from my apartment, La Fonda somehow made me feel like a tourist imposing on the locals of a foreign city.

"If you don't finish your dinner, no TV for you," the waiter said, pointing at a half-eaten bowl of the Colombian tripe stew called *mondongo*.

"But I ate all of the tripe," my friend said.

The waiter shuddered. "Brrrr," he said, "I won't eat that. It comes from the inside of a cow."

You should order at least an empanada or two: greaseless and crisp-crusted, corny and stuffed with a creamy forcemeat, served with a dip of cool, Colombian salsa that seems to be mostly scallion tops, chiles and salt. Empanadas are all the appetizer La Fonda needs, or seems to have on a regular basis, for that matter.

If you think of the meat as kind of a pot roast, the steaming of steaks might seem less barbaric, and the *carne sudada* here is good, a cumin-scented eye of round stained yellow with *achiote* and topped with stewed tomatoes and onions. *Sobrebarriga* is more or less the same thing done with brisket; the steamed beef tongue, rich, salty, with the gelatinous intensity of long-cooked meat, is even better. If you prefer your meat grilled, you might consider the *ave maria pues*: a thin, plate-size marinated steak, tasting strongly of the grill; a dense, spicy chorizo sausage; a dinner salad with a strong vinaigrette; a thick, smoky pinto bean stew (awesome); fried plantains, rice, *arepa* and a strip of pigskin. The crib sheet translates this mass of food as the "Holy Cow" plate.

LA FONDUE BOURGUIGNONNE

13359 VENTURA BLVD.. SHERMAN OAKS; (818) 501-9813. DINNER DAILY.

If you spent much time dating in Los Angeles in the '70s, you probably ended up at least once at La Fondue Bourguignonne, a small, fondue-intensive Westwood restaurant tucked away at the top of a long flight of stairs. Posthippie competitors like Alice's or the Aware Inn were respectable date places, nicely lit and striking an ideal midpoint between continental cuisine and carrot cake, but La Fondue was, you know, serious: dark enough for romance, cheap enough for a college student to afford sometimes but expensive enough for glamour, and stuffed with some of the thickest Gallic accents you have ever heard outside a Maurice Chevalier flick. Plus, the giggly single-mindedness of the thing, the wanton simmering in boiling wine, the really long forks, may as well have been designed as a way for couples to feed scallops to one another. La Fondue was like, wow.

A restaurant dedicated to the art of immersing things in hot liquid seemed a little old-fashioned even then. The fondue craze was a product of the late '50s, and the Sterno-fueled fondue pots many of our parents had gotten as wedding presents had been relegated to the attic more than a decade before. (My mother's bottle of *kirschwasser*, a cloying cherry brandy whose only known function is as a flavoring in cheese fondue, clearly predated the Vietnam War.) When La Fondue closed a decade or so ago, some of us were surprised that it had actually lasted as long as it did.

In the last few years, though, fondue has, along with Louis Prima and flaming *mai tais*, slowly crept back to respectability. Fondue sets are suddenly hot again in department stores and the pages of *Wallpaper*, and tony restaurants on Melrose serve the stuff.

I was stunned to discover not only that the Sherman Oaks location of La Fondue Bourguignonne had been there all along, but that reservations on a weekend evening were actually hard to get. Here are the dark wood, the gleaming copper, and the frilly curtains; the gallon jugs of California "burgundy" siphoned off into carafes; the tape loops of classical music that repeat so often you begin to suspect they are recorded on 8-track. The headwaiter answers the phone in the kind of heavy French accent you may associate with hockey goalies.

If you have ever eaten fondue, you probably know the drill. A waiter brings out a chafing dish filled with bubbling melted Gruyère, and you dunk stale hunks of baguette into the stuff, twirling until the cheese has completely coated the bread, inhaling sweetly alcoholic fumes from the cherry brandy and white wine incorporated into the mixture, occasionally pausing to munch on a tart little pickle or to take a swig of wine.

But at La Fondue, cheese fondue is just the beginning, at least when you order the three-course fondue combination dinner. Next comes the main-course fondue, a segmented tray holding bits of fillet mignon, chicken, scallops, and shrimp, plus chunks of mushroom and zucchini, which you spear on forks and cook in small vats of oil or wine that have been set to boiling over a burner in the middle of the table.

The oil fondue is a little problematic—nobody has ever really been happy with deep-fried steak—although with a little experimentation, you can just put an excellent seared crust on the seafood. The wine bath is kinder to the food (I loved the sweet lusciousness of long-simmered zucchini), but the meat is cut too thickly to cook in the quick, gentle *shabu shabu* style, and you lose the spectacular transformative effect that hot oil can have. However you decide to cook the food, you dip it afterward in one of five sauces arrayed on your platter, tiny pill cups of richness that range from béarnaise to spicy tomato purée.

And finally comes the chocolate fondue, a seething pint of melted goo ready to coat strawberries, grapes, melon slices, none of them particularly ripe, as well as all the marshmallows you can eat.

More detailed than *Boogie Nights*, more intense than an entire season of *That '70s Show*, La Fondue is a museum of *Love, American Style*-California, a *Three's Company* restaurant set come to living, breathing life.

LAKE SPRING CUISINE

219 E. GARVEY AVE., MONTEREY PARK; (626) 280-3591. DAILY, 11A.M.–
3P.M.; 5P.M.–10:30P.M.

The most delicious thing to eat in Los Angeles, including spareribs at Phillips',
Yujean Kang's lobster with fava beans, and Campanile's grilled-cheese sandwiches,
is a reddish-brown blob about the size of a hubcap, floating like a jellyfish in a
murky, dense sea of sauce. The blob, red-cooked in the traditional Shanghainese
style, is a specialty of the Lake Spring Chinese restaurant in Monterey Park.

Lake Spring, a sleek, Shanghai-style bistro, is the prettiest Chinese restaurant
in a neighborhood of hundreds of Chinese restaurants, all mirrors and deco
sconces, indirect lighting and silk-flower arrangements, and Chinese American
customers who look as if they subscribe to Paris *Vogue*. Mercedeses and BMWs
clog the parking lot, and the tables (Lake Spring is strictly BYOB) groan under
the weight of rare bottles from Bordeaux and Alsace.

The blob, described on the menu as "noisette of pork pump," is a whole,
anise-scented pork shoulder.

(The first time I asked a waitress what it was, she smiled mysteriously and
gestured toward her shapely outstretched calf.) The "pork pump"—a typo that
has been perpetuated on Los Angeles Chinese menus at least since Mon Kee
opened in the late '70s—is simmered in soy sauce and rock sugar for hours, until
it is so soft a probing chopstick easily penetrates the whole sweet mass of delicious,
melting fat. At the core is a fist of the tenderest imaginable pork, the sort of thing
all pork might taste like if the President's Council on Physical Fitness had never
been convened, sort of a platonic ideal of pig. A handful of Chinese greens
luxuriate in the gravy, and the slight bitterness tempers the incredible richness of
the pump. You can smell the garlic and spices from across the room—pork pumps
glisten on at least half the other tables in the restaurant.

Of course, there is more to Lake Spring than pork pump. The place is locally
famous for a dish of sea cucumber braised with shrimp roe, a dish I never got
around to trying.

There are unusual appetizers: "neutralize ham," which is bean curd that has
been braised, smoked, and pressed into a facsimile of Chinese ham slices, served
with a sneaky chile oil that is spicy enough to close your throat; "neutralize duck,"
which tastes and looks a little like chunks of Chinese roast duck; chewy slices of
a cured-pork terrine, bound with a clear Chinese aspic; wonderful braised celery,
scented with sesame oil and served cold with a soy-wasabi dip. Ask for the smoky
house condiment made with salted vegetables, fermented black beans, and peanuts: it goes with almost everything.

Steamed Shanghai pork dumplings, full of fragrant juice, are served with a dip
of shredded ginger and pungent black vinegar, and are worth every second of the

half-hour they take to cook. (The fried dumplings aren't nearly so good.) There are perfectly ordinary stir-fried leeks with scallops, chicken slicked with sweet sauce, things like that. There is something delicious called "jade shrimp"—tender baby shrimp stir-fried with a creamy spinach purée. The plump fried crabs, served with a subtle, ginger-spiked brown sauce, are fine.

Most spectacular is the fish-head casserole, a smooth chowder in an enormous earthen casserole. The broth is thick with puréed yellow beans, whose slight, fermented tartness enriches the casserole like crème fraîche, but without the heaviness; the sweet flesh of the fish is poached until barely set.

Lake Spring has inspired dozens of local imitators, none of which, save its sister restaurant Shanghai Palace, really begin to resemble its wildly inventive approach to traditional Shanghainese cooking. But I keep fantasizing about Wolfgang Puck discovering the great specialty and importing the recipe to Chinois—roomfuls of cholesterol-conscious westsiders chowing down on what is essentially pounds and pounds of braised hog lard: Pump it up!

LA LOUISIANNE

5812 OVERHILL DR. (AT SLAUSON), LOS ANGELES; (213) 293-5073. MON., THURS., 11:30A.M.–10P.M.; FRI., 11:30A.M.–MIDNIGHT; SAT., NOON–MIDNIGHT; SUN., NOON–10P.M.

Slauson Avenue, as it courses toward Ladera Heights, is something of a late-'50s museum, with smart '50s flower shops and groovy '50s motels, spectacular '50s neon and Sputnik-era churches that appear untouched by time. At the top of Slauson stands the hulk of the Wich Stand, which was the apex of nutty '50s coffee-shop architecture when it opened as a drive-in (now it's a health food restaurant), and whose javelin-through-roof look still seems at least as contemporary as *The Jetsons*.

Across the street from the Wich Stand is the Jet Age building that houses the swank Creole restaurant La Louisanne, and to come in for dinner here might be one of the most profoundly nostalgic acts a native Angeleno can commit. La Louisanne might have good crawfish étouffée and the house band might play a little too much Grover Washington, Jr., but otherwise, this restaurant is a step back to Los Angeles 1959, when people dressed for dinner, sipped Tom Collinses instead of Chardonnay, the parking lot was filled with brand-new Buicks, and appetizers at a fancy restaurant meant soup or salad instead of duck-sausage calzone.

When I was a five-year-old living a few blocks south of here, the La Louisanne space was occupied by a restaurant called Poor Richard's, a musky, Shirley Temple–serving wonderland decked out with teddy bears, whizzing toy trains, and giant pandas swinging on trapezes. Poor Richard's was the favorite special-occasion restaurant of just about everybody in kindergarten at Fifty-fourth Street School. Several years later, the building became the site of the best reggae club in town, where dub poets ruled and deejays blasted Augustus Pablo records through a really good sound system.

Now the restaurant is plush and continental, lit with a few dim spots and about a million tiny green lights, too dark to read the menu without holding it up to one of the globe candles that decorate every table. In a velvet coffin of a dining room in back, you settle into chairs that are a cross between plush CEO-model office chairs and the pods from the old Monsanto ride at Disneyland.

Here comes the maître d', looking diffidently at you over his shoulder as he leads you to a table near the front. He figures you for newcomers to the place, and as soon as you are seated he mumbles his recommendations: "Number one, the filé gumbo. Number two, the jambalaya. Number three, the étouffée."

The gumbo, black and dangerous, thickened with filé instead of okra, is crammed full of sausage, crab, and shrimp and has a complex yet powerful spiciness that tails off with a filé top note of newly mown hay. The jambalaya is a saucy thing, a tasty, soupy glop that seems to include at least as much spicy tomato sauce as rice, blanketed with chicken, shrimp, sliced hot sausage, and smoky slivers of ham—a distinctly inelegant plate of food but basically a good one, and served in a portion that could probably sate the entire defensive line of the Bruins. Crawfish étouffée involves a dozen or so crawfish, a mound of rice, and a dark, peppery sauce that is the single most delicious thing in this restaurant.

With the dinners comes salad—iceberg lettuce, shredded carrots, blue-cheese dressing on the side—or a decent bowl of clam chowder, the creamy kind, dotted with tender bits of clam.

After the big three dishes, the food can be hit or miss at La Louisanne—the Cajun-spiced grilled catfish with crab stuffing is good, while the snapper is just okay; the tomato-y chicken Creole sort of boring, while the Southern-fried chicken is crisp and tasty; the Cajun chicken has obviously been reheated, the stuffed crab—read, in the Creole manner, "crab stuffing"—not as interesting by itself as same substance sandwiched between two juicy pork chops. La Louisanne is pretty good for Los Angeles Creole, which is not to say it would be a threat to great Creole New Orleans restaurants like Eddie's or Dooky Chase. But it's as close to New Orleans as you're going to get within five minutes of the Santa Monica Freeway.

LANGER'S DELICATESSEN

704 E. ALVARADO ST., LOS ANGELES; (213) 483-8050. MON.-SAT., 8A.M.-
4P.M.

Langer's Delicatessen is in the pulsing Latin core of the Westlake district, smack among the 99¢ stores and fly-by-night swap meets, a short walk from Home Boy Taco, convenient to many ancient beer bars and cater-corner from MacArthur Park. Here's the kind of shoulder-to-shoulder sidewalk jostling that's not supposed to exist outside of Manhattan or Chicago's Loop.

On the block anchored by Langer's, sidewalk vendors sell sunglasses and a wide selection of gory Mexican tabloids. From an upturned bucket across the street, a Guatemalan woman occasionally does a thriving business in cigarettes and cucumbers. If this ever resembled a Jewish neighborhood—and forty years ago, it apparently did—Langer's HOT PASTRAMI sign is the last visible remnant.

As a current resident of New York, with free and easy access to pastrami sandwiches at Katz's, Pastrami Queen, and the Second Avenue Deli, I still find myself daydreaming about Langer's.

The fact is inescapable: Langer's probably serves the best pastrami sandwich in America—on a block better suited to Salvadoran cow's-foot soup.

A pastrami sandwich may not seem like much, I guess, but a good counter-man's skills can be as finely honed as a sushi chef's. The ones at Langer's do. Behind the deli counter, Langer's seasoned professionals prod the steaming slices as they work, occasionally pushing aside a piece that is less than tender. Langer's bread, a perfect seeded deli rye, comes from a secret source (actually Fred's Bakery on South Robertson). Most delis get their corned beef and pastrami from one of only a couple of sources; it's the final preparation that counts. The meat, preferably hand-cut, should be well spiced, steamed to softness, and piled neither too skimpily nor too high (actually, there should be slightly too much meat; it allows the *alte kakers* who make up much of any deli's clientele to custom-adjust their sandwiches to taste), with enough variation in the thickness of the pastrami to make each bite texturally different from the last. The seeded rye should be thickly cut, crisp crusted, and soft inside, with a slightly sour tang that cuts the richness of the meat. Yellow mustard, of course.

There is also pastrami and tomato on rye, with a dollop of sweet Russian dressing, and pastrami on rye grilled with sauerkraut and Nippy Cheese, and a platter of pastrami with gritty chopped liver. Corned-beef sandwiches are nice, sort of like the pastrami only a little less so, and the hot tongue sandwich is tender and juicy. Langer's has no sandwiches named after celebrities, but there is something called the "Fresser's Special" that's too baroque even to contemplate. Chicken soup can be pale; tasty matzo balls, though. The latkes are mushy and a little bitter. A herring appetizer consisted of about an ounce of fish and a half-pint of sour cream. Romanian tenderloin—skirt steak—is profoundly beefy, but can be as tough to chew as a steel-belted radial. For dessert, sweet noodle kugel can be rich and delicious, but can also suffer from something that tastes very much like freezer burn.

So, the pastrami's good here, and some other stuff is uneven. And if you don't like it, there's always the cucumber lady across the street.

LA PARRILLA

2126 CESAR E. CHAVEZ AVE., EAST L.A.; (323) 262-3434 (OTHER LOCATIONS IN NORTHRIDGE, TARZANA, LOS ANGELES); DAILY, 8A.M.–11:30P.M.

Here we are at the Mexican steakhouse La Parrilla, on Cesar E. Chavez Avenue in East L.A. And here come the mariachis, the sixth or seventh crew within a couple of hours, swaggering in from the restaurant across the street, looking for a customer to buy a song or two.

The leader of the trio, handsome in his *charro* vest, nods a hello to an itinerant stuffed-animal salesman on the same route, and he groans. The restaurant at the moment is populated mostly with non-Mexicans, who are rarely in the market for his songs or almost as bad, request things like "La Bamba" or "Guantanamera," which he sometimes has to play more than ten times a night.

We are happy to see him. Usually the bands are wonderful: sweet, close-harmony crooners or piercing trumpet-led trios, ready to play almost anything from the last century of Mexican music for a five-dollar donation. But the last band, a ragged quartet, featured perhaps the worst saxophone player on the planet, a man whose entire repertoire consisted of a single descending scale that he felt appropriate to just about any open space in any song his colleagues played. It was worth five bucks to just about anybody in the dining room to cleanse their ears of that honking sax.

La Parrilla is a wonderful place, with smooth, cool guacamole mashed to order in giant stone mortars and Mexican beer served so cold that it crusts over with ice crystals on a hot afternoon. The restaurant, like El Chamizal in Huntington Park, specializes in marinated, charcoal-grilled meats—thin beef fillets, pork coated in a ruddy chile paste, chorizo sausage, sweetly sauced spareribs, and chicken served in various combinations.

If you order a *parrillada al brasero*, the meat comes to the table piled on a little grill.

There are hand-patted corn tortillas, unless they've run out. Combinations are served with rice, grilled scallions, and little bowls of spicy *charro* beans made smoky with bacon, and mostly the grilled meat is very good.

Beyond grilled meat, La Parrilla serves the usual sort of upscale Mexican entrées—chicken in a wan pumpkin-seed-based *pepian* sauce, dryish grilled Cornish game hen, bland chicken mole—that you might find in a chain restaurant. Better are the many dishes based around grilled beef: *puntas de filete*, grilled chunks of steak tossed with pickled jalapeños and topped with melted cheese; filet in a smoky sauce of chipotle chiles.

Between mariachi songs, the waitresses are likely to push something called *molcajete Azteca*, a large granite mortar heated to a ferocious temperature, then filled with, among other things, bits of steak, grilled cactus paddles, chicken, a thin smoked-chile salsa, and a big slab of *panela* cheese, which bubbles and smokes where it touches hot stone. It might seem peculiar, this Mexican variant of the Korean *bi bim bap*, and you might wish for a longer fork, better to avoid scorching your wrist, but the *molcajete* is a delicious bowl of food.

LAS PALMAS

11671 VICTORY BLVD., NORTH HOLLYWOOD; (818) 985-5455. LUNCH AND DINNER, TUES.–SUN.

In its original West African form, *fufu* is usually a basketball-size lump of pounded yams or fermented cassava, that is almost tasteless until you mix it with a few tablespoons of curried goat or potato-leaf stew. Across most of the Caribbean, *fufu* has retained its bland integrity, even when it is jerry-rigged—I have in my possession a *fufu* recipe that calls for equal parts Bisquick and instant mashed-potato buds. A sort of plantain, *fufu* goes under the name *monfongo* in Puerto Rico and the Dominican Republic, and though it is loaded with pork products, it too functions primarily as a plain starch accompaniment to a chop or ladleful of stew.

But as Cubans have tended to do when adapting their African heritage—as they have with polyrhythmic music, storytelling, and painting—they got *fufu* wrong, but gloriously so. Behold *fufu de platanos*, as prepared at the North Hollywood Cuban restaurant Las Palmas: a compact, beige mound rising from its plate like a miniature Staples Center constructed of fried pigskin, garlic, and green plantains, oozing oil and melted lard, fragrant enough to make the guy across the room look up from his *Investors Daily* when the waitress brings it to your table. *Fufu* is as unobtrusive—even in this garlic-soaked room, as Shaquille O'Neal would be sitting at a corner table.

Perhaps *fufu*'s time has come. One expensive restaurant in Manhattan actually pairs *fufu de platanos* with tangerine-glazed tuna. And Las Palmas's *fufu de platanos* appetizer, with its variegated soft parts and chewy parts, juicy bits and crispy bits of swine, subtle sweetness and vicious lashings of salt, is—like Cracker Jack or Cajun popcorn shrimp—one of those dishes impossible to stop eating until you see the shiny surface of the plate.

Las Palmas is a small, tidy place in a part of the Valley dominated by recording studios and body shops, decorated with little more than a couple of tourist posters and a few palm-tree prints. The waitress tend to dress up as if they were just moonlighting from jobs in the D.A.'s office, and the crowd includes freshly pumped bodybuilders bursting out of tank tops; shaggy, bleary-eyed studio musicians; and squadrons of men in dark suits who take out a dozen lunches to go at a time.

A certain amount of the restaurant's business seems to revolve around its subscription lunch program where, for a set amount of money a week, Las Palmas will deliver you lunch every day. And while the menu is abbreviated, the list of off-menu specials is endless and ever-changing. You can usually get a plate of *fufu de platanos* as well as the archetypal Cuban tuber stew *ajiaco*, the roast chicken and the sweet, raisin-laced, ground-beef dish *picadillo*. There is sometimes a creditable version of the dried-beef dish *tasajo*, which is more or less the Cuban equivalent of Mexican *machaca*—less intense, less chewy than the wonderful *tasajo* at El Chori in Bell, but nice, glazed with a mildly spicy tomato sauce.

I had overlooked Las Palmas for the last several years because its version of my favorite Cuban side dish, *moros y cristianos*—Moors and Christians, black beans sautéed with rice—is always a bit on the dry side. Also, the restaurant was fairly extensively reviewed a decade ago, mostly by critics who assumed its specialty was *paella* (which I'm not even sure it serves anymore), rarely the best call at a Cuban place unless you like your rice tinted with a soap factory's worth of *achiote* instead of the proper Spanish saffron.

But in addition to the *fufu de platanos*, Las Palmas has the best fried green plantains I've had since the lamented Cuban-Chinese restaurant Chaos closed a decade ago: crunchy on the outside but quickly giving way, like a perfect bagel, to a resilient softness inside, tasting of starch and salt and clean oil, without a trace of the usual fishiness: French fries with a graduate-school education.

There is usually an inch-thick slice of Cuban roast pork, *lechon asado*, decorated with tangles of caramelized onions in a puddle of a brown sauce that could be either an insanely reduced brown pork stock enriched with an insane amount of salt, or a little olive oil fortified with a bit of a bouillon cube. At this extreme and appropriate level of saltiness, exact judgments are sometimes hard to make. The pork chops, trimmed of very little of their fat, are all crispness, oil, and garlic, like something from a page of the *Mambo Kings*—or come to think of it, from most of the pages of the *Mambo Kings*—brought to breathing, odiferous life. The waitress will insist that you finish with a demitasse of espresso that is perfectly undrinkable until you sweeten it with two packets of sugar . . . at which point it unaccountably becomes exactly right.

LA TAQUIZA

3009 S. FIGUEROA BLVD., LOS ANGELES; (213) 741-9795. DAILY FOR
BREAKFAST, LUNCH, AND DINNER.

The tacos from the truck behind El Taurino on weekends are remarkable. The *gorditas* at Roast To Go in Grand Central Market are swell. The *flautas* at Ciro's are unsurpassed. But the best single Mexican *antojito* in Los Angeles may be something called a *mulita* at La Taquiza, a sort of steroidal quesadilla good enough to make a grown man yelp with joy.

La Taquiza is a cheerful restaurant a block north of USC, a bright, high-ceilinged place festooned with air plants, what looks like a salute to the USC women's volleyball team, and a lonely bull skull set high above the cash register. The walls are splashed with painted slogans and parables: *"Aquí su salud es primero"*—"Here, your health comes first"—reads one particularly comforting slogan that stands in defiance of the cholesterol content of the merrily sizzling lengths of chorizo on the grill.

If La Taquiza—the name means something like "taco party"—is trying to replicate the vibe of L.A.'s ubiquitous healthy-Mex places, it fails in one respect: The food is superb.

Dudes from the local car-repair places, neatly dressed MBA students, families, snarling undergrads, and at least a table or two of cops are usually in attendance here, noshing on enchilada plates and powering down big bottles of Crush or Mexican Pepsi. There is a juice bar toward the front of the room churning out fresh pineapple, carrot, and orange juices, along with their equivalent *licuados*.

La Taquiza is well known among USC students for its tacos—massive, minimalist things equal in weight to three ordinary tacos, freshly griddled tortillas laden with a quarter-pound or so of grilled steak, stewed beef tongue, crisp bits of spit-grilled pork *al pastor*, or nicely seasoned chorizo sausage. You fold the tacos yourself and garnish them at a modified salad bar stocked with chopped onion, spicy pickled carrots, and four kinds of salsa, any one of which is good enough to make the guys at Baja Bud's stare at their Pumas in shame.

You can also get tacos of *suadero*, cubes of meat sliced from roasted spareribs, which have the high, funky sweetness of slightly overcooked pork, but the meat is usually too chewy, and it is almost impossible to eat one of these tacos without dumping half the contents on your lap.

The burritos are fine, tightly wrapped monsters stuffed with meat, creamy beans, and a little too much rice. The *sopes*, grilled cornmeal saucers piled with meat, beans, lettuce, and pungent Mexican cheese, are good. Even the *fajitas*, served still seething on a superheated iron platter, suffice—a little oversalted perhaps, but fresh and clean and good.

Still, the *mulita* . . .

177

Two thick corn tortillas, made seconds earlier, are slapped down on a griddle, glazed with Mexican cheese and freshly made guacamole, sprinkled with a few grams of meat snatched off the fire and then welded together into kind of a sandwich. The cooks here have a deft touch with *masa*, the corn dough that is the basis of Mexican cuisine, so that the tortillas, while bulky, have the illusion of great lightness and a fluffiness that comes only with consummate skill.

There is a crisp, toasty brittleness where the *mulita* has rested against the griddle, which gives way to an almost puddinglike softness inside, the sweet, roasted smack of grilled corn, and—finally!—the paired richnesses of the cool avocado and the hot melted cheese, and the chile-tinged chewiness of carbonized pork.

L.A. TOAD

4503 W. BEVERLY BLVD., LOS ANGELES; (323) 460-7037. MON.-SAT., 10A.M.-MIDNIGHT.

The Korean cafe called L.A. Toad is a favorite with Korean men, a good place to stop for a bite on the way home from work or before hitting the bars, the kind of clean, shirtsleeves restaurant with great food whose Anglo equivalent has all but slipped away: cheap enough for the average Joe, but with food so good that rich guys mob the place too. Inside, Toad feels like the Korean equivalent of one of those tiny, hidden trattorias in Rome, the smoky, tourist-free ones that never seem to make the guidebooks.

Toad isn't set up for non-Koreans, you understand: None of the waitresses really speak more than a couple of words of English, the food is unfamiliar, and the menu is untranslated.

The restaurant, once you get past the guard in the parking lot and the man with the portable phone who always seems to lurk right inside the front door, is a plain dining room, rather pretty actually, with pale wood, rice-paper screens, and a window that opens onto the kitchen. A carved wooden toad, the restaurant's mascot, sits on a sake box, looking out over the place. Behind the glass, a woman cooks Korean pancakes with a look of great seriousness, spreading oil onto the hot griddle and carefully measuring out blobs of batter: potato pancakes, oyster pancakes, crisp pancakes with scallions and fresh chiles, all of which are delicious dunked into a soy-scallion dip. Laughing groups of men raise ceramic pitchers and pour each other glasses of Korean rice wine.

The first time we tried to eat at L.A. Toad, the waitress panicked, not sure what to do with us, and finally showed us to a tiny table toward the rear. She looked around for help and then backed away. The cook peeked out of the kitchen.

A man in a white suit, looking a little like a Korean equivalent of the Christopher Walken character in *The Comfort of Strangers*, rose from the table where he had been eating dinner and walked over to our corner of the room. He bowed slightly. "You know," he said, quite formally, "this is a Korean restaurant, and at this restaurant you will find only Korean food. There are no hamburgers, no fried chickens."

He shuddered slightly at the thought of fried chicken, and reached up to tighten the knot on his tie.

"I believe you will find no barbecue here."

That night, through pointing and semaphore and walking around the restaurant to inspect other people's plates, we wound up with a very fine meal: crisp, griddle-fried potato pancakes with sprigs of chrysanthemum pressed into them; sweet, soft lengths of Korean blood sausage, and served with a tart chile dip; and warm, meaty-tasting slices of some cartilaginous animal part that we weren't able to identify but which was very pleasant with cold Korean beer. There was a dish that included slices of boiled pork, raw oysters, and a tangle of shredded radish kimchi, fiery-hot with chile—we wrapped them together in cabbage leaves and ate them like Korean tacos. We ate good, fist-size *mandoo*—like Korean kreplach—that floated in a peppery broth. We've been back and again, working our way through the pancake selection.

Good *bi bim bap* can be among the most delicious of Korean dishes, and Toad's is about the best in town. Arranged around the circumference of a flat bowl are a half-dozen little heaps of marinated vegetables—bean sprouts scented with sesame, stewed bamboo shoots, boiled spinach, that sort of thing—meant to be mixed together with hot rice, possibly augmented with the meat of a freshly fried fish. The contrast of hot and cool, salt and tart, soft and chewy is spectacular, and every bite offers a new and striking combination of flavors, right down to the bottom of the bowl. We didn't miss the barbecue at all.

LITTLE MALAYSIA

3944 N. PECK ROAD, NO. 8, EL MONTE; (626) 401-3188. TUES.–SUN., 11A.M.–9P.M.

We all know what happens when cultures collide in Los Angeles: strange hybrid foodstuffs like sashimi burritos or *kalbi* 'n' grits, odd cuisines like Salvadoran-Chinese, Japanese-Italian, and whatever the stuff at Eurochow is called. Most of the new restaurants on the Westside are awash in both risotto and wasabi vinaigrette, chipotle mayonnaise and Cajun seasoning. Quesadillas are likely to contain anything from Southwestern lamb stew to Chinese roast duck and, sometimes, even cheese. Nouvelle-cuisine chefs compete with Little Tokyo grandmothers for the best *yama imo* in the store.

But the concept of mix-and-match cuisine is nothing new in the world, and the whole cultural interaction thing was going on long before there was a Peter Sellars or David Byrne to note its existence. Look at Armenia, where Middle Eastern cooking runs headlong into the heavy peasant stews of Eastern Europe. Look at Malaysia, where Hokkienese food coexists with the spicy cooking of the immigrants from South India and the native, Indonesian-inflected cuisine of the Malay Muslims. Malaysian Chinese food is unlike any Chinese food in the world.

There aren't many Malaysian-Chinese restaurants in Southern California, and Little Malaysia is one of the best, a spare mini-mall joint in a strangely deserted stretch of El Monte. You've been to a hundred places like this one, with travel posters on the walls and soft hits on the radio; hot tea in water glasses and paper place mats on the tables. The owner's family serves, cooks, stuffs dumplings, and answers the phone. Little Malaysia seems to concentrate in the cooking of Penang, an island off Malaysia's west coast: a hot and spicy cuisine, liberal with such root spices as ginger and turmeric, tending more toward clean, sweet-and-sour flavors than toward the coconut-milk richness of much Malaysian and Indonesian food.

"Penang rolls" are thin crepes rolled around lettuce leaves into fat, steamed egg rolls, which in turn are wrapped around a sweetened forcemeat of sautéed root vegetables and toasted garlic. The steaming concentrates the flavors in a marvelous way. Penang *laksa* is made with pencil-thick noodles in a great, tart, tamarind-spiked fish broth. There are Penang sausages, Penang *mee* noodles, and spicy, Penang-style vegetables on weekends.

Kway ka involves stew-meat-size nuggets of rice noodle blasted with soy and spices over high heat until the edges crisp and become smoky, sort of a platonic ideal of Chinese *chow fun*. *Pie tee* are crunchy, thumb-size thimbles of fried pastry filled with sautéed vegetables. Slabs of bean curd are stuffed with delicious fish cakes and braised in light brown gravy. *Nasi lemak* is a Muslim specialty of coconut rice garnished with little piles of curried shrimp, spicy stewed vegetables, and a salty, chewy anchovy-peanut condiment that rivals any Northern Chinese fish-peanut dish.

When multiculturalism rears its head at Little Malaysia, things happen on the plate. In Singapore and Malaysia, Hainansese chicken-rice is as easy to find as a cheeseburger is in Westwood, a staple at every food court and the mainstay of every coffee shop. The dish—rice simmered in stock, accompanied by a chile dip and a few pieces of poached chicken—is easy to like. Little Malaysia's version of the rice, subtly fragrant with ginger, grains separate and just barely oily, is very fine, and the flavor of the chicken is clear and distinct. Curried fish head, a standard at Singapore's Indian restaurants, is delicately flavored and tartly sauced here, although the job of digging out the fish's cheeks, jowls, and lips is hardly a dainty one. Indian-style pancakes, *roti,* are crisp and savory, served with a side of tasty curried potato. With the meal, you drink iced tea, coffee with milk, or pungent iced passion fruit tea that may be to the pale beverage served at multi-cultural Melrose restaurants what Guinness Stout is to Miller Lite.

LIVING FISH CENTER

4356 BEVERLY BLVD., LOS ANGELES; (323) 953-1740. MON.–SAT., 1P.M.–MIDNIGHT.

The first cold night of fall, I went to the Living Fish Center, a small, superbly named Koreatown restaurant in whose window a brilliant neon trout burns in permanent midleap. Inside, a school of scarlet fish stare dumbly out from their dim tank, and a bubbling glass raceway teeming with prawns runs just below the ceiling. I am always happy to see swimming prawns.

From its name I had always inferred Living Fish Center to be a vivarium, a Korean analogue to Maine lobster pounds or posh Chinatown seafood palaces, but the restaurant seemed more like a roadhouse, really, a basic Korean cafe, sparsely populated with students and elderly Korean couples and knots of workers still in their technicians' overalls. A chef stood mute guard over what looked like a refrigerated counter borrowed from an ice cream parlor, and cards on each table advertised fantastically expensive dinners in blocky Hangul script.

A waitress handed me a plastic glass half filled with tepid tea that tasted mostly of detergent, then slid a small dish of oily toasted-rice gruel onto the menu-imprinted place mat.

It wasn't particularly good. The rubbery squid sautéed in spicy-sweet bean sauce, the clumsy fish chowder churning in its black iron pot, and the sugared, fried seaweed were hardly better. On the Korean sashimi platter, the slabs of tuna were still frozen, the whitefish dull, and the salmon had the funny, off-orange color of marshmallow peanuts.

More dishes arrived, part of the typical Korean generosity, including a whole fried fish, a foil tray packed with sautéed onions and diced shellfish, and half of a live sea urchin, spines still describing circles in the air, packed with mild, briny roe. (Fresh sea urchin bears the same relation to the stinky stuff you get at sushi bars that fresh bluefin tuna does to a can of Star Kist.)

It is never easy to intuit an Asian cafe's specialty on a first visit, and Seoul-food menus, where non-Koreans tend to be steered toward bland stews and grilled meat dishes, are often the most unfathomable of all.

It wasn't until we looked at the prawns leaping about the tank, and the chef behind the bar, and what seemed to be on the plates of half the customers, that we figured out what the restaurant's specialty might be. I said a couple of words to a waitress, and the chef came out from behind his counter and climbed up to the raceway containing the prawns.

He dipped a hand into the tank and rippled the still, clear water until some of the prawns sprang up to nip at his fingers. He plucked out the liveliest specimens and brought them back to his counter, where he stripped them of their shells. A few seconds later, the prawns were served on a mound of crushed ice—heads intact and very much alive.

It was among the most unsettling experiences I have ever had in a restaurant, preparing to bite into a living creature as it glared back at me, antennae whipping in wild circles, legs churning, body contorting as if to power the spinnerets that had been so rudely ripped from its torso, less at that moment a foodstuff than a creature that clearly did not want to be eaten.

I have consumed thousands of animals in my lifetime: seen lambs butchered, snipped the faces off innumerable soft-shell crabs, killed and gutted hundreds of fish. I had, I thought, come to terms with the element of predation inherent in eating meat, and I am thankful to the beasts that have nourished me. But this was the first time I had ever come up against one of the most basic of nature's postulates: You live; your prey dies. In order to eat, you must first rip into living flesh—not by proxy, not from a distance, not with a gun or knife, but intimately, with your teeth.

I thought about the Hindu cabby who had driven me back into town from a Singapore seafood restaurant years ago, lecturing me the entire way on the spirituality inherent in a single prawn, and I thought about my vegetarian friends who refuse to eat anything that once had a face.

I bit into the animal, devouring all of its sweetness in one mouthful, and I felt the rush of life pass from its body into mine, the sudden relaxation of its feelers, the blankness I swear I could see overtaking its eyes. It was weird and primal and breathtakingly good. And I don't want to do it again.

LOS TRES COCHINITOS

803 W. PACIFIC COAST HIGHWAY, WILMINGTON; (562) 549-0921. OPEN SEVEN DAYS, TWENTY-FOUR HOURS.

The last few times I drove down to Los Tres Cochinitos, which is a bustling Mexican restaurant among the tire stores and oil refineries of Wilmington, the place was out of *cecina de res*. It sort of bummed me out because Wilmington is a pretty fair drive from almost anywhere, and the *cecina* is so good: flat slabs of Mexican dried beef, sliced thin as poker chips and fried until they are black and crisp.

Two wide pieces cover nearly an entire plate and bubble like freshly cooked bacon. Each brittle mouthful—you don't really cut the stuff so much as snap off pieces with your fork—shatters into nuances of citrus and garlic and extreme well-doneness; sprightly jigs of carbon and lime. As far as I know, Los Tres Cochinitos—the Three Little Pigs, if you feel like translating—is the only place in the Southland where you can get the crunchy kind of *cecina*, although the Oaxacan places make pretty good versions of the chewy kind. Los Tres's *cecina* tastes not unlike Thai dry-fried beef. *Cecina* and a good fresh-tomato salsa make something close to the perfect taco.

Los Tres Cochinitos is less of a family restaurant than a Mexican-American version of Canter's Delicatessen, busy twenty-four hours a day, staffed by waitresses with attitude, most of the food less revelatory than well prepared, and famous for the health-giving properties of its soup—in this case the intense, vegetable-studded *cocido* that comes with most entrées. The place is all green tuck-'n'-roll booths and sparkling Formica; strange green-and-red drinks churn inside glass machines.

Los Tres is also known for its sweet, intense beef *barbacoa*; its brick-red pork *posole* with a nice, toasted-chile smack, and its dish of pork stewed with tomatoes and tender strips of cactus, *nopales*, that tastes a lot like the kind my wife's grandmother Lupe used to make. *Chile verde* is thinnish, long-stewed, and vibrant, with the clean, bright flavors of citrus and fresh chile and, not incidentally, hot enough to melt your fillings.

The seafood—catsupy octopus ceviche; shrimp in an acrid hot sauce, mushy fried fish—is forgettable; the insipid refried beans are nothing to write home about.

But a *quesadilla norteña*, stuffed with chewy bacon and gobs of melted cheese, is sensational junk food, and *bistecitos a la poblana*, squares of thin, grilled steak tossed with melted cheese, tomatoes, and peppers, is a classic beer snack, like a plate of nachos somebody decided to make with beef instead of the chips.

LU GI

539 W. VALLEY BLVD., SAN GABRIEL; (626) 457-5111. DAILY FOR LUNCH AND DINNER.

Behold the Sichuan hot pot, a pint or so of scarlet liquid frothing in a chafing dish, spitting up bloody geysers, roiling and bubbling around bits of meat and tofu like a sulfurous brimstone pool. You have tasted hot Asian food, no doubt, searing Thai curries and blistering Korean stews, but this is a heat of a different order, truly corrosive stuff, a pure tincture of chile and spice, thick as cream.

So saturated with fragrant steam that from the outside it vaguely resembles a sauna, the Taiwanese restaurant Lu Gi specializes in the fearsome Sichuan bowl of red, a cook-your-own spectacular that may be the perfect thing to eat on a chilly winter night.

Like Pink's, Roscoe's, and Chili John's, Lu Gi is essentially a one-dish restaurant and every table in the place seems to host an induction burner and a bubbling pot. (It is permissible to nibble on Taiwanese snacks, perhaps a seaweed salad or cheeselike slices of pressed tofu in a fairly powerful chile sauce of its own.) And if you are not Chinese, a waitress may well try to dissuade you from sitting down at a table.

"American people do not like this food, I think," one told me, grimacing slightly. "It is too . . . too . . . spicy."

When you manage to convince the staff that you won't even think of demanding *kung pao* chicken or pan-fried dumplings, a waitress will fetch a hot pot: a big, stainless-steel vessel fitted with two bowls, one filled with an innocuous clear broth and the other with the Disco Inferno. She clicks on the hot plate, and the broths immediately bubble to life.

With the basic hot pot—the broths, tofu, and vegetables—it is customary to order foods to cook in the boiling brews, perhaps vivid pink, frozen curls of meat, sliced black mushrooms, slivers of freeze-dried tofu, or plates piled high with dark Chinese greens. As with *shabu shabu*, you pick up a bit of meat with your chopsticks and swish it through the boiling broth for a few seconds until it is just cooked through, or drop it in and fish it out with a little strainer.

The chile broth is a perfect medium in which to cook gamy shavings of mutton, gelatinous chunks of beef tendon, and quivering blocks of tofu that pick up and amplify the strong undertones of garlic and spice. Delicate little fish balls, fillets of bass, and fresh shrimp dumplings are best simmered in the clear medium, and a waitress may hover for a few moments to make sure you don't drown them in the overpowering sea of red. Vegetables—try the crunchy slices of Chinese wintermelon—go anywhere, as do slithery rice noodles, which cook surprisingly quickly in the boiling soup.

By the end of the meal, when you have finished simmering a tableful of meat and greens in the broth, and it has boiled down to almost an espresso thimble of red goo, it is probably as caustic as lye, which you may well discover when your guts knot up five minutes into the drive home. Sometimes there is no pleasure without pain.

LUK YUE

123 N. GARFIELD AVE., MONTEREY PARK; (626) 280-2888. DAILY, 7A.M.–3A.M.

Luk Yue is the quintessential Cantonese greasy spoon, all hanging ducks, surging crowds, and giant bowls of rice porridge, tucked alongside a Cantonese supermarket in the heart of Cantonese Monterey Park, and open until three A.M. Luk

Yue is the Cantonese equivalent of Denny's—fast, informal, and extremely cheap—and I would not be surprised to hear that the small, brightly lit restaurant turns over five-hundred meals a day. The waiters are always too busy to translate the specials that are posted on the walls.

Luk Yue is not a fancy place: as soon as people sit down, they instinctively wipe their spoons and teacups dry of detergent-scented droplets; five minutes after their food arrives, they may have already eaten and gone.

Of course, the Chinese idea of what might be acceptable to eat, even at two in the morning, is very different from what a Denny's customer expects, so instead of patty melts you find dried squid with pigskin; instead of French fries, great, crunchy piles of Chinese broccoli with oyster sauce; instead of chili, bowls of anise-scented Cantonese beef stew with turnip.

If you've had a little too much to drink, pork blood sautéed with leeks might soak up the alcohol as readily as *menudo*. If you're broke, a single order of the extraordinary pan-fried chow mein noodles with spareribs and black-bean gravy— or skinny rice noodles fried with hunks of duck and bits of salty preserved greens, or curry-tinged Singapore vermicelli—will amply feed two for less than five bucks. (Stick with the pan-fried noodles here; the noodle soups tend to be ordinary.)

Everybody seems to start with golden wedges of fried, stuffed bean curd, crunchy outside and steamy, almost liquid, within, that you dunk in bowls of soy-based sauce and eat while they're still hot enough to blister your tongue.

Within the Chinese community, Luk Yue is probably best known for its excellent Cantonese barbecue: soy-sauce chicken, pork hock, and crispy roast duck, served either straight up or over rice. An order of roast pig is essentially an excuse to eat the crunchy strips of pigskin, tasty nutritional nightmares that come with a quarter-inch of melting pork fat still attached, and which are almost too rich to eat without a dab of *hoisin* to cut the grease.

"Assorted-barbecue rice" is roasted with barbecued meats in a superheated clay pot, and the juices from the sausages, pork hock, and Chinese slab bacon give the rice the deep, sweet flavor of really fresh pork. A drizzle of salty barbecue juices from the bowl served on the side moistens the rice further into sort of a Chinese risotto. The ginger-scented clay-pot rice with spareribs and black bean sauce may be even better, the kind of rank, powerful, utterly delicious Cantonese soul food that hardly ever makes it past the staff meal at Chinese restaurants any swankier than this.

LU'S GARDEN

534 E. VALLEY BLVD., SAN GABRIEL; (626) 280-5883. DAILY, 11:30A.M.–
1A.M.

The best restaurant in town? Who knows? And reasonable minds may disagree
on which restaurant offers the best value per dollar spent. But Lu's Garden is
hands down the fastest restaurant in Los Angeles County, a Taiwanese porridge
cafe where your food magically appears at the table about thirty seconds before
you do, a place where it is not unusual for patrons to eat lunch, pay, and leave
in less time—and for less money—than it takes most people just to pick up a
Big Mac at the drive-thru.

A few years ago, there were dozens of Taiwanese porridge restaurants in the
San Gabriel Valley, places specializing in a bland rice gruel spiked with soft
chunks of boiled sweet potato. A few cents got you a big bowl of the stuff; another
buck or two bought a few grams of minced beef, stewed tofu, or Chinese pickles
from a big steam table up front. Rice porridge fortified with sweet potatoes—a
cheap stew that can keep a human technically alive—was the invariable ration of
wartime Taiwan, and the porridge fad, which spread across both the San Gabriel
Valley and Taiwan itself, may have been more or less the equivalent of the American craze for Dean Martin and dry martinis.

At first glance, Lu's Garden is a fairly forbidding place. At noontime the line
extends out the door; at midnight the bare, low-ceilinged dining room resonates
with more dialects of Chinese than are taught in the East Asian languages department at Harvard. And unless you have actually spent a bit of time in Asia,
this is a style of eating you probably haven't experienced before. People behind
you will grumble if you haven't ordered your meal a couple of seconds after
you've reached the head of the line, and when you get to your table, it might
take a while to figure out what to do with the mounds of braised fresh soybeans,
the coils of pig intestines, the heaps of tiny whole anchovies that you may have
chosen in your panic.

Actually, Lu's classic porridge-house cooking is similar to the food you may
have eaten at places like Mandarin Deli; there is a wide assortment of simmered
things—dried tofu, hog parts, sautéed chicken, plus an assortment of Chinese
salads—but fortified by the gruel rather than by the more usual noodles and
dumplings. This tends to be the sort of homey fare you might see at dinner at a
Chinese friend's house, but rarely in restaurants: whole tiny squid sautéed in dark
soy sauce; ground pork simmered with a handful of winter pickles; briskly garlicked seaweed salad; cold, chopped mustard greens. And it's easy to order—you
get three items per person for the lunch special; at supper time, when the portions
are three times the size, you order the dishes one by one to be shared family style.
Go for fish, a pickle, and a vegetable. Try something you've never seen before.

The women behind the counter are always helpful, eager to explain that the sliced pig's belly with leeks is a better bet than the stewed pork stomach, to subtly guide you toward a plate that's both balanced in flavor and nutritious. There are no translation problems at Lu's: If you want the fried belt fish (and you should—the crisp, salty, oily lengths of the imported fish are worth every one of the bones you are going to have to pick out of your teeth), just point at it.

Lu's is not the sort of restaurant for people who are phobic about food touching on a plate. In fact, creating ideal combinations of meats and vegetables in your bowl of porridge is rather the point of the exercise, the sweet grease leaking out of a sliced Chinese sausage providing ideal counterpoint to the tartness of pickled mustard greens; the smoky heat of cold, sliced tripe slicked with chile oil contrasting just so with bland, juicy slabs of broth-simmered tofu.

M

M & M CAFE

9506 AVALON BLVD., LOS ANGELES; (323) 777-9250. TUES.-SAT., 8A.M.-
8P.M.

M & M soul-food restaurants, most of them good, are nearly as common as
Burger King in South Central Los Angeles. But the original restaurant in the
sprawling chain, a small, window-barred cafe on a tidy strip of auto-repair shops
and storefront churches a few blocks north of Watts, is, simply, what most of us
are hoping for every time we step into a soul-food cafe: a spare, well-scrubbed
place, decorated with a state-map calendar from a Mississippi funeral home, that
serves gargantuan portions of perfect southern food.

A jukebox is well stocked with soul oldies. Firey-brand hot sauce and pepper
vinegar sit on the tables. A security guard hangs out in a corner, perpetually
nursing a plate of chicken wings. The dining room always smells like Thanksgiving. In a part of town where "country" can sometimes be taken as an insult, the
M & M Café is country in the best sense of the word, an outpost of rural
Mississippi in one of the most urbanized areas on earth.

Each day, there are about half a dozen entrées to choose from. You get to
choose three side dishes with your meal: stewed collard greens, candy-sweet yams,
rice and gravy, green beans cooked with potatoes so long that they fall apart when
you look at them, and perfect, creamy macaroni and cheese. This is the place for
sweetened iced tea served in tumblers so immense you can barely get one hand
around them; fresh lemonade that tastes the way your grandmother's probably
did; crusty, dense corn muffins with slabs of margarine.

A pan-grilled T-bone steak, blackened and sinewy, comes to the table, well
done but still full of juice, smacked with black pepper, garnished with a big pile
of black-rimmed grilled onions and a puddle of steak gravy—it may be the manliest meal in Los Angeles.

Short ribs, an occasional daily special, are bigger than most restaurants' long ribs, smoked and peppered like pastrami, glazed with brown gravy; oxtails, stewed to the gelatinous richness you might associate with a $50 *queue de boeuf* in a Michelin-starred Parisian restaurant, are as good as you'll find outside of l'Orangerie. Fried catfish—two whole fish to an order—are crisp and meaty; even turkey wings with stuffing are swell. If you have not stuffed yourselves insensate, there are giant bowls of peach cobbler. If your belly isn't distended, you don't feel like taking a nap and you don't have a stunned, happy smile on your face, you haven't really given M & M its due.

MA DANG GOOK SOO

869 S. WESTERN AVE., KOREATOWN; (213) 487-6008. DAILY, 8A.M.–10P.M.

Tokyo has its share of noodle shops; so do, one must concede, Taipei, Hong Kong, and Seoul. But Los Angeles may have a bigger variety of Asian noodles than any city in the world, bowls of *pho* and skeins of *soba*, hand-pulled *mein* and hand-pulled *udon*, Filipino *mami* and Polynesian long rice, Malaysian *laksa* and Sumatran *bakmi*, noodles from Thailand, Burma, Cambodia, Laos, Sri Lanka . . . from practically every noodle-eating culture in the East.

Not least among these are the many noodles of Korea, which range from delicate herb-scented North Korean noodles to the robustly chewy potato starch noodles that dwell at the bottom of funky bowls of cold organ-meat broth, from the pencil-size rice noodles sautéed in chile paste to the extremely Korean version of hand-thrown *chachiang mein*. Korea is as much a noodle culture as Vietnam (the latest Korean craze is Vietnamese noodles; a dozen or so brand-new *pho* parlors, all serving a B-minus version of the ubiquitous Vietnamese beef-noodle soup, popped up last year in Koreatown).

I have eaten hundreds of bowls of Korean noodles over the years. But not until I stumbled into Ma Dang Gook Soo, a Korean noodle shop tucked into a corner of a big Koreatown mall, had I ever tasted what are probably the signature noodles of Korea, the thin, handcut, wheaten noodles known as *gook soo*. To understand Korean food without trying a bowl of *gook soo* is almost like trying to understand the concept behind Italian pasta without ever having tasted spaghetti. Everything else is just a noodle.

Ma Dang is a homey place, a tiny bit of Korean countryside fitted next to a *soontofu* place and facing out, past an iron security fence, onto churning Western Avenue. The walls are lined with rustic rice-paper screens, like the Korean equivalent of Japanese shoji, and are hung with mural-size photographs of a muddy Korean village that seems largely populated by chickens. A long line of people usually curls past the wooden benches outside the door of the restaurant, and even-

189

tually a waitress will come out to take your order, which will be ready—along with a few different kinds of *kimchi* and a cup of barley tea—as soon as you sit down.

There is a decent sort of *bi bim bap* at Ma Dang, mounds of simmered "mountain vegetable," bean sprouts and greens topped with a runny fried egg, and vegetarian sushi—the establishment is liberal enough in their definition of "vegetable" to include a little sliver of hot dog in the roll. You can get most of the common kinds of Korean noodle here too, elastic potato-starch noodles in chile paste, sweet rice-cake noodles, noodles made from mung beans, and noodles made from buckwheat. But mostly, there is *gook soo.*

Gook soo, especially as interpreted here, is a marvelous noodle, flat and slightly stretchy, about the size of fettucine but more fragile somehow, knife-cut from a thin sheet of rolled dough. The basic *gook soo,* identified on the menu as "handmade noodle," is served in a broth based on dried anchovies, clear and slightly earthy, garnished with seaweed, *kimchi,* or bits of meat, concealing a few chunks of boiled potato, and adding a presence—a depth—to the noodles, which seem almost to melt into it. (Chicken *gook soo* is bathed instead in a thick, white chicken broth, whose body—like that of Korean beef soup—seems enriched with the milky meat proteins that Western cooks tend to filter out.) You can eat the *gook soo* as is or spike it with the restaurant's marvelous chile-scallion condiment.

A Korean friend practically collapsed with nostalgic longing when she tasted Ma Dang's cold *gook soo* bathed in fresh soy milk, embellished with julienned cucumber, a few drops of sesame oil, and very little else, a minimalist noodle for the hottest day of summer.

MADHU'S DASAPRAKASH

11321 E. 183RD ST., CERRITOS; (562) 924-0879. TUES.-SUN., 11:30A.M.-2:30P.M. AND 5:30P.M.-9:30P.M. (FRI. UNTIL 10P.M.); FRI., SAT., AND SUN., 11:30A.M.-10P.M. ALSO 12217 SANTA MONICA BLVD., WEST LOS ANGELES; (310) 820-9477.

If you give it half a chance, you may become as infatuated as I am with the *pessret* at Madhu's Dasaprakash, which is a thoroughly discovered South Indian vegetarian restaurant a short *iddly*-toss to the west from Artesia's Little India strip. *Pessret,* which at first glance may look more like a working maquette for an Eero Saarinen structure than like anything you might possibly eat, is a beige, lentil-flour pancake with the dull, smooth sheen of a freshly pressed pair of gabardine slacks, as big around as a phonograph record, and bent into a kind of postboomerang curvilinear shape. The thin, crisp edges work to a slight, sour chewiness at the center. The pancake encloses a mixture of green chile and minced raw onion—a sort of elegant counterpoint of slight bitternesses—and the package is as spicy-hot as an East L.A. taco.

Pessret, of course, is not the only decent thing at Madhu's Dasaprakash, nor is it even considered a house specialty. The waiter, in fact, may insist that you try the restaurant's famous version of *masala dosa,* a rice-lentil pancake wrapped around a mound of spicy onion-potato glop, before he will let you order the *pessret* at all. Dasaprakash is truly an international house of pancakes. *Rava dosai* are crisp, lacy pancakes made from the South Indian equivalent of Cream of Wheat; *oothapam* are lentil-pancakes with tomatoes or onions. At the end of your pancake feast, the table will be littered with little steel bowls of *sambhar,* the thin, lightly curried lentil broth that is to South Indian pancakes what maple syrup is to American ones.

Dasaprakash, which is affiliated with a family-run chain of hotels back in South India, began its life here as a hippyish place up on La Cienega before it moved to a Cerritos shopping center near the hub of Little India. Many people in the Indian community consider Dasaprakash—along with Rajdoot in Artesia and perhaps Chameli in Rosemead—to be one of the very few serious Indian restaurants in Southern California. And a newish branch perched atop a fancy West L.A. mini-mall brings world-class Indian food to that side of town for the first time.

The intricately spiced cashew fritters called *pakodas* have the crumbly texture of pecan sandies; the fried bean patties called *medhu vadai* look like Donut Gems but taste of cardamom and clean oil. *Idli* are the usual steamed, madeleine-size discs of fermented rice, but the version called *conjeevaram iddly* is studded with cashews, chiles, and whole spices, and tastes like a Christmas cookie possessed by the devil. *Bondas* are fried, blandish Ping-Pong balls of lentils or mashed potatoes that benefit from a dab or two of the spicy mint-laced chutney. A *thali* plate, more or less an Indian TV dinner, includes the crisp puff called *puri,* and a trayful of *sambals* and sauces in which to dip it.

After the fritters and pancakes, you should probably get *uppuma,* a dramatic mound of steamed semolina that is flavored with sweet onions but that is probably two-thirds butter by weight—a teacupful of the stuff serves about six. *Bisi bele huli anna,* which might be the South Indian version of the Venetian rice dish *risi e bisi* (you'll have to consult Marco Polo), combines rice, lentils, a slug of chiles, and probably an entire stick of butter—to incredibly rich effect. Great Southern Indian cooking may be vegetarian, but it's not precisely health food.

MAE PLOY

2606 W. SUNSET BLVD., SILVER LAKE; (213) 353-9635. DAILY, 10A.M.–
10P.M.

Hard by a Silver Lake swarm of Colombian, Salvadoran, and Filipino dives, near the famous wounded-foot sign that spins outside a podiatrist's office, Mae Ploy is the kind of Thai restaurant that everybody needs in their neighborhood, a place stocked with egg rolls and stir-fries and *pad Thai* noodles but also terrific Bangkok-cosmopolitan food: hot curries, Isaan-style salads, and complex, vegetable-laden soups.

Thai customers seem mostly to order to-go food from a steam table out front, stocked with the usual curries and chile-speckled fried fish; everybody else—black and white, Asian and Latino, gay and straight, affluent and slacker—crowds into the separate dining room, pounding Thai iced tea and crunching sweet-sauced wedges of fried bean curd. (For some reason, a lot of my favorite Thai restaurants have a large Central American following.)

As at a lot of Bangkok-style restaurants, the best food involves salads and snacks. Eggplant salad is smoky and warm, garnished with thinly sliced red onions and crumbles of soft tofu; a warm duck *larb* is nice if a little livery; bamboo-shoot salad, gritty with toasted rice, has the pungent gaminess peculiar to that vegetable.

There is a good version of the northern Thai salad *nam sod*, ground pork sautéed with chiles, peanuts, citrus, onions, and vegetables. It's served barely warm, with the traditional crunchy garnish of pig's ear that most places leave out, but its crunchiness and slightly gelatinous richness gives the dish its special character. Another salad involves catfish, coarsely chopped, mixed with slivers of hot chile, then fried into a tan, porous mass: rich yet not too oily, dressed with chile, fish sauce, and citrus, superbly crunchy.

And if the main dishes tend to be less interesting than the specials and the first courses, most of them—whole fried pompano served with the usual sweetish chile sauce, chicken in a gentle green curry, pepper-garlic shrimp—are at least competent.

MAGIC CARPET

8566 W. PICO BLVD., LOS ANGELES; (310) 652-8507. MON.–THURS.,
11A.M.–10P.M.; FRI., 11A.M.–3 PM; SUN., 9A.M.–10P.M.

As an agricultural center, Yemen produced the world's first coffee. As a center of music, it inspired much of what passes for Israeli dance music. But in Tel Aviv, where much of the huge and ancient Yemenite-Jewish community has gathered in the last hundred years, Yemenite culture may be most appreciated around dinnertime: Yemenite soups and salads—and the ubiquitous peppery Yemenite spice blend called *hawaiji*, fragrant with cardamom and turmeric—can be found almost everywhere in Israel.

Magic Carpet is widely considered to be the best kosher restaurant in Los Angeles. It is also probably the best Middle Eastern restaurant of any sort on the Westside, the equal of Hollywood's Marouch and Alhambra's Wahib's. In Tel Aviv, Yemenite restaurants are known for their bewildering array of eggplant condiments, and Magic Carpet may have more kinds of cool eggplant salad than all other restaurants in town put together. There are a coarse sort of eggplant pâté and slivers of marinated eggplant; a fiery-hot eggplant jam called *madbucha* and a cool salad of chopped eggplant with tomato; garlicky Bulgarian eggplant and a smooth, unctuous eggplant in tahini, which is the restaurant's version of *baba ghanoush*. On the eggplant combination plate, the salads are arranged like spokes on a wheel. And for another couple of bucks, you can add Moroccan spiced carrots, hummus, and the house's pale, minted version of tabbouleh, much heavier on the bulgur wheat than the Lebanese tabboulehs you may have tasted.

It took me a surprisingly long time to discover this restaurant given that my first apartment, a tiny walkup over a kosher butcher shop, was just a couple of blocks from here. If I had tasted Magic Carpet's *melawach* back then, I might never have moved. *Melawach*—a bronzed, pizza-size fried Yemenite pancake that seems to have a hundred levels of wheatiness, a thousand layers of crunch and the taste of clean oil—is one of the greatest dishes in Los Angeles. You can do practically anything with a *melawach*, and Magic Carpet does, topping it with cinnamon and toasted nuts or crumbles of ground beef, a spicy confit of sautéed vegetables or an omelet.

The best way to eat *melawach*, perhaps, is one of the simplest: sprinkled with the spice mixture called *za'atar*, whose sumac-tartness and wild-thyme pungency marry perfectly with the rich denseness of the pancake. (*Melawach* with *za'atar* is a kissing cousin to the *za'atar* bread Armenians eat for breakfast.) *Melawach*, eggplant, and a bowl of the divine lentil soup—who could ask for more?

The hot appetizer plate includes warm stuffed grape leaves; the ubiquitous Moroccan "cigars," crisp thumbs of fried pastry stuffed with a highly spiced meat paste; and some of the best falafel balls you will ever taste. The *margaz*—tiny, coarse lamb sausages similar to the Moroccan *merguez*—are quite spicy; the bland little *kibbe*, fried bulgur-wheat capsules stuffed with beef and pine nuts, are not.

Unfortunately, as at almost all Middle Eastern restaurants, the main courses are almost beside the point: juiceless lamb shanks, dryish chicken stained yellow with saffron and turmeric, tilapia fillets glazed with chile-intensive tomato sauce.

The beef dishes on the menu are marked with asterisks denoting "Lubavitch meat," which I assume is as kosher as it is possible for beef to get, but the kebabs and the cardamom-laced beef stew are tough, without much flavor.

Desserts at Magic Carpet run toward the mousse cake and the tiramisu, and, since this is a kosher restaurant, toward the dairy-free versions of those. Still, as this will not be the lightest meal you have ever eaten, why not finish with a pot of fresh-mint tea?

MAGO'S

4500 S. CENTINELA AVE., CULVER CITY; (800) 900-MAGO. LUNCH AND DINNER, MON.–SAT.

We can be proud of many things, we Americans, from the Declaration of Independence to Elliott Carter's string quartets, from quantum physics to the interstate highway system, from Martha Stewart to the . . . Spamburger. Which is to say, an inch-thick slab of Spam, seared on a hot griddle and slid into a toasted hamburger bun with ketchup, mustard, tomatoes, and lettuce. A Spamburger is crisp, the Spam part of it anyway, which is abundantly speckled with those crunchy black bits, and sort of sweet—actually, very sweet, a corrosive, penetrating sweetness that lingers on your palate for about the same length of time as the faded pomegranate notes in a great, old Côte Rotie. You've heard of those nuanced lunch-counter hamburgers where each ingredient lends its own layer of crunch and the meat patty acts almost as a savory condiment? This isn't that, baby. A Spamburger is all about the Spam, its cloying, porky essence, the overgenerous nature of salty, fatty food manufactured for and revered by folks for whom salty, fatty food is, or used to be, the ultimate in unobtainable luxury. Spam is what this country is all about, two cars in every garage and a pig in every can. Spam tastes like America.

Spamburgers with sliced avocado and teriyaki sauce taste even more like America, or certain parts of it anyway, at least as served at Mago's, the Culver City hamburger stand that is to Westside Japanese-Americans what El Tepeyac is to Eastsiders and Pancho's is to people who grew up in the South Bay. I used to go to Mago's a fair amount in the late '70s, and even then I was astonished by the diversity of the burger stand's menu. You could get a million different kinds of shakes back then, and every variety of fast food prepared in every possible way. I also had such oddities as fried calamari tacos, teriyaki sticks threaded with avocado, *taquitos* with soy-laced guacamole, and a cherry soda so good that I can still conjure up the particular tingle of it today. (None of which are on the menu anymore, although you can still get regular teri sticks, *taquitos*, and fried wonton.)

Mago's may have been chopped and channeled, outfitted with an indoor seating area and a beer-and-wine license, acres of bright Formica and an array of smiling cat totems, but it really hasn't changed much—if you discount the fact that nothing about the place really seems that weird anymore. There are a whole lot of Hawaiians in the neighborhood now, so the existence of classic teriyaki plate lunches—one scoop mac, two scoops rice—is less than an oddity.

The neighborhood (and the staff) leans Chicano—across the street from Mago's is the classic, East L.A.–style Taqueria Sanchez—so the street-level fusion, the tricultural incorporation of Asian ingredients into Mexican structures with American flavors, seems almost natural. Witness the delicious tacos stuffed with slippery chunks of ripe avocado and slices of sweet, red-rimmed barbecued pork. Note the fat burritos swelling with grilled strips of teriyaki-greased beef, avocado, and cheese, or the hamburgers composed of *chashu* and avocado, or really, the resplendent Spamburger. Which, as we've previously noted, tastes like America. Don't miss the banana shakes.

MAMITA

714 S. BRAND BLVD., GLENDALE; (818) 243-5121. SUN.–THURS., 11:30A.M.–8:30P.M.; FRI. AND SAT. 11:30A.M.–9P.M.

Papas a la huancaina, a potato appetizer from Peru's central Andean highlands, may be the closest thing there is to a Peruvian national dish. It is the automatic appetizer in nearly every eating place in the country, from the most basic *picanterías* to the fanciest white-tablecloth restaurants; it is served at bus-station snack bars and in airplane meals, at high mountain inns and seaside resorts. The standard form of the dish—cool, sliced potatoes in a violently yellow sauce of cheese, annato, and mild chiles—is about as simple as it is possible for food to get, only slightly more challenging to prepare than a tuna sandwich. In a country as obsessed with its hundred-odd kinds of potatoes as the French are with their cheeses, *papas a la huancaina* may be the only potato dish everybody in the country can agree on.

I suppose I have tasted three or four dozen versions of *papas a la huancaina*, from chefly, caviar-topped hors d'oeuvres served with *pisco* sours to giant, peasanty logs of spud. Still, although I tend to order the dish in Peruvian restaurants as reflexively as I do guacamole in a Mexican place, I've never really understood the point of the stuff. Most of it tastes like liquefied Velveeta on refrigerator-cold potatoes; something to douse with fiery green Peruvian chile purée—*ají*—and nibble before the real food shows up.

Mamita is a clean, solid Peruvian cafe on Glendale's auto row, the friendly, basic kind of restaurant you'd be delighted to discover in a working-class quarter of Callao. The menu, though almost 120 items long, essentially rings variations on the half-dozen Asian-tinged dishes you'll find in Lima's Chinese-run dives. It is hard to have dinner here without eating about a half-pound of sweet red onions, which the chef seems to throw, sautéed or cut into thin rings, into everything but dessert.

Mamita, like most Peruvian joints with seafood-restaurant ambitions, is fairly deft at deep-fried stuff, most of it on the well-done side: marinated squid, fish, or chicken *chicharrones* fried to resemble salty, crunchy pork cracklings; garlicky fried spare ribs that have the almost appealing funkiness of overcooked pork; and a decent *jalea*, the famous Callao-style equivalent of the Captain's Platter at Long John Silver.

There are the basic, Peruvian-style stir-fries—Chinese technique applied to Peruvian ingredients—ubiquitous in L.A.-area Peruvian restaurants: *tallarin*, which is *saltado*, and *chaufa*.

Mamita serves the definitive *papas a la huancaina* in Los Angeles: room-temperature sliced potatoes cooked just past al dente to a point where they are just about the consistency of thickly sliced jack cheese. I like the dance of contrasts between the dense sauce and the slightly denser spud, between the clear, slightly acid flavor of the potato and the richness of the cheese, all of which project the illusion that you are eating a single substance with many complexities, as opposed to a tuber with a sauce. *Papas a la huancaina* may be more or less the Kraft Dinner of Peru, but when executed carefully, it can be powerfully good.

MANDARIN DELI

727 N. BROADWAY; (213) 623-6054. SUN.–WED., 11A.M.–8P.M.; FRI. AND SAT., 11A.M.–8P.M.

For a long time, everybody went to the original Mandarin Deli, which was the essential sticky-table noodle shop in Chinatown, all giant bowls and gusts of garlic, little plates of jellyfish, wall signs, and hungry crowds looking longingly at your chair. There were dumplings that turned out to be filled with soup when you bit into them (now off the menu), great fish dumplings, and the best potstickers anyone had ever tasted. The potstickers were the quintessence of fried food: crisp, flat, and slightly charred on the side where the dumplings seared in the pan, soft and rounded on the other side, stuffed with a mince of pork and scallion. Mandarin Deli's potstickers were—and are—seemingly greaseless but bursting with juice and garlic and the flavor of hot oil.

Then branches and spinoffs seemed to open everywhere there was a substantial concentration of Chinese. The newer places tended to be a bit grander, a bit spiffier, and the Chinatown location lost a little of its allure. Around lunchtime,

The Little Tokyo Mandarin Deli almost seemed like an adjunct of the *Los Angeles Times* cafeteria.

But while the other branches of the chain may serve Mongolian beef and *kung-pao* shrimp, ice water and Japanese beer, the Chinatown restaurant remains almost Stalinist in its noodle-shop rigor: What you get here are noodles and dumplings, with maybe a few marinated cold dishes to nosh on while you wait. It is the essential Chinese deli menu, and the food is primal and good. If you ask for rice, you may be directed to a restaurant at the other end of the mall. If two people split one bowl of noodles between them, the waiters may scowl until you tack on an order of dumplings or a pressed-tofu salad or something.

And while there may be better noodle shops now, the Mandarin Deli is still the standard by which all Chinese noodle shops may be judged. Like the pastrami sandwich at Langer's and La Brea Bakery bread, the existence of Mandarin Deli is a solid argument for living in Los Angeles.

Seaweed salad—julienned strips of the crunchy sea plant as elusively briny as a Hog Island oyster—is slightly sweet and sour, seasoned with an astonishing quantity of garlic; an order may be the best two bucks you could ever spend in a restaurant. Peanuts boiled with star anise and celery become something halfway on the continuum between nut and vegetable. Stewed tendon comes to the table still warm, a plate of slippery, luxurious food, heavily garlicked and vibrating with the sharp taste of fresh scallion greens. Even the stewed beef tripe is good, chewy and fragrant with soy sauce and anise.

The key to ordering noodle dishes at any Mandarin Deli is to specify the handmade noodles, which means you'll get wide, thick, square-cut noodles that are something like fettucine on steroids. They taste much better in rich pork stock or in a searing chilied broth than the spaghettilike noodles you would get instead. Handmade noodle soup with spicy chile: that's the ticket. "Ground flour" soup noodles are a little like Chinese spaetzle, in a sort of thick, egg-spiked broth; "square noodles" are little pasta hankies in more or less the same eggy soup. The cold noodles tossed with sesame paste, slivered cucumber, and chicken are exemplary.

The best reason to choose the Chinatown Mandarin Deli over the other branches is the availability of fish dumplings—airy, steamy things filled with a loose, fragrant mousse of whitefish and chopped greens that could serve as a specialty of any high-priced "Pacific Rim" restaurant in town. Except these are much better.

MANDARIN HOUSE

3074 W. EIGHTH ST., KOREATOWN; (213) 386-8976. LUNCH AND DINNER DAILY.

In the heart of Emilia-Romagna, twenty miles east of Modena and ten minutes in a rented Alfa from the tiny town of Nonantola, the single best pasta restaurant in the world sits in the middle of the grape fields, a simple, farm-structure-looking thing with a half-dozen Lamborghini tractors parked out front and some picnic tables out in back, crowded with shirtsleeved businessmen who've downed too much homemade grappa to make it back to Modena without a cab. The hand-rolled *garganelli* in Bolognese sauce, a fugue of slippery texture and long-simmered spice, are good enough to bring tears to your eyes; the paper-thin *tagliatelle* are hardly worse. It's the kind of pasta made by women who measure weeks in flour and seasons in egg yolks, and every fold and crevice of noodle can seem eloquent as a sigh.

I think about that plate of *garganelli* whenever I tuck into an order of *chachiang mein* at Mandarin House, an unassuming Chinese place in Koreatown that serves extraordinary hand-pulled noodles.

The pasta, spaghetti-shaped strands varying from phone-wire-thick to vermicelli-thin, are heaped unadorned into one large soup bowl; the sauce, a musky, tar-black thing made with garlic, fermented black beans, sautéed onions, and both ground and shredded meat, occupy most of another. The noodles—stretchy, bouncy things, perfectly al dente, with a slight surface tackiness and a nicely developed wheat flavor—are delicious enough to eat a lot of either by themselves or daubed with a bit of the fresh-chile condiment on the table.

Topped with a few spoonfuls of the sauce, the noodles become extraordinary, trapping quantities of meat and oil that vary from strand to strand, and each mouthful is different enough to power a hungry person to the bottom of the noodle bowl—a hungry person obsessed with finding the perfect bite, anyway. With the Korean-style free appetizers—slivers of raw onion served with thick salty soy jam, which is better than it sounds, and really fiery pickled cabbage—a bowl of noodles can be a dinner for two.

If you didn't know these noodles were here, you'd never find them. Mandarin House is as average as a Chinese restaurant can get—a low building stuck in a Koreatown mini-mall, furnished with red vinyl booths and sticky tables, dining room stacked with cases of beer. And if you attempt to order anything but the hand-thrown noodles, you will wonder why you bothered.

MANDARIN SHANGHAI

970 N. BROADWAY, CHINATOWN; (213) 625-1195. DAILY, 11:30A.M.– 9:30P.M.

Caught up as some of us are in pursuit of the impossibly great Chinese restaurant, we are sometimes blinded to the not inconsiderable virtues of the pretty good Chinese restaurant: a place that is conveniently located, open early and late, cheerful about takeout, and blessed with both easy parking and a huge menu of fresh and amusing food. At a great Chinese restaurant, it is easy to worry too much about whether you are ordering properly, whether the steamed carp is a better choice than the rock cod, or whether the Chinese-language signs on the walls represent amazing seasonal delicacies you will never get to taste. At a pretty good Chinese restaurant, you eat what you always eat.

In the last ten years, I suppose I have eaten as often at Chinatown's Mandarin Shanghai as I have at any other Chinese restaurant. There have been quick mid-afternoon meals; takeout on the way home from work; Chinese dinners out with assorted toddlers; intimate, long lunches; and elaborate dinners before the opera. The neon-lit Mandarin Shanghai, affiliated somehow with the family that runs the Mon Kee seafood restaurants, was once reputed to be the best Shanghainese restaurant in Los Angeles, with a broad repertoire of the sweetish braised and baked dishes of eastern China. It has been surpassed by several San Gabriel kitchens, but there was a time when if you wanted roast yellow fish in brown sauce, sea cucumbers with shrimp roe, or a dish of sautéed eel, this was pretty much the only place to go.

If you've eaten in many Shanghainese restaurants, you know what to expect: appetizer plates of bony, smoked fish; hacked bits of cool chicken marinated in rice wine; a vivid pink terrine of cured pork; chewy vegetarian "duck" sculpted from black mushrooms and bamboo shoots. You won't do badly with the standbys of shredded pork with salty pickled vegetables, Chinese watercress sautéed with preserved bean curd, or coins of sliced rice noodle fried with pork and leeks.

The same few dishes seem to make it onto on the tables of almost all the Chinese customers. Here you'll find what used to be the definitive version of dry-fried string beans in Los Angeles, seared in a blistering hot wok, glazed with a classically pungent sauce of pork, garlic, black beans, and too much oil, slightly smoky, with that crisp-tender sweetness that usually stays locked within string beans. The steamed lion's-head meatballs may be the best food in the restaurant, big and fluffy, decked out with ruffly manes of cabbage, fragrant with garlic and star anise, bathed in half an inch of the mother of all brown sauces.

The restaurant specializes in earthen-pot entrées, soupy things served in great clay vessels as big around as satellite dishes, and first among these is the fish-head earthen pot—the front half of a gigantic carp stewed in an aromatic stock, laced with sharply spicy chiles, and mellowed with bean paste. The rest of the fish, one presumes, finds its way into the popular dish of fish tail braised with a seemingly infinite amount of garlic cloves.

I've had better braised fish tail—sharper, more finely textured, less oily—and you probably have too. The fish head, like most of the food here, is merely pretty good. But pretty good is enough sometimes, and Mandarin Shanghai is one of the most useful restaurants in Chinatown.

MARIO'S PERUVIAN SEAFOOD

5786 MELROSE AVE., HOLLYWOOD; (323) 466-4181. MON.–THURS., 11A.M.–8P.M.; FRI. AND SAT., 11A.M.–9:30P.M.; SUN., 9:30A.M.–8P.M.

In polyethnic Los Angeles, where Japanese cooks prepare Jewish-Mexican food for African Americans and Thai people make Italian food that Salvadorans like to eat, Peruvian restaurants are sometimes the most polyethnic of all.

The most famous Los Angeles Peruvian restaurant is, of course, Matsuhisa, the Peruvian-inflected Beverly Hills post-neo–sushi bar that most people think of as straight Japanese even though the chef douses the fish with an awful lot of garlic.

As in much of South and Central America, the restaurants in Peru are mostly run by cooks of Asian descent. In Los Angeles, what we think of as Peruvian food is often Peruvian-Chinese food, a cuisine inflected by Asian flavors and cooking techniques, of Peruvian ingredients and appetites. It's what Peruvians expect when they go out to eat, if not exactly what they eat at home.

In a mini-mall on the corner of Melrose and Vine, down the street from the musician's union, Mario's Peruvian Seafood Restaurant is as bi-ethnic as they come. The cooks are Asian; the waitresses Peruvian. The walls are decorated with pictures of *campesinos* and llamas and gory bleeding Jesuses; above the serving counter sit plaster Japanese good-luck cats, paws raised in greeting. Across the street is a well-stocked liquor store where you can pick up a six-pack of Sapporo to drink with your dinner. (Mario's has no alcohol license, and the house beverage, a plum-colored corn drink violently flavored with cloves—*chicha morada*—may be too close to Kool-Aid for your taste.)

The repertoire of Asian-Peruvian cuisine consists essentially of variations on just three dishes, and Mario's prepares them as well as anyone. *Chaufa* is Peruvian fried rice, which is a spicy, garlic-drenched version of the standard Chinese-restaurant stuff. *Saltado* is a salty, delicious stir-fry that includes limp French fries as the main vegetable ingredient and plenty of onion, tomato, and chile. *Tallarin* is chow mein made with spaghetti, stir-fried in a hot pan until it chars slightly

200

and picks up a nice smoky flavor you might associate with decent Cantonese *chow fun*. You can have any of these fried with chicken, shrimp, or a spicy mixture of squid, octopus, and shrimp.

Still, the orthodox Peruvian food at Mario's tends to be more interesting than the straight *chifa* stuff. Mario's serves a classic version of the Peruvian shrimp chowder *chupe de camarones*, a big bowl of chile-red soup, mellowed with milk, thickened with great quantities of beaten egg, and topped with a giant crouton of freshly fried bread. Half a boiled potato is sunk at the bottom of the bowl—in a Peruvian restaurant, you're never far from a potato—and several big shrimp, still in their shells and barely jelled by the heat of the broth, float at the top. The basic taste is not unlike a shrimp-flavored variation on peppery cream gravy. (*Sopa a la criolla*, which is basically the same thing made with beef in place of the shrimp and noodles in place of the crouton, isn't nearly as good.)

Chicharron de pollo is something like Peruvian Chicken McNuggets, heavily breaded chunks of bird fried hard to resemble pigskin and served with an herbed, citric dipping sauce as vividly yellow as a happy-face emblem. And on Sundays there's usually *tallarin verde*, Chinese spaghetti sauced with an intense, creamy pesto and topped with a thin grilled steak. *Tallarin verde* is the kind of tri-ethnic dish that could only have originated in Peru.

MAROUCH

4905 SANTA MONICA BLVD., HOLLYWOOD; (323) 662-9325. TUES.–SUN., 11A.M.–11P.M.

The Lebanese cafe Marouch is probably the best-known Middle Eastern restaurant in Los Angeles, an East Hollywood mini-mall storefront with a clean '80s look, TV sets blaring belly-dance videos, and large photographs of cedars plastered in niches. Mercedes and stretch Rolls-Royces mingle with primer-colored B-210s in the parking lot out front—the prices are what the kind of people who have too much money call "practically free."

If you go to parties in Silver Lake, you've probably eaten Marouch's rice-stuffed grape leaves and *baba ganoush* a few more times than you realize.

When I lived in the neighborhood, I stopped by Marouch at least twice a week, midmornings for a piece of baklava and a thimbleful of Turkish coffee, late afternoons for a bowl of dense lentil soup, on Tuesday nights for the special stuffed eggplant, and Thursdays for baked *kibbe*. When I didn't feel like cooking, sometimes I'd take home a whole roasted chicken, wrapped like a giant burrito in a soft, oil-stained sheet of the Armenian bread *lavash* and accompanied by a white, blindingly powerful garlic sauce that had the consistency of mashed potatoes. When you sit down for a late-afternoon drink, the waiter brings out a plate of carrot sticks and soaked almonds to nibble with your tiny bottle of the Lebanese beer Almaza.

Despite the whirling towers of beef on the *shwarma* spits, the crisp-skinned quail on the charcoal grill, and the platters of pounded raw veal, Marouch's salad-heavy menu is vegan-friendly, making the restaurant one of the best places to go for lunch in Los Angeles with somebody who doesn't eat meat.

Los Angeles is also home to plush Lebanese dining palaces with a dozen different kinds of hummus and Casey Kasem as a steady customer, Middle Eastern grills more specifically Moroccan or Russian-Armenian than Marouch's familiar Lebanese-Armenian blend, and the energy in local Middle Eastern restaurants sometimes seems elsewhere—even, for a while, at Marouch's own short-lived Beverly Hills venture. But still: Marouch is as good as ever.

Order the combination dinner consisting of everything on the left side of the menu, and out comes smooth, cool hommus, dressed with a splash of olive oil and garnished with a pine-nut or two; the tart Lebanese sour cream *labneh*; the pounded paste of veal and bulgur wheat called *kibbe*, served both raw, as kind of a Lebanese steak tartare, and formed into vaguely Sputnik-shaped capsules and deep fried around a ground-beef forcemeat. The bitter, herbal bite of the tabbouleh, chopped parsley tossed with soft kernels of bulgur, is sharp contrast to the richness of *baba ganoush*, or the earthy power of the fava stew called *fool*. *Fattouch* is a wonderful salad of sweet peppers, onions, and tomatoes, spiked with crunchy chips of toasted pita bread, sprinkled with the tart Middle Eastern spice made from dried sumac berries and tossed with a lemony vinaigrette.

Armenian *sujok* are pretty good here—sliced, fried sausages flavored with cumin and hot pepper—but I'd been to Marouch maybe a hundred times before I discovered the wonder known as *makanek*, fat little beef links half the size of your thumb, sweetly seasoned with cinnamon and cloves, crisped in a frying pan and served in a ceramic bowlful of lemon and oil, pretty much everything you hope for when you order an unfamiliar sausage.

There are turnovers stuffed with tart spinach purée and fried pastry rectangles, *borek*, stuffed with cheese, hot-pink pickled turnips, and chile-red slices of the cured beef *basturma*. It can be overwhelming, facing down a dozen plates of food and realizing that grilled quail, kebabs, and stuffed lamb shank may be yet to come.

The best dessert at Marouch is a tricky, soft pastry available only at Easter, but there is rice pudding that tastes like a rosewater-sweetened version of *panna cotta*, and what a waiter describes as cheesecake: a square of syrup-soaked pound cake sitting on a lake of salty melted cheese.

MARSTON'S

151 E. WALNUT ST., PASADENA; (626) 796-2459. TUES.–FRI., 7–11A.M. AND
11:30A.M.–2:30P.M.; SAT., 7-11:30A.M. AND NOON-2:30P.M.

Pretty much anybody will concede that the coffee shop DuPar's serves the best French toast in Los Angeles—essentially supermarket balloon bread transformed into a rich, eggy bread pudding, slicked with melted butter, and dusted with confectioners' sugar. In good French toast, milk and egg invade a slice of bread the way the creatures in *I Married a Monster From Outer Space* took over police officers. The French toast served in swank brunch places is at the other end of the spectrum: thick slices of a challahlike substance, perhaps smeared with damson jam, but practically unbreached by liquid.

The French toast at the Pasadena breakfast place Marston's stands somewhere in the middle: thick slices, nearly saturated, dipped in crumbled corn flakes before frying for a crunchy, golden crust. Fanny Farmer *auteur* Marion Cunningham attributes the corn-flake wrinkle to James Beard, who attributed it to dining cars on the Santa Fe Railroad, whose tracks passed not fifty yards from the restaurant. This may bring things full circle.

Marston's is a converted old house across from Memorial Park, serving strong coffee, crisply fried potatoes, and orange juice dense and sweet as a Creamsicle. The place feels like the best restaurant in a small college town, and in a way it is. Sometimes, with all the customer chatter about guest lectures and Maranatha meetings, Marston's seems like an adjunct of Fuller Theological Seminary down the street.

At lunch, the restaurant serves clean, considered California cooking: white chili made with lots of chicken and jack cheese; grilled-fish tacos that taste like something taken from an issue of *Cooking Light* magazine; Cajun whatevers and spicy jicama salad instead of fries, if you like. There are alfalfa sprouts on the hamburgers, marinated black beans on almost everything else; club sandwiches and Cobb salads.

At breakfast, though, Marston's serves exactly the sort of food a missionary might crave after a stint in rural Chile, and it is not uncommon to hear someone here commenting on the first pancakes he's eaten in three years. The thin, buckwheat-based blueberry pancakes are dense and dark, pliable as crepes, barely sweetened, studded with fruit—blueberry pancakes for grown-ups. The macadamia-nut pancakes are basically thin scrims of buttermilk-pancake batter stretched between crumbs of roasted nut, served with a shot of maple syrup, and dusted with more nuts.

Marston's may be a little Calvinist in its hours—it closes on Sundays and stops serving breakfast abruptly at 11:00 A.M., perhaps guided by the notion that laggards don't deserve to eat anything as good as its French toast.

MATSUHISA

129 S. LA CIENEGA BLVD., BEVERLY HILLS; (310) 659-9639. MON.-FRI., 11:45A.M.-2:15P.M., 5:45P.M.-10:15P.M.

I have noted the hush that fell on a roomful of gangsta rappers when Quincy Jones walks into the studio, and seen a roomful of fiction writers breathe the words of a Raymond Carver story as the emphysematic author struggled through a reading late in his life. I've seen the ecstatic look on an oboist's face as she was singled out for praise by Pierre Boulez. I've even hung out with twelve-year-old girls at a Hanson concert. (Don't ask.) But I have never, I think, seen the un-muted awe that Nobu Matsuhisa commands when he strides through the Japanese fish wholesalers just east of downtown Los Angeles.

Matsuhisa hits the markets several times a week when he is in town, but business still crashes to a halt when he is in a store, so great is his reputation as a buyer of fish. Sushi men peer over his shoulder, admiring his ability to find the three great *hamachi* in a shipment of merely good ones, the perfect bluefin tuna, *kumamoto* oysters so lively that you half-expect them to leap out of their shells. Matsuhisa engages senior fish men in conversations that seem to consist of three grunted words. Young sushi apprentices cower behind headless tuna, afraid to approach. One well-known sushi chef, pretending to be ab-sorbed in the contents of a crate of mackerel, gasps when Matsuhisa puts his mark on a box of sculpin, like a chess master realizing that an innocuous pawn sacrifice is going to cost him the game fifteen moves down the line. Even the live abalone, swaying like hula dancers in their little wooden crates, seem to move in tribute to the chef.

If Matsuhisa were nothing more than a gifted sushi master, running a suc-cessful restaurant in Beverly Hills and training a couple of apprentices a year, he would still be exalted in these chilly refrigerated warehouses. But he is not. He is the one who changed the game. And as such, as the baron of a sushi empire that stretches from London to Aspen and the inventor of a strange, new cuisine, he is perhaps the only Japanese chef in America whose influence is felt as strongly in Japan as it is in his adopted United States—and it's felt pretty strongly here.

God himself couldn't get an nine o'clock reservation at the tempura bar at Matsuhisa on a weekend, not unless He had an in with Robert DeNiro.

Matsuhisa, whose restaurant is probably the most influential California restau-rant since Spago, is a Japanese sushi chef who spent several years working in Lima and who—unlike most formally trained Japanese chefs even there—actually picked up an appreciation for the spicy, fish-intensive cooking of coastal Peru, which is home to some of the most varied seafood on earth. So in a certain way, the rise of Nobu Matsuhisa should have been something I've been waiting for half of my life, a truly new, undeniably sophisticated cuisine born from the collision of Japanese technique, Latin flavors, and American marketing.

But I have never really subscribed to Matsuhisa's cult. Even from his first years in the restaurant, a sticky place adjoining a taco stand called Chicken on Fire, even as the originality of his cuisine was praised by Wolfgang Puck and half the A-list talent in Hollywood, I was the guy with the puzzled look on his face waiting at the valet stand, fingering the maxed-out Visa card in his wallet and trying to figure out why he hadn't gone for sushi in Little Tokyo instead.

If you have eaten even a few meals at a traditional Japanese *izaka-ya,* or pub, you have undoubtedly tasted something very like the braised cod cheeks, the pâté of monkfish liver, and the lightly seared tuna *tataki* that lies at the heart of Matsuhisa's repertoire. Good sushi chefs have always known that squid scored with quick, small slashes becomes especially tender. To sauté the resulting squid with garlic as if it actually were the shell pasta it resembled seemed coarse, obvious. Miso-broiled cod, often described as Matsuhisa's greatest invention, is a classic of Japanese home cooking sold premarinated not only at Japanese fish counters but also in half the supermarkets in Seattle. And the cross-cultural inventions that seemed so creative to the rest of the food press struck me as far less exciting than the ceviches and *tiraditos* I'd tasted on the streets in Lima.

Matsuhisa's prices are high: tabs at the Beverly Hills restaurant easily run two or three times higher than they do at comparable restaurants. And the secret rituals of the restaurant can get on your nerves after a while: the annotated forty-page menu, the clandestine specials you only read about in magazines, the six-seat tempura bar that may be the most exclusive club in America not actually requiring Senate confirmation.

But what I'd thought was the secret of Matsuhisa—like certain Chinese chefs, he seemed to draw crowds by adding peppers and garlic to nearly everything—may have been moot. What Matsuhisa seems to have done, with comparatively little effort, is to redefine the modern restaurant kitchen as a place with a sushi bar at its core.

For "new-style sashimi," for example, a dish of thinly sliced fish dribbled with a warmed, ginger-laced mixture of *ponzu* sauce with sesame and extra-virgin olive oils, Matsuhisa's sushi chefs cut the fish, arrange the plate, and monitor the preparation. The actual "cooking" of the dish (i.e., the heating of the oil) is secondary. *Tiradito,* a pinwheel of fluke or octopus fillets, glistening with citrus juice and polka-dotted with tongue-charring dabs of red-chile purée, is composed by sushi chefs; so is the sashimi salad (slabs of raw seafood, moistened with a sort of daikon-enriched salsa, hidden under limestone lettuce leaves stacked neatly as playing cards) and the rounds of finely minced *toro* tartare served hip-deep in a sweet, wasabi-fired miso sauce. The basic ingredients for such cooked dishes as squid "pasta," seared *toro ta-*

taki, and even the delicious grilled Kobe beef *tiradito*, which may be the chile-smeared steak of your dreams, flow from basic sushi preparations too.

Everybody knows that the best way to run through a meal at Nobu is to specify *omakase*, chef's choice, which nominally will bring forth an improvisational menu based on available ingredients and the whim of the chef, but which in fact usually brings on a flurry of the restaurant's best-known dishes, possibly shifted around a bit to reflect the progress of the seasons. *Omakase* has become as stylized as a *kaiseki* meal: fish tartare, sashimi salad, "new style" sashimi, miso-broiled fish, sushi, and dessert.

But Matsuhisa, unlike its New York counterparts, does always seem better, livelier, when you sit at the sushi bar, where I have had some of the best sushi meals of my life. The sushi chef noticed my predilection for strong, fishy fish the last time I was in, and served course after course of perfect, rich food: smoky, slippery lotus sprouts with rice vinegar; mackerel, jack, and sardines glazed with lemon and sprinkled with flaky salt; monkfish liver in a sharp *ponzu*; tiny live abalone in a candy-sweet miso purée; warmed lobes of sea urchin roe set on pickled *shiso* leaves, which in turn were balanced on broiled sweet shrimp: an explosive combination of sharpness and sea-sweetness.

Matsuhisa obviously lets each of his chefs improvise, shine as individuals in a way that wouldn't be possible if each plate of food had to be vetted by an executive chef. At the restaurant, where even nonsushi dishes travel through the sushi bar, individual sushi chefs *become* the line, empowering the kinds of efficiencies—and quality control—Escoffier could scarcely have imagined.

And the man knows how to buy a fish.

MAY FLOWER RESTAURANT

800 YALE ST., CHINATOWN; (213) 626-7113. DAILY, 10P.M.–10A.M.

On an quiet corner near the western fringe of Chinatown, near the benevolent societies and across the street from the park where elderly Chinese do their *tai chi* exercises early in the morning, May Flower Restaurant is a modest Cantonese lunch counter whose outside wall is decorated with a painting of a bowl of noodles. One wall is dominated by a picture window (if you get a window seat you might see a funeral parade wind its way past the restaurant, complete with twenty white limos and a hymn-playing brass band), and another wall by a huge glass display case that holds a few roasted ducks. Small red shrines are scattered about the room.

May Flower is where to find perfect Cantonese beef stew—long-braised, anise-flavored chunks of brisket and meltingly tender beef tendon that's among the richest foods on earth—or plates of sweet, crisp-skinned "village-baked" chicken, or stewed pig's trotters that are slithery and delicious. Mustard greens braised with salty oyster sauce are very good. Spareribs and barbecued pork are not as good. But basically, May Flower is a place to slurp things out of bowls.

If you've looked down your nose at wonton since you were a kid, this is the place to try them again—herbed pork balls wrapped around bits of shrimp crunchy enough to remind you of water chestnuts, and in turn wrapped with floppy cloaks of pasta. The wonton, more of them than you might expect in a three-dollar bowl of soup, bob in deeply flavored pork stock, along with noodles if you want them, and bits of duck or village-baked chicken or trotters or beef stew or whatever you'd like. Smear the wonton with a little of May Flower's pungent house black-bean chile sauce. Dribble a little of the fragrant black vinegar into the soup.

You can have your noodles—the dense, eggy kind—without wonton but with the soup and all the other stuff, or fried—chow mein—and spareribs with black beans, barbecued pork, or with anything else they have lying around. (May Flower may do only a few basic things, but it combines them in a lot of different ways.)

And here is Chinatown's definitive *jook*, rice porridge, thick and savory and spiked with spicy strands of fresh ginger, which comes with basically every combination of stuff—try it with peanuts. Or with village-baked chicken. Or with strips of tripe. Or with the house combination of chicken, shrimp, liver, and kidney, which flavors every drop. It may not have a whole lot to do with the elegant, wan *jook* commonly ladled from Thermoses on fancy dim-sum carts, splashed down with a plastic tumblerful of hot tea, but May Flower's *jook* can be a real power breakfast, with enough complex carbohydrates to slingshot you through the toughest day at work.

MEI LONG VILLAGE

301 W. VALLEY BLVD., #112, SAN GABRIEL; (626) 284-4769. DAILY, 11:30A.M.–9:30P.M.

Of all the Chinese cuisines represented in California, and probably in China itself, Shanghai-style cooking may be the most delicious: long-braised meats; juicy dumplings; lots of pork and river fish; all sorts of preserved vegetables; and sweetish, subtly flavored brown sauces amped up with wine, roasted garlic, and long-aged black vinegar.

The center of Shanghainese cooking in America, which for so long was New York's Chinatown, shifted to the San Gabriel Valley several years ago, and there are probably more good Shanghainese restaurants in San Gabriel and

Monterey Park than anywhere this side of, well, Shanghai. Not least of them, among the chic new-wave Shanghai bistros and the gutsy Shanghai noodle houses, the straightforward Shanghai cafes and downscale Shanghai dumpling joints, is Mei Long Village, a sleekly traditional restaurant in the inevitable San Gabriel mini-mall.

Mei Long Village is a tasteful, earth-tone place—no neon, no black marble— that looks as if it were decorated to appeal to the parents of the chic Chinese kids who hang out at Lake Spring; a restaurant comfortable both for the extended families who crowd the great circular tables at dinnertime and for the fortysome- thing Chinese couples who come for quiet meals by themselves. The list of bev- erages can resemble that of a purist country-western club (the last time I was in, it was Bud or nothing), and the restaurant is not particularly vegetarian-friendly— the chef seems to put pork in just about everything.

But even if Mei Long Village served nothing but dumplings, it would be worth a visit. There are delicious steamed *bao* stuffed with either sweet red bean paste or a pungent mince of strong greens and black mushrooms; crusty pan-fried *bao*; flaky sesame-flecked pastries, called vegetable cakes, filled with root vegetables and bits of pork; and pork-and-vegetable cakes, flying saucer-shaped discs of flaky dough wrapped around sautéed leeks.

First among the dumplings here are what are among the most delicious Shang- hai soup dumplings anywhere: pleated Ping-Pong balls of ultrathin dough, ten to an order, that explode into soup and pork and garlic when you pop them in your mouth. The crab dumplings, enriched with the sweet taste of the fresh crustacean are even better.

Not quite everything is completely great at Mei Long Village, though nothing is actually bad. The stir-fried stuff—*kung pao* chicken and walnut shrimp and ginger beef—may not be much better than it is at your favorite neighborhood takeout; the dry-fried string beans have been underseasoned and overcooked.

Mei Long Village is a perfect place to try any of the famous Shanghai stan- dards: sweet, fried Shanghai spareribs dusted with sesame seeds; garlicky, whole cod braised in pungent hot bean sauce; the big pork meatballs called lion's head, tender as a Perry Como ballad, that practically croon in the key of star anise. The new-wave Shanghai classic jade shrimp, stir-fried with a spinach purée, is especially good here; firm, subtly garlicked, garnished with deep-fried spinach leaves that are improbably glazed with sugar, a combination that by all rights should be bizarre but tastes as familiar as something you've been eating since you were a child. Even the jellyfish head, a stir-fried dish that is not a euphemism for anything, is good—slightly sweet, and smacked with ginger.

The pork pump, that peculiar star of California Shanghainese menus, is es- pecially fine here—a pork shoulder braised with rock sugar, soy, and a host of aromatics, drenched in a brown sauce that one suspects is mostly drippings and served on a bed of spinach. Mei Long Village's pork pump, far more than most, seems more of a soft insinuation of richness than twenty thousand calories on a plate.

MESSOB

1041 S. FAIRFAX AVE., LOS ANGELES; (323) 938-8827. SUN.-THURS., 11A.M.-11P.M.; FRI. & SAT., 11A.M.—MIDNIGHT.

As long as anyone can remember, the short stretch of Fairfax Avenue south of Olympic has been a center of ethnic restaurants in midtown. For decades, the block was an Eastern-European stronghold; later, it became a locus of the Sunday-night Chinese-restaurant district before that moved to the southern border of Beverly Hills.

A few years ago, South Fairfax coalesced into something like the Ethiopian equivalent of Mulberry Street in Manhattan or Greektown in Detroit, an enclave where an Ethiopian could buy vegetables and dinnerware, get her hair done, and stop for a cup of Ethiopian coffee, but also a tourist-friendly strip lined with restaurants whose menus seem virtually identical. On Fairfax, the sweet, mephitic odors of cardamom, smoldering incense, and roasting coffee overpower even the high burnt-meat stink of the local Carl's Jr.

Nyala is the hippiest restaurant on the strip, with Ethiopian bands on weekends and a low-key vibe John Shaft would have recognized. Blue Nile may be the family restaurant, and Rosalind's is the one in which ex-Peace Corps workers feel at home.

Messob, on the other hand, is the Ethiopian version of a checked-tablecloth Italian joint, a homey, dim-lit mom-'n'-pop with signed celebrity photos on the walls, sketches of Haile Selassie, and a steady green glow from the neon signs in the window. On half the tables sit bottles of exotically tart Ngok beer, which used to be imported from the Congo in big, thick bottles but is now, I think, brewed in Torrance. Stacks of freshly made *injera*, the sour, floppy bread that is the basis of Ethiopian cuisine, are plastic-wrapped for takeout in the back of the restaurant. Dim Ethiopian polyrhythms pulse from speakers in the ceiling, the kind of music you'd imagine lava lamps would probably make if you found a way to run them through your stereo.

You've eaten at Ethiopian restaurants; you know how the tune is supposed to go. A stew called *wot* will be simmered in a fiery, multispiced sauce colored brick-red with dried chiles; a mild stew identified by the word *alitcha* will at some time or another be fried with wilted onions. *Fitfit* is a stew tossed with pieces of sour *injera*, served on the usual sheet of *injera*, and customarily eaten (like all other Ethiopian dishes) using still more *injera* as a spoon, making the whole thing a fairly *injera*-intensive proposition. (The tomato *fitfit*, a bitingly tart *injera*-based condiment, is terrific.)

Everything is seasoned with one or two of the holy trinity of Ethiopian cooking—spiced butter, hot dried chile paste, and a hot *fresh* chile paste—and almost everything sings with high notes of garlic, ginger, and cardamom.

Most people order one combination plate or another, giant metal platters lined with *injera* and mosaicked so intricately with little varicolor heaps of *tibs* and lentils that it almost seems as if you should be able to make out Lincoln's face among the mounds of spiced collard greens, split peas, and freshly made curd cheese. Like the number-two dinner at a Mexican restaurant, a Messob combination is undemanding, tasty, and fun.

Kifto, as close as Ethiopia comes to a national dish, is usually referred to as a version of steak tartare, finely minced raw beef tossed off the flame with quarts of melted, spiced butter. *Kifto* can be overcooked and gritty here unless you specify that you want it rare, or better, raw. Try rare *gored gored* instead, which is essentially the same dish made with larger strips of meat. The subtle gaminess of raw beef here acts as just another top note in the complexly spiced, sharply cardamom-scented stew, which is spectacular.

Don't miss the special Ethiopian coffee, roasted to order in a lidded pan, brewed, and poured into little cups from a ceramic Ethiopian coffee pitcher that is brought to the table on a tray that also includes a fuming coal of incense. The old Bagel delicatessen made a great cup of coffee in the street's last incarnation, but Messob's Ethiopian cup really is an improvement.

MIKE'S HOCKEY BURGER

1717 S. SOTO ST., VERNON; (323) 264-0444. MON.–WED., 6A.M.–7P.M.;
THURS. & FRI., 24 HOURS; SAT., UNTIL 7P.M.

Welcome to Mike's Hockey Burger in scenic Vernon, California, an industrial town that looks like an enormous, truck-choked loading dock. The restaurant, marked by a roof sign depicting a giant hockey player, is within sight of the bulbous Vernon water tower, which resembles an alien spaceship docked in a parking lot. At noon, the groups of sheriff's deputies and truck drivers double up two or three to a table, and the short-sleeved factory managers do the sidewalk cafe thing at the picnic tables outside among billows of diesel smoke. In Vernon at lunchtime, Hockey Burger is the only place to be.

Meet Mike Chitjian, who owns the joint—he's the guy with a black mustache, scowling in the corner by the fryers. Mike used to play a little hockey himself, and has the pictures to prove it. There they are, surrounded by Kings pennants and autographed photographs of hockey greats, right up there on the Hockey

Burger Wall of Fame. Another wall boasts autographed photos of celebrities—Dolly Parton and Larry Hagman, among others. Mike has friends in high places, and hockey trophies too.

There are cheeseburgers at Mike's restaurant, and tuna sandwiches, and pastrami dips dripping with peppery grease. A Mike's Special includes roast beef, melted cheese, and plenty of onions stuffed inside a pita, but is nothing that would make the guys at Philippe's lie awake at night with worry. Mike, who is of Armenian descent, also serves something called a Hye Pie—a small Armenian pizza, *lahmajiun*, folded around onions, tomatoes and Armenian string cheese and grilled until the outside becomes crisp and the cheese melts into the tomatoey meat mixture inside. The Hye Pie is very good.

What Mike is proudest of is the Hockey Burger itself, which is essentially a cheeseburger garnished with a sliced, grilled Polish sausage. "Number-one first-quality," Mike says. "It is patented and registered."

Some theorize that the concoction is called a Hockey Burger because the burger symbolizes the puck and the sausage the hockey stick; some say that the trisected sausage resembles the grille on a Zamboni machine. Some people think that Mike is just a fool for hockey. But although the Hockey Burger may be fearsome to behold, it is actually pretty delicious: the lightly toasted poppy-seed bun both crisp and chewy; the lettuce crisp; the tomato ripe; the spicy sausage providing an unctuous foil to the slightly bitter tang of the thin hamburger patty. You will finish it in about a minute, no matter how resolved you may be toward moderation. You will also feel it, for the rest of the day, as a small, indigestible lump.

MI RANCHITO

12223 W. WASHINGTON BLVD., CULVER CITY; (310) 398-6106 MON.-THURS., 11A.M.–10P.M.; FRI., 11A.M.–11P.M.; SAT., 10A.M.–11P.M.; SUN., 10A.M.–10P.M.

The best Veracruz-style restaurant on the Westside has always been Culver City's Mi Ranchito, which served the only Veracruz-style *chilpacholes, salpicons,* and *jarocho* plates in the area, although most of the antiques dealers and studio craft-services guys who frequented the place came for the cheap burritos, perfect *carnitas* plates and bottles of Dos Equis so cold that they formed little ice caps when you poured them into a glass. The current Mi Ranchito is a seamless simulacrum of the old one: walls and ceilings encrusted with farm implements, old cooking tools, and vintage tavern photographs, porcelain figurines and flags of all nations, burbling fountains, musical instruments, T-shirts, posters conjugating obscene Spanish verbs. *Ranchera* music still blares from the sound system—there are even speakers broadcasting out onto the sidewalk—and the same guys in big hats slump over the same giant bowls of *cocido*.

Carne asada is exemplary, well marinated, crusted with black pepper, chewy, beefy, and hot; the *carnitas* are lean and moist, but full of flavor. The beef in red chile sauce is well made, if not especially exciting; the pork *chile verde* is spicy, tart, and balanced. Mi Ranchito has always been known for its soups: abundant beef *cocido*; rich chicken soup; a wonderful *albondigas* soup flavored with mint. The first-rate *posole* has the funk of hominy, the bite of hot chile, and the slightly gamy understate of long-stewed meat, but the chunks of boiled pork taste freshly cooked, and the soup has flavor even without the usual additions of chopped onion and oregano.

The food at Mi Ranchito, it must be admitted, is wildly inconsistent. When the *machaca* is on, it is a great old-fashioned version, crisp at the edges, properly chewy, seasoned with what seems to be whole shakerfuls of black pepper. Sometimes it is bland and too eggy by half.

And oddly, Mi Ranchito falls short on some of the crucial Veracruz seafood classics—where one might expect the restaurant to shine. The *huachinago la Veracruzana* is often somewhat overcooked; the seafood-stuffed burrito *jarocho*, while a couple of notches better than similar burritos served at, say, Señor Fish, suffers from the tinny taste of canned shellfish. The *chilpachole*, a thin, intense seafood soup bathing a whole snapper or a crab, is flavored with handfuls of a special *epazote* that the restaurant's owner imports from his home village, Caleria, but can be too edgy, too medicinal to fully enjoy. But one bite of the minty Caleria-style *salpicon* is enough to make you forgive the restaurant almost anything: warm, coarsely chopped beef mixed with minced radishes, onions, and fresh herbs, tossed with lime juice, served with thick flour tortillas and great mounds of oily rice. A restaurant with *salpicon* this good could probably get away with serving Moby Jacks.

MISHIMA

8474 W. THIRD ST., LOS ANGELES; (323) 782-0181. DAILY, 11:30A.M.– 10P.M.

Mishima might be kind of a heavy name for a noodle restaurant, carrying as it does intimations of gonzo jingoism and tortured personality crisis, four-volume novels and ritual suicide—at least if the place is named after the late Japanese novelist. One supposes that if the noodles clumped together, Mishima's chef might feel compelled to ritually disembowel himself in disgrace.

But like an Izozaki exterior or a Commes des Garçons–suit, Mishima's pasta is admirable for simplicity of line and elegance of execution, even when it doesn't exactly thrill you.

Pencil-thick *udon* noodles, thick, white worms with the al dente bite of good Italian pasta, are slippery enough to elude your chopsticks three falls out of four, and have a solid, wheaty taste. *Soba*—thin, buckwheat noodles—are firmer, almost chewy, and have an earthy pungency of their own that sings through Mishima's tart, clean soy broth. The ceramic bowls are pretty, too.

Most Japanese noodle shops, at least in Los Angeles, specialize in *ramen*, the garlicky, spaghetti-shaped, pork-brothy stuff that Japanese consider to be Chinese noodles, but although Mishima serves only *udon* and *soba*—the austere "Japanese" stuff—you will find many subtle variations thereof.

The house specialty, *tanuki soba* (or *udon*), tempers the severity of the plain noodles-and-broth with tiny Rice Krispies puffs of fried tempura batter; *chikara soba* (or *udon*) has gooey, grilled *mochi* rice cakes lurking in its depths. Curry *soba* (or *udon*) is spiked with white-meat chicken and has its broth thickened with yellow Japanese curry, the mild, turmeric-heavy kind you find mantling curry rice at Japanese lunch counters.

Wakame udon resonates with the pungent iodine flavor of seaweed—it should; a solid inch of kelp floats on the surface—and *mentaiko udon* includes a pink, thumb-shaped sac of spiced cod roe. There is a decent version of the traditional *zaru soba*, chilled buckwheat noodles coiled on a bamboo mat, ready to be dipped in a saucer of chilled soy-citrus sauce, and a few varations on that theme. You could probably eat an entire bowl of any of these noodles and ingest less fat than you would from eating a single French fry.

The theme of fashionable minimalism continues in the side dishes: *edamame* boiled in brine; the fried tofu puffs called *inari* stuffed with rice and sweet pickled vegetables; *onigiri*, compact rice cakes studded with bits of seaweed, pickled plum, or the spicy herb *shiso*; and amazingly good sticks of fried fishcake, dusted with shredded, dried seaweed, that might get Mrs. Paul to thinking about *seppuku* herself.

MUSSO & FRANK GRILL

6667 HOLLYWOOD BLVD., HOLLYWOOD; (323) 467-5123. TUES.-SAT., 11A.M.-11P.M.

Around three o'clock at Musso & Frank, with the counter mostly emptied of its flannel-cake stragglers, a busboy smooths out white linen napkins for the dinner crowd. An ashtray smell of cold, burnt wood comes off the grill behind the counter's middle, and a man pokes among the dead ashes for a while before walking over.

"If you hear a little explosion," he says, "don't worry. I'm turning on the grill. If you hear a big explosion . . . run like heck."

Within a couple of minutes, he coaxes the grill into crackling life. The warm scent of woodsmoke spreads across the room. A red-jacketed waiter comes over and pours a clear, cold martini from a pony into a tiny, frosted glass, then carefully spoons Welsh rarebit from a metal salver onto crustless toast. Other waiters bustle about the empty restaurant, preparing for the evening rush.

It seems very much a perfect gentleman's lunch, here in these worn, wooden swivel chairs beneath the ancient hunt-scene wallpaper. The rarebit is rich, warm, a little grainy, not a platonic Fannie Farmer vision of the classic cheese dish but very good anyway, especially when cut through with the chill, bitter snap of the gin and topped with salty crumbles of bacon you've sprinkled on yourself. The service is solicitous, but mostly leaves you to your own thoughts.

Musso's, the oldest restaurant in Hollywood, is an easy place to be happy, and it seems a privilege to be able to come here every once in a while.

In a sense, it's impossible to describe Musso & Frank as a restaurant rather than one's own relationship to Musso & Frank. Like the Griffith Park Observatory or Ramon Navarro's star on Hollywood Boulevard, Musso's just is, canned asparagus and musty crab Louie and all. Faulkner and Fitzgerald and M. F. K. Fisher drank here, and practically everybody has an opinion of the place, none of which is wrong.

You may dislike the flannel cakes—thin, plate-size pancakes that taste something like rubbery fortune cookies—but almost everybody else adores them. You may subscribe to the conventional wisdom about the place (stick to steaks, chops, and martinis), but thousands of others can recite the unchanging list of daily specials by heart.

Curious about jellied consommé? Quivery brown stuff, sort of refreshing with a squeeze of lemon, mounded in a tiny, iced bowl. Combination Louie? Cooked, chilled shrimp, crab, and lobster piled on a bed of lettuce, with little paper cups of horseradish—catsup sauce and spicy Thousand Island dressing on the side. Finnan haddie? A giant, naked haunch of smoked haddock, intimidating but sort of delicious really, served with good tartar sauce and boiled new potatoes. The sheer size of the menu, which doesn't seem to have changed much since the restaurant opened in 1919, makes it possible to eat as Jay Gatsby may have, or Nora Charles, or Mr. and Mrs. Bridge.

At the counter, all sorts of possibilities arise that probably wouldn't occur to you in a booth. You can split a club steak or a Wednesday order of sauerbraten with a friend without feeling cheap. You can strike up a conversation with the person sitting next to you, who might be a B-movie character actor, or a composer, or a seedy Brit who's just had his car stolen and wants to borrow twenty bucks just till next week.

"What's in a chicken pot pie?" asks a man at the end of the counter.

"For chrissakes," his friend says in disbelief. "Chicken."

If you've sat at the end closest to the door, you can watch the waiter Manny croon Hank Williams songs or make silk handkerchiefs disappear. Manny also makes the best Caesar in the joint, garlicky and awash with pungent anchovies. (If you're a pretty girl, and you look longingly enough at him when he's tossing one, he might slip you a few leaves free of charge.) You can order coffee and bread pudding and people-watch for hours during the pretheater rush. You can eavesdrop.

"Taylor's is where you go for a steak," said the woman sitting next to me one evening. She reached over and stabbed a forkful of Caesar salad from my plate. "Musso's is where you come for, well, a bowl of peas." She ordered a hot turkey sandwich for herself and a hot chicken sandwich for her friend, and under the gobbets of brown gravy, one sandwich not only looked but also tasted exactly like the other. I let her have a big piece of my steak.

NICE TIME DELI

140 W. VALLEY BLVD., NO. 209, SAN GABRIEL; (626) 288-0149. DAILY, 11:30A.M.–10P.M.

I have stared down okra gumbos so gooey that a spoonful of broth snapped back into the bowl as sharply as a stretched rubber band. I have enjoyed tacos made with a corn fungus called *huitlacoche*, which looks like gangrene on a plate. I have sampled dried Icelandic seaweed that smelled like the set of a porno movie, and green-tea salads that had the caffeinated kick of a pound of Yuban. I am no stranger to the fabled Javanese stinky bean named *pete*.

But in the world's pantheon of hard-core vegetables, surpassing skunk cabbage, Japanese mountain yam, and possibly even the toxic Indonesian bean so delicious that its devotees eat it despite the certainty of excruciating kidney pain, the most intense may be Chinese bitter gourd, a warty, pale-green thing the size of a large cucumber, as bitter as envy, as bitter as hot tears.

Sautéed bitter gourd, as prepared at the Taiwanese-style Nice Time Deli in San Gabriel Square, has the funk of the green beans they used to serve at your elementary school cafeteria, and the luscious succulence of ripe honeydew melon. Your first taste of the stuff, mellowed by the sweetness of shredded pork and the small pungency of fermented black beans, may remind you of braised celery—until the onset a second or two later of the aftertaste, a shocking, penetrating bitterness with all the subtlety of a tongue piercing, not chocolate bitter or even tea bitter, but cancer-medicine bitter, a bitterness that will still be with you four hours later. There is something oddly appealing about bitter melon. You really should try it.

Taiwan, more than other culinary regions of China, still retains a bit of its pre-Chinese past; the strong flavors of the coastal south are muted by neither the agricultural abundance that shaped Cantonese cooking nor the urbane sophistication of Shanghainese cuisine. You may find fermented shrimp, bitter vegetables, and fish innards in most Chinese kitchens, but the Taiwanese seem to have more of these things. If a fast-food place in a Chinese food court serves you bowls of soup that seem to contain more congealed pork blood than actual broth, or wedges of fried tofu you can smell across the room, you have probably stumbled into a Taiwanese joint.

Nice Time Deli, a small, plain Taiwanese noodle shop on the second level of the huge San Gabriel Square mall, may attract a more purely Taiwanese crowd than any restaurant in town: shirtsleeved business dudes doing deals over big plates of clams; Chanel victims clutching shopping bags from the mall's department store; high school students stretching three dollars into a bowl of noodles.

While technically a Chinese deli, Nice Time doesn't really serve much of the fun stuff—dumplings, hand-pulled noodles, scallion pancakes—most people associate with Chinese delis. This is plain, rigorous food, almost Scandinavian in its simplicity.

Nice Time's soothing version of *czech-a* noodles, perhaps the most austere noodles in the Chinese pantheon, seems to be little more than thin Chinese vermicelli in a mild stock, embellished only with a gram or two of burnt onion; goose-noodle soup—a goose leg, rice, and a sprinkling of bean sprouts—comes in a clear broth any grandmother would recognize. Coins of sliced rice cake, sautéed with a few shreds of pork and very little oil, would be totally bland if not for a blast of dried-shrimp stink. Eel noodles, on the other hand, in a thick, cornstarch-gooey sweet-and-sour sauce, taste more like sex than like anything you might ordinarily contemplate as food.

A ginger-intensive dish of minced pork layered over rice and garnished with red-cooked Chinese *chicharrones* is absolutely basic Chinese home cooking, the kind of thing that makes it onto Chinese restaurant menus about as often as tuna casserole does onto American ones.

Almost everybody seems to supplement their starch with snacky stuff identified on the menu as dim sum: fried lozenges of fish cake not dissimilar to Thai *chao tom;* not particularly distinguished capsules of fried tofu; broad, thin, fried pork chops that take over a plate like the pork tenderloin at Hoosier greasy spoons. Meatballs come encased in a stretchy rice-flour wrapper that seems to have the physical characteristics of Flubber; fried chicken egg rolls seem to be the exact same thing passed through hot oil long enough to give it a crackly crunch.

The northern-style side dishes will be familiar to anybody who has ever ventured into a Mandarin Deli: marinated seaweed topped with fusillades of garlic; strips of pressed bean curd dripping raw soy; Chinese lunch meat with bean sprouts. But the great dish at Nice Time may be the squid "potage," a giant bowl of cornstarch-thickened broth with plenty of vegetables, noodles if you want them, and extraordinary little fish dumplings, the size and shape of candy cigarettes, that have tiny, chewy slivers of squid at their core. The potage is flavored with a few drops of Taiwan-style barbecue sauce, vaguely sweet-sour, with a powerful smokiness; each bite of soup (as with all great Chinese dishes) is radically different from the next. Awesome. But austere.

NICK'S CAFE

1300 N. SPRING ST., LOS ANGELES; (323) 222-1450. MON.–FRI., 5:30A.M.– 2P.M.; SAT., 6A.M.–11:30A.M.

The best ham in Los Angeles may be the stuff they serve at at Nick's Cafe downtown, a plateful of thick slices fried to smoky denseness, ribboned with sweet fat, fibrous and chewy in a way that only real ham can be and blackened crisp at the rim. There are ham omelettes here, sandwiches made with ham alone, and hard-core sandwiches made with ham and a fried egg, but the best way to have the ham may be straight up, doused with the restaurant's searing house salsa, with a bland pillow of hash browns on the side. If the world were just, Nick's would be as reknowned for ham 'n' eggs as the Dodgers are for baseball.

Nick's is one of those basic breakfast spots that seem to have passed intact from the '40s, an ancient joint on the part of North Spring by the railyards, a haven of quilted aluminum and dad's-den wood paneling, old railroad signs, and hog paraphernalia. A clean, masculine aroma of fried ham and strong coffee hangs in the air. The shirtsleeve clientele seems mostly made up of the big-city guys who make factories run. A plush pig hangs upside down from its cloven hooves; oldies radio blares Sam the Sham; an electric train whirs around the small diner on tracks set a foot below the ceiling.

Outside, through the window, trains couple and decouple on the tracks, and you can look up past Chinatown to Dodger Stadium. Conversation around the U-shaped counter may touch on a big mariachi concert or the news from city hall, but it always, always turns to the LAPD. (The restaurant is actually owned by a couple of homicide detectives, and the gossip around the counter here is usually more accurate than anything you'll see in the *Times*.) There may be plenty of meatloaf, thick-patty hamburgers like Mom used to make, tuna melts, and grilled cheese.

"Pretty much everything is made from scratch here," the waitress says, rolling her eyes as if she thinks roasting turkey for the Friday cold-turkey sandwich special is an affectation. "I think the only things they buy in packages are the condiments, the mustard and catsup."

525 SUMNER ST., BAKERSFIELD; (661) 322-8419. DAILY SEATINGS AT NOON AND 7P.M. ONLY.

Some people stop in Bakersfield for a burger and a tank of gas on the way to Fresno. Others go on purpose to hear the country & western music, or to throw back a bourbon-and-water in one of its many old bars. Antique collectors like to rummage through the city's junk stores, finding plaster cats, rusted Lucky Strike marquees, and complete sets of uranium-red Bauer soup tureens that are invariably as expensive as they would be on Melrose but seem fantastically attractive when set off by clean, desert light and storekeepers who accept American Express. The entire downtown looks as if it took its blueprint from the pages of one of the better David Goodis novels; the place is a wonderland for aficionados of noir.

But what draws me to Bakersfield is the hearty cowboy cooking at its Basque-American restaurants, garlic and cholesterol and all-you-can-eat, and when I drive the hundred-odd miles over the Tehachapis, old crockery and Buck Owens are usually the farthest things from my mind.

The first thing to do when you pull into town is to seek out the Basque-restaurant district around the intersection of Baker and Sumner streets a few miles east of downtown. To an outsider, this restaurant row looks a lot like skid row, a gray neighborhood of taverns, machine shops, and sizzling neon, of Hopperesque poolhalls and the odd grizzled drunk. Even on a Saturday night, the area seems empty and drained of life. But if you walk into one of the bars on a weekend afternoon—Noriega's, Wool Growers, or the Pyrenees—you'll find it smoky and teeming, filled with people arguing about farm politics and Fresno State football in Spanish, French, and Basque.

The drink of choice in Basque Bakersfield is something called Picon punch, a bittersweet cocktail made with brandy, soda, grenadine, and a bitter Basque liqueur named Amer Picon. You may think the cocktail is a tourist affectation, but rest assured: you will see a burly farmer thrust his gut toward a barkeep and snarl, "Gimme Pi-*cahhhn*." A Picon goes down smoothly but gnaws at your brain for hours, and costs little more than a beer. What more could you ask from a beverage?

Hop from bar to bar, have a Picon punch or three, but get to Noriega's by seven o'clock sharp, because the food is better, the family crowd friendlier, and there's just one seating for dinner—make sure to call ahead and reserve before you leave L.A. You sit at long communal tables side-by-side with ranchers, schoolteachers, and real cowboys, which is more than you can say for dinner at Black Angus.

Once I sat next to a local sheepman who commented on the abilities of every shepherd at the table "That blond guy down at the end, he's the best," he said. "Knows a lamb is sick before she knows it herself."

The routine of a Basque-American meal is well established. Most of the restaurants in the area adhere to the pattern, which seems most appropriate for those customers who come to dinner straight from two back-breaking weeks of manual labor with the flocks. You serve yourself boardinghouse style from communal platters brought to the table, and wash everything down with juice glasses full of cold red wine. Bread is sliced from simple French loaves, fresh and chewy. At Noriega's, where there's no menu, you eat what you're served.

First there are tureens of vegetable soup, heavy on the cabbage, which you enrich to taste with a couple of spoonfuls of spicy Basque tomato salsa and a dose of boiled pinto beans. Then you are passed a platter of thinly sliced pickled beef tongue—cool, rich, and slick with garlic—a big bowl of very fresh lettuce dressed with a simple garlic vinaigrette, and possibly a bowl of cottage cheese flavored with mayonnaise and chopped herbs. Though the tongue can be more succulent elsewhere in town, Noriega's beans are nonpareil, its salad crisp.

Next comes the entrée, typically a big plate of oxtail stew with carrots, or perhaps a dripping, gravy-sodden, garlicky lamb stew that seems like the most delicious thing you've eaten in your life, and after that, a platter of overcooked spaghetti in spicy tomato sauce. When you're sure you won't need another bite of food until next Tuesday, the main course comes out—fried chicken, or better yet, incredibly crisp beef ribs whose flavor is the soul of grease and garlic—accompanied by mountains of thick, fresh-cut French fries. Then a waitress passes cool slabs of strong blue cheese and little dishes of liqueur-spiked ice cream or flan.

One time a kid sitting next to me reached over and tugged on my sleeve. "Hey mister," he said, "you and your friend come and play." We followed the kid and his brother out of the dining room to a massive, concrete jai alai court adjoining the bar and tossed around a tennis ball until their mom dragged them away. Several Picon punches and about two pounds of lamb stew into the evening, we'd finally had enough.

NORTH WOODS INN

7247 N. ROSEMEAD BLVD., SAN GABRIEL; (626) 286-8284 OR (626) 286-3579. MON.–THURS., 11:30A.M.–10P.M.; FRI. & SAT., 11:30A.M.–10:30P.M.; SUN., 11:30A.M.–9P.M.

If you grew up in West Los Angeles, you probably have primal yearnings for Lawry's roast beef that you don't fully understand. If, like me, you hail from the Southside, you may long for Poor Richard's, a '60s wonderland of Shirley Temples and chugging model trains up on Slauson near Crenshaw. Former Valley kids lull themselves to sleep by imagining the old trout stream running through Sportsman's Lodge.

But for generations of kids growing up on the Eastside, in the vast expanse of flatland stretching from the L.A. River out to Azusa, Whittier, and beyond, memories of big meat begin and end at Clearman's North Woods Inn, a vast, timber-themed steak house ensconced in a log cabin the size of the Twin Cities Metrodome, home to sizzling lumberjack steaks, frothing schooners of root beer, and huge baked potatoes smothered in whipped cheese-food topping. To a nine-year-old, it has never gotten any better than the North Woods Inn.

The North Woods Inn has spread into an empire—Clearman's owns half a dozen restaurants, and its cheese butter sits next to the Hooters hot-wing mix at supermarkets all over the Southland—but the mothership has always been the San Gabriel restaurant, anchoring a trappers-theme mall that includes a place to buy Ye Olde Ruger semiautomatics among the usual craft stores and gift emporia.

The main dining room is a dim, soaring space, punctuated with animal heads and rusted lanterns, lined with long wooden tables, speckled with glowing oil paintings in the style of Goya's *Naked Maja* as rendered by the caricature guy at Disneyland. The piano player, a youngish dude who looks as if he is probably concealing half a dozen piercings underneath his barbershop-quartet outfit, is bold enough to leaven his sets of Gershwin and Kern with the occasional chorus of Green Day or the Offspring. As soon as you are seated, a waiter comes over, props menus up in front of you like so many targets in a shooting gallery, and upends a bowl of peanuts onto your table, instructing you to throw the shells onto the floor.

There is a ritual to a dinner at North Woods Inn, as inviolable as the sacrament of the spinning salad bowl at Lawry's or the pageant of the flaming Jet Pilot at Trader Vic's, and while it is technically possible to order just a sandwich and an order of fries, I have never actually seen anyone do so. Where Chasen's used to serve Parmesan toast, the North Woods Inn serves cheese bread, a couple of slices per person. It is an unusually soggy toast, actually wrapped in foil for maximum floppiness and crusted with enough garlic and cheese to pave the bed of the Rio Hondo. Salads come in pairs, a tart red-cabbage slaw and a lettuce salad in a mild solution of blue cheese, which you are instructed to toss together into something resembling a decent college-dormitory-style salad with creamy Italian dressing.

Steaks come in all the usual shapes and sizes here—chunks on skewers, petite fillets, and expensive New York cuts—but the house specialty is a top sirloin called the lumberjack steak. It is fairly safe to say that the lumberjack steak will not wipe the memory of steaks at Jocko's or the Palm from your memory circuits, but it is fair enough in its limited way: not crusted with char but at least tinged with smoke.

Do not miss the pumpkin-size baked potato with cheese butter, probably 1,800 calories without breathing hard, which ranks with the Hollywood Bowl, MOCA, and the outlet mall in the old Babylonian tire plant as a true cultural icon of California.

NYALA

1076 S. FAIRFAX AVE., LOS ANGELES; (323) 936-5918. SUN.-THURS., 11A.M.-MIDNIGHT; FRI.-SAT., 11A.M.-2A.M.

At the south end of South Fairfax's African restaurant row, Nyala is the grooviest of the Ethiopian hangs, a dark, cavernous restaurant with ochre-stippled walls and African-shield screens, silhouettes of antelopes, and lighting that manages to highlight the cheekbones of everybody in the room.

When you walk in, a sweet Al Wilson soul ballad might be blasting over the big speakers, four sharply dressed men clustered around the turntables arguing whether next to play Lakeside or Cameo. Or perhaps you have arrived in the midst of Abyssinian Oldies Night, to a swirl of Motown and Isaac Hayes. Sometimes they even play traditional Ethiopian music—modal, dark, appealing stuff that sounds just a little like Led Zeppelin played backward and underwater.

A Lakers game flickers eternally on a large-screen TV over the bar; no matter what time you show up, you will probably leave before nine-tenths of the people in the room, who tend to treat Nyala as a clubhouse. There are a lot of other Ethiopian restaurants in this neighborhood now, but Nyala is the place to go on a hot third date, elegant yet exotic. The central fact of Ethiopian cuisine is *injera*, a pale, moist, platter-size pancake with which you scoop up your food. *Injera* serves the same purpose as the tortilla in Mexican cooking and the pita in Middle Eastern food, but somehow more so—it acts as plate, utensil, condiment, and bread, and is an ingredient in about half the stews.

Ethiopian cooking is unthinkable without *injera*'s profound sourness, or without the central flavorings of onions, ginger, red pepper, and perfumed lakes of spiced butter. Before the Italians invaded the country in 1935, Ethiopians flavored even their coffee with salt and the fragrant spiced butter. Ethiopian cooking is anything but light.

There is a fine version of the chicken stew *doro wot*, thick with hot spice and glistening with butter, that includes only one chicken leg and one stewed egg per order but whose sauce will flavor a stack of *injera*; there is spicy stewed lamb, *yebeg wot*, and the tough, tasty beef stew *yeawaze tibs*. *Minchetabish* tastes like a fiery Ethiopian take on Texas chili. There's a good vegetarian red-lentil "chili" here too, *yemiser wot*.

Kifto, steak tartare, is more or less the Ethiopian national dish, raw strips of hand-chopped lean beef tossed with warm spiced butter and herbs, and can be transcendentally delicious here, greasy and wonderful, wrapped in *injera* with a few crumbles of Nyala's house-made Ethiopian cheese and a bit of the mustard-green stew *yeabesha gommen*.

As is customary at Ethiopian restaurants, hearty Italian dishes occupy half the menu—things like angel-hair pasta with sautéed vegetables and garlic, or spaghetti with an exotically spiced Bolognese sauce. If you're not Ethiopian yourself, you'll probably never get around to ordering them. Because you can't eat pasta with your hands.

O

OKI DOG

5056 W. PICO BLVD., LOS ANGELES; (323) 938-4369. MON.-SAT., 9A.M.–
10P.M.

For a while in my late teens, long before I could have told you the difference
between a quesadilla and a quenelle, I ate at Oki Dog more often than I did at
home. About one in the afternoon, when the artist I worked for took the first of
his habitual breaks for Thai stick and Rainer Ale, I'd sneak out of his studio and
walk down the block to the Pico Boulevard Oki Dog. About two in the morning,
after an evening of slamming to the Germs or the Dead Kennedys at the old
Starwood, I'd end up with everybody else at the Oki Dog in West Hollywood,
which was the closest thing there was at the time to a punk-rock after-hours club.
If your hair resembled a chemotherapy side-effect, Oki Dog seemed a logical place
to go.

The West Hollywood Oki was always the famous one, a magnet for punks
and hustlers, groupies and teenage runaways, for everybody who was happy that
a single teriyaki burrito was enough to fill three bellies for a day. TV shows
featured it, hip magazines touted it, a thousand and one members of the purple-
mohawk brigade sang its praises on beer-soaked stages. Pumped-up countermen,
crazy as the clientele, shouted back at you in a pidgin version of the gruff Japanese
the family who owned the place spoke behind the grill.

The original Oki Dog was too colorful for its own good—after a decade of
neighbors' complaints, the city finally managed to close it down. But the Pico
operation always served better, fresher food, a relentlessly transglobal blend of
junk cuisines that was more or less the fast-food equivalent of what they were
doing across town at joints like Chaya Brasserie and Chinois.

The most famous Oki creation is the eponymous Oki Dog, a couple of hot
dogs wrapped in a tortilla with chili, pickles, mustard, a slice of fried pastrami,

and a torrent of goopy American cheese, a cross-cultural burrito that's pretty hard to stomach unless you've got the tum of a sixteen-year-old.

A teriyaki steak sandwich must contain half a pound of sweet, grilled beef, thinly sliced and plopped into a French roll with lettuce and mayo. French fries—you get something like two pounds—are freshly cut, fried to order, and usually overcooked. Pepsi comes by the quart. Five bucks will get you enough food for two, with a quarter left over to play a round of Ms. Pac Man.

Still, the best of the Oki creations, a Chinese-American-Jewish-Mexican thing made by Japanese cooks for a mostly African-American clientele, is the pastrami burrito: a foil-wrapped grease bomb the size and weight of a building brick, bursting with fried pastrami, sautéed cabbage, onions and peppers, mustard and pickles, and a healthy glop of chili. It's enough food to feed a medium-size family—or three punk-rockers—for a week.

P

PALM STEAKHOUSE

9001 SANTA MONICA BLVD., WEST HOLLYWOOD; MON.–FRI., 12P.M.–
10:30P.M.; SAT., 5P.M.–10:30P.M.; SUN., 5P.M.–9:30P.M.

Somehow, somewhere, fondness for the Palm has to be classified as a psychiatric disorder, because everything about the place triggers a warning bell in the deepest recesses of the unconscious mind. The famous celebrity caricatures on the wall constitute essentially a museum of '70s excess, for one thing, enshrining Cher and O. J., Burt and Loni, Redd Foxx and the guy who used to play Banacek, forming sort of a living Trivial Pursuit portrait gallery. The booths underneath those portraits are packed out with a deep concentration of what used to be known as the suits. The waiters, flat-footed Italian guys who cultivate Bronx accents as lovingly as Sean Penn at the Actors Studio, are widely reported to be rude, though what this means in practice is that they expect you to keep the repartee on a fairly snappy level.

It is one of the great puzzles of California, how a place can be so totally New York–inspired and still breathe the essence of L.A.

The wine list, although abbreviated, is no more overpriced than it is at, say, Spago, and includes wonderful small-production California wineries as well as the usual blockbusters from Mondavi—try the insanely concentrated Andrew Murray Syrah from Paso Robles. Appetizers tend toward simple things done fairly well: shrimp cocktail, perhaps, or clams casino good enough to make you wonder why everybody serves *insalata caprese* now instead.

But mostly there is the best steak in Los Angeles, a huge New York strip for two: a charred, oblong blob with the oddly irregular, misshapen appearance most great steaks seem to have, drenched in a puddle of its own brown, glistening juices, probably enriched with melted butter.

Sliced open, the steak is the vivid purple of raspberry sherbet, barely lukewarm at its broad center, with the extraordinary texture of *toro* sashimi, almost alive beneath your teeth, with a startling mineral tartness that evolves like the bouquet of an old St. Emillon in your mouth. This is an extraordinary piece of meat. The first time I tasted it I barely noticed the waiter forgot to bring the cottage fries—and I generally consider fried potatoes to be proof of the continuing presence of a loving God.

The Palm's cheesecake, a cracked, sunken thing with the pure, tart essence of soured milk, is as perfect a creation as you will find on this earth.

PALM THAI RESTAURANT

5273 HOLLYWOOD BLVD., HOLLYWOOD; (323) 462-5073. SUN.–THURS., 11A.M.–1A.M.; FRI. AND SAT., 11A.M.–2A.M.

Palm Thai may be the most famous Thai supper club in Hollywood, and it seems as if it has always been around, anchoring a mini-mall that also includes a Thai buffet restaurant and the Thai-Chinese stronghold Ruen Pair. Thai tour buses often park out front. I used to go to Palm Thai with the late DJ Jac Zinder—the restaurant was the best place in Los Angeles to see touring Thai pop musicians—and although we would usually eat a few quail and an order of beef salad or something, the cooking seemed tangential to the music.

Now Palm Thai may be my favorite restaurant in Hollywood. On a crowded Saturday night, the band onstage tumbles through a set that sounds like the *Totally Awesome 80s* songbook translated into Thai, all breathy vocals and swooshy synthesizers, drum machines and guitar solos mailed in from backstage at a Journey concert. With the music come bottles of Singha. And with the beer, you eat Thai bar snacks: crisp-skinned Thai sour sausages hot from the grill, served with fried peanuts and raw cabbage; beef jerky, fried to a tooth-wrenching chaw; deep-fried little quail, glazed with salt and pepper, as crisp-skinned as Cantonese squab, whose strong-tasting dark meat oozes juice.

There is a proper papaya salad, the unripe fruit shredded into crunchy slaw, with taut chile heat, sweet-tart citrus dressing, and the briny sting of salt-preserved raw crab. The chicken-foot salad is a good call here: ghost-white shards of slithery meat tossed with slivers of raw red onion and assorted fresh herbs, sluiced with citrus, supercharged with a perfectly balanced spiciness. Palm Thai prepares the best version in Hollywood of *seua rong hai*, northeastern-style barbecued beef, a fatty, garlicky, well-charred cut, which tastes like the end piece of a really good roast beef, sliced and served with an intense, rust-colored chile purée that is the Thai equivalent of chipotle salsa.

As in most great Thai places, finding the restaurant's actual specialties requires a bit of persistence. Non-Thai customers are routinely brought a roster of the familiar cooking of suburban Thai restaurants—the pad Thai noodles, mint-leaf chicken, and naked shrimp you've seen five hundred times. Or you can request a second menu, which includes most of Palm Thai's best dishes: fiery salads, Isaan-style bar snacks, and elaborate soups. Much of the restaurant's exotica is confined to still a third, untranslated menu tucked inside the second one, and if you ask nicely, a waitress may translate a few items for you.

Try the red curry of wild boar, quite hot but tempered with coconut milk and flavored with lime leaves, *galangal,* and unripe green peppercorns still on the branch. The boar itself, sliced thinly and simmered in the sauce, has good flavor, like pork gone wild, and is chewy enough to occupy your teeth for hours. (Boar is not a meat for people who prize tenderness above all virtues.) Venison, done exactly the same way, tastes more like the deer your uncle Fred shot last season in Lone Pine than like the clean, denatured New Zealand venison you find at restaurants with valet parking. The braised quail is worth asking for, curried and stewed down into something that resembles a gamy Thai *salmi.*

Steamed trout, served with vegetables, comes in a heavy, fish-shaped chafing dish that sits over a Sterno inferno. As you eat the fish, seasoning it to taste with a chile-inflected fish sauce, you spoon light, lemongrass-infused broth from a tureen into the chafing dish and into your bowl. By the end of the meal, the trout and vegetables have added body and flavor to the bubbling broth, which has become a light, sophisticated fish soup on its own: spectacular.

Frog is available in a thin, fermented-bamboo curry which has the aroma of a clean barn and the heat of a Bessemer converter.

"This tastes good now," says the owner. "But it will hurt your butt in the morning."

Instead, stick to the pepper-garlic frog, crunchy, fried bits of the amphibian set on a layer of fried, minced garlic so thick that it looks at first like a plateful of granola, as much garlic as even a Thai person could want. The third time we ordered this dish, the frog was garnished with thin, moss-green, disconcertingly crunchy croutons of . . . deep-fried frog skin. What gave the game away were the bits of skin that had been slipped off the frog's feet, long, wrinkly toes and all, which were rolled elegantly at the top and bore an uncanny resemblance to opera-length frog gloves that Barbie might wear. Frog gloves: Accept no substitute.

PAPA CRISTO'S TAVERNA

2771 W. PICO BLVD., LOS ANGELES; (323) 737-2970. TUES.-SAT., 9A.M.-6:30P.M.; SUN., 9A.M.-4P.M.

C & K Importing is not a secret, exactly—it is among the best-known ethnic markets in Los Angeles—but if you haven't been in for a while, the vibrant

Greekness of the place may surprise you: the trays of baklava, the whole butchered lambs, the steaming pans of roast meat.

C & K is a couple of blocks away from Loyola, traditionally the highest-toned of southern California's Catholic high schools, and right across the street from the big Greek Orthodox church, but it is sometimes surprising to poke your head inside the old market on a Sunday and see a crowd that looks demographically closer to the neighborhood as it looked in 1949 than to the way it looks now. It's a place you'd expect to find on Halstead in Chicago, or somewhere in Astoria, Queens, but not on the Guatemalan fringes of Koreatown.

Papa Cristo's Taverna, a Greek restaurant at one side of C & K, is sometimes as crowded as the Pico bus at rush hour, a high-ceilinged takeout counter alive with the smells of garlic, cinnamon, and charred meat.

The menu at Papa Cristo's is simple practically to the point of nonexistence, and includes few of the dishes traditionally associated with Greek cooking; neither salvos of stuffed grape leaves nor fusillades of flaming cheese, complex stews nor elaborate shellfish plates.

What you get at Papa Cristo's is grilled animal: lamb chops or beef or whole fish or *loukinika* sausage, served as they would be at a church picnic that featured some spectacularly talented cooks. Everything comes on a plastic plate, nestled between a heap of creamy Greek-style fried potatoes and a tiny Greek salad. If the cook remembers, there will be a round of fresh pita bread hot from a smoky fire. There will definitely be a little plastic cup of *tzatzaki,* a powerfully tart sauce made with yogurt, garlic, and fresh dill that both overwhelms and improves everything it touches. And you will have a Mediterranean meal superior in every way to what costs three or four times as much in Brentwood or Beverly Hills.

PASEO CHAPIN

2220 W. 7TH St., LOS ANGELES; (213) 385-7420. DAILY, 10A.M.–9P.M.

Local TV newscasts may characterize the neighborhood around MacArthur Park as the center of crime in the civilized world, and it is certainly an easy place to buy a forged green card, but the area is a crossroads of Central-American commerce in Los Angeles. If you need to buy a bundle of banana leaves, Honduran-style bread, or papier-mâché statues of jungle birds, this is the place to go.

You could check out the entry-level capitalism at any of a zillion swap meets. You could walk around the lake and watch the fountain for a while, visit the rusty George Herms sculpture that looks a little like a miniature of the one they tried to kick out of Beverly Hills, or just scope the surrounding '20s architecture, which is almost a Raymond Chandler landscape come to brick and stone.

And after you're done, if you haven't filled up on chile-dusted mangoes from the street vendors or pastrami sandwiches at Langer's, you can walk across the street to Paseo Chapin, which may be the best place in Los Angeles for a Guatemalan lunch. On the walk to the restaurant from the (guarded) parking lot around the corner, you will almost certainly be afforded at least one opportunity to buy a bogus driver's license.

Once called Guatelinda, a slightly grimy restaurant where it sometimes seems everybody in town ate his first Guatemalan meal, Paseo Chapin is tubbed and scrubbed, soaringly high-ceilinged, with glass-covered tablecloths and walls painted the color of mint-chip ice cream. Tables are set up where musicians once wailed away on oversize marimbas; booming jukebox ballads pour from big speakers near the ceiling. The restaurant even smells good, in a meaty, garlicky, dinner-at-grandma's kind of way.

Guatemalan food is simple stuff, hearty and a little peasantlike, dominated by corn and beans and strong Mayan herbs, as close to pre-Colombian cooking as you'll find in Central America. Paseo Chapin's *pepìan* is a forceful version of this Maya stew: ground, spiced squash seeds, fortified with burnt bread and toasted chiles and thinned out with broth, overwhelming the boiled chicken that floats in it but also giving the rather ordinary bird substance. *Pollo con crema* is a revelation, a Latin American standard given life with an elegant, thin cream sauce, as tart as citrus, made from bell peppers and tart Guatemalan sour cream.

Paseo Chapin's *revolcado*, a gamy stew of pork parts, may mist the eyeglasses of expatriate Guatemalans, although it is probably more palatable chased down with a stiff shot of nostalgia. The grilled thin steaks and pork tend to be dry and a little dull; the meat-stuffed chiles rellenos are nothing to write home about. But everybody might like *longaniza*—little, coarse-textured sausages, hot with black pepper, laced with pungent dried herbs and grilled crisp, served with a fresh, chile-laced tomato salsa that has a deep, smoky bite.

The restaurant has a strong specialty in tamales: *cuchitos*, which are not unlike traditional Mexican corn-husk tamales, glazed with chile but slightly bland; *tamalitos de chilpìn*, more or less *cuchitos* laced with Guatemalan mint; and tamales Chapin, the house specialty of pork-stuffed masa steamed in a banana leaf, that has the wetness and herbal complexity of a Nicaraguan *naca tamal*. *Paches*, fluffy as if they were knitted from vicuña wool, are unusual banana-leaf tamales made with mashed potatoes instead of corn, tinted pink with chile.

Most dishes are served with a dollop of puréed beans, black as ink, a couple of caramelized bananas with salty Guatemalan cream and some brothy rice. The fried plantains are probably sweet enough to stand as dessert on their own, but once in your life, you should try a real Guatemalan *mole de plátano*, tart slices of fried plantain blanketed with a thick, dangerous sauce made with toasted seeds, cinnamon, and the bitterest imaginable chocolate.

PHILIPPE THE ORIGINAL

1001 N. ALAMEDA ST., LOS ANGELES; (213) 628-3781. DAILY, BREAKFAST, LUNCH, AND DINNER.

Late in the afternoon at Philippe the Original, the restaurant mostly emptied of the last of the lunch crowd, a waitress stretches and yawns behind the stainless-steel service counter as if she's just awoken. She counts·out seven olives from a bin in the back, five cents apiece. She smacks a cardboard "Closed" sign in front of her station. Her shift ends in a minute, and she hums to herself as she slices big, assymetrical slabs off the outside of a leg of lamb. She lets a French roll soak in a bowl of salty pan drippings just a second or two longer than is strictly necessary, but not so long as to soften the crisp edges of the slash in the roll's top. She cuts slices from a block of good American blue cheese thinly and sort of laminates it to the roll with a brisk twist of her knife. She is happy to be serving her last French dip sandwich of the day, and she seems to savor the wine order. "Silver Oak," she says, rolling the words around in her mouth. "Silver is very lucky for the new year. It means you will make a lot of money." She walks over to the Cruvinet at the rear of the service area, and measures out a healthy slug of wine. She smiles. "To a prosperous new year," she says.

Time moves slowly at Philippe's when you sit at a chest-high table in the main dining room, reading somebody's wrinkled old sports section and crunching saw-dust beneath your feet. The lamb sandwich is wet and rich, with something of the gamy animal stink of old-fashioned roast meat; the cabernet is a strong, deep-purple wine that tastes of blackberries and sharpened pencils and vanilla-scented new-oak barrels. All around the restaurant you can see nostrils flare when people hit little depth charges of Philippe's hot mustard in their sandwiches. Philippe's is a fine place to have lunch. Philippe's is so much a part of old Los Angeles that sometimes it feels as if it isn't a part of Los Angeles at all, as if it belongs to a city much older, much more attached to its distant past than this place where historic preservation committees work to save old branches of McDonald's. A 1951 newspaper column mounted on the wall actually begs Philippe's not to mess the place up with chrome, a substance that was the travertine marble of L.A.'s Golden Age. Everybody who has lived in Los Angeles more than a year knows the story of the restaurant, how Philippe himself supposedly invented the French dip eighty years ago when he accidentally dropped a sandwich into some gravy, how the coffee still costs a dime, how it is one of the very few places that cost-conscious county supervisors are allowed to eat expense-account meals.

I am one of the few Philippe's apostates—I happen to believe that the French dip was "invented" at the slightly older Cole's P. E. Buffet at 6th and Main, which has not only a slightly better sandwich but also Ritterbrau on tap—but I still find myself at the restaurant more often than I sometimes believe.

PHILLIPS BARBECUE

4307 LEIMERT BLVD., LOS ANGELES; (323) 292-7613. MON.–SAT., LUNCH
AND DINNER.

Phillips Barbecue is situated at the hub of the Crenshaw district, in the shadow
of the old Watchtower complex, right where Crenshaw and Vernon run headlong
into Leimert. The restaurant, tucked into a mini-mall between a liquor store and
the local chapter of Alcoholics Anonymous, is a little hard to see from the street,
but if you keep your window open, you should be able to sniff out the hickory
from half a mile away.

The order line snakes from the takeout window, through the long, narrow
lobby, out the door, onto the sidewalk. The inside of the restaurant itself is nearly
as vast as two well-smoked phone booths placed side to side. On weekends, the
line veers left where it seems in danger of spilling into the cars that roar though
the parking lot. When the wind is right, the line bastes in a pungent haze of
woodsmoke. At Phillips, supper sometimes takes more dedication than some people think is strictly necessary. But is Phillips worth the fuss? Yes. This is the best
barbecue in southern California. Spareribs, crusted with black and deeply smoky,
are rich and crisp and juicy, not too lean. Beef ribs, almost as big around as beer
cans, are beefy as rib roasts beneath their coat of char, tasty even without the
sauce. (The big Styrofoam containers of extra-hot sauce, with a scary, solid inch
of whole chile peppers floating on top, can be pretty exhilarating for a pepper
freak.) House-made beef hot links, denser than some, are gently spiced, closer to
bouncy bratwurst than to intense, coarse-ground monsters. Chicken, smoked
through to the bone, retains all its juice, though overcooked sliced beef does not.
Even the beans taste good, packed with more smoke and spice than most places
manage to get into their ribs.

That's why everybody was surprised one Saturday when a guy toward the
middle of the line actually left without any food: "I got takeout here just last
Tuesday," he said. "I think I'm going to get me some chicken somewhere else."
"Last Tuesday?" said a woman two places back. "Dear, I come here three times
a week. You can't get better food than at Phillips." But really, I think she was
pleased to be thirty seconds closer to her small-end dinner, extra-hot sauce. Mr.
Phillips himself, natty in suit and tie, peered out the front end of the place and
grinned.

PHO 79

727 N. BROADWAY, SUITE 120, CHINATOWN; (213) 625-7026. DAILY, 8:30A.M.–7P.M.

In a city thick with Vietnamese noodle shops specializing in fragrant beef noodle soup, one of them has to be the best. And among the hundred-odd I've tried, there is no contest: Pho 79 simply serves the best *pho* (pronounced "fur") in town, as its precursor did in Saigon, and as its sister Pho 79s do in Westminster, Long Beach, and Monterey Park.

If you like noodles, you might agree Pho 79 serves the perfect breakfast, light, tasty and just exotic enough, inexpensive and filled with vitamins. There's sweet, freshly squeezed orange juice—also lemonade and the tropical fruit drink *guanabana*—and also soy milk for the lactophobe. The strong, dark-roasted coffee, dripped at table in individual stainless-steel French filters, is great.

As in most Vietnamese noodle shops, Pho 79's best dish is listed first on the menu: *pho dac biet*, house-special *pho*, with slices of brisket, tendon, tripe and rare beef laid atop slippery rice noodles and submerged in a beef broth fragrant with garlic and cinnamon, onion and herbs. If you hesitate more than an instant when ordering, a waiter may bark "Number One?" Even before ten in the morning, two-thirds of the people here are slurping the giant bowls of *pho*.

No two people eat *pho* the same way. You can squeeze a little lime juice or squirt some chile or hoisin sauce into the soup, or mix in bean sprouts, sliced hot chiles and leaves of fresh Vietnamese basil from a plate of herbs, making the dish something of a salad. The soup, tasty enough on its own, becomes obscenely good. If you order the variation called *pho tai*, noodles with rare beef, you can ask for the beef on the side; you dip the slices of raw beef in hot soup until they turn opaque, then dip them into a special chile paste. Other versions of *pho* include higher or lower proportions of brisket or tripe, or include beef meatballs that are gamy with Vietnam's ubiquitous fish sauce: the dish is almost infinitely customizable.

Almost everything at Pho 79 that isn't beef soup has something to do, somehow, with the combination of cool rice noodles and garlicky barbecued pork. With *bun cha*, the grilled bits of pork—marinating in *nuoc cham*, the clear, sweet garlic-fish sauce that is to Vietnamese cooking what soy sauce is to Chinese—are served, garnished with ground peanuts and fried chips of garlic, in a separate bowl. Plain vermicelli comes in a second bowl, crisp romaine lettuce in a third. The idea is to roll it all up into bundles of food, like little noodle-filled lettuce-leaf burritos, then dip them in *nuoc cham*.

Bun thit nuong is more or less the same thing, except the lettuce and the pork are on top of the noodles in a bowl and you add the *nuoc cham* to taste; *bun tom thit nuong* throws in a couple of charbroiled shrimp; *bun thit nuong cha gio* includes some chopped up Vietnamese spring rolls tossed right in there with the noodles; *bun bao*, not as delicious, substitutes sautéed beef. For a change, you can have the terrific fresh egg rolls called *goi cuon*, which is a fresh spring roll made with our old friends pork, shrimp, lettuce, and vermicelli wrapped up in a sheet of edible rice paper, ready to dip in the chile-spiked hoisin sauce called *nuoc leo*.

The fried spring rolls, *cha gio*, stuffed with thin noodles and a crab and pork forcemeat, come seven to an order, hotly spiced with black pepper. You wrap the crisp dumplings with marinated carrots in leaves of romaine as you do the *bun cha*—during the summer there are sometimes four or five different herbs to wrap in with them, mint, cilantro, and two or three kinds of fresh basil—and dip it in yet another bowl of *nuoc cham*. (Without fail, your party will end up with several bowls of fish sauce apiece and enough greenery to feed a gerbil for a year.)

Of course, Pho 79 does have a few drawbacks. On weekend mornings, you may have to wait. They haven't changed their one Vietnamese easy-listening tape in more than a decade, and if you go every week, you get to know the songs pretty well. And they're invariably closed the one day in the middle of the week you decide to carpool from downtown for lunch. Call ahead.

PHUONG

710 W. LAS TUNAS DRIVE, SAN GABRIEL; (626) 282-6327. DAILY, 11A.M.– 10P.M.

Phuong, sometimes called Pagôde Saigon, is a mini-mall palace of Vietnamese beef. There is *pho*, of course, as well as barbecued beef balls, grilled beef, and beef ribs served with spring rolls over rice.

Mostly though, Phuong is devoted to the Saigon cult of all-beef dinners, the famous feast known as *bo bay mon:* seven courses of cow brought to you one after the other until you drop.

The first thing you've got to know about the seven-beef dinner is that it's labor-intensive in a way that makes Korean barbecue seem like white-glove butler service. Until you get bored with the process halfway through the meal, you wrap each bite of food into a little rice-paper burrito with herbs and vegetables, then dip each bundle into a dish of sauce. And it takes a little technical work to get it right.

The basket of herbs includes Vietnamese purple basil and plain old regular basil, mint and cilantro, crisp leaves of romaine, and a spiky Vietnamese herb, *rau ram*, whose flavor can remind you of the sensation experienced when you accidentally bite into a piece of aluminum foil. There are marinated matchsticks of carrot and daikon, paper-thin slices of cucumber, mounds of bean sprouts, and acerbic slices of raw eggplant. The rice paper comes in a tall, moist stack, and the trick is to peel off a single sheet of paper without tearing it in half. The deeply weird pineapple-anchovy sauce *nam mem* comes in a communal crock, from which you spoon out a portion into a little private bowl and add chile or not as you please.

First up come slices of rose-red raw beef, fanned out on a plate. You swish the beef a slice at a time through a tabletop pot of boiling vinegar just until it whitens, then wrap it in rice paper with vegetables and a splosh of the *nam mem*. A big, fluffy steamed meatball studded with clear noodles is something like a loose, sweetly spiced Vietnamese pâté, if you are the type of person to scoop up pâté with shrimp chips. A platter of stuff midway through the meal includes grilled meatballs, tough strips of grilled beef already rolled around vegetables (which doesn't excuse you from having to roll them up again in rice paper), and little cylinders of minced beef wrapped in Hawaiian *la lot* leaves, which either do or do not have a narcotic effect, depending on whom you believe.

Item six is a sautéed-beef salad in a powerful vinaigrette. Item seven is a powerfully flavored beef soup, clear and concentrated, pungent with ginger and garlic, with a tablespoon or so of rice at the bottom. You don't wrap the soup.

Bo bay mon is surprisingly cheap, and the staff doesn't seem to mind if two split just one dinner.

PIE 'N BURGER

913 E. CALIFORNIA BLVD., PASADENA; (626) 795-1123. MON.–FRI., 6A.M.– 10P.M.; SAT.–SUN., 7A.M.–9P.M.

Pie 'N Burger is an unprepossessing place, a neighborhood hamburger joint with a long counter, a couple of tables, and the sort of wood-grain Formica that brings to mind stereo-speaker veneer. Regular customers slide onto their regular stools, their regular orders long memorized by the waitresses.

Of course the neighborhood is just around the corner from Pasadena's elegant Lake Avenue shopping district and just a couple of blocks from Caltech, which means the guy next to you may be reading a long physics proof over his ham and eggs as if it were the morning paper, and the Barbara Bush pearls the woman at the end of the counter is wearing could very well be real. Pie 'N Burger is locally famous for its big omelets, its pancake breakfasts, its crisp, slightly oily hash browns. This is one of the few places anywhere where a truck driver, a socialite and a Nobel Prize–winning chemist might sit side by side.

Like all good hamburgers, a Pie 'N Burger burger is about texture: the crunch of lettuce, the charred, slightly friable surface of the meat, the outer rim of the bun crisped to almost the consistency of toast. When compressed by the act of eating, the hamburger leaks thick, pink dressing that is somewhat more tart than it may look; soft, grilled onions, available upon request, add both a certain squishiness and a caramelly sweetness.

The slice of American cheese, if you have ordered a cheeseburger, does not melt into the patty, but stands glossily aloof from it, as if it were mocking the richness of the sandwich rather than adding to the general effect. The burgers here come jacketed in white paper, and are compact enough to remain generally intact through three-quarters of their life—it's kind of a genteel thing, a Pie 'N Burger burger, not one of those greasy monsters that explode into pungent goop.

French fries, the finger-thick kind that taste mostly like potato, are great, crisp outsides giving way to steamy, firm interiors, and a single half-order is easily enough for two. Cokes are hand mixed with syrup and seltzer, which means you can order them to your liking; the chocolate shakes are dense as plutonium.

For dessert, as you may have inferred from the restaurant's name, there are pies: ultra-sweet pecan pies, custardy coconut creams with marshmallow topping, banana creams oozing from beneath tall lashings of meringue, fresh-strawberry and fresh-peach pies in season and classic canned-cherry pies, none of them perfect, but an ideal conclusion to a genteel hamburger lunch.

THE PINES

4343 PEARBLOSSOM HIGHWAY, PALMDALE; (805) 947-7455. DAILY, 7A.M.–2P.M.

To get to the Pines, you speed down the Pearblossom Highway from Palmdale, through a landscape of dirt, Joshua trees, and squeaky-new housing tracts, past dozens of billboards advertising master-planned communities, toward low, red buttes that thrust into the teal sky. It used to be in the middle of nowhere; now the Pines is in the middle of nowhere special. You'll probably cruise right past the tiny pine grove that's just about the only thing of the restaurant you can see from a distance on the road, that and one of those dim bent-arrow things you sometimes see by desert gas stations. If you pass the local swap meet, you've gone too far. The Pines is the kind of place where the waitresses joke about being picketed by Weight Watchers; where biscuits automatically come blanketed with luscious cream gravy that must be the stuff of every cowboy's dream. Inside, the Pines is tidy, a couple of picnic tables covered with oilcloth, and a worn lunch counter eight stools long. There's a funk of coffee and fried onions and cigarettes in the air: It smells like breakfast in those parts of the country where green vegetables are still thought of as a communist plot. A cook wears a button that reads "Eat and Go Home." The walls are trimmed with shellacked Dad's-den paneling and hung with old Antelope Valley rodeo posters. It's a family restaurant,

236

but mostly to the sort of families where Mom wears faded Led Zeppelin T-shirts and Junior's known how to ride shotgun on a Harley since he was three.

Visualize an enormous oval restaurant plate, then imagine that plate blanketed with a golden, oval pancake half an inch thick. Sliding across the surface of the pancake, a robin's egg of melting butter leaves a salty trail. Next to the plate is a little bowl of fresh tomato salsa, juicy in the Central California manner rather than spicy, and another of chopped jalapeño peppers. The pancake, an occasional Pines special called a tortilla cake—the batter is enriched with masa, cornmeal and ground hominy—tastes the way you've always wanted a tortilla to taste, warm and soft and sweet as corn, fragrant, slightly burnt around the edges. It's a full pound of pancake. Or picture the same plate striped like the flag of some obscure African republic: yellow of a three-egg omelet, white of biscuits 'n' gravy; sandy brown of a half-pound or so of well-done fried potatoes, a weighty analog to the nouvelle presentation of a Michael's or a Le Dome but no less carefully done.

The Pines also specializes in something they call a "*Quiki*," whole yellow hominy scrambled with eggs and things like jack cheese, country ham and Ortega chiles, the whole meltingly good. (A *Quiki* might be a frontier interpretation of a traditional Indian dish; then again, it might not.) The Loco Quiki, an incredible 1,500-calorie grease bomb screaming with peppery chorizo, is the one you should try.

I'd first heard about the place from two guys who ran a rock 'n' roll diner in Hollywood, an expatriate Brit and a Western-swing crooner whose obsession with post–Dust Bowl Americana included frequent road trips here. Their own restaurant, an eight-stool lunch counter, was littered with such Pines touches as battered chalkboard menus and chipped coffee cups, as well as gallons of 30-weight cream gravy. Behind the counter, the guys would pour coffee and fry bacon and rave about the fantastic, badger-size hamburgers served just an hour's drive north. And sad as I was when their diner changed hands, since the first time I finally made it up to the Pines, I've hardly missed it at all.

The three-quarter-pound Pine Burgers are the hugest things, bigger in diameter than some asteroids, the best conceivable version of a coffee-shop hamburger—the thousand island dressing is homemade, but it's still thousand island, if you know what I mean—and almost worthy of the computer-printed sign on one wall that says something like "Best Hamburger on Planet Earth: The Pines—Voyager 2." (There's a smaller burger, but you've driven all this way, why bother?) Chicken-fried steak is the *pièce de résistance* of the cowboy *cordon bleu*. The Pines' is of the no-frills variety, just a thick, batter-fried slab of protein, but the crunchy gold bubbles of crust soften just so under a white blanket of gravy, the meat has the fibrous resistance of a really good steak, and you can actually taste the beef: perfect. Save room for the raisin pie.

PINK'S

711 N. LA BREA AVE, HOLLYWOOD; (323) 931-4223. OPEN DAILY FOR LUNCH AND DINNER.

Pink's, of course, is the legendary Hollywood chili dog stand, opened in the '30s by hot dog king Paul Pink, conveniently open after the bars close, and decorated with more signed 8×10 glossies than all the dry cleaners in Beverly Hills.

But have you ever been to Pink's when it opens in the morning, when the giant blocks of chili in the steamtable haven't yet completely melted into orange grease, when the customers consist mostly of cops and copy-shop dudes, when you talk yourself into believing chili dog breath before noon may not be a liability?

Consider the Pink's dog, uncouth and garlicky, tapered and uncommonly slender, skin thick and taut, so that when you sink your teeth into it, the sausage ... pops ... into a mouthful of juice. The bun is steamed, just so, soft enough to sort of become a single substance with the thick chili that is ladled over the dog, but firm enough to resist dissolving altogether, unless you order your hot dog with hot sauerkraut. Crisp chunks of raw onion provide a little texture; a splash of vinegary yellow mustard supplies the hint of acidity that balances the richly flavored whole.

Pink's also serves hamburgers, but I can't say that I have met anybody who has actually eaten one.

POLLO A LA BRASA

764 S. WESTERN AVE., LOS ANGELES; (323) 382-4090. 16527 S. VERMONT AVE., GARDENA; (562) 715-2494. DAILY, FOR LUNCH AND DINNER.

The first thing you may notice about Pollo a la Brasa, a Peruvian chicken joint on a traffic island near the edge of Koreatown, is the wood smoke, great billowing draughts that perfume downwind noodle shops and coffee bars, make the nearby Salvadoran cafés smell as if they served barbecue instead of *pupusas* and occasionally offer a whiff of disaster in the night to high-floor apartment dwellers.

Split logs are piled everywhere—behind the restaurant, blocking the front door, behind fences and in the kitchen, spilling over onto half the square footage of the wedge-shaped parking lot.

Inside the restaurant, a tiny takeout place that seems no smokier than, say, the inside of a chimney, most of the floor space is taken up by an assembly line in the back, guys impaling chickens onto thick steel skewers, jamming threaded chickens into a vast, flame-licked apparatus, hacking chickens into parts with the dexterity of machete-wielding orthopedists and tossing them onto piles of French fries. Chicken and fries is about the extent of the menu here.

The chicken here is remarkable, well garlicked, slightly spicy, marked with pungent smoke, clearly the marriage of a chicken and a smoldering log. The softness of the meat betrays slight over-marination, but the flesh is juicy, the herbal flavor clear, the skin caramelized and crisp.

With the chicken comes a standard salad and little plastic cups of *aji*, a smooth mint-green chile purée that is almost hot enough to sear the skin off your lips. The fries are made from fresh-cut potatoes, but cooked in that limp, peculiarly Latin American style that accentuates the musky sweetness of potatoes rather than their potential crispness. To drink, you'll find the usual cans of Inca Kola and the Peruvian purple corn beverage *chicha morada*, which always sounds more exotic than the vaguely clove-scented Kool-Aid it turns out to be.

There is also a small grill devoted to *anticuchos*, garlicky little shish kebabs of beef heart. In Lima, street vendors manage to make beef heart taste better than steak—smoky, a little blackened, as meltingly juicy as prime fillet. The *anticuchos* here may not be quite the charbroiled pencil-erasers you'll find as appetizers at certain South Bay Peruvian restaurants but are probably not the dish that will persuade you that cow organs are worth eating.

PORTOBANCO'S

5779 W. VENICE BLVD., LOS ANGELES; (323) 937-5144. DAILY, 11A.M.–9P.M.

Once the site of Keste Demena, the best Ethiopian restaurant Los Angeles has ever known, the Nicaraguan bistro Portobanco's sometimes feels less like a restaurant than like a movie set of a restaurant circa 1979: tablecloths protected under glass, travel posters placed a little too randomly on the walls, the bar just 10 percent too elaborate for a place where nobody has ever had a stiff drink.

On weekends, Portobanco's serves *nacatamals*, which are soft, brick-size tamales steamed in banana leaves and stuffed with vegetables and meat, not the epochal *nacatamals* that used to be a specialty of the late Highland Park Nicaraguan restaurant La Plancha, but plenty good. *Repochetas* are crisp, oily turnovers stuffed with slabs of chewy, salty Nicaraguan frying cheese, sprinkled with crumbles of sharp grating cheese, and smeared with a melting tablespoonful of thick, Nicaraguan *crema*, which has almost the decadent, nutty, mega-butterfat groove of a French Explorateur: a deep-fried dairy extravaganza.

Portobanco's makes a proper version of Nicaragua's national salad, *vigoron*— logs of steamed yucca arranged into the rough shape of a pinwheel, layered with tart, spicy cabbage slaw called *curtido*, then strewn with slabs of fried pigskin, crunchy, a little chewy, meaty yet bland. *Vigoron* has the play of flavors you might expect from a legendary folk food, the almost Play-Doh-like consistency of the starchy tuber playing off against the cool crackle of the cabbage, the jerkylike chaw of the pigskin working against yucca's bland inertness, but where *vigoron* sometimes snaps—a great *vigoron* goes pretty well with a cold beer—Portobanco's version is a little monochromatic, a little too much like poverty food.

Entrées, as at most Nicaraguan restaurants, are served with rice, black beans, and a little square of the chewy fried cheese. *Fritanga*, a traditional Nicaraguan combo plate, is dominated by well-marinated chunks of deep-fried pork. *Puerco asado*, pan-fried pork, tends to be a little stringy and overcooked. *Pescado estilo Tipitapa*, a fried perch done in the style of Tipitapa, a town near Managua, is tasty, topped with a sauté of tomatoes, onions, and peppers that's slightly astringent against the crisp, salty fish.

Not everything's great here. A roast garlic chicken tastes a little like last night's Versailles bird. *Tostones*, fried green plantains, are dry, chunky things. On the other hand, *salpicon*, the salad of chopped beef, onions, and diced radish you will find on pretty much every menu between Guadalajara and Tierra del Fuego, can be swell, coarsely chopped, gently fragrant, blood warm and a couple degrees more well-done than usual, so that the dish may remind you of the browned bits left in the bottom of the pan after you cook a roast.

Don't miss the *cacao*, a cold drink made from crushed whole cocoa beans and spiced like an exotic pudding.

THE PRINCE

3198 ½ W. SEVENTH ST., LOS ANGELES; (323) 389-2007. OPEN DAILY, 4 P.M.–MIDNIGHT.

The Ambassador district was one of the swankiest areas in '50s Los Angeles, home to leather-booth steakhouses, to tony supper clubs, to intimate cafes where swooning love couples were serenaded by White Russians playing gypsy violin. The fanciest restaurant in the Ambassador district—and one of the three or four swellest places in the city as a whole—was the Windsor, just east of the Ambassador Hotel, a dim-lit cave that served food of a formality almost impossible to imagine today.

Generations of Angelenos passed through the Windsor, learning to eat sweetbreads, dining on things like veal *forestiere*, Sea Breeze salad and lobster Thermidor that were finished tableside by tuxedoed waiters. The Windsor was the last place in town that still served old-fashioned flaming desserts like crepes Suzettes and cherries jubilee.

But the neighborhood changed. The half-dozen hotels that provided much of the restaurant's clientele closed down, and the average age of a Windsor patron crept up toward Bob Hope's. Just at the point a couple of years ago when retro chic might have saved the place—the bar was on the verge of becoming a hip hang for the Young Hollywood crowd—the Windsor shut down.

Only in Los Angeles could a place like the Windsor be transformed into a smoky Korean singles joint, the Prince. Imagine a Korean pub shoehorned into the fanciest restaurant in Los Angeles circa 1953, complete with the lawn jockeys at the top of the stairs, oil paintings of earls above the oxblood leather banquettes, and an Esquire Haute Cuisine Award plaque that was probably there on the wall when Wolfgang Puck was in grade school.

Where the Windsor used to have a characteristic scent of Sterno and grilling chops, the Prince is heavy with the smell of *kimchi* and fried fish; where you once heard a lot of Johnny Mercer from a cocktail pianist, you hear Whitney Houston and bouncy Korean pop music today. About the only constant is the traveling businessmen who still gather in shirtsleeves at the bar, eating fish, chain-smoking, and looking wistfully at the secretarial pool, except these days the suits' home offices tend to be in Seoul instead of Hartford or Kokomo.

The food, you understand, is not exactly the point at the Prince, which seems to specialize in grilled Korean sausages, American dishes that might have been inspired by Quad Cities Rotary–banquet menus from 1963, and plates of fried shrimp and fish not all that different from what you'd get at the local Long John Silver. Still, if you like Korean bar snacks, you can eat pretty well.

Korea may have one of the subtlest, varied, most intensely regional cuisines of the world, but Korean bar food is something else: universally spicy, salty, sweetish stuff whose basic purpose is to persuade you to buy another bottle of beer. The basic unit of currency at the Prince is the *kimchi* pancake, a thin mass of egg batter laced with the tart fermented cabbage, lashed together with scallions, then fried to an exquisite, oily crispness. *Kimchi* pancakes come free with your drinks, which makes sense, because the greasy heat of the things, the salt and tart, are enough to power you through couple of double-size bottles of Korean Hite beer. There's a lot of dried fish here—the chewy squid and minnows and whatever that are the Korean equivalents of Beer Nuts—and peppery Korean meatballs as compelling as Slim Jims.

Mostly what you get at the Prince are vastly proportioned Korean versions of basic Chinese stirfries, lumps of meat or tofu deep-fried, then braised with vegetables in an appealing glop of bean paste, red chile, and garlic. These stirfries—whether shrimp, pork, or squid—seem identical, right down to the relaxed state of the onions and sauteed red bell pepper and the handful of sesame seeds scattered on top.

Say what you will about spicy sautéed octopus: any posh restaurant whose idea of romantic date-night cuisine involves fried tentacles and half a pound of garlic is a restaurant whose time has come.

R

RAJDOOT

11833 ARTESIA BLVD., ARTESIA; (562) 860-6500. DAILY, LUNCH AND
DINNER UNTIL 10:30P.M.

The restaurant Rajdoot marks the northern edge of Artesia's Little India neighborhood, the Pioneer Avenue drag of sari merchants and jewelry joints, Indian
music stores and posters that advertise Parsi-Gujarati spectaculars. Indian snack
shops, Indian fast-food places, and fragrant grocery stores well stocked with fresh
turmeric run two or more to a block. In this part of town, *samosas* are as common
as tacos, turbans as frequently seen as cowboy hats are in Texas.

Rajdoot, owned by a consortium of Indian-American businessmen (including
the owner of the splendid snack shop Standard Sweets a mile down the road), is
Little India's fancy place, softly scented and gently lit, with soft cloth napkins on
the tables and bowls of breath-sweetening cardomom pods placed strategically by
the door. Each dish is served in gleaming copper tureens and is a couple of dollars
more expensive than it would be at one of the less formal restaurants down the
street. Everywhere you look are glittering knickknacks, rich fabrics, even an
Indian-art coffee-table book or two strategically propped in a wall niche. Weekends, a sitar player, who may be the equivalent of the harpist in a tearoom, drones
serenely from a low, pillow-covered stage. Rajdoot is not a curry joint.

The items on the menu are each rapturously described in English, making it
easy to pick out a meal, and though you will probably end up drinking big bottles
of excellent, smoky Taj Mahal beer from Bombay, there is a lengthy wine list.
Rajdoot is still where the local Indian community holds its intimate recitals and
fancy receptions, so it is a good idea to call before making the long drive from
Los Angeles.

When Rajdoot opened several years ago, it featured a chef from Hyderabad
and a dozen or so dishes that had never been seen in the Southland, exotic

vegetable concoctions and elaborate *pulaos*. Now the menu has settled down into more or less the familiar trans-Indian mode of a lot of other restaurants, but Rajdoot's food is creamier, more elegant, more complexly spiced than you'll find at other local Indian places, closer to chef-driven cuisine than to folk cooking.

There is a light tomato-herb soup, a turmeric-yellow mulligatawny that conceals bits of lamb in its spicy depths, and cubes of fresh, white cheese that are lightly battered and cooked until they are crisp and melting. *Pappadum* crackers are light as air, served with a pair of chutneys. Tandoori chicken is crunchy and fiery red, rushed sizzling from oven to table; *paneer tikka*, tandoor-roasted cubes of marinated fresh, white cheese, are bland and soothing as a young, pretty singer of *ghazals*. *Samosas* can be leaden as West Coast knishes, but breads—crisp garlic *naan*, sweet onion *kulcha*, potato-stuffed *paratha*—tend to be superb.

The tomatoey Goa-style fish curry—sort of a South Indian equivalent of *huichinago a la Veracruzana*—is tart and sweet and wonderful, and the *kadai murgh*, sort of a spicy, northern-style chicken stew, is good. The most successful main dishes here, though, tend to be vegetarian. *Dal makhani*, a gingery dish of stewed black lentils, seems closer to great Tuscan hearth-baked *fagioli* than to the usual thin yellow glop. *Navratan korma*, cauliflower and peapods and such, is simmered in a spectacular, richly sweet cashew-cream gravy. A startlingly delicious dish of stewed okra manages to be smoky and herbal and blistering hot all at once.

Perhaps because of its connection with Standard Sweets, Rajdoot is one of the few local Indian restaurants where the desserts measure up to the food. Check out the cool, spice-scented rice pudding or the wonderfully sweet, steaming-hot carrot compote.

REDDI-CHICK

IN THE BRENTWOOD COUNTRY MART, 225 26TH ST., SANTA MONICA; (310) 393-5238. MON.–SAT., 9:30A.M.–7:30P.M.

You may have heard people expound with Talmudic subtlety on the nuances of a perfect dish of *cholent*, the exact species of marine life that might make their way into a proper bouillabaisse, and the range of permissible textures in a dish of Lebanese minced lamb. You may have friends who claim to know where to get the best duck-tongue noodles, where the Liberian *fufu* is fluffiest, whose soufflés rise the highest. But everybody thinks they know where to get the best roast chicken in town. On the Westside, the answer is likely to be Brentwood Country Mart.

Brentwood Country Mart, at the nexus between Brentwood and the pricier stretches of Santa Monica, is a more sprawling courtyard mall patinated with the sort of homey rusticity best pulled off in an area with no actual farmers. There's a pretty good bookstore shoehorned in toward the entrance, a tony baby-clothes store, and a non-Starbucksian place to buy latte. The market itself is small but has a pretty good butcher shop and real Connecticut-suburb feel.

But to most people in the exalted reaches north of Montana, the Country Mart is synonymous with Reddi-Chick, whose roaring fire and golden-skinned roasting fowl exude an aroma almost powerful enough to reach down into Santa Monica Canyon. The usual call at Reddi-Chick is the chicken basket—half a roast chicken buried beneath a high mound of fries—and generations of Westside kids have learned how to customize their chicken basket with extra dollops of barbecue sauce, smears of sour cream, and giant gobs of Dijon mustard. They have tried the other menu items at Reddi-Chick. They know to stick to the basket.

Because while Reddi-Chick's staple product is probably not the best chicken you've ever had—the breast meat could be somewhat less dry; a little fresh garlic wouldn't hurt—it's really good. Westsiders like to compare the bird with the earthier, ultimately better chickens at Zankou, but a Reddi-Chick is more like an ideal version of the chickens that twirl in heated supermarket cases, mildly seasoned but crisp, with bits of caramelized skin that stick to your teeth, and a developed, mellow sweetness that will scent your hands for the rest of the day no matter how many Kiehl's products you apply to them.

RED LION

2366 GLENDALE BLVD., SILVER LAKE; (323) 662-5337. DAILY, 11A.M.– 2A.M.

All half-timbers, dark lights, and Ritterbrau on tap, Red Lion is a Teutonic Disney fantasy at the eastern edge of the Silver Lake district, where beer is served in boots, the waitresses wear peasant dresses tight-fitting enough to give Helmut Newton night sweats, and your dinner makes its way upstairs from the kitchen in a dumbwaiter that pulleys the heavy, basic German food into a kind of sauerkraut-scented armoire. (It's enough to make you respect the wonders of high technology: a private elevator for *schweinenbraten*.)

Squadrons of beer steins, most of them for sale, are displayed behind glass on the walls. In the men's room, the week's California *Staats-Zeitung* is strategically mounted behind Plexiglas for convenient stand-up reading. Sometimes there's an accordion player who will play "Eine Polische Mädchen" for a small donation. More often, a guy bangs out stuff like "Bette Davis Eyes" on a small but intensively programmed synthesizer, sometimes accompanying himself on alto sax.

Early in the evening, there's usually a scattering of native Germans at the bar, though lately they've been outnumbered by arty Silver Lake dudes and the kind of shaggy music-scene guys who always know where to find the best suds in any neighborhood. The Red Lion serves Bitburger on tap, and the various shades of Ritterbrau, but the beer to get is Spaten Weissbier, tart as limeade, refreshing with a slice of lemon on a hot summer night.

Open late, populated but rarely overcrowded, Red Lion may not be the most refined restaurant in Los Angeles, but it has always been a good place for a beer and a wurst—knockwurst, bratwurst, weisswurst, bockwurst, German-style wieners—as well as the tasty smoked pork chops called *kasslerrippchen* and the jiggly pork hock called *eisbein.*

Leberkase, or veal loaf, is more or less like a flat, soft sausage without the skin, about the size and thickness of a slice of Wonder Bread, with a smack of garlic and smoke that is astonishingly like that of a Dodger Dog, garnished with an egg hard-fried to a beef-jerky chewiness for contrast. Red Lion's farmer's plate includes one sausage stuffed with a sweetly seasoned mixture of blood; another filled with something like hot, loose liverwurst; and a slab of bacon cut thickly as steak.

The sausage platter may be even more spectacularly caloric: a giant plate covered with chunks of bratwurst and knockwurst, cut into chunks and bristling with dozens of the kind of fancy cellophane-tufted toothpicks that classy coffee shops use to fasten your BLT, the polar opposite of a vegetarian plate.

Vegetarians, of course, will find little here that doesn't have at least a lashing of bacon fat for ballast. But oddly enough in this palace of meat, the best dish may be the fish dish called *rollmops:* cool, silvery slabs of marinated herring, cleanly fishy, so heavily vinegared you can choke a little on the fumes if you take too big a first bite. The herring comes with a great pile of something close to the perfect potatoes, fried crisp in bacon grease and dotted with wilted onions—in other words, just the sort of fish for which liter-size beer mugs were invented.

RED'S CAFE

1102 E. 22nd ST., LOS ANGELES; (213) 745-9909. DAILY, 8A.M.–4:30P.M.

If Norman Rockwell had palled around with Chester Himes, he might have come up with something like Red's Cafe, a soul-food diner tucked away off Griffith Avenue, a U-counter fried-chicken peep into America's recent past, only five minutes southeast of downtown. Red's is about forty years old but seems even older, a long, narrow storefront that fills up at noon and is as much a part of the neighborhood as the streetlights or the grocery stores.

At the turn of the century, most of Los Angeles probably looked like this area—tidy Victorian houses on the residential streets, gabled two-story apartment buildings on the thoroughfares, corner markets scattered every few blocks—

though now it feels more like the old parts of Portland or San Francisco. The corner of the central city least touched by redevelopment—even Beaux Arts redevelopment—this may be one of the few remaining parts of town still laid out for pedestrians.

At Red's, a coolerful of fresh lemonade is usually on hand, a framed photograph of a policeman sits next to some sports posters on the wall, and a crowd of regulars, most of them men in shirtsleeves and ties, sits along the long, U-shaped counter and tucks into huge southern farm dinners. In front of each place sit bottles of two kinds of hot sauce, plus a cruet of pepper vinegar to splash on the greens. A television set high in a corner blasts *Oprah* most afternoons.

"Do you like the lemonade?" the owner asks one day. "Because everybody just goes crazy for this lemonade. I don't understand it . . . it's just lemonade."

The menu at Red's is posted on a signboard high on a wall, but though it changes from day to day, the bill of fare is eternal: you basically have a choice of pig's feet, fried chicken, or slabs of long-braised meat. Sometimes you'll find sweet-potato pie for dessert, sometimes just a handful of peppermints. To go with the cooked animal there might be black-eyed peas—sharp-tasting and buttersoft—or pillowy stewed pinto beans, intensely flavored collard greens, or pungent heaps of simmered cabbage.

Oxtails are beefy and gelatinous, melting mouthfuls of meat; neckbones are leaner, stronger-tasting; short ribs are luxurious slabs of long-cooked protein that fall apart with the prodding of a fork. The fried chicken is extraordinary, a full half-chicken to an order: crisp crusted, well spiced, juicy, full of flavor, something close to a platonic vision of soul-fried bird. Steaming hillocks of rice and gravy are a given. At Red's, almost all of the customers leave with foam containers of leftovers.

It's easy to become a regular here—when I stopped by once a day or two after the '92 riots, the owner greeted me with a "Hiya, chicken"—after my usual lunch order—and then asked me what I'd managed to loot. "I didn't get anything myself," she winked. "I've never much cared for swap-meet clothes."

RENU NAKORN

13041 E. ROSECRANS AVE., NORWALK; (562) 921-2124. DAILY, 11A.M.– 9:30P.M.

There is a certain type of man for whom hot food is never hot enough, who adores the green fire of Peruvian *ají* sauce, and splashes chile into Korean soups that are already hot enough to smelt tin. This brotherhood—they're *always* dudes—reek of garlic, keep certain rib stands in business, and like to cook each other stir-fries that consist mostly of habanero peppers. These are the men whose personal Everest can be identified by the words "spicy hot for adventure."

Forget Sichuan or Mexican—Thai food is practically the only stuff hot enough for them, along with Bhutanese dishes and certain Punjabi curries. Better yet is Isaan cooking, from the northeastern part of Thailand, which can be hot enough to stun even natives of Bangkok even though it's mostly salads. The summit of Isaan cooking is a grilled-beef dish called *suea rong hai,* which is reputed to be delicious enough to make a tiger weep with hunger.

At the splendid Isaan-style restaurant Renu Nakorn, which is still among the very best Thai restaurants in the United States—even after longtime chef Saipin Chutima decamped to Lotus of Siam in Las Vegas—*seua rong hai* may be the single mildest dish on anybody's table. A trip to Renu Nakorn can be a little like taking your tongue to the Leather Castle.

Renu Nakorn is a small restaurant in a Norwalk strip mall, down the street from burger stands and Western bars, next door to a working dairy. (In the parking lot at night, you can smell cows even if you can't see them.) Though it seems to be at the end of the universe, it's only twenty minutes south of downtown.

There is a blistering *larb* of finely ground catfish seasoned with lime, chile, and nutty-brown ground toasted rice; there are the thinnest sour strands of shredded bamboo shoot or shredded green jackfruit dressed the same way; there is an extraordinary, coarsely chopped Isaan version of steak tartare that was so delicious it could've seared the hairs out of your nostrils. (Renu Nakorn, which may serve more kinds of *larb,* sort of a minced Thai salad, than Shakey's does pizza, also does *larb* of squid and chicken and browned duck, among other wonderful things.) The waiter will bring a side plate of sliced cucumber and cabbage on a bed of crushed ice, which you nibble on between bites to cool down, and little straw baskets of sticky rice, which you're supposed to roll into balls and use to scoop up the food. The *seua rong hai*—sliced, grilled rare, and served with a gamy, tart dipping sauce—is almost benign, a pleasant, meaty intermezzo between fire-breathing salads. Fatty chunks of grilled pork neck taste like the stuff you trim off a steak and then eat by yourself over the sink after the kids are asleep.

Renu Nakorn's food is spicy, but what makes it wonderful is the fresh play of tastes, a fugue of herbs, animal pungencies, and citrus that is quite unlike anything at your corner Thai cafe. The endorphin high on the way home can be tremendous.

The menu is pretty extensive, but you'll get more of the best stuff if you choose a couple of dishes from the "Renu Nakorn Special" area of the menu and look plaintively at any untranslated dishes when the waiter comes. You can negotiate a real Isaan meal with minimal effort—sweet-hot tendon soup and papaya salad studded with chunks of salted raw crab; whole deep-fried catfish, crunchy and sweet, whose caramelized crust has the smack of Thai iced tea; or dry-fried beef that tastes like the world's best beef jerky, served with a smoky chile dip close to a thick chipotle salsa. Maybe you'll get the grilled shrimp. But try to finagle the grilled beef flanked with chopped raw chiles above and sliced raw garlic below. That dish, one of the strongest things I've ever been served in a restaurant, is pungent enough to bring tears to the eyes of ten tigers and an elephant and all the cows next door.

RINCON CHILEÑO

4354 MELROSE AVE., HOLLYWOOD; (323) 666-6075. TUES.–THURS. AND SUN., 11:30A.M.–10P.M.; FRI. AND SAT., 11:30A.M. to 11P.M.

If you have not reserved a table at Rincon Chileño, you will probably be exiled for a while to the delicatessen next door, where the smell of freshly baked empanadas will drive you mad. More than once, I have surveyed the chances of getting into the restaurant, and settled instead for a car picnic of empanadas, a bottle of Cousiño Macul Antigua Riserva Cabernet, and a sandwich, *chacarero*, that involves grilled beef, tomatoes, and slivered green beans. (The restaurant's fiery green hot sauce, *pebre*, makes the sandwich just about perfect.) For dessert, there are flaky Chilean pastries filled with thick homemade caramel. Rincon Chileño is conceivably the only restaurant in L.A. where it can be pleasurable to be turned away.

Rincon Chileño is an old-fashioned ethnic restaurant on the eastern end of Melrose, closer in atmosphere to the Spanish restaurants in New York's West Village than to the divier ultra-authentic places you now expect in Hollywood. Rincon Chileño has clean tablecloths, attractive prints on the walls, and starched, almost formal service, as well as an extensive list of hard-to-find Chilean wines, which is what the wine geeks have been nattering on about since the good Italian reds got too expensive.

It's sort of splendid inside, really, with a Saturday-night buzz in the air, garlic and smoke, a handsome crooner who sings sad songs along to the recorded guitar tracks on his tape machine. The singer flows into an early Elvis song, and a man escorts his date into a clearing in the middle of the main dining room, then leads her, with the starchy snap of a professional tango instructor, through some precise *Happy Days*–style choreography. A waiter shows some customers a flier advertising a soccer match pitting the restaurant against a rival cafe, then mimes a header . . . *goooooooooalllllll!* Rincon Chileño is as much community center as it is restaurant.

Chile is a long, thin country that is almost all seacoast, and the cold-water currents that rush past its shores nurture some of the oddest seafood in the world.

Some of this makes its way to the restaurant fresh, but most of the shellfish, unfortunately, comes from cans: marinated canned Chilean abalone with potato salad, marinated canned pink clams, various marinated canned shellfish with bits of finfish in a mixed ceviche. These appetizers are actually fine—chewy, slightly spicy, freshened with lime—but you might want to avoid ordering more than one of them. The seafood soup *paila* can taste more of the can than it does of the seafood.

The famous fish of Chile, aside from the Chilean sea bass that is ubiquitous in swank Westside grills, is something called *congrio*, a tasty, white-fleshed fish that tastes a little like halibut might taste if halibut had any flavor, and comes in long, firm fillets. *Congrio* is delicious fried in a light, crisp batter, looking like nothing so much as something off a giant fish 'n' chips platter, garnished with a chopped-tomato salad that tastes like a Chilean *pico de gallo*.

The Chilean-style tamales called *humitas* are terrific here, sweetly spiced, intensely corn-flavored, with the consistency of a steamed pudding. Steaks are thin, marinated, and chewy in the South American tradition, and might come garnished with a fried egg or with a side of the wonderful, spice-fragrant, yellow-bean stew *parotos granados*. *Pollo arvejado* is a chicken that has been stewed with a large quantity of canned peas, which is homey in its way, but perhaps not a dish worth the journey. *Pastel de choclo*, a pan-Andean favorite and probably Chile's best-known dish, is a sweet, nutmeg-laced corn pudding that conceals a chicken leg at its core.

But the restaurant's great specialty might be the appetizer of marinated sea urchin, whose powerful iodine smack seems nearly tamed by the flavors of citrus and finely minced onion. The sea urchin may be delicious, and crammed full of the aphrodisiac nutrients that make this dish so popular with dating Hollywood types, but is really too rich to eat in great quantity.

A waiter sees a few bites of uneaten sea urchin and shakes his head sadly.

"You didn't like it," he says. "I knew the flavor was too strong for Americans."

ROMANTIC STEAKHOUSE

119 E. VALLEY BLVD., SAN GABRIEL; (626) 307-5558. WED.-MON., 11:30A.M.-10P.M.

Romantic Steakhouse is a dim-lit restaurant near the great San Gabriel mall, a Hong Kong–style chophouse known for its surf 'n' turf platters, fried Cornish hens, and steaks in black-pepper sauce. Little overhead spotlights cast a precisely calibrated glow onto the tablecloths of each cozy booth; soft music is periodically interrupted by the fortissimo sputtering of filets mignons being rushed into the dining room on superheated metal platters. Couples dress up for dinner here, at least a little bit, and talk softly, drinking wine. One thing is clear: For at least some people in the neighborhood, dinner at Romantic Steakhouse qualifies as a Hot Date.

Very little here hints of cooking more exotic than lobsters with butter or pork chops in mushroom sauce, and the table is set with knives and forks instead of chopsticks. Give or take a wine piña colada here or there, or a dish of vegetarian cuttlefish, the menu is pretty much the same as those at the dozens of other East-West restaurants in the San Gabriel Valley. But while Romantic Steakhouse may effectively function as the Chinese-American equivalent of the fanciest French restaurant in a small Indiana town, the owner is from Burma, and the restaurant has a strong subspecialty in the kind of Burmese food Chinese people like. If you ask the owner politely, he'll bring out Burmese dish after Burmese dish, until you beg him to stop.

Burmese-Chinese food is strong stuff, slightly oily, sour in ways you've never contemplated, and overlaid with a scrim of ginger, toasted garlic, and citrus that seems to flavor each dish. The orthodox Burmese food served locally at Whittier's Golden Triangle restaurant is subtler than the Burmese-Chinese food at Romantic Steakhouse, more cleanly spiced, swayed more by the surrounding influences of Thailand, Laos, and Islam—probably even more elegant. But sometimes you want to nibble on a delicate salad made from river-washed tea leaves, and sometimes you just want to power your way through a bowl of burnt-onion noodles.

There's usually a noodle salad at Romantic Steakhouse, slicked with garlic oil and ginger, tossed with slivers of vegetables and shavings of cold chicken. Rice fried with vegetables and bits of Chinese sausage has the smokiness that comes from brief cooking in a very hot wok, with perfectly separated rice grains, a high topnote of garlic, and a burnished sweetness from the sausage—it's one of the best plates of fried rice in town.

Chicken curry here is quite different from both Indian and Thai conceptions of the dish—tinted yellow with turmeric but smacking more of onion, garlic, and chile than of exotic spice, and neither cream nor coconut milk tempers the spiciness of the sharply delicious dish. The owner often suggests a uniquely Burmese chicken dish, awash in red oil (he apologizes for the oiliness in advance), fried with an astringent Burmese vegetable that has the texture of spinach but a pointed, bitter sourness that suggests a mixture of grapefruit peel and sorrel.

After you've been to the restaurant a couple of times, the owner might bring out a platter of crisply fried pig intestines with the numbing richness of freshly fried pigskin. These fried intestines may be more alarming to look at than they are to eat—cut in cross-section, they vaguely resemble an H. R. Giger drawing of sliced figs—but they go down pleasantly, and have few of the lingering side effects you may associate with chitlins.

Moh hin ga is sometimes considered the Burmese national dish, a catfish chow-

250

der spiked with transparent vermicelli, enriched with a dribble of coconut milk, and given color with blackened onions. Romantic Steakhouse serves a fairly classic version of the soup, almost gritty with toasted chickpea flour, sparked with an elusive, many-leveled sourness. What seem like a dozen flavors unfold one by one: fermented fish, citrus, ginger, turmeric, the earthiness of catfish. There are other decent soups here—a complex hot-and-sour, a simple broth of fish sauce and vegetables—but *moh hin ga* is the soul of Burmese cuisine.

The inevitable dessert at Romantic Steakhouse, at least after a Burmese-Chinese meal, is something called *faludi*—not christened, as far as I know, after author Susan—which tastes very much like Strawberry Quik spiked with slithery cubes of grass jelly. *Faludi* may seem a little too much like a nursery sweet, but rest assured: It may be the only dessert in the house that doesn't come complete with a candle and three waiters singing "Happy Birthday" in Cantonese.

ROSCOE'S HOUSE OF CHICKEN & WAFFLES

1514 N. GOWER ST., HOLLYWOOD; (323) 466-7453; 830 N. LAKE AVE., PASADENA; (626) 791-4890; 5006 W. PICO BLVD., LOS ANGELES; (323) 934-4405; 106 W. MANCHESTER BLVD., LOS ANGELES; (323) 752-6211. SUN.-THURS., 8:30A.M.–MIDNIGHT; FRI.-SAT., 8:30A.M.–1A.M.

Tucked away on a Hollywood side street, Roscoe's is the Carnegie Deli of Los Angeles's R & B scene, a place where everybody goes mostly because everybody goes there. At odd hours of the night, Roscoe's hops with hip-hop gangstas and old-time crooners, funkateers and exponents of new-jack swing, athletes and body-guards.

If you're in need of a particular gospel bass player or the guy who did the arrangements for Luther Vandross's last tour, you'll probably run into him if you hang out around a chicken-liver omelet long enough. Roscoe's may be the only restaurant in town where you can see both Roberta Flack and MC Eiht. The pleasant reek of heated syrup is sometimes discernable from more than a block away.

Roscoe's branches have popped up in a lot of places, one (now closed) on the site of the legendary Tommy Tucker's Play Room, another in a '50s coffee shop on Pico, and another on Manchester in South-Central Los Angeles. There's a gleaming new Roscoe's on the fringe of the Bungalow Heaven neighborhood in Pasadena.

Considering its legend, the original Roscoe's is surprisingly small. The squarish, mirrored dining room is paneled with rough wood in a way that echoes mixing-room decor and is set up in a baffling circle-in-square floor plan that resembles the two-tier layout of a forty-eight-track control room. Maybe the secret of Roscoe's success among musicians is this: It's a restaurant that looks like a recording studio.

The hard-core dish at Roscoe's, preferred by many of the customers who look as if they'd once spent a fair amount of time on the offensive line of the Rams, is something called Stymie's Choice, a daunting mountain of fried chicken livers sluiced in gravy, swamped in grits, and garnished with a couple of eggs. Some people swear by the hot-water corn bread served at the beginning of the week, others by the house's filling, bland version of red beans and rice.

The basic currency of Roscoe's, of course, is fried chicken and waffles: big, round waffles that look and taste a little like Eggos on steroids, surmounted with egg-size pieces of whipped butter that will eventually swamp each crevice in the waffle when it melts. There are chicken-and-waffle combinations of every description: white meat or dark, smothered in onion gravy or left alone, served with grits or biscuits or stewed greens.

The combination of chicken and waffles may be a time-honored one in American cooking—Thomas Jefferson brought a waffle iron back from France in the 1790s, and the combination popped up in cookbooks not long after that—but as far as I know, nobody has cleared up the mystery of exactly how you're supposed to eat chicken and waffles together.

Do you wrap the waffle around a chicken leg and gnaw, watching carefully for bones, as if it were a pig-in-a-blanket? Should the waffle assume the essentially ornamental nature of the fried tortilla at the base of a tostada, or the more fundamental role of the bread supporting an open-face hot-turkey sandwich?

Or do chicken and waffles just happen to coexist on the same plate, having not much to do with one another besides the occasional happy splash of maple syrup on a succulent fried wing? We may never know.

RUEN PAIR

5257 HOLLYWOOD BLVD., HOLLYWOOD; (323) 466-0153. DAILY, 4P.M.– 3:30A.M.

Ruen Pair has everything you'd want in a Hollywood Thai restaurant late at night: interesting food, a guarded parking lot, and a scruffy late-night scene. The place shares a mini-mall with a laundromat, a doughnut shop, and a popular Thai nightclub; almost empty at 8:00 P.M., it picks up momentum at 10:00 and becomes packed by midnight.

At Ruen Pair, there are actually two menus: one a standard pad-Thai/cashew-chicken takeout sheet; the other a yellow four-page menu that lists the restaurant's real specialties—and even translates them all. You will probably have to ask for the yellow menu, but it is worth the trouble.

Ruen Pair is the best Thai-Chinese restaurant in Hollywood. Its strong, clean flavors are overlaid with a characteristic Thai funkiness, and its casualness of presentation is strictly Chinese. In non-noodle-shop Thai restaurants, most of the Thai regulars eat Thai style, with spoon and fork; at Ruen Pair, almost everybody uses chopsticks. Fried flower stems are typically Thai-Chinese; so are anise-scented roast fowl and fried Chinese sausage.

As you walk into the place around 2:00 A.M., you can spy the plates on the crowded tables, under the fish tank, toward the blaring TV; everybody is eating more or less the same thing: omelets and morning-glory stems. The omelets are the flat, crisp, well-done Thai kind, fried in oil, frizzled brown at the edges, studded with firm fragments of coarsely chopped shrimp, little cubes of turnip, or a handful of peppery ground pork—not unlike streamlined versions of an Italian frittata, without the mellowness or the height. With the omelet comes a small dish of fire-red chile sauce, a little dab of which goes a long way.

Morning glory stems are hollow little things, slightly crunchy, with a peppery, watercresslike sweetness, fried with an immoderate amount of garlic and bursting with green juice. Morning glory becomes even better if you drizzle on a bit of vinegary fish sauce, enlivened with a confetti of chopped bird peppers, which acts much the same as pepper vinegar does for soul-food collard greens. As far as I've been able to tell, the dish has none of the narcotic effects for which morning glory was esteemed in the '60s. Tastes pretty good, though.

You will also use the vinegar dip with the so-called goose stew—sliced roast-goose, golden-skinned, richly flavored, scented with star anise and cloves, better than at any Chiu Chow dive in Los Angeles; great Chinese food with a distinctive Thai twist. The duck stew is tasty too, if less unusual. Among the soups is a strange, delicious potage of pork broth, ground pork, and puckery, salt-preserved vegetables.

Salads include firm, gelatinous slivers of preserved egg, translucent black, hotly spiced with chile, dressed with lime, arranged around a heap of red onion, cilantro, and chiles; salty, pungent bits of fried, preserved fish tossed like croutons into a delicious Thai salad; raw, marinated shrimp, slick and scented with chile and lime, slightly chewy, splayed on a bed of lettuce.

Sweet Chinese sausages are sliced thinly and fried into chips, too crisp to pierce with a fork and impossible to resist. Crumbles of ground pork are sautéed with Chinese preserved olives, which have the spongy texture and gamy, intensely salty smack of the burnt Kalamatas that stick out of the top of La Brea Bakery's olive bread: a spectacular dish.

Thai friends had warned me off Ruen Pair for years, claiming the cooking was somehow inauthentic. But the restaurant couldn't be more authentic. Authentically Thai-Chinese.

SAFETY ZONE CAFE

3630 WILSHIRE BLVD., LOS ANGELES; (213) 387-7595; DAILY, 11A.M.–
11:30P.M.

On the roster of ethnic-restaurant insecurities, somewhere between the fear of having to toast a colleague with a native liqueur that smells like carburetor cleaner and the shrinking sensation experienced when you realize you've just ordered two courses of barbecued spleen, is the feeling that you might be Ordering the Wrong Thing. This is most common in Chinese restaurants, of course, where no satisfactory English translation exists for many weird but tasty fishes or for most of those obscure, imported vegetables that are in season for only three days a year. It also happens in Italian or Latin-American restaurants that turn out to specialize in the last thing on the menu you might think of ordering—say, Peruvian squid-ink risotto—which you'll see later in the travel section of *The New York Times*.

And sometimes you might have the sneaking suspicion that you've ended up in a Cambodian equivalent of Denny's or the Salvadoran version of Taco Bell.

The first time I stepped into the Safety Zone, a plush Koreatown restaurant where I was meeting a reporter for the *Korea Times*, I was almost too awestruck to breathe: the place is a Smithsonian-quality masterpiece of bad 1970s restaurant design. Plaster baby elephants, mounted on lamp bases, are poised to climb Doric columns toward glowing globes of light. Potted fake poinsettias line the rim of a drained reflecting pool, and lime-green satin bordello curtains open up onto a private dining room. Artificial yellow roses soar against the walls; tilted Roman-style eaves spill down from the lilac-purple ceiling toward the seagreen carpet. The faux-bronze sea-shanty lighting fixtures look kidnapped from the fourth-most-elegant seafood house in Tulsa, Oklahoma.

The first three times I visited the restaurant, everybody around me seemed to be getting the same thing, the identity of which I couldn't figure out. We ate good fried rice with kimchi, a thick, chile-red plate of stuff into which the waitress folded a freshly fried egg; *bi bim bap*, a vegetable mélange into which you fold the rice yourself; and barbecued eel. There was a creditable version of Korean steak tartare mixed about with strips of Asian pear, and floppy, beef-stuffed-Korean dumplings, *mandoo*, that brought to mind *tortellini in brodo*.

And finally, we learned the restaurant's terrible secret—two-thirds of the people in the restaurant were eating steak and potatoes. Safety Zone may not be a joint for connoisseurs after all, but you can hardly go wrong by ordering the wrong thing.

SAHAG'S BASTURMA

5183 SUNSET BLVD., HOLLYWOOD; (323) 661-5311. OPEN MON.–FRI.,
8A.M.–8P.M.; SAT., 8A.M.–9P.M.; SUN., 8A.M.–4P.M.

The Armenian cured beef called *basturma* may be the most powerfully flavored cold cut in the world, less a foodstuff than a force of nature, with a bit of the chewy translucence of first-rate Italian *bresaola*, a ripe, almost gamy backtaste, and then—*pow!*—the caustic, bright-red slurry of hot pepper, Middle Eastern herbs, and garlic hits your palate with the subtle elegance of a land mine. It's sort of an acquired taste, *basturma*, a meat that makes its cousin pastrami seem like the kind of thing a duchess might nibble on white bread with the crusts cut off. I would not be surprised to find out that a particularly pungent *basturma* had the power to affect the weather.

The best place to try *basturma* in Los Angeles, and possibly in the world, is Sahag's Basturma, a small, fragrant Armenian deli in the heart of East Hollywood, stacked floor-to-ceiling with bagged spices and bottled grape molasses, jars of roasted peppers and big cans of Lebanese cherry jam. A glass counter displays most of the usual Armenian meats and cheeses, plus a few that you've probably never seen before, and there always seems to be an elderly man or two reading the Armenian newspapers at one of the deli's two tables. There is a certain improvised, picnic quality to a meal at Sahag's, washed down with Armenian yogurt sodas you fetch from the cooler yourself, supplemented with the tart green olives and beet-red pickled turnips the deli gives away with its sandwiches.

Behind the counter, almost always, is Sahag himself.

"Do I make the *basturma?*" Sahag asks pensively. "Three generations my family makes *basturma*, first in Lebanon, now in Hollywood. This is *basturma*—my *basturma*. I am the king of *basturma*. Nobody makes *basturma* like me."

Basturma may be consumed in pita, or sliced with olive oil like *carpaccio*, but maybe the best way here is in a sandwich, layered on freshly toasted lengths of

French bread, garnished with tomatoes and pickle wedges, in a combination that will ooze out of your pores long after you are finished with lunch.

Sahag also makes sandwiches from the grilled link sausage called *maanei,* strongly flavored with mint and garlic, crunchy with pine nuts, slightly sweet; sandwiches with a thick lashing of the Armenian sour cream *labneh* where you might expect the meat to be; sandwiches of *sujuk,* the most famous of the Armenian sausages, a rich, coarse-ground dried sausage that, when fried, acquires something of the texture of thick-cut fired, salami and has the exotic sourness of Middle Eastern herbs.

"You can get a chicken sandwich anywhere," protests Sahag if you should happen to order one, but the grilled chicken sandwich here is fine, dosed with garlic and dusted with the sour spice *za'atar.*

If you manage to talk Sahag into it, he may make you a sandwich with a dried, highly spiced Armenian cheese, explosively pungent, that has the stinging, dried-chile wallop you might associate with a straight *ancho* purée.

"This cheese is too expensive," says Sahag, hefting a baseball—size lump. "But I tell you: take it home, slice it, and make it into a salad with sliced onion, sliced tomato—biggest kind—and a little good olive oil . . . you know, it's not so bad."

I bought a smallish lump—six bucks. I made the salad. And you know . . . it wasn't so bad.

SANAMLUANG CAFE

5176 HOLLYWOOD BLVD., HOLLYWOOD; (323) 660-8006. 12980 SHERMAN WAY, NORTH HOLLYWOOD. 1648 INDIAN HILL BLVD., POMONA. DAILY, 9A.M.–4A.M.

At 2:30 A.M. on a Sunday morning, Sanamluang Cafe, the crown prince of Thai noodle shops, may be the busiest place in Hollywood. Cars triple-park in the lot, outdoor tables bustle, crowds jostle for a chance to be the next party of seven to cram into a booth designed to seat four.

After midnight, Sanamluang is popular with musicians winding down after gigs at Spaceland, sad-eyed German tourists, and Thai teenagers devoted to alternative lifestyles—it is not unusual to overhear somebody at the next table proclaim that his life's great ambition is to become the Thai Liza Minnelli.

Named after a park in Bangkok famous for a ceremony marking the start of the growing season, it is as brightly lit as a Burger King. Everybody's drinking giant tumblers of iced coffee or vanilla-scented Thai tea, striped at the top with a halo of half-and-half instead of the traditional sweetened condensed milk.

More perhaps than any other restaurant in Los Angeles, Sanamluang feels like Southeast Asia—crowded, noisy, high with the smells of garlic and fermented fish, a city place to duck in and out of in twenty minutes. This is the place to come for vast plates of rice fried with mint leaves, seafood, and immoderate amounts of chiles; for big, comforting bowls of chicken soup flavored with toasted garlic; for wide vegetarian noodles fried with Chinese broccoli and what seems like five bucks' worth of shiitake mushrooms; for broad, mild "emperor's noodles" stir-fried with egg, garlic, and pork; for morning glory stems fried in bean sauce. The Indian curry noodles, with beef, boiled eggs, and an extremely spicy, coconut-laced curry, are great.

There is a good version of the traditional combination *cha-po*: duck, crunchy bits of deep-fried belly pork, rice and fish sauce. Chinese broccoli fried with the crisped belly pork is utterly garlicky and rich. Green papaya salad may be an undistinguished version of the northeastern Thai standard—like many Thai noodle shops, Sanamluang is better on the Chinese end of the Thai-food spectrum—but other salads, especially the warm squid salad and the salad made with slivers of Chinese roast duck, can be fine.

Sanamluang used to be famous for its complicated menu, with whole categories of dishes that could be ordered only after 10:00 P.M. or before noon or on Tuesdays and Thursdays; a dish of barbecued pig uterus available only at the Pomona location; and things like "rice flak soup with assorted pig offal" that were probably better left to the imagination. Fried cockles in spicy sauce were on the menu as a late-night special for more than a decade, though nobody I knew ever managed to snag a plate. When I finally did succeed in obtaining a bowl of Chinese spaghetti, a sad little pasta with chicken broth and salty Chinese pickles, I understood why the restaurant served it only on Sunday mornings.

But the General's Noodle—which could be christened after the deeds of a historical Thai leader but was probably named for the fully uniformed Thai man, apparently a real general, who directs traffic in the cafe's parking lot on weekend afternoons—is extraordinary: thin egg noodles, penetratingly garlicky, garnished with bits of duck, barbecued pork, crumbles of ground pork, a couple of shrimp, and a teaspoon of sugar, either dry or submerged in a clean, clear broth. A bowl of General's Noodle Soup, enlivened with a few slices of the vinegared Thai chiles from the little jar on the table, may be the most soothing thing possible at the end of a long night.

SANG DAO

1739 W. LA PALMA AVE., ANAHEIM; (714) 956-8105.

If, ten years ago, somebody had asked you to come up with the still center of postwar Orange County, you could have done worse than the intersection of Euclid and La Palma, which is near the leafy heart of old Anaheim, the football powerhouse Servite, and great stretches of pleasant '50s bungalows that all but defined the GI bill–financed California dream. La Palma Chicken Pie Restaurant, whose menu might conceivably have been imported straight from Moline, Illinois, is right down the block.

Today this corner of Anaheim is cosmopolitan as any few blocks of Hollywood or San Gabriel, populated with authentic Mexican *taquerias*, Salvadoran *pupusa* shops, Thai grocery stores, and a mall full of Chinese chain restaurants whose sister cafes line the streets of Monterey Park.

Half a block west of here lies what might be the only Lao strip center in southern California, with a couple of Lao markets, a Lao hardressing salon, and a gaggle of Lao teenagers who flirt with one another from the front seats of Japanese sedans. At the heart of this center, Sang Dao may be the first serious Lao restaurant in Southern California, an inconspicuous diner masquerading as a neighborhood Thai-Chinese dive. It would be possible to eat here twenty times without suspecting there was anything more to the restaurant than ginger beef.

Mostly, the stuff on the printed menu is Thai, the usual beef with Chinese broccoli, hot-and-sour seafood soup, and nice version of the dish usually called "ginger fish" in Thai-Chinese restaurants. Lao barbecued chicken is almost indistinguishable from Thai barbecued chicken; fried Lao noodles are more or less *pad Thai* by a different name. Even the Lao version of *pho*, the famous Vietnamese beef noodle soup, has a complex sourness you might associate with Thai food. This makes a certain amount of sense: Laos and Thailand share a long border, and the one Lao cookbook in English includes recipes for dishes that are extremely similar to Thai *nam sod* and chicken-coconut soup.

The majority of the Lao dishes here, transliterated but not translated on a chalkboard by the door, seem more like the Isaan-style food of northeastern Thailand (abutting Laos) than like the relatively more tropical Vietnamese or Cambodian cooking: lots of raw vegetables, basketsful of exotic herbs, and sticky rice served with everything.

Many of the Lao dishes at Sang Dao, pungent, chile-hot finger food, is meant to ease down a cold Heineken or two. Crunchy fried quail, elusively flavored with something that tastes like but probably isn't five-spice powder, is cut into bite-size quarters and served with a dipping sauce of puréed chile. Deep-fried Lao sausage, crusty-edged, sour with lemongrass, has a deep, cured-pork flavor that is somehow reminiscent of great Bolognese mortadella, though Lao sausage would never be confused for mortadella in a police lineup. Lao beef jerky is sweet, edged with black, delicious.

A lot of the Lao specials tend to be fiery-hot salads dressed with chile and lime, tossed with a fragrant powder of coarsely ground toasted rice, pungent with raw garlic, and pounded eggplant and herbs. Duck *larb* is dark and gamy, flavored with bits of cooked duck liver; a salad of warm grilled beef tongue is terrific, the animal richness of the tongue cut through nicely by the raw garlic's bite. One grilled-beef salad involves slabs of raw steak and an abundance of green chiles; a *larb* of beef, thinly sliced, is almost alive with the fragrance of fresh mint.

After all the fire, it would be inconceivable to leave Sang Dao without at least one order of ripe mango with sticky rice. If the new multicultural Orange County were all it is cracked up to be, mango with sticky rice would become as ubiquitous in summer as strawberry pie.

SAN PEDRO FISH MARKET AND RESTAURANT

BERTH 78, 1190 NAGOYA WAY, SAN PEDRO; (310) 832-4251. MON.-THURS., 11A.M.-9P.M.; FRI., SAT. & SUN., 11A.M.-9P.M.

The San Pedro Fish Market and Restaurant occupies a crumbling wharf in the Ports O' Call complex, swarming with children, besieged by gulls, vibrating with mariachi trumpet bleats and *norteño* music from a dozen radios, blasts from the stacks of passing cruise ships, and orgiastic seafood consumption that rivals anything in Tom Jones.

Picnic tables sag under the weight of baroque, stinking pyramids of fish skeletons and shrimp shells, crumpled paper cups, dessicated limes, and yard-long shanks of margarine-yellow garlic bread that look as if they've been gnawed on by wolverines. Tanned, shirtless men stagger under the weight of fried fish big enough for Hemingway to have bragged about. The beer line seems to stretch half a mile. Teenagers, buzzing on gallons of sugary *horchata*, pound on crabs with little wooden mallets, impatiently trying to free fugitive nuggets of sweet meat from tricky interstices of shell. *Mariscos* nirvana. Lobster heaven. Dungeness-crab paradise. You are reminded that the Mexican population of Los Angeles is larger than that of Guadalajara.

San Pedro can sometimes seem almost a magical place, a vast, roiling stew of oil refineries, canneries, and docklands where giant cranes hoist objects as large as office buildings and ornate Emerald Cities of steel and earth belch satisfying gouts of rank yellow, flame.

In years gone by, *Pee*-dro was where you caught the seaplane to Catalina, ate rubbery abalone steaks aboard a decommissioned ocean liner, and made your parents drive half a dozen times back and forth to Terminal Island on the Vincent Thomas Bridge. As a teenager, you may have gone to hear punk rock in yawning old San Pedro warehouses—Saccharine Trust! The Minutemen!—or taken your fake ID out for a spin in the Pacific Avenue bars where Charles Bukowski abused his liver. Before the Balkan wars, San Pedro was to be home to a dozen huge, dark restaurants of indeterminate Adriatic origin, where ten bucks bought a carafe of bad red wine and an acre or two of grilled meat.

But today—as gentrified as San Pedro's downtown has become—it is hard to imagine a better outdoor dining experience in Los Angeles than this fish market, this low, sprawling place hard by Ports O' Call's dense concentration of chainlike seafood restaurants.

To get to the fish market from the parking lot, you walk in past the churro stand through a sort of food court and outside to the main dining area, where one of your party should stake a claim to a table while the rest of you tackle the lines for the fish. Though this may seem like the most chaotic place on earth, the protocol is strict—the San Pedro fish market is essentially L.A.'s biggest exemplar of the You Buy, We Fry paradigm.

The first area you should visit, to the left of the entrance as you walk in, down a narrow passageway and into a separate room that echoes with the sound of rushing water, is the shellfish concession, dominated by low, concrete tanks that teem with crab—both meaty dungeness and the scrawnier local crabs—and lobster. In Chinese restaurants, crabs are fished out of tanks for you; here, you are handed a long pair of tongs and you bag your own damned crabs—lively, vicious things, claw action distinctly unimpaired, that will take a decent, sporting shot at the meat of your arm before you present them to be steamed.

To the right of the entrance is a long (and sparsely attended) fish counter, stocked with the usual fillets and steaks. A little farther on, an antechamber practically bursts with oceansful of whole, impeccably fresh fish on ice, hundreds of them, pink New Zealand snapper and glistening trout, sea bass and needlenose barracuda, catfish and all manner of rock cod, and probably a stray Santa Monica Bay croaker or two—all ready to be scaled, gutted, deep-fried, and eaten quickly with chile sauce.

A counter near the eating area sells garlic bread and sandwiches (even hamburgers), beer, and soft drinks. The most popular concession is probably the one that sells giant mounds of spicy shell-on shrimp, grilled with peppers, chiles, and onions, and heaped six inches high onto plastic cafeteria trays. They're a little leathery, but as hard to stop eating as potato chips. Shrimp, beer, and boats—what more could you want out of life?

And after you've powered through a school of shrimp, a couple of fried sea robins, and a dungeness crab or two, listened to a thousand choruses of "Cielito Lindo" and drained a few glasses of Bud, you can grab a fresh, greasy *churro* from the stand outside the door and be happy as a three-year-old. If you actually *are* a three-year-old, you will often find a selection of charming, wee carnival rides at the end of the parking lot.

SANUKI NO SATO

18206 S. WESTERN AVE., GARDENA; (310) 324-9184. MON.–FRI.,
11:30A.M.–2:30P.M., 5:30P.M.–10P.M.; SAT.–SUN., 11:30A.M.–3P.M.,
5:30P.M.–9:30P.M.

In the great tradition of Tokyo secret addresses, Sanuki No Sato isn't the easiest place to find. It's stuck in a sort of industrial strip, for one thing, equidistant from the Japanese shopping centers of Gardena and the gleaming low-rise Japanese corporate campuses of Torrance. The signs that identify it are untranslated, and the flags that hang down over the doorway can seem more like a barrier than a welcoming touch. Once you're inside, you may be momentarily shocked when you leaf through a takeout menu and discover that it is in elaborate Japanese script as well.

Like most serious Japanese noodle houses, Sanuki No Sato specializes in delicate buckwheat *soba* and pencil-thick wheat-flour *udon*, cold or hot, plain or in soup. The noodles here won't change your life like the fragile *soba* at Honmura-An in New York might, or even like the stretchy hand-pulled *udon* at Kotohira down the street, but they're elegant, light, better than okay.

Plus, the actual tableware is just spectacular: pickle plates striped with the organic subtlety of jellyfish markings; rough noodle bowls whose murky glaze glimmers with deep-forest green; lacquered wooden *bento* boxes with interior geometry as intricate as a microchip.

Kyo nishin, a dense, sugar-cured herring, seems sort of small for a $7.50 side order—you've probably won bigger fish at a church-carnival Ping-Pong ball toss—but has the intensity of Shanghainese smoked fish. Fresh *inari* sushi, vinegared rice stuffed into fried-tofu pockets, is leagues better than the packaged stuff you pick up in the supermarket.

Udon come in all the standard flavors, topped with crisp buttons of tempura batter, in a plain soy-enriched broth, with slices of cooked beef, with chewy bits of rice cake, with exquisitely slimy Japanese mountain yams. The *udon* have a mild wheat flavor and the proper, pronounced firmness to the tooth.

Udon served in hot, rustic-looking iron kettles—identified on the menu by the root word *nabe*—are different somehow from the *udon* served in bowls: softer, stretchier, more luxuriant, more like key ingredients in a stew than objects in their own right. *Yukinabe udon,* buried in its broth beneath half an inch of grated radish, a sprinkling of freshly grated wasabi root, and a ferociously spiced cod egg-sac the size and shape of a thumb, is almost refreshing in spite of its bulk—an exotic bowl of noodles you could eat every day.

Where a perfect *soba* noodle is fragile enough practically to fall apart under the pressure of a harsh glance (buckwheat, the principal ingredient, has almost no gluten), the *soba* at Sanuki No Sato are on the hard side, almost stiff. Though they're fine in soups, they haven't quite the delicate nutty flavor you'd want for *zaru soba,* which are plain cold noodles served with a delicate soy-based dip. (*Zaru soba* is the traditional test of a Japanese noodle shop.)

At lunch, there is the *tojuki bento,* a multi-course banquet in a lacquered Japanese box, a *bento* experience easier to eat than to describe: two, maybe three kinds of vinegared seaweed; a small slab of salt-broiled salmon; a foil candy cup filled with vinegared daikon and a teaspoonful of salmon eggs; rice tossed with bits of toasted seaweed and sharply salty fish, garnished with julienne strips of a paper-thin omelet; sashimi of tuna and octopus; pretty good tempura—shrimp, eggplant, fish cake, and Japanese pepper—and a bowl of dipping sauce; a prawn simmered in sweet wine and a little beef stew with mushrooms and vegetables; one bowl of *udon* and another one of egg custard; and a wedge of the Japanese omelet *tamago.* That this all fits into a *bento* box is a testament to Japanese engineering: I have seen buffet tables with less food on them.

If you are slightly less hungry, you can't go wrong with the *nabeyaki udon.* With three or four different kinds of fish cake, simmered bamboo shoot, spinach, two broth-softened tempura-fried shrimp, a handful of tempura-batter cracklings, chunks of boiled chicken, and an elegant vegetable that looks a little like Chinese broccoli but probably isn't, it's something like a one-dish rendition of the USDA food pyramid.

SA RIT GOL

3198 W. OLYMPIC BLVD., KOREATOWN; (323) 387-0909. DAILY, 11A.M.– 11P.M.

If there were such a thing as a Korean cowboy bar, it might look a little like Sa Rit Gol, a rustic Koreatown barbecue place decorated with raw wood and Korean beer posters, and full of two-fisted drinkers. The owner, a bluff, friendly guy, is likely to cuff you on the shoulder the second or third time you come in, and it's not that unusual to see a brawl out in the parking lot the kind of brawl where the parties involved bear-hug after a missed swing or two, and then come back inside for a teary reconciliation. Even the name—it translates as "The Valley of Bushes"—seems like the title of a *Gunsmoke* episode.

As at many Korean restaurants, the tabletops at Sa Rit Gol have grills built into their centers, on which you cook your own entrée. As at practically all Korean restaurants, you are brought little plates of *panchan* as soon as you sit down— the classic, pungent, marinated cabbage *kimchi;* radish *kimchi;* bean sprouts fragrant with sesame oil—in addition to a selection that may include chile-marinated cuttlefish, dried fish, vinegared cucumber, squid, whatever's around. There will be a metal bowl of bland soup per person, and lidded metal capsules that contain the rice. If you are not Korean, the waitresses may seem amazed that you are willing to eat cuttlefish or *kimchi*, or casseroles hot with chile, as if they are sure you are there only because the lines are too long at the Sizzler down the street.

Sa Rit Gol is locally famous for its pork barbecue—thin loin strips soaked in a sauce of red chile and garlic, which cook up brick-red on the tabletop grills. The meat caramelizes black in spots and glistens with juice, becomes slightly chewy, and is as subtle a creation as you might reasonably expect from food that you essentially cook yourself. (Don't let it sit on the grill too long. It will become indistinguishable from chile-smeared rawhide.) If you like, you can dab the pork with a bit of fermented yellow bean paste and fold it into a crisp leaf of romaine, creating a sort of Korean equivalent to *tacos de adobado*, and eat the package with your fingers.

Or grill fat slices of belly pork, like uncured bacon, until they are charred and crisp, and then dip them into a little saucer of sesame oil and salt. It is classic Korean drinking food, rich enough to absorb any amount of rice wine, and perhaps a little decadent for the American taste. (Belly pork appears on the menu in Hangul script only, but you should ask for it.) Grill sweet, marinated slices of flank steak, gritty with black pepper, or snipped wedges of marinated short-rib meat that become crisp and juicy over the flame. Grill—or more likely, have grilled for you in the kitchen—marinated squid, cuttlefish, or the needle-nose saltwater pike that the Japanese call *sanma*.

Of course, barbecue and *kimchi* are not all there is to Sa Rit Gol. (Barbecue and *kimchi* are not all there is to any Korean restaurant, no matter how much the proprietors may try to persuade you otherwise.) There is a delicious casserole of baby octopi, tender tentacles and such waving out of a sweet chile-scallion stew; braised shiitake mushrooms with spinach, full-flavored and bosky; crisp, eggy pancakes that enclose aromatic shredded vegetables; giant, bubbling casseroles of crab; pungent fish soups served seething in superheated iron bowls.

Dessert will inevitably be a thin, chilled broth, garnished with pine nuts, that tastes like a tea made from ginger snaps.

SEAFOOD STRIP

140 W. VALLEY BLVD., NO. 212, SAN GABRIEL; (626) 288-9899. DAILY, 11A.M.–3P.M. AND 5–11P.M.

Here we are again, back in the Chinese mall called San Gabriel Square, where the air smells garlicky as heaven and great Chinese restaurants rub up against one another like friendly whales in the sea. And here we are on the second level, in a grand restaurant that may serve the best Taiwanese seafood in California. Seafood Strip is pretty swank for a Chinese restaurant, all glass and pastels, with sleek lacquered chairs, neo-deco detailing, and giant fishtanks. The customers don't look dressed up, exactly, but as if they were born into tailored dresses and nine-hundred-dollar Italian nipped-waist suits.

In the way you can find at least a couple of Italian dishes on most Ethiopian restaurant menus, you might detect a relic or two here from the days of the Greater East Asian Co-Prosperity Sphere. It is, in fact, possible to eat something very much like a Japanese meal at Seafood Strip. You might start with a large sashimi platter: raw tuna and yellowtail and octopus and salmon prettily arranged around a nest of grated radish, garnished with an egg-size lump of wasabi. It's good sashimi, impeccably fresh, though not quite up to the standard set by the best sushi-only restaurants. Whitefish fillets float in a Japanese-style miso soup, whose richness in this context suggests less the free stuff ladled out at sushi bars than the fragrant yellow-bean soups of Shanghai. Grilled fish with soybean paste has a slipperiness, a subtle sweetness, that is not unlike that of the broiled, sake-lees-marinated cod that is a standard dish in *izaka-ya*-style Japanese pubs.

Still, Seafood Strip is no Japanese restaurant. As free appetizers, you are brought the little dishes—tart, crunchy radish pickles, peanuts boiled with star anise, or soft, fragrant strands of stewed seaweed—that are the staples of Chinese delicatessens. There are plenty of deep-fried dishes, but they have nothing to do with tempura: crunchy, thick battered cubes of tofu that you paint with a sticky, garlicky soy reduction; chewy, fried cuttlefish balls that spurt hot juice when you bite into them; musky oyster-leek rolls wrapped in tofu skins; and fried cuttlefish, with a pepper-salt dip, that tastes like the world's best calamari. There is a crunchy, sweet salad made from shredded jellyfish, which is more delicious than it sounds, and a vividly flavored appetizer of cold, sliced boiled goose.

As an ordering strategy, most people order an expensive major dish—soft-shell turtle with chestnut, or a blandish mixed-seafood casserole, or the enormous clay-pot stew called "monk jumps over the wall"—and then a bunch of sautéed vegetables or stir-fries, less distinctive, to round out their meal. Squid sautéed with Chinese celery, spinach fried with garlic, and eggplant fried with basil are delicious. The famous Taiwanese dish of tiny whitebait fried with peanuts and chile—closer to crunchy fried noodles than to anything you might think of as fish, albeit crunchy fried noodles that stare back at you with tiny black eyes—is as hard to stop eating as a basket of fries.

One unusual specialty involves crisp, melting slices of broiled eel, glazed with sweet soy sauce and mounded on a large heap of brown sticky rice that has been cooked with spices and diced mushrooms and little chunks of taro. It is an absolutely spectacular plate of food. (The same sticky rice is served with a plump steamed crab, but the eel's sweetness seems more appropriate.) A sweet, intensely gingery version of the Taiwanese classic three-glass chicken, called "chicken cas-serole," is encrusted with caramelized juices, soy, and rice wine, seasoned with plenty of fresh basil, and hacked into meaty, bite size chunks. There is a host of chafing-pot soups: one especially fine one involves jerkylike strips of dried squid and chocolate-brown slices of fresh conch melding into a broth whose peaty smokiness reminds me of old single-malt scotch.

Hong Kong–style seafood palaces are well represented in Los Angeles. But although Taiwanese immigrants outnumber Hong Kong immigrants two to one in Los Angeles County, Taiwanese seafood, an exotic amalgam of Northern Chinese, general Asian, and native Formosan dishes; fried frog, braised catfish, and sautéed sea snails—is much harder to find. Seafood Strip is a Taiwanese treasure.

SEÑOR FISH

422 E. FIRST ST.; (213) 625-0566. DAILY, 10 A.M.–9P.M.; 618 MISSION ST., SOUTH PASADENA; (626) 403-0145. DAILY, 11A.M.–9P.M.

Since it opened a decade ago in a single former burger shack, the Señor Fish chain has become an institution: its scallop burrito is a rare Sure Thing in an otherwise inconstant time.

Here are spicy fried-fish tacos like the ones they serve on the Ensenada waterfront, burritos filled with fat scallops, and plates of sautéed shrimp *mojo de ajo* so powerfully seasoned that you can almost feel the garlic vibrate in your teeth. The famous seafood quesadilla, widely copied, is exemplary—a large flour tortilla, filled with stretchy cheese and a garlicky panful of sautéed fish, shrimp, and scallops, griddled to a browned crispness and brushed with a smoky chile salsa: the sort of trashy, irresistible mess you might throw together for an impromptu dinner at a rented beach house, knowing everybody will ask for seconds.

There are certainly weak spots in the menu. The shrimp in the rather ordinary shrimp cocktail are often flabby and overmarinated; the octopus tostada can be flabbergastingly good one time and mediocre the next.

But grilled trout—at less than five bucks—splayed and salted and slicked with lime, served with rice and beans, is wholly satisfying; grilled salmon is nicely rare and enough for two. The whole deep-fried snapper, all crunch and salt and steamy, fragrant flesh, is cooked with the sort of finesse you might expect from an expensive Hong Kong–style fish house.

You'll even find stuff for vegetarians: lardless beans, quesadillas, wonderful crisp-shelled tacos filled with mashed potatoes. And the vegetarian enchilada—sauced with a stinging green purée, filled with sautéed zucchini, cheese, and herbs—is great. Long live Señor Fish!

THE SHACK

185 CULVER BLVD., PLAYA DEL REY; (310) 823-6222. DAILY, 10:30A.M.–
10P.M. ALSO AT 2518 WILSHIRE BLVD., SANTA MONICA; (310) 823-6222.

The Shack is loud on a Sunday afternoon, really loud, with four sporting events playing on four screens, Bob Seger pounding from the stereo, and a bar four deep with tanned dudes shouting at the top of their lungs: *WAHHHHHHHH.* A surfer guy comes in and bellows, "Somebody's got my seat, *maaaan,*" and a smaller man slides off the end stool. Everybody there seems to know which seat the surfer means. He swaggers to his stool, pats it, and starts to scream with his buddies before he so much as orders a drink: *WAHHH WAHHH WAHHH.*

There are some women here, even some beach moms with children in the small cluster of tables near the food counter, but few of them seem unescorted: the Shack is a manly place, a place that hosts Jaegergirl promotions, a place where you can watch the Clippers on TV and drink Carlsberg on tap.

The Shack is an archetypal beach hamburger dive, a crowded joint in the heart of Playa Del Rey with a sister restaurant on Oahu and another in Santa Monica, an all-shorts dress code and a weathered-wood nautical roadhouse vibe that looks as if it's been too long from the sea. Bright fliers advertising Mexican Night, Spaghetti Night, and cheap Saturday-night prime-rib specials paper the walls, though most of the clientele seems to treat the food as something convenient for soaking up the beer.

Patty melts are sweetened with great gobs of Beaver mustard; guacamole burgers are greased with spicy green glop. A Fire in the Hole slicks two open-face hamburgers with house-made, kidney-bean-rich chili, the kind of stuff that can repeat on a guy who likes his beer. A 'Shroom burger is garnished with fried mushrooms and Swiss cheese.

But the Shack's most magnificent achievement is something called the Shack Burger, a quarter-pound of ground meat and a Polish sausage crammed together in a bun. The sausage is ruddy, garlicky, grilled crisp; the hamburger patty is charred in a way that you may associate with backyard barbecues, totally carbonized but oddly appealing in its acrid blackness, kind of dense, and extremely well done. The Shack Burger seems repellent on the surface, and it will seem repellent an hour after you eat it, especially if you help it down with bargain tequila shooters, but at the time it is irresistible, all grease and smoke and snap. The Shack Burger is dude food, the secret ethnic cooking of the Dumb White Guy.

12225 E. CENTRALIA AVE., LAKEWOOD; (562) 402-7443. TUES.-SUN., 11A.M.-10P.M.

Mirch ka salan is my kind of vegetable. What we're talking about is essentially a stew of jalapeño peppers, dozens of them where you might expect to see okra or spinach floating among the spices, and the result is hot enough to sear your esophagus into steak-o-bob. It's one of the specialties of the Pakistani-Muslim restaurant Shahnawaz, where the house beverage seems to be ice water served by the pitcherful, and you can see why. *Mirch ka salan* is less a dish than a chemistry experiment in a bowl, a thick stew the approximate yellowy tan of a camel's flank, heady with the scents of garlic and ginger, bound with a pungent, grainy mortar of ground spice. Garnishes of lemon, cucumber, and fresh shredded ginger are served alongside in a gleaming metal salver; in a straw basket are smoking-hot ovals of freshly baked *naan* bread with which to scoop up the stew.

I've never been to Shahnawaz without ordering the *mirch ka salan*.

The restaurant can seem forbidding at first, a small dining room filled with chain-smoking men, a ball game blaring from a corner TV, a loud, finger-pointing argument with occasional phrases like "fast break" and "slam dunk" like islets in the rapid stream of Urdu. Sometimes you may wait fifteen minutes at a table before anybody realizes you are there, and you will probably have trouble getting anybody to explain the several untranslated items on the menu. Sometimes everybody in the restaurant will have their noses buried in the newest edition of the local Pakistani press. Every so often, you will run across a waiter who finds it hard to believe that you really do want to try the spicy, delicious minced brains *masala*.

The chapter on Pakistani cookery in the Time-Life *Foods of the World* series is entitled, "Pakistan: Muslims Who Live on Meat," and jalapeño stew or no jalapeño stew, it's not as if Shahnawaz serves a lot of vegetables—a lentil *dal*, a blandish dish of spinach and potatoes, and something called *baghare baigun* that is essentially *mirch ka salan* with chunks of Asian eggplant in place of the chiles, may be about it.

Nehari is a spicy beef stew flavored sharply with ginger; *haleem* is a gentle mash of pounded meat cooked with grain. *Paya* is a rich, clove-scented stew of beef and ox tendon cooked to a melting tenderness. On weekends, there is a very nice *biryani*, basmati rice cooked with butter, sweet spices, and lamb.

And consider the tandoori mixed plate: a rare lamb chop, subtly smoky, crisp at the edges; a few pieces of bright-red marinated chicken *tikka* that spurt juice like chicken Kiev; a ruddy, whole chicken leg; several inches worth of clove-scented minced-lamb kebab; a tart pile of yogurt-marinated roasted beef—all for about the price of a movie ticket.

SHAHREZAD FLAME

1422 WESTWOOD BLVD., WESTWOOD; (310) 470-9131. SUN.–THURS.,
11:30A.M.–11P.M.; FRI., 11:30–MIDNIGHT; SAT., 11:30A.M.–3P.M.

Of all the ethnic neighborhoods in the Southland, Westwood Boulevard's strip of Iranian shops and restaurants is at the same time one of the best known and least touristed, a quarter-mile of signs in curling Farsi script located south of the skyscrapers and megaplex movie theaters at just about the spot where you can find vacant parking spots on a Westwood Saturday night. Some of the best Iranian cafés stay open until long after the late show; some of the boutiques and grocery stores sell exotic items you'd never in a hundred years expect to find within a block or two of All American Burger.

Shahrezad Flame is a sleek, modern restaurant smack in the middle of the strip, all clean lines and slick surfaces, with chicly dressed customers, candles everywhere, and tables speckled robin's-egg blue. Iranian American pop—stuff that sounds sort of like Julio Iglesias with a head cold—pours out of the stereo, sometimes alternating with circa-'81 new wave hits. There will always be at least one guy, munching on a steak sandwich the size of his head, chattering animatedly into his cell phone, engaged in a Persian-to-Persian call.

The cornerstone of Shahrezad Flame, the reason you pay a couple of bucks per person more here than you do at other restaurants in the neighborhood, is a spherical, tandoor-type oven that looks like a giant blue eyeball set under a massive cylindrical ventilation hood. Into the oven go sheets of dough. Out of it comes fragrant sheets of soft, hot flatbread, perforated like matzo and mottled with crisp bits of carbonized flour, that are brought to your table one after another until you burst. To nibble with the bread, you might try *sabzi khordan,* which is a platter of fresh raw herbs and a slice or two of salty feta cheese; or *torshi liteh,* a powerfully sour marinated-vegetable salsa; or a whole head of raw, tender, marinated garlic. If you manage to eat it before it stiffens, the bread, called *tanori,* is among the most seductive Middle Eastern breads in existence.

Shahrezad has kebabs—pretty good ones, in fact—but they're about the least interesting food in the restaurant, little more than charcoally chunks of marinated protein that help you get down the humongous mountains of egg-yolk-stained Iranian rice.

Better to start with *borani,* what the menu calls "eggplant delight," an extremely tasty glop of fried eggplant and sesame paste, topped with Shahrezad's signature tangle of blackened fried onion. Grape leaf bundles, *dolmeh,* are stuffed with meat, raisins, and pungent Iranian spice. Soups include *ash reshteh,* sort of a delicious Iranian version of Mediterranean *pistou* that is fragrant with dill and garlic, thick with beans and noodles.

If *sabzi polo* happens to be offered, order it: the giant mound of green, dilled rice pilaf is topped with chunks of crusty, perfectly grilled whitefish, redolent of its herbed marinade. *Tahchin* is an enormous, crisp-crusted brick of saffron-yellow rice, the size of a cinder block, that is stuffed with braised lamb and garnished with bittersweet barberries, a native Iranian fruit. *Baghali polo* involves a nicely seasoned lamb shank completely buried underneath dilled, lima-bean-spiked rice.

Fesenjan, the popular Iranian dish of chicken sauced with a purée of pomegranate and ground walnuts, is less sweet than usual and of clear pomegranate flavor, but less exotic than the ingredients might lead you to believe. *Karafs,* on the other hand, described on the menu as fried celery, is terrific, the pungence of long-braised celery tamed with lime and mint.

I like the stews: *gormeh sabzi,* with dried lime, kidney beans, and spinach cooked until it collapses into a dark-green purée; *badjeman,* eggplant cooked in a steely tomato sauce with veal; and *ghaimeh,* a thick split-pea thing. (You can have any two of the stews on a slab of crunchy rice crust, called *tah dig,* as an appetizer. Do—it's the biggest bargain on the menu.)

And for dessert, tea served in water glasses, with wafers of homemade caramel.

SHAKAS

2300 S. GARFIELD AVE., MONTEREY PARK; (323) 888-2695. SUN.-THURS., 10A.M.–10P.M.; FRI. & SAT., 10A.M.–MIDNIGHT.

There is sushi. And then there is Spam *musubi.* Spam *musubi* is a brick of vinegared sushi rice, the size of a chalkboard eraser but with twenty times the heft, burrito-wrapped in a sheet of dark-green nori seaweed and stuffed with a pink, glistening slab of the luncheon meat. It's substantial, Spam *musubi,* sweet, salty and faintly tart, porky more in its aftertaste than in its first full-frontal assault, with a density just this side of lead. You could, I think, wrap your knuckles around a Spam *musubi* and knock out a punk in a bar.

Spam *musubi* is a specialty of the other Pacific Rim cuisine, the spectacular miscegenation of Asian flavors and vernacular American technique that has made up street-level Hawaiian cooking for decades. Spam *musubi,* not the baroque, Frenchified concoctions of mahimahi, papaya, and baby ginger that prettify the menus at hotel restaurants, is the real soul food of Hawaii. So are square meals of *saimin* noodles, teriyaki and deep-fried pork with curry; shave ice, chili rice, and vast hamburger steaks with soy-flavored gravy.

The classic form of the Hawaiian plate lunch—two neat scoops of rice flanking a single scoop of macaroni salad, a few shreds of the Japanese pickled cabbage called *tsukemono,* and a heap of teriyaki pork or grilled short ribs—is as traditional and unchanging as a McDonald's Quarter Pounder Meal or, more to the point, a southern diner's meat and threes. Hawaiian food, in its purest form, tends to be . . . basic.

One of the best of the local Hawaiian places is Shakas, a Formica-clad takeout restaurant near the southern edge of Monterey Park, in an area where the Chinese restaurants give way to somewhat older Japanese restaurants, pastrami stands, and vast electronics stores. There are always a few potential nose tackles in here—Shakas does not serve diet food—as well as a handful of kids eating powdery shave ice, and skinny computer geeks who can do serious damage to a teriyaki bowl. Shakas (a *shaka* is a hand sign, basically a fist with pinkie and thumb extended, indicating kinship), while wonderful in its way, possesses slightly fewer amenities than a Burger King.

You'll find Spam *musubi* at Shakas, of course, and the fried Japanese dumplings *gyoza*, and a mild chicken curry with potatoes. The plate lunches—the gravy-soaked hamburger steak called *loco moco,* the fried chicken cutlet, the Spam and eggs—are absolutely classic, mounds of rice standing proudly as the nuclear domes up the coast from Trestles, and the macaroni salad even has a little flavor, though I couldn't actually tell you what flavor it is.

Teriyaki beef is a mellow variation of the stuff you find topping the rice at Beef Bowl. For something closer to what we all grew up thinking of as teriyaki, try the sweet Korean-style grilled short ribs, aka *kalbi*. Sesame chicken, goopy deep-fried drumettes dipped in syrup and rolled in sesame seeds, is strictly steam-table grub, though after a couple of bites you may find yourself powering through a pound of the things.

Best of all is *kalua* pork, the stalwart of the luau pit, baked at low temperature until the meat collapses in on itself, fatty, unbelievably rich, disconcerting at first because it is utterly unseasoned, but ultimately as satisfying as stringy North Carolina–style barbecue. Shakas knows how much of the stuff you'll ultimately eat—*kalua* pork is sold primarily by the pound.

SHANGHAI PALACE

932 HUNTINGTON DR., SAN MARINO; (626) 282-8815. DAILY, 11:30A.M.–3P.M. AND 5P.M.–8:30P.M.

Shanghai Palace is a Chinese restaurant on an ivy-covered San Marino commercial strip that looks a little like Carmel, nestled among studios that will produce an oil portrait of your grandfather or teach your seven-year-old to twirl like a sugarplum fairy. San Marino families flock to Shanghai Palace, blond broods with perfect teeth and retroussé noses who look as if they've just stepped out of Tommy Hilfiger ads, supping on orange chicken, egg rolls, and sweet-and-sour pork. The restaurant, one of the very few open for dinner in what is probably Los Angeles's wealthiest suburb, is on one level not so different from Chinese restaurants in Montecito or Greenwich, Connecticut—although unlike those suburbs, San Marino still has dry laws in effect, which means that Shanghai Palace serves nothing stronger than Slice.

But San Marino is becoming more Asian by the week. More than half of the students in San Marino schools are Chinese-American; a guy outside washing his Lexus on a Saturday is as likely to be Asian as WASP. The city is bordered on its south by San Gabriel and Alhambra, two of the best Chinese restaurant cities on the planet, and it makes sense that San Marino might finally have a serious Chinese restaurant of its own.

Shanghai Palace, the sister restaurant to Monterey Park's splendid Lake Spring Cuisine, has always had good food if you looked beyond the sticky-sweet neighborhood-restaurant stuff, but it used to serve a sort of Cantonese variant of Lake Spring's creative Shanghainese cooking—wonderful, quirky versions of classic Hong Kong–style banquet food. These days, with the exception of the occasional jellyfish plate or dish of mayonnaise-fried shrimp with candied walnuts, Shanghai Palace is solidly Shanghainese, with brown sauces, extravagantly scented braises and carefully constructed slices of vegetarian goose, fish-head casseroles and pork with preserved vegetables.

How many great Chinese restaurants are there in the San Gabriel Valley? Enough so that it is actually possible to forget about a place like Shanghai Palace, to pass the place a couple of times a week on the way to Chinese restaurants in San Gabriel or Rosemead without being tempted to slow down the car.

Plainly a mistake: The house soup is a mammoth clay pot of milky-white broth filled with tofu, slivers of Chinese squash, and a whole fish, which the waitress lifts from the pot and anoints with a musky, thin sauce. Another clay pot holds delicious lion's-head meatballs, orange-size clouds of anise-seasoned ground pork that fall apart at the touch of a spoon.

A spicy, chewy tangle of duck webs fried with basil, chiles, and dark soy could pass for Thai food nine times out of ten, as could braised Japanese eggplants. Slices of Chinese winter melon are cooked down to a fragrant lusciousness with smoky bits of Virginia ham. Sweet Shanghai-style spareribs, glazed and fried, are as hard to stop eating as buttered popcorn.

There are bits of frog cut up small and fried with spicy salt, tossed with a few rings of serrano chile, and there is a wonderful dish of fish cut into quarter-inch dice and fried simply with chopped red and green bell peppers and a handful of pine nuts. That frog is one of the best salt-and-pepper dishes I've ever eaten, utterly crisp but still moist and amphibian; that fish is a lesson in the interplay of flavors, the high, cinnamon-tinged muskiness of browned pine nuts bringing out the sweetness of the flesh.

If you ask for some *ong choy*, a hollow-stemmed Chinese water vegetable that isn't on the menu but is usually available in decent Chinese restaurants, it comes to the table as a warm, khaki-color heap tasting of salt, garlic, and the particular bittersweetness of the vegetable. Even the sautéed shrimp, a usually boring dish I order all the time because my young daughter likes it almost as well as she does ice cream, is great, slicked with garlic, and garnished with sweet, fried scallions.

Do not miss the phenomenon known as stuffed hen. Have you ever had one of those weird-looking green things from a dim-sum cart, lotus leaves wrapped around a filling of sticky rice and vegetables and bits of sweet Chinese sausage? This is a little like the best version you've ever had of that, except instead of the lotus leaf, the softball of sticky rice is stuffed inside of a boned-out game hen and deep fried. The rice becomes saturated with the hot chicken juices; the skin of the hen becomes as crunchy as a potato chip. Although the bird is cut up in a way that implies it is meant to serve six people, you could probably inhale the whole thing yourself before you knew what hit you, driven into the kind of feeding frenzy that leaves you with rice grains stuck in your hair, a greasy aureole around your lips, and the feeling that the world may be all right after all.

SHAU MAY

15 E. VALLEY BLVD., ALHAMBRA; (626) 282-2262. DAILY, 11A.M.– MIDNIGHT.

Shau May is a bare-bones Taiwanese snack shop near the epicenter of Chinese Alhambra, a loud, neon-lit buffet a block away from the city's big Hong Kong–style seafood houses, and sandwiched between a cavernous Chinese movie theater and a print shop that specializes in embossed Chinese menus.

The café hops late at night when it fills with Chinese teenagers and their friends, local businessmen in shirtsleeves, dudes reconnoitering after an evening of Jackie Chan. But Shau May is more than a cheap feed, more than a bowl of Taiwanese pig-foot noodles. It is also the best place in town for Taiwanese slush, the light Chinese dessert that is as ubiquitous in the San Gabriel Valley as frozen yogurt is in Encino. Shau May is essentially the Chinese answer to Baskin Robbins.

Most Asian countries have something like Taiwanese slush: the Philippine ice parfait called *halo halo*, the sweet Indonesian ices spiked with things like baby coconut and avocado, the fruit-flavored snow cones sold in Singaporean hawker centers.

The Japanese, who are reputed to have started the ice-dessert fad sixty years ago during the days of the Greater East Asian Co-Prosperity Sphere, are famous for the shaved ice served locally at sweet shops like Mikawaya in Little Tokyo Plaza, and the Japanese version is clean, typically austere.

Taiwanese slush, though, is perhaps first among Asian ices, an ultracold block of ice whirred against a sharp steel blade, a shower of fine, dry powder snow moistened with an expert squirt or two of milk.

Beneath the snow, plopped down on your plate like stew at a mess hall, are four ladlefuls of sweet stuff you choose from an array of sixteen. On the plate, canned peaches run into chunks of boiled taro in syrup, and soft boiled peanuts settle against translucent, vaguely herbal lozenges of grass jelly or sticky heaps of sweet red beans. Little translucent BBs taste like congealed honey; puffed grains in syrup taste a little like a bowl of Super Sugar Crisp that have spent too long in water. These sweets, most of which are nonfat, flavor the ice, add a compelling richness, and melt on your tongue.

There's an art to composing your slush, I guess—the most popular formula would seem to include one canned fruit, one legume, one squishy thing, and one starch—but the women behind the counter don't sneer at you even if you choose all beans.

Shau May is the logical place to stop for dessert after a big Chinese meal. I once took cookbook author Marion Cunningham to Shau May after a Muslim Chinese dinner at the big San Gabriel mall, and the great cook, who has written more books about desserts than most of us have even read, was immediately taken with the idea of buying up a fleet of pushcarts and becoming the Colonel Sanders of Taiwanese slush. Sometimes it takes a woman who has tasted everything to realize the elegant simplicity inherent in a dessert of canned fruit under ice.

SHIANG GARDEN

111 N. ATLANTIC BLVD., MONTEREY PARK; (626) 458-4508. DAILY,
11:30A.M.–10:30P.M.

Shiang Garden, formerly Charming Garden is a clean, bright place, spare of ornament, with fresh tablecloths and formal service, waitresses rushing in and out of a warren of banquet rooms off to one side. It is the most serious Hunan-style restaurant in Southern California.

Here comes a waitress, slinging a tray like a cigarette girl, hawking an assortment of cold hors d'ouevres that cost just a couple of dollars a pop: tender, young bamboo shoots cooked in a sweet chili sauce; marinated cubes of jicama; parboiled snap peas brushed with sweetened sesame oil. If you're fortunate, there will be smooth, cool slabs of chile-marinated beef tendon. Tiny, dry-fried anchovies tossed with fiery-hot chiles may be the kind of bar snack you have been waiting your entire life to taste.

What you're going to want next is the house-special bean curd, a smoking clay pot that ends up on every table, where it sputters and spits like a volcanic hot spring and is violently flavored with chile, garlic, and leeks. It couldn't be more delicious. Bean-curd sheets are fried crisp into simulations of Peking duck skin, then daubed with bean sauce and wrapped in pancakes. Steamed lotus-leaf rolls look suspiciously like Greek *dolmas,* but you are supposed to unwrap the rolls and scrape out the gooey filling of chicken and pork, or you will become a figure of fun to everybody in the restaurant—as a friend was horrified to discover.

Hunan honey ham, which you tuck into cunningly sliced chunks of Wonder bread, may be blander than the best versions, but goes nicely with the rest of the food. Strangely spiced noodles with "hot herb sauce," pungent with Sichuan peppercorns, tossed with ground pork, and coated with an intriguing grayish powder are weirdly astringent yet totally compelling, a taste like nothing you've ever experienced before.

And lunch isn't even the best meal at Charming Garden.

House-smoked pomfret, bronzed and gleaming, might be the most beautiful plate of food in the San Gabriel Valley, like some patinated artifact displayed on a handsome platter. The large fish, which the restaurant flies in from Taiwan, smells strongly of smoke—almost too strongly—but the rich, pale flesh is surprisingly delicate, like perfect sturgeon, and almost needs the aid of the pepper-laced salt with which it is served.

One soup involves raw fillets of whitefish barely poached in the mild broth a waitress pours over them from a teakettle; another, a savory slurry of minced squab served in little bamboo cups, is as complexly resonant as a first-growth Bordeaux. There are shredded bits of pork stir-fried with twice their weight in fresh red chiles; crunchy fried strips of eel tossed with candied walnuts; and crisply fried chicken heavily scented with numbing Sichuan peppercorns.

I have been disappointed just once: rosy slices of pheasant breast, looking like nothing so much as proscuitto, are dipped in a taro batter and fried at a tableside cart, but never do manage to become crisp.

But in a stunning twist on the famous Cantonese dish of minced squab in a lettuce leaf, Charming Garden chops fresh shrimp fine, sautés them with garlic, tosses them with crunchy bits of fried bread, and wraps them like tacos in leaves of iceberg lettuce; the contrast between the cold lettuce and the hot shrimp, the sweet garlic and the crisp mineral tang, is superb.

When a waitress brings the unpromising sounding "steamed stuff chicken" to the table at dinnertime, she unwraps a big foil packet, snips the knot tied in an ovenproof plastic bag, and reveals a whole red-cooked chicken, fragrant with soy and spice, enveloped in a puff of anise-scented steam. You've heard of chicken so tender it falls off the bone? This chicken is so tender that the bone itself has mostly dissolved, and the calcium-enriched flesh has absorbed so much flavor that it seems like something else apart, chicken evolved to a higher astral plane.

SHIN CHON

244 S. OXFORD AVE.; (213) 384-2663. MON.–SAT., 9A.M.–11P.M.

When you walk into Shin Chon, a nondescript mini-mall restaurant near the northeastern edge of Koreatown, you know what you're going to eat, the waitress knows what you're going to eat, and all the other customers know it too. Shin Chon is a restaurant devoted to the cult of Korean beef soup, *sol-long-tang*, to the extent that there is no menu and no other item served. There is also no language barrier: you don't order, you nod. There's even a neon depiction of the *sol-long-tang* in the front window. The beef soup is pretty good.

Sometimes you'll see men in the parking lot, staggering under the weight of a dozen or so to-go orders, or entire Korean Airlines flight crews slurping soup still in uniform. Shin Chon is a democratic institution, as Koreán as Nate 'n' Al's is Jewish.

Almost as soon as you sit down, you are brought two dishes of fresh *kimchi*— one of pungent cabbage, one of crunchy radish, both of which are intensely garlicky, also fiery hot. Then come small metal bowlfuls of lukewarm barley tea, then little canisters of hot rice, then beer if you've ordered it. Before you've had time to nibble more than a leaf or two of the cabbage, out comes the soup, steaming hot in a straight-sided pottery bowl, smelling like the quintessence of beef.

Good *sol-long-tang* is milky white, the result of long, patient cooking and the essence of many bones. In its ideal form it is as healthy and digestible as chicken soup, protein-rich, pretty much skimmed of all its fat, just the thing for a rainy spring afternoon, or as ballast for a night of serious drinking. *Sol-long-tang* seems to be almost as common in Koreatown as ramen is in Little Tokyo or *pho* is in Little Saigon, the universal snack, quick lunch, or light evening meal. (Actually, Korean-speaking *pho* shops popped up all over Koreatown this year: beef noodle soup is beef noodle soup.) You can be in and out of any of the many Koreatown *sol-long-tang* joints in less than thirty minutes; you can recognize the *sol-long-tang* joints by the ubiquitous neon bowl of soup. And at least one Koreatown place will even deliver the *sol-long-tang* to your door.

Shin Chon's *sol-long-tang* is opaque enough to conceal its load of thin noodles and long-simmered slices of brisket, practically an incandescent, glowing white. If the milky, wholesome groove seems appealing, you can stir in most of your bowl of rice, which turns the dish into a satisfying gruel.

The soup is unsalted—you season it to taste with a half-teaspoon or so of coarse salt from a container on the table, also freshly chopped scallion greens, which soften quickly in the hot broth, and possibly a spoonful of Shin Chon's chile paste, which tints the soup flamingo-pink.

The soup is also served in a bottomless bowl, more or less, because the waitresses will bring out more noodles, more *kimchi,* more broth, and more barley tea if you want, and then package the "leftovers" to go.

SKY'S GOURMET TACOS

5408 W. PICO BLVD.; (323) 932-6253. MON.–THURS.. 11A.M.–7:30P.M.; FRI. AND SAT., 11A.M.–9P.M.

Sky's Gourmet Tacos, an African-American taco stand, is . . . different. The walls are lined with pictures of jazz musicians where you'd expect to see *norteño* stars, and the stack of periodicals in the corner includes black entertainment tabloids and black business journals instead of frayed copies of *La Opinión.* The music on the radio is R&B. And the smell in the air, the indescribable cooking aroma that can pinpoint your location in the world far more accurately than any GPS, is somehow closer to a cumin-scented Caribbean restaurant than it is to East L.A.

Sky's are not the tacos your mother used to make. Or rather, they probably *are* the tacos your mother used to make, unless you happened to grow up in a Mexican household: two thick corn tortillas mounded with turkey, shrimp, or beef, gilded with orange cheese, buried under shredded lettuce, and doused with the sweet-hot house salsa. If you want what you might ordinarily call a taco, ask for the smaller *"tacolitas"* instead.

The steak in the tacos, rubbed with spices and seared to a blackened medium-rare before it is sliced, is pure Mom's cooking too, much closer in flavor to a Southern T-bone than it is to the usual thin, tough, citrus-scented *carne asada;* the shrimp are clumsily spiced, but also practically exude a homemade quality.

Open-face "burritos" are more or less the tacos written in triplicate: huge masses of meat, lettuce, and cheese layered onto bulletproof flour tortillas, luxuriating in pools of tasty orange grease and slicked with big clots of cool sour cream . . . fork-and-knife burritos. And just the thing for a quick lunch, perhaps sluiced down with a quart-size glass of homemade lemonade. Sky's is a different sort of authenticity.

SOOT BULL JEEP

3136 EIGHTH ST.; (213) 387-3865. DAILY, 11A.M.–11P.M.

Soot Bull Jeep is the archetypal big-city Korean barbecue: noisy, smoky, loud, always crowded, with all the bustle you'd expect in the heart of a great city. Here we are, crammed around a table, battling great gusts of secondhand meat smoke that shroud the restaurant in blue, garlic-scented fog. Guys in suits pound back endless shots of Jinro, a kind of smooth, low-proof Korean vodka distilled from yams, poured from bottles designed to look like J&B Scotch. Tabletop grills briefly explode into fountains of yellow flame.

There is a noodle dish or two to be had here, but you will certainly order barbecue. Even before the waitress drops a menu in front of you, she scatters a trowelful of glowing hardwood coals into the pit set in the middle of your table. A greased wire screen fits above the charcoal; around the pit go a dozen or so dishes of pickled cabbage, steamed spinach, and the rest of the little appetizers and condiments that come with a Korean meal.

Soot Bull Jeep is one of the few Korean restaurants in town that use the traditional live coals for their tabletop barbecue in place of the more common gas grills, and the meat takes on a delicious savory tang. Dinner at Soot Bull Jeep is an atavistic thing: not just good liquor and platters of raw meat, but also smoke, fire, and showers of small cinders that can transform a good linen shirt into something that looks like Wile E. Coyote after an encounter with an Acme exploding cigar.

If you are new to this sort of thing, a waitress will unceremoniously dump raw, marinated protein onto the grill in front of you, returning periodically to turn the meat when it is done, scissor it into bite-size chunks, and maneuver it away from the heat so that your ignorance of cooking times injures the meat no more than it absolutely has to. When the flames leap too high, she scatters ice chips that bubble and dance as they hit the hot grill. When the food is burnt irreparably, she sighs and scrapes the salvageable bits onto a fresh screen.

Short ribs turn nicely chewy, but retain their juice on the grill; pork loin is marinated in a spicy chile paste that blackens and turns crisp; bits of marinated spencer steak are sweet and tender, but overcook in a flash. Slabs of eel become sweet, crisp, and pleasantly oily over the flame; off-menu baby octopus gets crunchy around the tips of the tentacles, deliciously chewy toward the thickest part of the body.

When a bit of meat is cooked to your liking, you can drag it briefly through a soy-based dip or wrap it in a scrap of lettuce leaf with perhaps a few shreds of marinated scallion and a schmear of pungent fermented-bean paste. Unmarinated spencer steak is served frozen, shaved into rounds the approximate size and shape of beer coasters, which the waitress flicks onto the grill like a gambler dealing out a hand of cards, and you eat it with a salt-sesame oil dip instead.

For dessert, Soot Bull Jeep features a special kind of perfumed chewing gum that smells like hand lotion, perhaps the only gum in the world that makes Juicy Fruit seem restrained in comparison.

SPOON HOUSE

1601 W. REDONDO BEACH BLVD., GARDENA; (310) 538-0376. DAILY,
11A.M.–9P.M.

My late friend Jac Zinder used to run a Hollywood nightclub, Third Eye, devoted
to the odd and wonderful carom shots that result when Punjabis take a stab at
Bee Gees–style disco or a band of seventeen-year-old Colombian kids poke at the
Rolling Stones catalog, music that sounded at the same time both familiar and
unspeakably exotic. When an artist takes on an unfamiliar culture, something
vital is invariably lost in the translation—I heard a Japanese Led Zeppelin tribute
band at the Whisky once reproduce "Dazed and Confused" right down to Jimmy
Page's wrong notes—but something important is gained too.

Look at what Picasso found when he tackled African sculpture: cubism. Look
at what the Japanese came up with when they reinterpreted Italian cooking: spaghetti sandwiches. Japanese sometimes eat spaghetti doughnuts too.

A spaghetti sandwich, *supageti sando,* comes with meat sauce, and is served
either on white bread or with the noodles stuffed inside a split French roll. A
Tokyo novelty, the spaghetti sandwich is an Italianate spin on the rather more
common *yakisoba* sandwich. You can find both of them in the underground
arcades near subway stations, where the food stands specialize in handy commuter
snacks.

You can find meat-sauce sandwiches, though neither spaghetti sandwiches nor
yakisoba sandwiches, at the Spoon House in Gardena, a tidy Japanese-Italian
spaghetti joint, with a California bear painted on the window and a line spilling
out the door.

The Spoon House is packed with first-generation Japanese: posses of teenage
girls, middle-aged couples taking a break from shopping, young families with very
young, smeary-mouthed children who point and giggle and wave. The chef, behind a sushi-bar-like glass counter, manipulates the octopoid controls of what is
labeled the Al Dente System, a complicated water-boiling carousel that cooks
pasta to order. A sparkling room decorated in late-'70s high-tech, Spoon House
looks as if it were designed to resemble the background in a Patrick Nagel poster.

The food—a Japanese take on an American take on Italian cooking—resembles nothing you've ever encountered. Picture a plate of noodles layered with
Chef Boyardeeish meat sauce, topped with hot dogs that have been sliced thin
and fried, topped in turn with a fried egg and crowned with two neatly crossed
rashers of bacon. This is the Spoon House version of spaghetti Bolognese. Or
imagine spaghetti tossed with fried cabbage and thick, Spamlike slices of canned
corned beef. Or a thin, runny *carbonara* sauce that tastes overwhelmingly of
pepper. Spoon House pasta seems designed to feed a Japanese nostalgia for the
ration-maximizing cuisine of the postwar American occupation.

But once you get past expecting anything here to taste like Italian food, some of the Spoon House specialties are actually pretty good. Spaghetti is tossed with butter and cod roe until the mixture coats every strand, then tossed with sea urchin roe, cool slices of squid, and seaweed: the subtle oceanic flavor, cut with the sharp bite of the Japanese herb *shiso,* is remarkable. You can get noodles sauced with basil and *shiso,* or with *shiso* and tart bits of pickled plums, or with squid and a thinnish, hottish tincture of wasabi. Spaghetti with Japanese clam sauce comes with *shiso,* meaty sautéed shiitake mushrooms, plenty of garlic, and a big heap of clams—it's the kind of thing you'd be happy to find for three times the price at Chaya Brasserie.

STANDARD SWEETS & SNACKS

18600 PIONEER BLVD., ARTESIA; (562) 860-6364. TUES.–SUN., 11A.M.– 8P.M.

The people behind the counter at Standard Sweets & Snacks are as brusque as they are at any delicatessen, perfectly willing to skip on to the next guy if you take a little too long choosing between the fried lentils and the spicy mix, to ignore you altogether if you ponder the subtle difference between the *burfi* made with cashews and the *burfi* made with pistachios. It is easy to lose yourself in the complex geometry of a stack of *jalebi,* tubular spirals of fried rice-flour saturated with heavy syrup.

Espresso-color *gulab jamun,* caramelized cheese patties, bob in the syrup in which they've been poached. Rows and rows of milky halvahs, some sprinkled with nuts, some adorned with ultrathin sheets of pure silver foil, march into the near distance.

"Please!" barks a counter woman, gesturing at the glass-front case with the sweeping motion you may recall Carol Merrill making toward Curtain No. 2 on *Let's Make a Deal.* "These are all just milk and sugar, cooked together in different ways."

Standard Sweets is among the best of the many sweet shops in Artesia's Little India district, a place to stop for a cup of tea after shopping for saris or golden nose rings, coconut scrapers or bootleg tapes of Sufi trance singing. There may be nothing quite so soothing after a spicy meal as a great Indian *rasmalai,* freshly made cheese with the open, slightly spongy texture of really good fresh mozzarella, simmered in sweet cream and then chilled, sprinkled with crushed pistachio nuts, perhaps flavored with a bare hint of rosewater and the sweet, pure essence of milk ... unless, of course, it's *rasmalai* and a cup of milky, cardamom-scented *masala* tea.

Tea and carrot halvah at Standard Sweets is almost an automatic stop after an

Indian meal in Artesia, the Indian equivalent of espresso and cannoli at a Mulberry Street bakery after a pasta dinner in New York's Little Italy.

I had been going to Standard for years before I ventured beyond dessert. The restaurant, which prepares vegetarian dishes from all over India, is not quite as specialized as some of the shops in the area, a couple of which carry mostly the sweet yet fiery snacks from the midwestern state of Gujarat, others specializing pretty explicitly in sticky Punjabi concoctions.

At Standard, you can get fresh tandoori-baked garlic *naan* that is neither quite so buttery nor so flaky as it can be at tandoori specialty restaurants. But it is good enough, served with a Styrofoam plate and a cheerful invitation to dip out spinach with cheese, curried vegetables, lentil *dal* and cool, spiced yogurt from the steam table in the corner. You can also get a very passable version of the Gujarati dish *bhel puri*, a sweet-and-sour salad made with crunchy bits of toasted noodle, chickpeas, potatoes, and a stiff slug of tamarind chutney.

Dahi vada resembles a spiced Punjabi lentil cookie cosseted in cool, sour yogurt. The crisp tricornered *samosas* are stuffed with the inevitable curried potato. *Chana,* or curried whole chickpeas, come with a deep-fried puff of yogurt bread that comes out from the fryer almost the size of a basketball before it deflates into something that tastes like Navajo fry bread. You'll find most of the usual South Indian snacks—the steamed rice cakes called *idli,* the lentil pancake *uttupam*—and a sensational version of the Ping-Pong-ball-size bread *pani puri,* which you crack open, stuff with potatoes, and dip into thin cilantro sauce.

But everybody around you will be eating the *masala dosa,* a burnished crepe rolled around gently curried potatoes into a cylinder the size of a Louisville Slugger, served with a small metal bowl of vegetable curry.

For customers more interested in nostalgia than taste, Standard sells packets of the imported snacks called *nam keen* from a famous Indian manufacturer, salty tidbits that are basically the Indian equivalent of Chex mix—sold for the same reason, one supposes, that a bakery catering to expatriate New Yorkers might feature Devil Dogs alongside its cheesecake and loaves of pumpernickel.

STEVIE'S ON THE STRIP

3403 CRENSHAW BLVD.; (323) 734-6975. SUN.–THURS., 11A.M.–10P.M.; FRI. AND SAT., 11A.M.–11P.M.

Stevie's is a brightly painted Creole restaurant near the top of the Crenshaw Strip, an immaculate, sweet-smelling former fast-food joint tucked into a corner that always seems too small for the cars that crowd into the lot. If you could sit at a corner stool here for long enough, nursing a tall cup of pink lemonade, you'd probably see half of the city walk through the door for takeout. Stevie's fried chicken, crisp, peppery stuff that is run through a smoker before it is coated and deep-fried, is a staple in South Central L.A.

Stevie's used to be one of the biggest local advertisers on the legendary hip-hop radio station KDAY, and you can probably tell a true old-school rap fan in Los Angeles by his or her ability to hum old Stevie's commercials—half rapped, half sung, the ads were better hip-hop jams than half the records on the rotation. Stevie's is still a big advertiser on black radio, and it not unusual to hear a Stevie's promotion on the R & B ballad station that always seems to be blasting in the restaurant itself. Smoky fried chicken, the radio says. Short ribs. Gumbo on Fridays. Register to win free concert tickets.

Stevie—Stephen Perry—pushes his food with a vigor some may think more appropriate to selling used Oldsmobiles.

"Look out," he yells back to the cooks. "I see an order of gumbo getting out of his car right now."

About thirty seconds later, a nattily dressed older man comes through the door and walks up to the counter. "Gumbo?" Stevie asks. "Lemonade?"

The man nods and reaches up to adjust his driving cap.

"See," Stevie says to the cooks. "I told you."

On Fridays, if you arrive before the pot runs dry, Stevie's has an extremely good gumbo, dark and rich, poured over a handful of rice, full of smoked chicken, plump shrimp, a couple different kinds of sausage, and crab legs that are notched so that you can get at the meat without spattering your shirt with viscous black goo. The flavor is equally earthy and marine, heightened by the murky herbal complexity that only filé can lend, garlic from the sausage, smoke from the chicken. The seafood is nicely poached in the broth, in contrast to the vast majority of gumbos—including most of the gumbos in Louisiana—in which the shellfish is cooked to tough strings.

"How is the gumbo served?" Stevie says to a customer, raising an eyebrow. "The gumbo is served real good."

On days that are not Fridays, you might as well try the smoky fried chicken, the decent fried-oyster po' boys, or the chitterlings sold by the pint. The side dishes are almost all good—long-cooked collard greens, black-eyed peas sharp with the tang of bay leaves, ultrasugary yams, hand-cut French fries, rice 'n' gravy. Red beans and rice, served with a dryish fried pork chop or a hot link, is somewhat underseasoned, but you can bring it up to strength with a squirt or two of hot sauce. Short ribs, dense hunks of meat, ruddy and chewy, tinged with char, are plenty fine enough to take you through the other six days of the week.

But as I say, show up early on Fridays. A friend was once beaten out of a bowl of gumbo by an MTA driver who stopped a full Crenshaw bus outside during rush hour, ran in, and copped the last order. Denied!

Behold Sushi Bar Golf, a Korean restaurant at the heart of a neighborhood that can't decide whether it is Filipino, Salvadoran, or Japanese. Although Sushi Bar Golf is in plain view, it seems a little like a secret restaurant, with its valet parking and entrance hidden in the rear of a busy Union Oil station. When you wheel around the Nissans and battered Mavericks at the gas station's pumps, you will find Golf's small parking lot filled with Lexuses, Infinitis, and a smattering of the newest BMWs.

Somebody at Golf must play a round every so often, and there are the photographs, autographed scorecards, and course souvenirs to prove it. The deep, wooden booths are decorated with pictures of Augusta fairways rendered in glowing tones that suggest black-velvet Elvis paintings. Back in the corner, a poster of Tiger Woods occupies a favored niche. On video monitors hanging from the ceiling, golf tournaments silently play themselves out, except on the one screen that usually seems to be broadcasting sushi-making instructional tapes. If you look carefully, you will even find an autographed glossy of the golf-mad Korean comedian Johnny Yune.

Golf occupies a former coffee shop that for most of the '70s and '80s was a Japanese place called Alps, famous for its passable *yakisoba*, hamburger patties spiked with minced onion, and beautiful waitresses in very short skirts. The '90s saw Alps' transformation into Hassho, which was an *izaka-ya*—Japanese pub— whose seared albacore and simmered cod was positioned almost exactly between the simple food at the popular pub chain Yoro No Taki and the exquisite nibbles at expensive joints like Yuu and Ita-Cho.

Where classic Japanese sushi is a delicate medium, Korean sushi is Technicolor-bright, pungently seasoned, and served in meaty, Flinstonesian slabs. Golf brings to this venerable space the Korean paradigm of sushi as a great bar snack, and indeed, most of the men sitting around the sushi bar itself seem to sluice down their tuna rolls and live-shrimp sashimi with vast amounts of Dewars and Johnny Walker Red. The traditional Korean liquor *sojuk,* a low-proof sweet-potato vodka, seems almost too feeble for the cuisine.

First, there is a little bowl of boiled soybeans to nibble on while you scan the menu, and then a small assortment of the Korean appetizers called *pan chon,* which may include the usual *kimchee;* sweet, thinly sliced turnips; a black sea vegetable; maybe something marine and slithery that you suspect to have once been a sea creature's unmentionables.

Tempura—a few vegetables, a couple of shrimp, a slice of lotus root—comes in an attractive iron basket, and has the distinct oily-sweet smack of fresh crullers. Once, the waitress brought over, as casually generous as a taco-shop waitress with a basket of chips, a whole, deep-fried scorpionfish for each person at the table, and the nightmarishly ugly scorpionfish, poison spikes and all, tasted a little like a freshly fried cruller too.

The menu at Golf, printed in English and Hangul—but not in Japanese—is rich in teriyaki plates and mackerel dinners and such, but seems to emphasize the sashimi assortments known as Par, Birdy, and Eagle, glacial moraines sculpted out of shredded daikon, then salted with fishmarkets-full of fresh sliced fish: salmon striped with pale fat; rich, red tuna; various halibuts and yellowtails; shrimp fished from the tanks behind the sushi bar; various bits of abalone and clam.

The sushi here is fine, hand rolls stuffed with strips of grilled salmon skin, rather overvinegared mackerel sushi, beefy tuna, piers of grilled sea eel, house-special rolls that resemble vegetable-rich tuna rolls paved with curved scallops of thinly sliced avocado.

But nothing may go better with a brimming glass of *sojuk* than Golf's *hwe do bap*, Korea's great contribution to the world of sushi, bits of impeccably fresh sashimi topped with vinegared slivers of cucumber, strips of toasted seaweed, black sesame seeds, and a raw quail egg, which you toss at table with sweet bean sauce and a bowl of hot rice. Fore!

SUSHI GEN

422 E SECOND ST.; (213) 617-0552. MON.–FRI., 11A.M.–2 P.M., 5:30P.M.–10P.M.; SAT., 5P.M.–10P.M.

There are, of course, many sushi experiences available in the greater Los Angeles area: sushi served by reggae singers and sushi served by tap dancers, sushi bars that specialize in firecracker rolls and sushi bars that refuse to prepare anything that wasn't available in Meiji-era Japan, sushi bars that double as singles bars, and sushi bars—very good sushi bars—whose chefs are as strictly demanding as any dominatrix you could ever hope to meet.

If your taste runs toward sushi plucked off little toy boats or sushi sent your way on conveyer belts, sushi you order by computer or drive-through sashimi burritos or sashimi carved off a living sea bass that stares at you as you eat—you are in the right place. There are so many sushi bars in Los Angeles—and so much demand for sushi—that experienced chefs reportedly command salaries heretofore paid only to studio electricians and Jaguar mechanics.

But in the midst of apparent raw-fish plenitude, in a town with both the cheapest and the most expensive sushi restaurants in North America, what's hard to find are great regular-guy sushi bars, places populated neither by tentacle-waving partiers nor by effete crab-brain-eating purists, places that will sell you a California roll if you want one but also take pride in their cured mackerel.

Which brings us to Sushi Gen, a dim, wood-lined Little Tokyo place with the festive, hazy look of a smoke-filled saloon. There are cheap teriyaki plates and big bowls of *chirashi* sushi, salads with radish sprouts and complicated preparations of lobster, sashimi platters and weird boiled things. And sushi. But you knew that.

It is relaxing to sit at the long bar in the middle of a lunch rush, to watch the chefs whittle sides of tuna down to two hundred pieces of sashimi and a heap of what looks a little like cat meat, to strip one hundred clams, cut fifty pieces of yellowtail, cause slivers of halibut to leap free from a massive side of fish. And when the chef finally looks up at you after having broken down a bluefin, it almost seems like magic when he seems to anticipate your request, slashes his blade into the heart of the fillet, and liberates a few blocky slabs just for you: perfect. (In the evenings, when the chefs have the time to concentrate mostly on their sushi-bar customers, there isn't quite the same illusion of precious, stolen moments.)

Sushi Gen has everything you could want from a sushi bar: the white-fleshed albacore tuna, lightly seared at the edges to tighten the sweet flesh; ultrafresh halibut drizzled with sea salt and a few drops of *ponzu*; cool, unctuous slices of pickled mackerel whose taste practically oozes over the sushi's wasabi bite; crunchy, briny sheets of herring roe; crisp, broiled sea eel. The nutty, clean, slightly bitter *uni* is some of the best sea urchin I've ever had that wasn't attached to its shell—the stuff is usually too funky for me, but this *uni* still tastes of the sea.

Ankimo, monkfish liver, while lacking a little of the gorgeous luxuriousness of the same preparation at the late Shibucho, is pure, almost spartan, under its sprinkling of shredded daikon and tart *ponzu* sauce. And the sushi of giant longneck clam, sliced so thinly that you could count the grains of rice underneath it, is fine.

In the end comes the customary omelet *tamago*, tender layers of egg knit together tightly as fine silk. Or possibly a salmon-skin hand roll, laver rolled around generous lashings of radish sprouts, seeds, rice, *gobo* root, and the crunchy, oily bits of toasted skin itself, then bound at the bottom with a second piece of seaweed so that the juicy mixture won't drip out onto your lap.

Is this transcendent? No.

But it is a good place to eat lunch.

SUSHI SASABUNE

11300 NEBRASKA AVE., (310) 268-8380. MON.-FRI., NOON-2P.M. AND
5:30-9:30P.M.; SAT., 5:30-9:30P.M.

Sushi Sasabune, a spare, discreetly marked restaurant on the site of the old Sawtelle Mexicatessen, may be the best sushi bar in Sawtelle Boulevard's Japanese
district. THIS RESTAURANT SERVES ONLY TRADITIONAL SUSHI, says a sign in the
window. WE DO NOT SERVE TERIYAKI, WHITE RICE, CALIFORNIA OR SPICY ROLLS,
ETC. THIS RESTAURANT IS BASED ON CHEF'S CHOICE.

You've probably heard of the two or three famously strict sushi bars in the
Valley, places where the chefs insist on ordering for you and pride themselves on
eighty-sixing customers who insist on spicy firecracker rolls, but Sushi Sasabune
may be the strictest of all.

A sushi chef sets before each of us a small dish containing rather overchilled
slices of raw albacore in a supertart *ponzu* sauce, and he studies us as we eat. Do
we season each bite with the proper amount of chopped scallions? Do we shake
off excess sauce from each bite? Do we fumble with the chopsticks? Do we pass?

He slices into a slab of tuna that is the glowing, translucent pink of a Barbie-
'n'-Skipper accessory, and with exaggerated deliberateness, he molds them onto
struts of rice that may as well have been engineered in Stuttgart.

"My sushi is very soft," he says, brandishing a piece of the stuff with his
work chopsticks, "and you must eat it correctly. Pick it up not like this, or like
this . . . but like so. Pour only a very small amount of soy sauce into your dish—
many people flood the dish with sauce, and that is displeasing. You may flavor
the soy sauce with wasabi if you like. And dip not the rice but just the end of
the fish, or it will all fall apart into the sauce."

Finally he sets two pieces of tuna sushi in front of each of us. I have eaten
sushi hundreds of times, but suddenly I am unable to gain purchase on the
slippery fish with my chopsticks. The rice begins to crumble. I give up and use
my fingers. The pupils in the sushi chef's eyes seem to contract with rage.

It is a good piece of tuna sushi, almost fragile, of the sort that dissolves in
your mouth rather than providing an intense, beefy chaw. The wasabi—the hot
green stuff—is so sparingly applied as to be nonexistent. The rice, still warm, is
more loosely packed than I have ever seen it, dissolving into individual grains the
instant it hits your mouth. If you can accurately assess a sushi bar from a single
piece of tuna sushi—and Japanese friends assure me that you can—Sasabune is
sushi bar as passive experience, less for sensualists than for aesthetes. Nobody at
Sasabune will ever ask you what you want to eat, only when you want to stop.

"Red snapper from New Zealand and halibut from Boston," says the chef as
he places more sushi in front of us. "No soy sauce. Please eat them in order,
closest sushi first." Both the fish are lean, mild, almost overwhelmed by the lem-

ony pucker of the marinade. Eaten one after the other, the progression of these sushi may be a comment on the slightly differing brininesses of the fish, or maybe not. It's sort of a minimal experience.

And so it continues. Marinated yellowtail, also tart, has none of the sweetness, none of the oiliness, none of the strong-tasting brown spots you may associate with the fish; *kanpachi*, a kind of Japanese yellowtail, is exquisitely tender, but mild as flounder. The restaurant's signature sushi—a microtome-thin slice of salmon, a crunchy, transparent wisp of kelp, and a sprinkling of sesame seeds— is a little rich, almost decadent by the standards of this place, though it too manages to have a clean, sour afterbite rather than the mellow fish-oil glow that usually lingers in your mouth after you eat salmon sushi.

Perhaps as a reward for not insisting on California rolls, perhaps as what he thought was the end of the meal, the sushi chef turns suddenly generous, half-smiling and handing us fat crab hand rolls as if he were presenting us with the keys to his Camry. The crab rolls, which are the size of Jamaican spliffs, are fairly minimal too, with none of the *gobo* root, shaved *bonito,* or radish sprouts that garnish most of their equivalents around town, but they were great anyway, almost precisely half crabmeat and half rice, with the sweet, vanilla taste of really fresh shellfish and the smoky toastiness of freshly grilled seaweed.

The course of marinated Spanish mackerel and marinated Norwegian mackerel is fairly anticlimactic, though I am sure it is meant to prove some abstruse point on the relative qualities of fish oils. The chef has our number—out come more spliffs, this time stuffed with crunchy, oozing bits of grilled salmon belly.

The chef seems to be smiling at something, so we turn to see what it is. HEART DISEASE RISK, says a sign on a pillar behind us, IS HALVED BY EATING 8 OZ OF SALMON PER WEEK.

SUSIE'S DELI

12238 ARTESIA BLVD., ARTESIA; (562) 860-7272. WED. AND THURS., 11A.M.–8P.M.; FRI. AND SAT., 11A.M.–9P.M.; SUN., 12P.M.–8P.M.

Among my correspondents is a Dutch guy named Johann, an enthusiast of In-donesian food who has been known to call before 7:00 A.M. when he is excited about a dish he had the night before. When I run into Johann in a local Indo-nesian restaurant, which happens more often than you might expect, he will wink conspiratorially and pretend he doesn't notice me, though I know he later points me out to the proprietor—I suspect he would sell his soul for an extra helping of the right *ayam goreng.*

Perhaps it is a genuine symbiosis, perhaps it is the experience of fighting together against the Japanese in World War II, perhaps it's the food, but there seems to be no closer relationship between a people and their former colonizers than there is between the Indonesians and the Dutch, whose cultures in the Southland are sometimes almost indistinguishable.

Local Dutch grocery stores stock as many Indonesian spices as they do Dutch cheeses, and books from Amsterdam sit side by side with those from Jakarta. To judge from market shelves, Dutch emigrants have a nostalgia for fiery curries; Indonesians for Dutch spice cakes and licorice pastilles. In Southland Indonesian restaurants, you are as likely to see large, intergenerational Dutch families as Indonesian ones.

Johann is particularly excited about an Artesia restaurant called Susie's Deli.

"It is quite authentic," he says. "I am always meeting old friends that I haven't seen since we were in prison camp together."

He urges me always to call ahead and ask if they're serving *ayam pangang klaten*, an occasional weekend special involving fried chicken, coconut milk, and ground Indonesian nuts. I have called ahead many times.

Susie's Deli is the usual family-run mini-mall restaurant, with a few shelves of Dutch-Indonesian groceries, batik on the walls, and a deli counter filled with shrimp chips and ultrasweet Indonesian desserts.

There is the usual assortment of exotic Indonesian ice drinks, flavored with jackfruit and rosewater and bright-green mung-bean squiggles, including at least one drink, *es campur*, that looks like the mysterious substance in a jar that occupied the attentions of an entire *Twilight Zone* episode. The menu is dominated by the usual Indonesian lamb *satay*, peanutty *gado-gado* salad, fried rice, and fried noodles, though the *bakmi goreng* noodles are nicely smoky and the insanely spicy fried rice is sensational.

A few Sumatran dishes show up here from time to time. *Empek-empek palembang*, essentially a fried, egg-stuffed empanada made with house-pounded fish cake in place of a crust, is served in slices, sauced with a thin, sweet soy broth, and garnished with noodles and diced cucumber. *Tahu bakso kuha* involves meat-stuffed tofu and a gently spiced broth. *Bandeng presto* is made from a bony fish marinated and pressed under a weight until its bones dissolve, at which point it is fried to an unusually savory crisp.

But the Susie's Deli experience revolves around the weekly chalkboard specials, things like ultracrunchy fried shrimp; fried fish in a bright-red chile sauce; spicy fried chicken wings; yellow rice garnished with stewed beef, toasted coconut, some chicken curry, and a chilied hard-boiled egg. And sometimes, at least thoretically, you can even taste *ayam pangang klaten*.

"Please?" I ask. "Do you have it *today?*"

"We don't," the waitress says, "but you may like this other one even better."

A few minutes later, she brings out a dish of fried chicken flavored with a tart, curried vegetable julienne that tastes like a postmodernist's deconstruction of a jar of picalilli. I don't know whether it's better than the *ayam pangang klaten*, but I suspect that Johann would approve.

SWASDEE

8234 N. COLDWATER CANYON BLVD., NORTH HOLLYWOOD;
(818) 997-9624. DAILY, 11A.M.–9:30P.M.

The Thai Buddhist Temple in North Hollywood is a massive thing, tile-roofed and streaked with gold ornament, grounds crowded with parishioners, and saffron-robed monks, and small children who run about as if the temple were a playground.

On weekend afternoons and during festivals, the air around the temple almost throbs with the smells of Thai cooking: meat grilling at *satay* stands, the wheat pancakes called *roti* sizzling on massive griddles, pungent, briny salt crabs being pounded for green papaya salad. This feast is more or less the equivalent of the meals of smothered chicken and collards served Sundays after the service at some African-American churches, and the inexpensive Thai feast is open to all. The temple may be the epicenter of Thai culture in the Los Angeles area, and some of the Southland's best Thai restaurants, markets, and video stores are located within a short drive.

Directly across the street from the temple, in a small strip mall where you can buy a packet of frozen durian or a tape of Thai hip-hop, where a Thai catering truck sells papaya salad and grilled Thai sausage instead of tacos and cheese sandwiches, Swasdee is the rare Thai restaurant with more soul than refinement, more guts than flair. Geared almost exclusively to a Thai clientele, Swasdee serves the kind of homey dishes you might expect to eat if you were invited to a potluck dinner at a Thai friend's house.

Seafood-fried rice is delicious, for example, a fiery thing of near-risotto creaminess, almost more fish than grain, but there is a rather heavy use of bright red imitation crab, and the rice is stained pink with what appears to be catsup. Rich slivers of roast duck, in a dense, musky brown curry almost grainy with spice, are simmered with exotic Thai vegetables, but also with little arcs of pineapple cut straight from canned pineapple rings. Hot-sour seafood soup is clear, balanced, intense, thick with shrimp, fish, tender bits of squid, and green-lipped mussels.

You would expect nothing less than authentic cooking in this neighborhood, and mellow green fishball curries, crisp-edged mussel omelets, Chiang Mai–style sausages of raw, cured pork, crunchy with bits of cartilage, arranged on a plate with fried peanuts and little cubes of raw ginger are nothing less than authentic. The grilled beef salad and the overdressed glass-noodle salad can be less than spectacular—this isn't, after all, an Isaan-style restaurant—but the ultrafresh green papaya salad is very good, tart, chile-hot, heady with the sharp, briny aroma of salted crab.

One dish, a blistering yellow curry of fermented bamboo shoots, smells of clean stables, not the genteel flavor note often found in a well-aged Châteauneuf de Pape, but a full-on horsey aroma that permeates every corner of the restaurant when you lift the cover of the clay pot in which it is served. But the curry is pretty good, the bamboo's tartness pushing hard against the extreme chile heat and the gamy wallop of salted fish—this is Thai cooking with the volume turned up to ten, and the dish is probably too strong for anybody not raised on the stuff to take more than a couple of tentative bites.

While they're in season, don't miss the soft-shelled crab, three whole ones to an order, coated in fritter batter, sizzling from the deep fat, crunchy as potato chips and served with both a sweet, pungent cucumber salad. You may never again experience the eerie sensation of eating crabs that have the exact airy crunchiness of a Rice Krispies Marshmallow Treat.

T

TACOS BAJA ENSENADA

5385 WHITTIER BLVD., EAST L.A.; (323) 887-1980. DAILY, 8A.M.–8P.M.

Ensenada has always been a world capital of Lost Weekends: popular with sport fisherman who measure out their afternoons in spent cases of Corona, the center of the universe for aficionados of stuffed armadillos and illegal fireworks, a major crossroads for vendors of polyester serapes (made in Taiwan), a final destination for cheap cruise-ship journeys that take half a week to go nowhere in particular. The city has long been famous for the loud, boozy cantinas—Hussong's! Papas Fritas!—whose stickers probably adorned the bumper of the jacked-up Yukon that cut you off on the 405 last week, and if you spend most of your time within a few blocks of the bars, Ensenada can seem like a tequila-fueled satellite of the loudest fraternity party in the world.

Once you get a few blocks away from the tourist district, though, Ensenada takes shape as a solid, working-class industrial city, a major port. And as surely as Oaxaca and Veracruz, Ensenada has a cuisine of its own (if a minor one), a sturdy style of local cooking with big flavors, tons of citrus, and lots of fresh seafood. *Taquerias* favor the decent local beef and pork—sometimes even turtle. Carts on every street corner sell shrimp ceviche and *patas de mulas*, spicy cocktails of lime, tomatoes, and the raw meat of bulbous black clams that really do resemble mules' feet. Baja spiny lobsters are split, fried in oil, and served with melted margarine and lime. Californians have always come to Ensenada for expensive breaded-abalone dinners. The local peppery version of seafood soup is famous all over Mexico.

Still, in the rest of Mexico and beyond, the words *estilo Ensenada* signify just one thing: fish tacos, specifically the fried-fish tacos served at stalls in the fish market down by the docks. And Ensenada's fish tacos are formidable things, small—a couple of bites each, tops—but mighty. And there may be no experience on Earth that quite matches the pleasure of an afternoon spent wandering around the Ensenada fish market, sluicing fish tacos down with oceans of slush-cold Tecate beer and watching locals haggle over yellowtail tuna and horse mackerel.

Oddly enough, despite the physical proximity of Baja and the presence of tens of thousands of Ensenada expatriates in the area, Los Angeles restaurants—with the possible exception of Señor Fish—have never been able to produce a really great fish taco. Until now.

Tacos Baja Ensenada is a cheerful restaurant in a converted hamburger stand near the heart of East L.A., a Formica palace echoing with bouncy *ranchera* music and decorated with maps, posters, and postcards of La Bufadora, the sea spume twenty minutes south of Ensenada. Tacos Baja smells right, homey and oniony, like a Mexican grandmother's house, without a hint of seafood funk, and the various seafood cocktails—octopus, shrimp, clam, though not the *pata de mula*—are fresh and good. You'll find the usual *sopes* and *carne asada* plates; more to the point, there are tiny, crisp tortillas mounded with tart, rich ceviches of crab, shrimp, or fish.

You've come, no doubt, for what may be L.A.'s finest fish tacos: crunchy, sizzlingly hot strips of batter-fried halibut, folded into warm corn tortillas with salsa, shredded cabbage, and a squeeze of lime, sprinkled with freshly chopped herbs and finished with a squirt of thick, cultured cream, lightly done, delicately flavored. Entire religions have been founded on miracles less profound than the Ensenada fish taco—you could eat four in a minute and a half, and no doubt probably should, before they have a chance to cool.

But in your lust for the tacos, don't miss the spectacular *cahuamanta estilo Sonora*, a robust, fragrant dish of Baja stingray simmered with vegetables until it reaches the consistency of poached chicken, then served as a sharp, celery-scented soup or shredded and folded into comfortingly bland, vaguely marine-tasting tacos. Stingray tacos! Revenge on every creature that ever buried its barb into your ankle at the beach! The manliest taco in the sea!

THE TAM O'SHANTER INN

2980 LOS FELIZ BLVD.; (323) 664-0228. SUN.-THURS., 11A.M.-9P.M.; FRI. AND SAT., 11A.M.-10:30P.M.

"Ladies and gentlemen," says the piano player, "let's take time out for a brief liquormission," and at the Tam O'Shanter Inn there is a move to the bar, to the snifters of single-malt Scotch and flagons of McAndrews Scottish Ale, to the freshly fried potato chips that are a feature of this friendly piano bar. Many of the customers—gray hair, expensive sweaters, craggy foreheads—look as if they have been coming to the Tam since they were at USC Law School on the GI Bill, and many of them are capable of singing "Surrey With the Fringe on Top" without even a hint of irony.

Pianist Frank Day has been in the piano-bar biz for half a century, much of it in his Sunday- and Monday-night stints at the Tam, and he has a repertoire that ranges from Cole Porter to Jerome Kern, from Puccini medleys to the inevitable "New York, New York." He is, simply, the finest cocktail pianist in Los Angeles. And when he drinks a screwdriver at the keyboard, he has been known to stick the straw in his eye for comic effect.

A couple of blocks from the golf courses of Griffith Park, smack between the L.A. River and the industrial district of Glendale, the Tam O'Shanter Inn is one of the oldest restaurants in Los Angeles, a '20s roadhouse enlarged into a sprawling special-occasion joint, a half-timbered barn that sometimes seems like an infinite warehouse of Scottish-themed kitsch.

The Tam, run by the old L.A. family that owns Lawry's Prime Rib, spent a time in the '70s as a restaurant called the Great Scot, one of the "Ye Olde Sir Loin of Beefe"–style places popular at the time. The waitresses wear the smart tartan uniforms of that departed era of American restaurants; unfortunately, most of the restaurant's cooking, weirdly bland toad-in-the-holes and rarebits and spinach salads, dates from the '70s too.

But the food served in the Pub, the large area up front, is fine, big sandwiches stuffed with roast brisket or pastrami or prime rib—Lawry's prime rib!—or freshly roasted turkey, nicely dressed, served with good coleslaw. If you ask for it, a waitress will bring you freshly ground horseradish, which adds a nostril-searing punch to any sandwich. If you like, you can usually get a basket of batter-fried seafood or a half-pound of steamed shrimp to go with your mug of ale. The Pub is one of the few thriving examples of the businessman's restaurant left in town, those sandwich-and-beer lunch places that seem to have been taken over by fast-food and salads.

In New Orleans, the famous cocktail is the Sazerac; the most enduring cocktail from New York may be the Manhattan; the great Los Angeles cocktail is probably the Moscow mule—a combination of vodka, lime, and strong ginger beer first mixed at the old Cock 'n' Bull on the Strip. It's the cocktail credited with introducing vodka to America. The Tam makes a great Moscow mule served in a pewter mug. The Cock 'n' Bull uses a copper mug, but otherwise the drinks are the same: spicy, not too sweet, and sneakily alcoholic.

And the waitresses can be a trip: "I have been having a rich but troubling affair with a gifted saxophonist in Laguna Beach," one says, setting down drinks in front of a couple of the best-known composers in America. "You're not musicians; I wouldn't expect you to understand."

"But we *are* musicians," says one of the composers, an actual Pulitzer Prize winner.

"That's so sweet," she says. She pats him gently on the shoulder. "You're trying to make me feel better."

The Tam is a big-city bar, where nobody knows your name.

TASTE OF TEXAS

301 N. AZUSA AVE., COVINA; (818) 331-2824. MON.–THURS., 11A.M.–9P.M.; SAT., 8:30A.M.–10P.M.; SUN., 8:30P.M.–8P.M.

Los Angeles County may be the best place in the country to find regional Mexican cuisine. A couple hundred Mexico City–style *taquerias* do business within its borders, as well as dozens of Guadalajara-style goat restaurants, Oaxacan lunchrooms, Colima-style *marisquerias*, and Yucatecan joints.

Taste of Texas, though, may be the only Tejano-style Mexican restaurant around here, a basic, sprawling place on the western edge of Covina, with T-shirts hanging from the ceilings and autographed testimonials from Texas congressmen on the walls, a splash of Selena paraphernalia, and a party room that occasionally sees shows by Tejano musicians. It is probably the only restaurant in the world that diplays autographed photos of both Hideo Nomo and legendary Texas organist Augie Myers.

A million onion-splattered chain-restaurant horrors have been perpetrated in the name of Tejano—Tex-Mex—cooking, but the true style is a regional Mexican cuisine in its own right, less the cooking that may have existed in Texas when it was still part of Mexico than a marriage of Northern Mexican aesthetics and American abundance: plenty of grilling, mountains of beef and lakes of melted cheese, clean flavors, thick flour tortillas, hefty portions stronger in chile pungency than in chile heat. Mexican-food purists—Rick Bayless, Diana Kennedy—abominate the sizzling fajitas platter, the bowl of chili, the cheese-soaked enchilada plate. The rest of us are too busy eating, at least when the stuff is good.

Taste of Texas is more of a self-serve restaurant than a place with table service, and it takes a couple of visits to get used to the routine. You grab a fistful of menus, maybe order a pitcher of beer and some nachos to tide you over, then grab a table before the family just piling out of their Sierra truck beats you to it. When you decide what you want to eat, you go back up to the cash register, order, and pay.

The chips, tinted red with chile extracts, are to the left of the cash register; the coffee and sodas in their respective machines; the salsa—the smooth, spicy blender kind—in mason jars kept cool in an ice-bath in the center of the room.

Eventually the food will come, big oval platters on red cafeteria trays, and you go back to the front of the room to pick the stuff up.

Here are probably the best *fajitas* in Los Angeles, not the soy-soaked kind that sputter on superheated metal platters but chewy, well-marinated strips of skirt steak, grilled simply with onions, tasting of citrus and beef and salt, served in a heap alongside a little dish of soupy beans, handmade flour tortillas thick enough to stop bullets, and a nominal iceberg-lettuce salad. It's the sort of meal you might expect to find heaped onto paper plates at a San Antonio church picnic.

There are unexpectedly good versions of some hoary chain-Mex favorites. *Carne guisada* (quite different from the Central American dish that goes by that name), bits of beef or pork stewed in a thick gravy, resonates with musky dried-chile flavor but are mild enough for a toddler to eat. Chile-soaked *picadillo* tastes like taco meat with a university education; tacos are made with the extra-thick flour tortillas.

Weekend breakfast plates might feature homemade chorizo, fried calf's intestine, and something called El Nicky Snicky Pronto Quicky Barbacoa; spicy stewed beef cheeks.

Taste of Texas, though, is sort of schizophrenic in nature, specializing not just in the enchilada dinners you might expect in a Tejano restaurant, but in chicken-fried steaks the size of manta rays, also in nominally Texas-style barbecue, heavily smoked and doused (unless you specify otherwise) in a thick, catsup-based sauce. Actually, the barbecue is pretty good here. Slices of brisket, soft, juicy, slightly oily, practically vibrate with the campfire flavor of mesquite smoke. Beef ribs, crunchy, charred edges working their way to an almost jerkylike chaw toward the bone, are almost the size and heft of Louisville Sluggers—not bad, if you scrape off the sauce.

TAY HO

IN GOLD WORLD PLAZA, 1039 E. VALLEY BLVD., SAN GABRIEL;
(626) 280-5207. TUES.-SUN., 9A.M.-8P.M. ALSO 9242 BOLSA AVE.,
WESTMINSTER; (714) 895-4796. MON., 9A.M.-4P.M.

Of the world's street-food specialties, *banh cuon,* Vietnamese wide steamed rice noodles, might on the surface seem to be among the less compelling. Similar to the ghost-white noodles that come under the oval metal hoods in dim-sum restaurants, *banh cuon* can be chewy and unsubtle. *Banh cuon* may be on the menu at most of the Vietnamese noodle restaurants in town, but it usually takes a distant second place to the *pho*.

But Tay Ho serves the Stradivarius of *banh cuon:* transparent, almost membranous noodles, with the slight, stretchy resilience of *caul* and a faint, fine-cloth nubbiness—the noodles are steamed over muslin—that catches bits of the thin, sweet fish sauce you ladle from a Disney-stenciled carafe. You can get *banh cuon* wrapped around ground dried shrimp, or around a filling of crumbled pork sautéed with black pepper and tree-ear mushrooms. Tay Ho's *banh cuon* may be among the most delicate noodles you have ever tasted.

In San Gabriel's Gold World Plaza, Tay Ho is little more than a bare dining room with a few posters on the walls, a refrigerator case toward the rear filled with squiggly Vietnamese drinks, and a line outside to get in. If you don't look Vietnamese, you will be brought a photo album illustrating every dish on the menu.

Order the *banh cuon* with *thit nuong,* and you'll get sort of noodle burritos stuffed with sweet Vietnamese barbecued pork; order them with *bi,* and there'll be a gritty julienne of stewed pork skin with ground, toasted rice. In any case, you'll probably get the house special, which includes both kinds of *banh cuon,* a shrimp-topped sweet potato fritter, and a kind of shrimp cruller spiked with green beans. Surrounding it all, like beams from a cartoon sun, radiate slices of Vietnamese pâté. Noodles, shrimp crullers, cold cuts . . . they go together like ham and eggs.

TAYLOR'S PRIME STEAKS

3361 W. 8TH ST.; (213) 382-8449. MON.–FRI., 11A.M.–4P.M.; SAT. & SUN., 4P.M.–10:30P.M.

Real urban steakhouses are becoming rare in central Los Angeles, two-fisted meat-and-martini joints where an account executive can blow his Pritikin thing straight to hell with a massive hunk of well-aged sirloin, places where a fellow can get a decent slab of protein without crossing the border into Beverly Hills. The steakhouse belt that once stretched miles west of downtown has mostly gone over to *pupuserias* and Korean restaurants. Edward's, Vince & Paul's, the Cove, the Windsor, the Original Barbecue, and Bull 'n' Bush, among other old places, are gone. The Pacific Dining Car prices its steaks out of the reach of anybody but corporate lawyers and Japanese tourists.

But Taylor's Prime Steaks, located at the point where Koreatown and Little Central America collide, is a real urban steakhouse, one of the last of the dimly lit breed, decked out with red-vinyl booths, horsey prints on the walls, and a pickle-nosed guy at the bar who laughs like Thurston Howell III. Prime, dry-aged steak dinners, complete with soup or salad and a plateful of cottage fries, run about half of what the Beverly Hills places charge. In the '60s, Taylor's was what passed for high-style cuisine in Los Angeles, and the entryway is hung with rave reviews that are mostly twenty years old.

Tripping up the stairs into the banquet room, coiffed and lacquered Hancock

Park matrons look straight ahead, flawless in their full-length minks, grimly facing their husbands' office parties. Groups of businessmen float toward the door, ties loosened, vests unbuttoned, wearing the sheepish look on their faces that says they've been drinking since early afternoon. WASPy nuclear families, headed by ruddy men wearing college sweatshirts, slouch on banquettes. A gaggle of arty Silver Lake dudes seems pleased to be drinking martinis in a place like this. I like the bartender's way with an old-fashioned.

Taylor's used to be famous for its wine card, a thin, eccentric pamphlet that still lists things like '28 first-growth Bordeaux and ancient vintages of La Tache alongside bottles of overaged generic California "burgundy" and miniverticals of Jordan Cabernet, but the wine service is a little unorthodox—the waitresses fill the tiny wineglasses right to the rim, and the maître d' periodically comes by to top them up whether you want him to or not. This may not be the place to try that special bottle of Latour.

This may not be the place to try shrimp cocktail, either—the last time I tried it, the shrimp hadn't quite thawed in their horseradish-spiked catsup. The bread's no good, and the pea soup has all the charm of military rations.

The thing to get here, obviously, is steak: steak and good cottage fries and an iceberg lettuce salad, which is crisp and cold and globbed with just enough blue cheese dressing. The filet mignon is soft, buttery, as rare as you order it, crusted with char; a New York steak is beefy and rich. T-bones and porterhouses come sizzling on metal trays. London broil, kind of stewy tasting, is served already sliced, with a horseradish–sour cream sauce on the side. Lamb chops are thick and juicy as a Jackie Collins novel.

And the glory of Taylor's is the prime culotte steak, a softball-shaped prime thing cut from the top of the sirloin. All the steaks here are aged, but the culotte is profoundly aged, so much so that the outside can be as gamy as a well-hung hare. If you order the culotte rare, its interior is scarlet, dripping juice, salted with morbidity, marbled with fat—bursting with the mineral sourness of great meat. Taylor's culotte may be the steak that time forgot.

TEXIS NO. 2

698 S. VERMONT AVE.; (323) 387-8890.

In Los Angeles, the best Thai restaurants have been ultimately unreproduceable, no matter how hard their owners try; all the best Mexican places are the products of single food-obsessed chefs. Good Salvadoran places, though, like good Chinese noodle shops, tend to clone themselves, and though great swaths of the central city contain as many Salvadoran *pupuserias* as gas stations, it can seem as if most are branches of only about a dozen or so chains.

The most consistent of the chains is probably Texis, named after a small town in El Salvador and made visually distinctive by the corporate policy of listing practically the entire menu in the window in blocky neon script. Where some Salvadoran cafes can be on the grimy side, Texises gleam like McDonald's franchises. Where some restaurants feature, say, a spectacular version of the minced-beef salad *salpicon* but stuffed *pacaya* that is bitter and unpleasant, you won't find a truly bad dish at any Texis. And the soft *pupusas*, hand-patted, griddle-baked corn cakes stuffed with cheese, pork, or the pungent Salvadoran vegetable *loroco*, are as consistent as anything this side of Pizza Hut.

Most Salvadoran menus are fairly standardized, give or take a stew or two, but Texis goes out of its way to be user-friendly, with hamburgers for Americanized second-generation kids who would rather die than eat a *pupusa*; burritos and broiled beef for the Mexican-food crowd, and a fiery *salsa cruda* that would probably be unrecognizable in mild-sauce-loving El Salvador.

My favorite branch, nestled into an otherwise Korean mini-mall just a block south of the Wilshire Boulevard insurance district, is a deeply eccentric place, with ferns sprouting out of the ceilings, music that veers back and forth between Los Bukis and Whitney Houston, and a flashing message board that broadcasts the locations of the newest outposts of the Texis empire. A long wall is covered with a giant wallpaper mural of Vermont woods or something, the kind you find decorating roadside steakhouses in the Midwest, with a morass of jungle vines daubed onto it by an enterprising painter, as well as a palm or two and a crumbling Maya pyramid. Bubbling soft-drink machines, the sort that usually dispense fruit punch or Orange Bang, hold a vividly colored tamarind drink, and an orangeade-tasting version of *chan* that is almost crunchy with the pleasantly slimy seeds that make Chia Pets explode into loveliness.

Fried *yuca con chicharrones* is an exemplary rendition of the classic Central American salad: the tuber crunchy and light, the fried pigskin chewy, draped over a mound of the spicy cabbage slaw called *curtido*, and dressed with a mild tomato sauce. Fried slices of pork come with grilled onion slices and a big scoop of the beans-and-rice dish *gallo pinto*, or spotted rooster, that is good enough by itself to justify ordering the combination. The *salpicon*—cool, chopped roast beef dressed with citrus and tossed with diced onion and radish—is fine.

Carne guisada is a sturdy, bland beef stew of a sort you may not be nostalgic for, and the flattened fried hen is cooked longer than strictly necessary. But Texis even has food to make certain vegetarians happy: cheese-stuffed green squash battered and fried like *chiles rellenos*, the *pupusas*, and the aforementioned stuffed *pacaya*, which looks more like a boiled space alien than any flower has a right to do.

THAI NAKORN

8674 STANTON AVE., BUENA PARK; (714) 952-4954. SUN.-THURS., 10:30A.M.-10:30P.M.; FRI. AND SAT., TO 11P.M.

Beach Boulevard, as it cuts though Buena Park, may be the closest thing in the Southland to the cheerful vulgarity of the Vegas Strip, speckled with soaring dinner-theater castles and cavernous wax museums, lined with chain restaurants and giant neon motels that have high ratings from AAA. The cumulative effect of it all is to make you feel, as you cruise down the street, that you are small as a four-year-old.

A stone's throw away from Knott's, right next to the famous signboard that Love's Barbecue used to share with the local outpost of Jenny Craig, sits what is conceivably the most exotic restaurant in Orange County, a truly authentic Isaan-style Thai place. Thai Nakorn occupies what looks like a converted steakhouse—wood-paneling, red-leather booths, mounted animal heads—except that the chairs are the elegantly carved Thai type, and stacks of Thai-style chafing dishes teeter in the open kitchen. Plus, the chalkboard specials are all in Thai, and run more toward the anchovy dip than toward the surf-'n'-turf platter.

Isaan cuisine, the cooking of northeastern Thailand, is dominated by chile-hot salads: *larbs*, in which the primary ingredient is minced fine with herbs, and *yums*, which look a little like the salads you might get at Spago. Thai Nakorn has a superbly gamy grilled-beef salad, a minced-catfish salad with a richly marine taste, and a spicy tongue salad. There are warm, sour strands of shredded bamboo-shoot salad, almost gritty with dried chile, that you roll into a ball with sticky rice and eat with your fingers. (Actually, all the salads are great with sticky rice, which is served here in a traditional woven basket.) The squid salad is fine too.

Nam sod, which can sometimes seem like the most delicious thing you've ever eaten in your life, resembles a garlicky, salty pork salad, crunchy with toasted rice and tart with lime, shot through with bits of toasted peanut. *Nam sod* is one of the world's great bar snacks, perfect with a cold Singha beer.

In Bangkok, Isaan-style restaurants are at least as famous for their barbecued chicken as for their salads, and Thai Nakorn's version is nice, if unexceptional—you'll find it on the tables of most of the Thai customers here. Barbecued squid, a giant, smoky slab of the stuff, is wonderful.

We had *gaeng liang*, a mild, Isaan-style shrimp soup full of flavorful squashes, and *nuah dad deaw*, a garlicky sort of beef jerky that came with a smoky chile sauce. There was a fried blackfish, about 90 percent crunch, that had been sauced with a mint-chile goop that could probably make adobe bricks into a palatable entrée. "White pork," probably belly pork, was sweet and unctuous as a Wayne Newton show, but a lot hotter.

The desserts, a far cry from the jackfruit ice cream served at most Thai restaurants, include slippery green grass-jelly noodles in a sweet coconut broth and a warm, salty-sweet broth filled with many different kinds of delicious slime. I like the slimy stuff just fine, but it may not be the best thing to eat immediately before a ride on Montezuma's Revenge.

THUAN KIEU

123 E. VALLEY BLVD., SAN GABRIEL; (626) 280-5660. SUN.-THURS., 9A.M.-9P.M.; FRI. AND SAT., 9A.M.-10P.M.

Some specialist chefs work their entire lives perfecting a highly specific food: barbecue, *birria*, bread. There may be enough variables in pizza-making to occupy a diligent man for a lifetime. Japanese people go to one restaurant to eat hot noodles and another to eat them cool, one place for eel, a second for turtle, and a third for herring.

But no people's restaurants are as specialized as the Vietnamese, for whom the phrase *dac biet*, house specialty, practically rises to the level of a direct order. If you want charbroiled pork, you go to the place that advertises barbecued pork in the window; for spring rolls, the spring-roll place; for Hue-style noodles, see the Hue-style noodles man. Restaurants specialize in a single grilled fish, in *bun* or *pho* or *banh cuon*, in seven-course dinners all of beef. And if you keep your eyes open, you might run across one of the new Vietnamese cafes specializing in *com tam*, "broken rice."

Com tam (pronounced something like "gum-dum,") a specialty of central and southern Vietnam, is jagged bits of jasmine rice accidentally shattered during the harvest or during processing. In Vietnam, broken rice is a little cheaper than the best-quality jasmine rice; in the U.S., where it is available in most Asian markets, broken rice is actually a bit more expensive.

Com tam is one of the great Vietnamese working-class foods, the basis of a million plate lunches. You can still find entire streets in Saigon lined with *com tam* stalls, where for a few cents you can get a bowl of the broken rice garnished with shredded cucumber and chopped scallions steeped in oil, or perhaps a barbecued shrimp or a scrap of grilled pork.

The main drags of Vietnamese Santa Ana and San Gabriel have no shortage of *com tam* restaurants, but the best of them may be Thuan Kieu, a plain storefront diner in a neighborhood of Vietnamese businesses recently arisen just east of the big San Gabriel mall. Thuan Kieu is crowded at the usual times—you will probably have to share a table at lunch—and bare, save its dozen Formica tables and some slogans painted on the walls. There is fresh orange juice, strong iced coffee, and the usual mung-bean oozies to drink.

The menu may seem endless at Thuan Kieu, but what's listed are essentially variations on just a few things, a few noodle dishes plus broken rice with every imaginable combination of garnishes: broken rice with shredded pork, broken rice with shredded pork and baked egg, broken rice with shredded pork, baked eggs and charbroiled shrimp . . . like that.

Banh hoi, little mats of ultrathin rice vermicelli, come dressed with most of the same fried stuff that you can get with the broken rice; *bun*, thicker rice noodles, come tossed like big salads in bowls. There is a creditable version of the funky noodle soup called *bun bo hue*, shot through with yummy lozenges of steamed pig's blood.

The thing to get here, inelegantly translated as "broken rice with seven kinds of foods," is a big platter heaped with broken rice and a bit of everything in the restaurant that you could wish to taste. There are steamed balls of Vietnamese pâté, bright-orange wedges of a sort of Vietnamese quiche flavored with ground pork, and charbroiled slices of beef or pork, slightly blackened at the edges, bubbling with grease.

The platter also includes some of the best *bi* in town, shreds of roast pigskin tossed with herbs and ground rice, which has a slightly gritty characteristic that takes getting used to, but it flavors rice as nothing you've ever tasted.

Pounded shrimp appears on the menu in several guises: wrapped around a length of sugarcane and grilled, stuffed inside rice paper and immersed in hot oil, or wrapped in a thin sheet of tofu skin and fried to a delicate crunch. *Cha gio*, spring rolls, are coarsely textured and seasoned hard with black pepper, not quite as good as the crisply fried cigars at Golden Deli but serviceable. Sometimes you'll run across grilled pork chops, marinated either in a five-spice mixture or plain—"Korean style," the menu says—with soy and garlic.

And the rice itself, cooked with a little less water than its unbroken equivalent, is spectacular, firmer, with a bouncy resiliency a little like al dente pasta, a thousand chewy, jagged shapes beneath your teeth. Its subtle, toasted nuttiness is as different from plain boiled rice as risotto is from Rice-A-Roni. *Com tam* may be the most elegant example of culinary salvage in the world.

TITO'S TACOS

11222 WASHINGTON PLACE, CULVER CITY; (310) 391-5780. DAILY, 9:30A.M.–11:30P.M.

Though my mom's dog Mo liked Apple Pan Hickory Burgers, rare roast beef from Gelson's, Oat Thins, kosher salami, and basically anything from Jerry's Deli that isn't coleslaw, like my mom, what Mo liked best was hard-shell tacos from Tito's Tacos in Culver City. When mom went to Tito's for tacos for the dog, she always got them with extra cheese. Dogs love the taste of cheese.

Tito's is a taco stand near the fast-food corner of Sepulveda and Washington Place, next door to a branch of Lucy's Mexican Food, hard by the famous Johnnie's French Dip Pastrami. The lines can be long at Johnnie's and Lucy's, but the lines are always longest outside Tito's, Westwood-movie-line long sometimes, throngs of the kind of Westsiders who are portrayed neither on Baywatch nor on 90210: lawyers, gardeners, construction guys, students, Anglos and *sansei* and the third-generation Mexican-American equivalent of *sansei*, lots of kids, even the occasional knot of surfers. The lines are long, but they move fast.

Before they were replaced by Taco Bells on the one hand and Michoacan-style *taquerias* on the other, there used to be a lot of places like Tito's, Mexican-American joints where the tacos were always fried, *chile con carne* was always on the menu, and the guy behind the counter looked at you funny if you asked what was inside a burrito (meat, beans, and cheese . . . what else?). Thirty years ago, not many of us knew from *buche* or *cochinita pibil*.

Tito's is a high-volume place, where chips go from the fryer into giant galvanized trash cans that serve as storage bins, freshly fried tacos are stacked in long rows, and salsa is made in a drum. People eat at long picnic tables, either inside or out, behind the cardboard takeout cartons that form tabletop Stonehenges. The menu at Tito's, painted on a wall behind the counter, is not long; tacos and enchiladas and tamales, two kinds of burritos (with beans and without), tostadas and *chile con carne*, rice and beans. The menu boasts that Tito's uses 100 percent steer beef. Tito's has the deeply nostalgic bean 'n' chip smell of southern California childhood.

Enchiladas are cheesy and goopy; tamales are uncheesy and goopy; tostadas are crunchy, bean-smeared platforms that taste mostly of fresh iceberg lettuce. Inside the burritos are meat and beans, the meat being the same stewed (100 percent steer) chunks in a mild red-chile sauce that used to be served everywhere from El Coyote to the cafeteria in the UCLA student union that was my favorite restaurant in the world when I was eight. The beans are the fragrant kind that smell less like beans than like hot oil; the cheese is the bright orange salty kind that seems to exist solely to turn rubbery when it melts. For an extra six bits or so, you can get a little Styrofoam cup of guacamole that probably contains about as much actual avocado as "Krab" does crab, but which serves the essential purpose of turning things tart and green.

What you'll actually eat are tacos. With cheese. Just like my mom. And Mo.

TOMBO

2106 ARTESIA BLVD., TORRANCE; (310) 324-5190. TUES.-SAT., 11:30A.M.- 2P.M. AND 5:30-10P.M.; SUN., 5-9:30P.M.

Japan, of course, is home to the most refined food culture in the world, to fish fried so delicately that it appears less greasy than it did before it was immersed in oil, to sake that costs more per ounce than pure gold, to *kaiseki* meals so exquisitely calibrated to the seasons that an expert can set the calendar on her Rolex by an arrangement of root vegetables in broth.

But Japan, the birthplace of sumo one must remember, is also the home of the mayonnaise doughnut, the hamburger cutlet, and the octopus ball. Perhaps the most popular of Japanese street foods is *okonomiyaki,* a thick, circular pancake made from eggs, vegetables, meat, and ghost-white batter: crisp on the outside, substantial on the inside, the local equivalent of an Italian frittata or a Spanish tortilla, but . . . earthier somehow, uncouth, and generally cooked on a tabletop griddle. *Okonomiyaki,* like so many of Japan's other inexplicable culinary phenomena, arose in impoverished postwar Osaka, probably as a way to stretch scarce provisions into a filling meal, and became a way of life.

Okonomiyaki—sometimes called "Japanese pizza"—was fairly well known in Hollywood in the '80s, the specialty of an after hours place called Pannic House that was perhaps more famous for the skill of the dub DJ who manned the sound system than for its food. Pannic House's *okonomiyaki,* a bulky grease bomb fortified with nutritious vegetables, was capable of soaking up even more alcohol than a Tommyburger, and after Pannic House closed, it seemed as if half of Silver Lake was searching downtown for a replacement.

Now comes Tombo, a small restaurant in a sleepy Torrance strip mall, with a health-department *A* in the window and a faint smell of stale oil in the air, big bottles of Sapporo beer on the tables and a library of smutty Japanese comic books—apparently all but required in *okonomiyaki* joints—in a bookcase near the door. Each low, wooden table has a big sheet of metal recessed into its top, fired to a shimmering heat by big gas burners below the table.

Noodles, sushi, and *yakitori* are solitary foods, designed to be gulped at lunch counters, served in highly customized individual portions. *Okonomiyaki* is a social dish, meant to be shared with friends, and for students the local *okonomiyaki* parlor apparently occupies the same niche as the local pizza place does in U.S. college towns. If you stumble into Tombo at seven on a school night, you might find the place all but deserted; an hour later, every table is filled, the room is loud, and chopped onions all but fly across the room.

When you order *okonomiyaki,* a waitress lights the burner under your tabletop, films the griddle with oil, and plunks down a metal bowl containing pancake batter along with bright-red splinters of pickled ginger, slivered onion, and chopped cabbage, plus a raw egg. You grab a spoon, stir your batter like mad, and pour the goop out onto the hot griddle to cook.

A lot of the fun in *okonomiyaki* comes in tending your pancake, patting it flat with a big metal spatula, sliding it to a cooler part of the griddle when you sense it is starting to scorch, and glazing its surface with a sticky syrup flavored with Worcestershire sauce. When the mass is done, or at least brown and crisp on the bottom, you cut it into wedges, squirt it with mayonnaise and hot mustard from squeeze bottles, and season it with a thick dusting of powdered seaweed and *bonito* shavings from canisters on the table. If your pancake looks as if it has been tarred and feathered, it should be about right.

The standard *okonomiyaki* comes with three added ingredients—say, oysters, *kimchi*, and pork—but you can get more elaborate custom combinations, as well as Hiroshima-style *okonomiyaki* in which a mat of noodles is encased between two crisp layers of batter. Tokyo-style *okonomiyaki* has eggs fried right into the top of the mass rather than mixed into the whole.

Okonomiyaki may be the basic order at Tombo, but at least half of the tables will also be eating a dish whose name I didn't catch, which basically consists of a pot of soup spilled into sort of a ring-shaped battlement of shredded cabbage on the hot griddle and scraped up with a small metal spatula when it has boiled down to a thick, rubbery glaze. This dish, a classic postwar Japanese poverty food, may be fortified with things like cod roe, diced mountain yam, and cubes of cheddar cheese, but what you will remember will be the cabbage-studded broth itself, a sticky, salty, slimy ooze that has achieved the plastic consistency of Elmer's Glue.

TOMMY'S

BEVERLY BOULEVARD AT RAMPART STREET; AND MANY OTHER LOCATIONS. OPEN SEVEN DAYS, TWENTY-FOUR HOURS.

Los Angeles is the world capital of stuff with chili on it, and just as all pizza slices in Manhattan seem to originate from a place named Ray's, most of our chiliburgers come from stands named Tom: Tom's #5, Fat Tomy's, Big Tommy's, Tam's. The proliferation of all things Tom could derive from Ptomaine Tommy's, a long-defunct Highland Park lunch counter often credited with originating the gut bomb called the "chili size," but more recently, it almost goes without saying, it comes from Tommy's, the temple of the chili burger, the Rampart Division champ since 1946.

No Tom's, Tim's, Tam's, or Tums even come close. Late-night jaunts to Tommy's are a USC tradition, a UCLA tradition, and undoubtedly also a tradition at every institution of higher learning from the Fuller Theological Seminary to the Truckmaster School of Trucking. Tommy's, which is now past fifty, has probably been responsible for five hundred thousand cases of heartburn, 436 triple-bypass operations, and chili sufficient to sluice the L.A. River from Sherman Oaks to Wilmington.

Tommy's is a Los Angeles phenomenon. New Mercedeses crowd into the terraced parking lot next to decaying B-210s, vibrating boom cars next to Volvos just stopping by on the way home from the Hollywood Bowl. You can hardly call yourself a citizen unless you've stood at least once at the counter here, shoveling down chili burgers shoulder-to-shoulder with your fellow man.

Unlike the executive-size hamburgers served at places like Hamburger Hamlet or Cassell's, where half a pound of good beef is served largely unadorned, a Tommyburger is a sloppy, uncouth thing, oozing chili and raw onion, that takes over your system for the better part of a day. The high cumin smell of the chili seeps from your pores, haunts your breath, and adheres to your lips no matter how many paper towels you use to wipe the orange grease away.

There's no way around it: Eating a Tommyburger is an aggressive act. You can't stop at Tommy's and expect to go back to the office; you can't inhale a Tommyburger at one in the morning and expect your spouse to kiss you when you get home.

Tommyburgers aren't really street food—most Tommy's seem to be in distinctly pedestrianless locations—and they can't really be considered car food either, unless you're okay with orange grease spots on the upholstery and an aroma that lasts longer than most air fresheners. (Actually, the newish Hollywood branch of Tommy's, a drive-thru exquisitely positioned right off the Hollywood Boulevard exit of the 101, makes it possible to coast in off the freeway, load up on chili burgers, and cruise back toward downtown in a scant minute or two, though I wouldn't recommend it.)

Tommyburgers are generally measured out in units of double-chili-cheeseburgers: meat, chili, and American cheese on a soft bun with pickle, chopped onion, and a slice of beefsteak tomato that is usually one degree riper than you'd find at a supermarket. The cheese is sliced thick, more slab than slice, and melts directly into the chili as opposed to gilding the patty.

At a place like McDonald's, you're generally better off not tasting the meat; at Tommy's, the beefiness of the hamburger (the two patties are slammed directly together in the middle of the sandwich, boom-*boom*) seems to be pretty much the point. On the most primal level, a Tommyburger is as satisfying as a steak.

140 W. VALLEY BLVD., NO. 118C, SAN GABRIEL; (626) 288-6588. DAILY, 11A.M.–9:30P.M.

As you cruise up Del Mar toward the Chinese mega-mall called San Gabriel Square, young guys in pristine white Camrys curse one another as they compete for street parking, and the smell of frying garlic quickly broadens to a shout. By the time you come within sight of the hundred glowing ideograms of the center itself, you are ensnarled in a sea of honking cars, and the garlicky breeze starts to reveal hints of anise, ginger, and roasting ducks.

One knot of people gathers around a master noodle maker who quickly transforms a lump of dough into a skein of fine vermicelli, then lumps it back up and does it again. A larger crowd clumps in front of a makeshift stage near the supermarket, where a campy emcee conducts a karaoke contest, and sharply dressed young men glide up to you and press invitations for Taiwanese disco nights into your hands. Small children dart into a Vietnamese bakery, pressing their noses against glass cases that contain varicolor Chinese gelatins, green slabs of coconut cake, and yellow-bean pastries baked in the shape of little pigs.

Lines form outside the eighteen-odd eating places that form the core of the Chinese-mall experience. The biggest line of all, sometimes an hour long, still forms outside Tung Lai Shun, an Islamic Chinese restaurant that relocated to San Gabriel after almost a century in Beijing, a restaurant unique in the United States. (The big English-language neon sign says ISLAMIC CUISINE; the neon Arabic letters translate as "Chinese Restaurant.") You take a number from a woman in Muslim headcloth, and you take your place at the back of the line. You will have plenty of time to contemplate your dinner.

The first thing you may notice about Tung Lai Shun are the enormous rounds of freshly baked sesame bread that seem to be on every table, flaky, fragrant, multilayered things spiked with green onions, the size of Chicago pizzas, that are generally eaten here instead of rice. You can drag wedges of the bread through sauce, or stuff them with chopstickfuls of spicy braised Beijing lamb or even Mongolian beef. Tung Lai Shun is the only restaurant I can think of where "Mongolian beef" is actually worth ordering.

While you're waiting for the bread to come (it can take twenty minutes to bake), you nibble on cool, slippery slices of garlicked ox-tendon terrine, elegant as an appetizer at a two-star restaurant in France; thin, cold slices of delicately spiced beef; or chunks of cold braised lamb in an unctuous garlic jelly. There are steamed vegetable dumplings filled with a pungent, crunchy dice that is the color you've always imagined a rain forest to be, and a rather doughy crepe stuffed with a gritty mixture of chives that is one of the restaurant's few disappointments.

String beans, crisp and explosively juicy, are fried with hoisin and crumbles of beef and dried shrimp; eggplant is braised with soy, sugar, and spice until it is about thirty seconds from becoming a savory purée. Tea duck is ruddy to the bone, as smoky as Texas barbecue. Chicken with slippery mung-bean noodles—"ground green bean sheets"—is more or less a cool, spicy chicken salad strongly flavored with hot mustard. Beijing shrimp balls are crunchy little Ping-Pong orbs of ground shrimp, served with a little pile of ground spice to dip them in. Green-onion pies are 45-rpm-size discs of crisp, griddled dough, fried-food *satori*, even better when dipped in a tincture of chile and vinegar: easily the best green-onion pancakes in town.

Chinese Islamic cooking, which is robust, has its roots in the cuisine of remote places like Inner Mongolia, but is generally considered to have been raised to its highest level in the Muslim restaurants of Beijing. It is the get-down stuff Beijing's cosmopolitan set has always gone out for instead of, say, Mexican food.

Boiled lamb dumplings burst with juice and high flavor; lamb-and-cabbage warm pot is an enormous clay bowl of soup that contains lamb's funky soul, too much so for a lot of people. ("Lamb and pancake with special sauce" is basically the warm pot with a cut-up pancake floating in it.) Lamb fried with green onion is even better than the beef. At Tung Lai Shun, lamb tastes like the gamy, impolite essence of the meat, halfway toward mutton, one of the most delicious foods you can imagine.

UZBEKISTAN RESTAURANT

7077 W. SUNSET BLVD. (323) 464-3663. DAILY, 11A.M.–11P.M.

Onion-dome cutouts and minarets, Uzbeki hats on the walls, and a dome of *trompe l'oeil* sky overhead; the Uzbekistan Restaurant is a Disneylandlike essay on the joys of post-Soviet capitalism. Uzbekistan Restaurant, run by the man who opened the first privately run restaurant in the Uzbeki capital Tashkent, is a fairly swanky hang.

Some nights, the women, Ivana-wannabes, seem all but lifted from a Julie Christie movie circa 1967—beehives, clingy dresses, and all; at other times, there's more Chanel and Moschino here than the mind can comprehend. The men slouch in outfits so 1973-cool it's a wonder they don't moonlight in Beck videos. It's kind of a blast here on weekends, with the restaurant filled up with large parties, loud toasts every twelve seconds, and an organist pounding out Slav-style Jamaican ballads. (Bad reggae may be the universal language.) Every two weeks or so, an actual Uzbeki may show up for dinner amid all the Russians.

Out come the giant platters of kebabs, the mounds of herb-marinated tomato-onion salad, the slabs of house-smoked salmon, the peculiar but chewy and delicious Uzbeki bread that is shaped like a giant bialy and flecked with sesame seeds. Everybody seems to get platefuls of the flaky meat-filled pastries called *samsa*, a near cousin to the stuffed breads of northernmost China, and *chuchvara*, tiny fried dumplings with tomato sauce that bear more than a passing resemblance—though surely no kinship—to St. Louis toasted ravioli. Like the population of Uzbekistan itself, the food here, heavy on vegetables, intricately flavored with spices and fresh herbs, seems two parts Central Asian exotic to one part Russian suave.

Eggplant *samarkand* is the sort of cold sautéed eggplant in tomato sauce you have probably eaten at a dozen Middle Eastern restaurants; a pickled vegetable plate includes tart, powerfully garlicky pickled red tomatoes in addition to the usual cabbage and kosher-style dills; vegetables "*Buhara*"—tomatoes and onions and peppers and eggplant—are roasted in a small tureen. It is hard to imagine a meal at Uzbekistan Restaurant without an order of *hasip*, pungent, crisp-skinned sausages stuffed with rice and ground organ meat.

"Do you know what is in *hasip?*" the owner asked, after the third time I had ordered it.

"Sure," I said, suddenly uneasy. "It's liver, right?"

"No, ho, ho!" he said, and he held his stomach as if to contain his mirth. "Not liver . . . is *spleen*."

When you are not in the mood for spleen, there are always *chanum*, floppy, open-faced Uzbeki ravioli filled with a meat-tinged potato purée and served with sautéed vegetables and an almost hallucinogenic blast of fresh dill, or lamb chops, or a strangely charred stir-fry of peppers and mushrooms served in a smoking-hot cast-iron pan. *Lagman*, lumpy, hand-pulled noodles, are served either in a thick meat broth or fried with vegetables and bits of lamb, nearly as soft as a Central European noodle but with a bit of Asian stretchiness.

And *plov*, the grandfather of all rice pilafs, is dense and slightly oily, more like fried rice than the pilaf you may be familiar with, spiked with diced vegetables and crisp-edged chunks of lamb, flavored with a peculiar sort of Uzbeki cumin seed that is halfway to caraway. Don't miss the *plov*.

Before going out for dinner in Uzbekistan itself, I am reliably informed, it is customary to eat first: The restaurant tradition of the former Soviet Republic is not as far along as one might hope. But this place . . . of all the Russian restaurants in Los Angeles, with all the newly arrived émigrées, Uzbekistan Restaurant, easily the equal of the Georgian restaurants and Uzbeki restaurants in Brooklyn, New York, serves easily the best former-Soviet-Republic food in town.

VALENZUELA'S

11721 E. VALLEY BLVD., EL MONTE; (626) 579-5384. DAILY, 9A.M.–11P.M.

In August, what you might want to know about the Mexican restaurant Valenzuela's is that it serves what may be the coldest beer in town, chilled to a temperature somewhere around freezing, then served in mugs blast-cooled to the point that sometimes a little fog forms around them and the puck of ice frozen into the mug's base doesn't fall out until halfway through the meal. We've all seen beer cold enough to form little ice crystals on top; at Valenzuela's, the frozen layer at the top of your Bohemia is almost firm enough to skate on.

Valenzuela's is a roadhouse toward the eastern edge of El Monte, past the mall, past the car dealerships, past the miniature Statue of Liberty that sits in front of the civic center. (Valenzuela's parking lot is, not to put too fine a point on it, where the body of James Ellroy's mother was found forty years ago, and the neighborhood doesn't seem to have changed a bit.)

Inside, when the band isn't playing, the action is around the big TV screens at either end of the room; Dodger games, boxing matches, the Mexican soap operas called *novelas*. One Wednesday I was sure the three burly Stetson dudes in the corner were playing a high-stakes game of poker, but as the *novela* rolled its closing credits overhead, they sighed—Mariela was jilted at the altar!—and went out into the night. On a board near the door are inked the daily specials, which as often as not consist solely of six bottles of Corona in a bucket and an admonition to try one of the house's tasty seafood cocktails.

But though the fried *mojarra* is fine, and the garlicky shrimp decent enough, seafood isn't really the thing here. As you go to Ciro's for the *flautas* and to El Tepeyac for the giant burritos, Valenzuela's is almost synonymous with Jalisco-style *carne asada en su jugo*, beef roasted in its own juices.

The regular *carne asada* here is just a boring small steak; *carne asada en su jugo* consists of thin, massively heaped confetti of browned beef, flavored with bits of bacon, filled out with soupy beans, garnished with finely chopped onion, a handful of cilantro, and a spicy puddle of juice. On the side, a plate holds sugary roasted onions, grilled scallions, hot chiles that have been charred to an elusive sweetness, radishes, and lime. *Carne asada en su jugo* is a classically compelling dish, each spoonful subtly different—smoky, meaty, spicy, tart—with the promise of carnivorous nirvana in every bite. I have seen small, hungry people demolish giant piles of this stuff in just a couple of minutes.

Oddly enough, most of the customers here seem to order the *parrilladas*—small charcoal braziers brought to the table heaped with small steaks, grilled slabs of chicken, crunchy little sections of intestine, and oily grilled seafood—which are okay, but nothing you couldn't get better across town.

Better to try the proper Sinaloa-style *machaca*—made with true dried beef rather than the stewed beef you usually find in restaurant *machaca*—pounded to almost a powder with a mortar and pestle, and fried crisp with peppers and onions. The *machaca* here is a dense, powerfully salty dish that all but screams for another bottle of Valenzuela's cryogenically correct Mexican beer.

THE VENICE ROOM

2428 S. GARFIELD AVE., MONTEREY PARK; (626) 722-3075.

"The happiest place on earth," the bartender burbles when he answers the phone. He sounds as if he means it. And when you are a few Buds into the wind, the Venice Room may actually be the happiest place on earth, a dark, fragrant bar with black-light murals from the brush of some homeboy Canaletto: Venice, as seen from the windows of the Doge's Palace, painted in lurid, glowing tones of blue, orange, and pink. Gondolas throb with light; murky medieval canals course across the walls of the main barroom, almost vibrating to the thump of the Pat Benatar (or James Brown, or Tom Jones) that blasts from the big CD jukebox. And the Venice Room's happy hour stretches halfway to infinity. More to the point, at least for the purposes of this book, is the restaurant in the equally Venice-encrusted rear dining room, a restaurant whose sole offering is a full New York steak dinner for $7.50. The catch is you have to cook it yourself over a searingly hot commercial gas grill tucked into a corner of the dining room.

To get to the Venice Room, you cruise south from Monterey Park, past the informal demarcation zone separating the city's Chinese neighborhoods from its Latino ones, and into a part of town that feels very much like Greater Montebello, hard by the Pomona Freeway and just a nine iron north of the public golf course.

310

The Venice Room is marked by a swath of bright neon that looks like something from 1950s Chicago; the small parking lot is filled with pickup trucks and carefully tended old cars. When you order your steak, the waitress brings out a raw New York strip, a good one, decently marbled and rimmed with a full inch of creamy fat, plopped onto a plate with a foil-wrapped baked potato, a length of French bread, and a few pats of butter. You are allowed a pass at a flip-up salad station equipped with iceberg lettuce, a couple of different kinds of dressing, and matching heaps of shredded carrots and shredded red cabbage that seem imported from a junior high school cafeteria. The quality of your dinner is essentially up to you.

Seasoned veterans of the Venice Room hover over their steaks, slashing and battering them with knives and long metal prongs, lavishing them with garlic salt, cayenne, and bulk-packaged Cajun seasoning, drizzling them with oil, massaging cracked pepper and dehydrated onion flakes into the meat's bruised flanks. The cooking seems almost competitive, as if a gong is going to sound, a wall is going to open, and one of the dudes will be named the new Iron Chef.

Some people subject their steaks to elaborate regimens of higher heat and lower heat, acrobatic flips, and precise 90-degree rotations. Others just give their meat a hard, brief steakhouse sear—did I mention the grill was hot?—and enjoy their meat a perfect, drippy rare. One friend, a restaurant chef out on a busman's holiday, protects her steak like a mother hen, occasionally nourishing it with a twist of the pepper mill or a scattered palmful of salt, snatching it from the flame before the flesh has had a chance to cook through.

French bread crisps on the cooler edge of the grill, and almost everybody seems to improvise some sort of grilled garlic bread with garlic powder and butter. Baked potatoes, already pretty much cooked through, steam in their foil on the edge of the grill, except for the lone, butter-spurting, charred spud that somebody (OK, me) has decided to convert into a mickey.

Kids would love this place, but you have to leave them at home. The first time I walked in, I had a sleeping four-year-old draped over my shoulder, and the waitress couldn't have spoken more harshly if I had walked in carrying a barrelful of sloshing toxic waste. The Venice Room, she insisted, is a bar. And if you are younger than forty or so, chances are good that you will be carded.

But it is hard to imagine a simpler meal than a dinner at the Venice Room, or a meal more satisfying than grilled meat, garlic bread, a baked potato, and a pony of bar scotch.

"Do you eat here a lot?" I asked one guy who seemed to know his way around a two-pound shaker of garlic powder.

"Nah," said the guy, "this is only my second time. But I drink here a lot . . . a lot. A lot."

VERSAILLES

10319 VENICE BLVD.; (310) 558-3168. ALSO AT 1415 LA CIENEGA BLVD.,
(310) 289-3168; 17410 VENTURA BLVD., ENCINO, (818) 906-0756; AND
1000 N. SEPULVEDA BLVD., MANHATTAN BEACH, (310) 937-6829.

Everybody but me, it appears, adores the crisp-skinned roast chicken at the Cuban restaurant Versailles, loves the soupy black beans, the avocado salad, the mounds of bright-yellow *arroz con pollo*. And the walls at the restaurant are encrusted with reviews, a virtual history of the last fifteen years of Los Angeles media, played out in carefully laminated encomiums and glowing celebrity tributes. None of these clippings is mine—I tend to favor funkier Cuban restaurants, like El Comal just a few miles east, although I never mind coming to Versailles for lunch. By Eastside standards, Versailles isn't much; by the standards of Cuban restaurants within a five-minute drive of Fox and Sony, it is a miracle: garlic, squid, and cold red wine—who could object to that?

But sometimes the restaurant's famous citrus marinade, the dominant flavor in the chicken, seems less like a sauce to me than like a fizzy summer beverage. The roast pork, while certainly crunchy enough, is more stringy than luscious, and the *moros y cristianos*—beans and rice fried together, my benchmark of Cuban cooking—is too dry.

I always complain. And as usual, my friend Margaret, who has been known practically to live on this chicken alone, tells me I don't know what I'm talking about.

VICTORIA SEAFOOD

143 W. GARVEY AVE., MONTEREY PARK; (626) 280-5921. DAILY,
11A.M.–3P.M.

Twenty years ago, I thought authentic Hong Kong–style seafood was the greatest stuff in the world, fresh, direct, and a change from the gooey, Cantonese-American food we all grew up eating. The original Mon Kee was probably the first restaurant I ever went to with my own money—I used to take the bus to Chinatown when I was in high school the way my friends took the bus to the beach—and the straightforward, simple flavors of steamed fish, steamed shrimp, and cuttlefish stir-fried with broccoli were unlike anything I had ever tasted.

I frequented Yuet Lee in San Francisco for the phenomenal baked shrimp in spicy salt, and the big seafood restaurant where NBC Seafood is now, which was, I think, the first major Chinese restaurant in Monterey Park, for crab fried with ginger and scallions. I must have personally eaten a hundred steamed perch at the old Wonder Seafood in Alhambra.

But as the San Gabriel Valley swelled with new, prosperous Asian immigrants and the trickle of great Chinese food became a flood, I, and most of my friends, moved on to restaurants serving the food of Hunan, of Shanghai, of the shellfish-loving Chiu Chow people. Still, Cantonese cuisine is considered to have about the same relationship to Asian cooking that French cuisine does to European cooking.

And the first time I wandered into Victoria Seafood, I remembered why I liked Chinese cooking even back when it was Cantonese or nothing. There were live shrimp, whole schools of the things, plucked from the tanks and steamed, thin slices of boiled geoduck clam served over crushed ice, and first-of-the-season asparagus fried simply with garlic. Great platters were piled high with the best Chinese squid I've had in years, dipped in a thin batter of spicy salt, fried to an exquisite crunchiness and served with a garnish of sliced chiles that had been softened in oil. It was a wonderful meal.

Victoria Seafood is a small box of a place in Monterey Park, with big glass fish tanks wedged into every cranny, tanks filled with geoduck clams, hundreds of them, lolling out of their undersized shells like huge uncircumcised phalluses; tanks with dozens of mossy hard-shell crabs bound and gagged; tanks with big, thick-lipped fish that stare dolefully out into the room like Edward G. Robinson. Presumably named after the famous restaurant of the same name in Kowloon, Victoria is sometimes as crowded as Hong Kong, ten people at every table and a line spilling out the door, which is pretty good for a restaurant in a neighborhood with more Chinese restaurants than any other in America.

Victoria's fine version of Cantonese dried-scallop soup is thick, peppery, crowded with shredded root vegetables and crunchy tree-ear fungus like a classic hot-and-sour soup, and speckled with chewy bits of dried scallops, which add a sort of pleasant postcoital pungency to the broth. I like this soup—I've ordered it every time I've come to Victoria. Sometimes it's thin, but sometimes it has a fantastic muskiness that reminds me of truffles, and sometimes it's just a really good soup.

Sliced Chinese sausage and slabs of gamy Chinese bacon—"preserved meat"—cooked with rice in a superheated clay pot isn't bad exactly, but hasn't the paellalike texture, the delicate smokiness of the clay-pot rice served right around the corner at Luk Yue. In another hot pot, of oysters, tofu, and roast pork, the shellfish was overcooked, sabotaging the textural rhyme between oysters and bean curd that lies at its heart.

A house specialty, "BBQ chicken," turned out to be dryish deep-fried bird in a thick gravy; squid in "X.O." sauce had little of the dried-seafood intensity associated with the expensive X.O. condiment. Beef stew with turnips, a Cantonese standby, was dull, lacking even the expected shot of star anise. And the lunch specials, priced at less than half of the dinner-menu prices, are invariably less delicious.

Still, I'd go to Victoria again for the crisp-skinned fried squab, for the pea tendrils fried with garlic, for the crab with spicy bean curb.

Ultimately, the highest praise you can give a modest Hong Kong–style restaurant is that it doesn't screw up the fish, and steamed rock cod, flesh more fluffy than grainy, perfectly fresh, scented with ginger and scallions, is exactly what you want in Cantonese seafood: simplicity itself.

VIM

5132 HOLLYWOOD BLVD.; (323) 662-1017. DAILY, 11A.M.–10P.M. ALSO AT 831 S. VERMONT AVE.; (213) 386-2338.

Vim must have been one of the first dozen Thai restaurants in Los Angeles, a bright, fragrant storefront on a strip of South Vermont that anchored one of the city's original Thai neighborhoods. Composer Carl Stone named one of his earliest opuses after the restaurant, known for its particularly spicy food. A couple of critics, dazzled by the pineapple rice and fried oysters with ginger, still consider Vim the best Thai restaurant in town.

Alone, I think, among the early Los Angeles Thai restaurants, Vim developed a devoted Latino clientele, necessitating a trilingual menu that translates *tom kha kai* as both "chicken-coconut soup" and *"sopa picante de pollo con leche de coco."*

Now there is a second Vim, in the Hollywood Boulevard mini-mall space that used to house the Thai supper club Dee Prom, a bright, yawning place, as cheerful as a Burger King, with tomato-red banquettes and gleaming Formica tabletops, clean tile and fluorescent lights bright enough to illuminate an operating theater. A health department "A" is displayed in the front window in a spot that couldn't be more prominent if it were illuminated with a 100-watt bulb and framed in blinking neon. In this part of Hollywood, restaurants tend to be frequented mostly by Thais, but Vim is as multicultural as the neighborhood, hosting as many Spanish-speaking families as Thai ones, also Armenians, South Asians, and a smattering of the East Hollywood goatee crowd. Vim serves the strong, basic Thai food many of us fell in love with twenty years ago, neither particularly regional nor toned down to please the American palate, neither lightened nor laced with exotic produce.

Grilled chicken satay is the stuff you may remember from the '70s, strips of skewered bird stained yellow with turmeric and served with a spicy ground-peanut sauce slicked with red oil. Peppery, spongy hockey pucks of fried fish cake come with a tart salad of vinegared cucumbers. Great mounds of curried fried rice are as yellow as the Happy Face on your little sister's T-shirt. When you order fried pork with pepper and garlic, you get a plate of bare, thinly sliced meat, bereft of the mounds of caramelized garlic chips that usually accompany the dish, but intensely flavored and glistening with juice. Even the fried glass noodle with shrimp and egg is good, the dairy sweetness of egg and a smoky, pungent hint of black mushroom enlivening what sounds like the dullest dish on the menu.

Salads may not be the incendiary, gritty things you find at the newer regional restaurants, but they have a freshness, a purity of flavor, that has largely gone missing from suburban Thai joints: Chinese barbecued duck hacked into chunks, tossed with chile and lime; grilled shrimp, crisp at the edges; a chewy squid salad, quite hot. Seafood soup, strong, powerfully sour, with the dragon-breath smack of old-fashioned Thai food and teeming with fish, shrimp, and squid, may be the most popular dish among the Latino customers, a different flavor of a classic *sopa siete mares*. The chicken-coconut soup, if not as herbally complex as some versions in town, has a clean, concentrated lemongrass tartness glazed with chile heat and overlaid with the musky scent of what tastes like fresh *galangal*.

Vim may not be the best place to find eggplants the size of Ping-Pong balls, jungle curries of venison or bubbling clay pots filled with fermented bamboo. But when you're in the mood for *pad Thai* noodles or mint-leaf chicken, oyster omelets or *prik king* spicy enough to strip the enamel off your teeth, you can't do better. And Vim is cheap: Most of the dishes cost less than five dollars; a whole fried fish less than ten dollars.

W

WAHIB'S MIDDLE EAST RESTAURANT

910 E. MAIN ST., ALHAMBRA; (626) 281-1006. DAILY, 8A.M.–10P.M.
DINNER FOR TWO.

Wahib's Middle East, which may be the best Lebanese restaurant between Hollywood and the state of Michigan, is one of those timeless, big-city places, a cavernous old storefront with the garlic reek of a good delicatessen, high ceilings, and a takeout counter a city block long. Wailing Lebanese music blares from wall-mounted speakers, except when somebody puts on KROQ instead. Flags of all nations are mounted all around the room.

It's nice to come around in the late afternoon for a plate of smooth, cool *kibbe*, sort of a bulgur-studded Lebanese tartare of raw lamb; to munch on pickled hot peppers and sip a cold glass of Almaza beer.

Waiters rush around with the bowls of hummus, plates of pastry, fiery pickled turnips, and bowls of garlicky lentil soup that seem to come free with almost anything you order here. (You can get salad instead of the soup, or for a little extra, more of the parsley salad tabbouleh than it is possible for a man to eat.) A large family starts in on their kebab platters as if Dad had fired a starting gun. A handwritten sign announces the existence of something called the Homey Burger, for kids.

Dinners at most Lebanese restaurants seem to revolve around an endless array of *mezze*: communally served appetizers scooped up with pita bread. Here, because everybody gets hummus and tabbouleh as a matter of course, there is less emphasis on things like the smoky eggplant dip *baba ganoush* or deep-fried capsules of *kibbe* than there is on the main dishes. At the Middle East, dinner means lamb kebabs with rice, intensely herbed grilled quail, sweet nuggets of Armenian sausage, spicy-hot okra-tomato stew, or a curried-vegetable stew stained with turmeric, all served with mountains of rice.

If it's Thursday, there'll be delicious long-cooked spinach studded with chunks of braised lamb, or peculiar ball-bearings of couscous served with a grayish lamb stew (couscous is not, to put it mildly, a specialty of the Lebanese kitchen). If it's Monday, there'll be roast lamb over rice, and reheated-tasting whole chickens smeared with a paste of beef and pine nuts; if Wednesday, a Jordanian specialty called *mansaf* lamb.

Unlike most Lebanese restaurants, the Middle East makes something of a specialty of breakfast, giant affairs of eggs scrambled with the spicy Armenian sausage *sojuk* or ground beef or fresh tomato. *Fatch* is a fantastic mess of chickpeas, toasted pita, garlic, and pine nuts fried in olive oil and doused in homemade yogurt, which any sensible person would prefer to a Denver omelet. You can even, if you're so inclined, breakfast on fresh, raw lamb liver.

At Denny's a breakfast special may include a couple of sausages, an egg, some potatoes and a piece of toast. At the Middle East, the most popular combination is big enough to cover an entire table: a plate of the yogurt-tart homemade cream cheese *labneh* slicked with olive oil; a turnover stuffed with the thymelike herb *za'atar* and a squarish sort of danish stuffed with sweetly spiced ground meat where you might expect to find the prunes; a basket of pita; a plate of olives and pickles and another plate with onions, tomatoes, and fresh leaves of mint; two kinds of cheese, one sweet and rubbery, the other hard and pungent like an aged pecorino; a glass of hot tea; and finally a giant bowl of the herby, tart fava-bean stew *foul*. The spread covers every square inch of space on the table.

WOODY'S BAR-B-QUE

3446 W. SLAUSON AVE.; (323) 294-9443. SUN.–THURS., 11A.M.–MIDNIGHT; FRI. AND SAT., 11A.M.–2A.M.

You can no more influence a person's choice of barbecue pit than you can the brand of cigarette he or she smokes, and a lot of people think Woody's Bar-B-Que is the best barbecue place in Los Angeles. I tend to think it's the second-best barbecue place in Los Angeles, but on Sundays, when Phillips Barbecue (run by Woody's cousin) is closed, Woody's becomes my favorite for about twenty-four hours. And on weekends, Woody's stays open until 3:00 A.M.

Woody's is a simple place, a low building next to a mini-mall, chocolate-brown trim, lunch specials posted in the window. A mean-looking cartoon bull-dog painted on the wall outside has a thought bubble coming out of its head that says, I THINK Y'ALL BETTER HAVE SOME BAR BQ. A plastic menu board inside lists the usual slabs and sandwiches and dinners. Photographs of Dr. King, Malcolm X, and Mandela decorate the walls.

You place your order, pay, and sit on a communal bench until your number is called. If you come on a Sunday after church, when Woody's is at its busiest, you can hear a precis of nearly every sermon delivered in the greater Crenshaw area that morning.

What you get here is sweet beans, sweet-potato pie, eggy potato salad—the works. Which is to say, y'know, barbecue: crusty pork ribs spurting with juice; thick, blackened, hot link sausages with the chaw of good jerky; chewy, meaty little rib tips; giant beef ribs; charred, only occasionally stewy-tasting slices of well-done barbecued beef brisket that even Texans condescend to like.

The chicken is crisp-skinned, dense-fleshed, deeply smoky all the way to the bone like those fancy turkeys that cost a mail-order fortune. If a caterer decided to pull a fast one, the chicken would get a lot of compliments at a fancy society buffet.

The sauce is one of the sweet brick-red kinds, hotly spiced with red pepper flakes, seeds and all, which you sop up with slices of damp white bread until it is gone—one of those sauces that seems less like a condiment than like a way of life.

YABU

11820 W. PICO BLVD.; (310) 473-9757. MON.-SAT., 12P.M.-2:30P.M., 6P.M.-10:30P.M.; SUN., 5 P.M.-9:30P.M.

The Japanese *soba* noodle, properly executed, is one of the loveliest noodles in existence, a thin, square-cut strand of purest buckwheat, a yard long, with the clear, pinky-brown color of a mountain range ten minutes after sunset. Because true *soba* is made only of buckwheat, which contains little gluten, the noodle is delicate yet crunchy, full of the strong, musky toastiness of the grain, and seemingly apt at any second to disintegrate into a little pile of groats. Unfortunately, only one restaurant in the United States serves perfect *soba*, and that restaurant, Honmura-An, is in Manhattan and charges seventeen dollars a bowl.

"You may call this kasha," explained a waiter to a confused New Jersey customer the first time I stopped into Honmura-An. "In Japan, it is known as *soba*."

If you are in the mood for *soba* and you are neither in Tokyo nor in New York City, you might go to Mishima, which is a coolly austere place near Westwood, or to Kotohira in Gardena, where you'd really be better off ordering the splendid *udon*.

Or you might try Yabu down in West L.A., a sleek, busy hangout for UCLA students and the Westside Japanese crowd, which combines the standard *soba/udon*–shop menu with a nearly complete selection of Japanese pub snacks. Yabu is not a restaurant in which you contemplate pure, subtle flavors or the transient beauty of the changing seasons. It's kind of raucous, actually, filled with people sometimes more intent on their sake drinking than on the cuisine, but the food is pretty good and it's hard to get bored here. Think of Yabu as a Japanese equivalent to T.G.I. Friday's.

Essentially, most regulars order Japanese beer or sake and start off with an appetizer or three—clams steamed in sake, Japanese pickles, fat monkfish liver pâté, salty soybeans boiled in their pods–and then move on to a bowl of noodles.

There are composed salads of jerkylike, broiled salmon skin and greens; of seaweed; of cold slices of beef or albacore tuna, briefly seared on the edges but raw in the middle, arranged like petals around a plate and served with a tart soy dressing. Chunks of cod are marinated in sake lees and broiled to a crisp-edged tenderness, though broiled, salted yellowtail cheeks are perhaps overcooked. There are rich, oily rounds of fried Japanese eggplant in a sticky, almost caramelized miso marinade; tiny, salt-fried Japanese peppers; blocks of fried tofu, brown and crisp outside, almost liquid within, that are sprinkled with a couple tablespoons of thinly shaved flakes of dried *bonito* that dance in the heat like little sea monkeys.

And if the *soba* is less than spectacular—the restaurant stretches the buckwheat out with wheat flour, and the result is somewhat more resilient than *soba* really should be—it is at least very good, gamy and chewy, in a powerful broth of soy and dried *bonito*, garnished to taste with things like fish cake, Japanese greens, or crunchy bits of batter that have strayed away from frying shrimp in the tempura pot.

Best of all is the *zaru soba*, plunged straight from a boiling kettle into a basin of ice water to cool, heaped on a bamboo tray, served with a sprinkling of toasted seaweed and a soy-citrus dipping sauce. When you want your noodles straight, no chaser, cold *soba* is the way to go.

YAI

5757 HOLLYWOOD BLVD.; (323)-462-0292.

In Los Angeles, Thai restaurants are as common as burger stands, and Thai food has overtaken Mexican as basic date-night cuisine. Thai-style shrimp garnish chain-restaurant pizzas and are tossed with pasta in fusion restaurants; college students raised on Whoppers and Moby Jacks can discourse intelligently on the subtleties of one restaurant's *mee krob* and another's *tom kah kai*. When Angelenos move to New York or Paris, their nostalgia for *pad Thai* noodles is as keenly felt as the ache for a decent burrito.

Thai cooking here, though it may bear little relation to what you might actually be served in Bangkok, has become thoroughly familiar. This is an odd position for a cuisine in which nearly every dish is heated up with gut-wrenching quantities of fresh chiles, spiked with weird herbs, and seasoned with an exotic, smelly liquid pressed from fermented fish. Good Thai food should always be able to shock us anew—sometimes we forget that the authentic stuff, like certain French cheeses, may take a little getting used to.

In the rear of a dingy Hollywood mini-mall, Yai is as authentic as they come, a bare bones restaurant serving informal "people's food," and on a busy Saturday night it can take longer to grab one of the few tables than it does to order, eat, and pay at one of the less crowded joints in the neighborhood. On the walls are posters of what appear to be Thai pop stars, and notices for Thai disco shows.

The sort of thing you don't really find in the suburban Thai places is what Yai calls roast pork with Chinese broccoli: fatty, crispy chunks of pigskin on a forest-hued pile of greens whose vegetable bitterness cuts through the richness like a sharp knife. It looks something like a spinach salad, and fully half the customers here seem to have an order on their tables. The dish is bound together with a truly astonishing quantity of garlic, enough to induce a garlic sweat that may stay with you for days, and there's a pungent, searing chile dip on the side. It's not hard to like, this dish—in fact, it's rather delicious—but it is a walk on the wild side of the Western palate.

Yai serves a version of this dish with a slab of Thai dried fish in place of the pork, a big, bronze thing that combines heroic stinkiness with an awesome wallop of salt, and if you're not Thai, the waitress will look extremely startled when you order it. (The combination is supposed to be a favorite in working-class Bangkok neighborhoods, but I suspect that you have to grow up on the stuff to really love it.) On the other hand, you can find pedestrian renditions of regular Thai food here, *pad Thai* and beef with mint and *prik king*, but I can't see why you'd bother with them.

Tendon soup is more like it, a murky, intense beef broth spiked with anise, thick with bean sprouts and afloat with sliced beef and wonderful, gelatinous pieces of long-cooked beef sinew. Beef noodle soup seems to be more or less the same thing, with noodles in place of the tendons, but it tastes a little muskier, as if the stock was based partially on organ meats. Sweet dry-fried beef, gamy and jerkylike, comes with a smoky pepper sauce, like a Thai version of the ancho-chile salsa they serve at Border Grill—the barbecue-pit effect is very nice. Crunchy, bias-cut catfish slices fried stiff as potato chips are mounded with a terrific sweet curry paste.

And Yai is known for its spicy salads, particularly a grilled beef salad that really tastes of good steak under its bath of lime and chile, and a funky tripe salad. Try the most popular, an Eastern Thai-style salad made of shredded green papaya— closer to cabbage than to a fruit—tossed with carrots and scallions and such in a dressing of fish sauce and citrus that smells fresh and briny as a great oyster, served with a warm mound of sticky rice: shockingly good.

27 E. MAIN ST., ALHAMBRA; (626) 308-2036. OPEN FOR LUNCH AND
DINNER, TUES.–SUN.

The new Yazmin is a bright, high-ceilinged storefront in the heart of Alhambra's redevelopment district, decorated with a few Malay shadow puppets and colored lights that glow from hidden recesses. Malaysia was multicultural way before it was cool, and it seems as if every segment of Malaysian society is represented here on a Saturday night, Chinese and Malays and Indians, a couple of white guys, even a table or two of turbaned Muslims who presumably try to ignore the two or three pork dishes on the long menu.

Until it moved to Alhambra's Main Street, Yazmin was a small restaurant, a center of *rojak* salad and curry puffs at the back of a San Gabriel strip center where ethnic institutions were layered as intricately as circuits on a microchip. Yazmin was popular enough in its old location, but it was easy to forget amid the profusion of mini-mall restaurants that surrounded it. Now it seems to be a major Alhambra hang, as screamingly popular as Noodle Planet and the big, late-night seafood restaurants.

Hainanese chicken rice, one of the standbys of Southeast Asian cooking, is spectacular here: dry and fluffy, sharply flavored with garlic and ginger, served with a little dish of chile-ginger sauce fabulous to paint on everything but dessert, and garnished with a few slices of crisp-skinned roasted bird good enough to constitute an entrée of its own. Curry puffs are tiny, light turnovers filled with an airy mixture of curried potatoes and beef; the peanut sauce served with the chicken *satay* is to the Thai version of the sauce what Kobe Bryant is to Brent Barry.

Fish fillets or shrimp or chicken bubbles in Chinese clay pots with a mild, complex curry and meltingly tender slices of Japanese eggplant; there is an impeccable Malaysian version of the Indonesian dish beef *rendang*, cooked in spices and coconut milk until it falls apart at the touch of a fork. The *bah kut teh*, a version of the herbal "pork tea" that serves the same therapeutic function after a night of serious drinking in Malaysian Chinese culture that *menudo* does in Mexican culture, is a clean, intense pork bouillon perfumed with star anise. Vegetables too are good: hollow-stemmed *kangkong*, sometimes called Chinese watercress, sautéed with chile and fermented shrimp paste; string beans fried with dried shrimp; the turmeric-stained cabbage pickle called *acar*.

And Malaysian *rojak* can be one of the world's great salads: ripe mango, papaya, pineapple, cucumber, and jicama, sprinkled with chopped peanuts, garnished with crumbly cubes of fried tofu, and drizzled with a dark, sweet dressing spiked with red chiles and a bit of the stinky shrimp paste called *belacan*.

This isn't to say that Yazmin is incapable of bumming you out. *Takuwa goreng*, which you may be tempted to order because it comes to the table looking like a model of the Great Pyramid of Cheops sculpted out of fried tofu, is utterly bland; *pasembor*, a salad garnished with shrimp fritters and deep-fried vegetables that the Muslim street-food guys in Singapore sometimes sell as Indian *rojak*, is as watery as an airline Caesar. The crunchy shrimp crullers called *udang keropok* taste fine, but weep more oil than the face of a hormonally challenged teenager. If you order two curries that are substantially identical—say, the citrus-leaf-scented *limau pirut* chicken and the clay-pot chicken curry—nobody will bother to warn you. And finding a waiter can be as difficult as finding a cab on Madison Avenue five minutes after it has started to rain.

The Old Town Pasadena Malaysian restaurant Kuala Lumpur is certainly more elegant. But Yazmin may be the best place in town to explore the classics of the multicultural Malaysian noodle kitchen, the big, soothing bowls of *laksa* noodles in a bright-yellow Malaysian curry, as well as the sticky, wide noodles called *char kuei teow*, fried with thick Malaysian soy sauce and enough garlic to stun an elephant. (Malaysian dieters talk about *char kuei teow* in the tone of voice that fasting Americans use to discuss, say, a Big Mac attack.) And many of Yazmin's best noodle dishes tend to revolve around the slithery, egg-based *mee* noodle: *mee* Siam, vermicelli stir-fried with a tamarind-laced chile sauce and shrimp; Indian *mee*, stir-fried with a kind of homemade catsup; sweet, prawn-enhanced fried Hokkien *mee* as good as you'd find in a Ponang hawker's stall. Clay-pot curries can be very good, but sometimes, it's gotta be *mee*.

YONGSUSAN

950 S. VERMONT AVE.; (213) 388-3042.

Let Kansas City have its fried chicken, San Francisco its cioppino. Los Angeles is a world center of *kimchi*, the odiferous fermented vegetables that make up so much of the Korean table: briny bits of turnip, chile-sluiced cabbages, bittersweet daikon, stringy masses of seaweed and water spinach, and shoots of God-knows-what mountain vegetables, all cured in crocks, sold in bulk, neatly presented in little bowls. There is nothing like a good dish of cabbage *kimchi*, so garlicky that even silk flowers are tempted to wilt from the smell: chile-red, well salted, limp and yet resilient, as if each leaf had been individually wrung out by a special machine.

Korean restaurants live and die by their *kimchi*. A place can have crisp *bulgoki*, fragrant crab soup, springy buckwheat noodles, and still customers will avoid the place if the *kimchi* is subpar. *Kimchi* counters take up vast acreage in Korean supermarkets; shops devoted solely to *kimchi* thrive; homemade *kimchi* ferments in the cellars of half the houses in Koreatown, hundreds and hundreds of different kinds in all. I have tasted as much of it as I could.

And yet, I have never tasted anything like the *bosam-kimchi* at the North Korean–style Yongsusan in Koreatown—a green, round cabbage that has been hollowed out and stuffed, then wrapped up again and left to ferment whole; a *kimchi* as serious yet unpredictable as Kim Il Sung's foreign policy. The odor of this *kimchi*, a specialty of the North Korean region Kaesong, is off-putting at first, not strong, but overlaid with the kind of ripeness one might not ordinarily want to be reminded of at table—but it quickly resolves itself into a pleasing stink reminiscent of bubbling yeasts and runny French cheeses, and by the time you dig into the pale center of the cabbage and unearth vegetables, sweet nut-meats, pungent bits of shrimp, the perfume has somehow been transmuted into something as vibrant and heady as something bottled by Guerlain. *Bosam-kimchi*, at least at Yongsusan, is only lightly fermented (like a new pickle), and its sourness comes across as a mild thing, almost spritzy, deepening to a rounder, meatlike tang at the core. Sometimes it seems as if every flavor on Earth is contained somewhere in the soft, green orb.

Yongsusan is the Los Angeles branch of a small Seoul chain of Kaesong-style restaurants, an elegant, hushed place with plush banquettes and silk-covered walls, a warren of discreet private dining rooms, a tinkle of Korean classical music. If you are used to the smoky good cheer of the neighborhood's innumerable *soontofu* dives and *kalbi* parlors, the restaurant's formality may be a little surprising—as is its expense.

It may be technically possible to order a meal at Yongsusan dish by dish, but multicourse set dinners make up most of the menu at the restaurant, and the *bosam-kimchi* appears as the centerpiece of each. First comes a sweet squash porridge the approximate texture of library paste, then a sort of seafood salad not unlike Japanese *sunomono*, and a bowl of soft, almost transparent mung-bean noodles, *chung po mook*, flavored with beef and toasty little bits of seaweed that dissolve in your mouth with a final blast of brininess: very fine. *Ku jul pan* is the standard Korean fancy-dinner appetizer, thin crepes meant to be rolled around ribbons of egg, mushrooms, vegetables and meat. Roast pork, almost Italian in its voluptuousness, is served with a leaf or two of chile'd *kimchi;* a few slices of blood sausage veer very close to Colombian-style *morcilla*; oyster pancake with vegetables seems custom-designed to help down a bottle of Hite beer. Korean barbecued short ribs are an inevitable part of the meal. There is a sort of shrimp porridge spiked with vegetables and topped with a runny poached egg, and a bowl of soup with a dumpling or two, and delicious, stretchy buckwheat noodles—North Korea may be the world center of buckwheat noodles—in a cold beef broth. And a weirdly sweet persimmon punch. But mostly there is that Kaesong-style *kimchi*, the Chateau Lafitte of the *kimchi* world, and worth a visit on its own.

YUNG HO TOU CHIANG

533 W. VALLEY BLVD., SAN GABRIEL; (626) 570-0860. DAILY, 7A.M.–6P.M.

Pretty much everybody has eaten dim sum by now, the Cantonese dumplings wheeled along by cart-pushing waitresses, the great glassed-in trolleys of barbecued duck and grilled rice-noodle rolls. There are probably enough diners at dim-sum restaurants in the San Gabriel Valley on a Sunday morning to fill the Anaheim Pond.

Northern Chinese breakfasts are a little harder to find. They don't tend to be served in restaurants with dining rooms as large as the decks of aircraft carriers; the protocol is a little more complicated than the point-and-eat ordering that suffices at even the most monolingual of dim-sum restaurants. And for non-Chinese, the food can take a little getting used to: soy milk and piquant squid stew noodles are less accessible than barbecued pork buns.

But Yung Ho, a Taiwanese cafe in a corner of a pan-Asian mini-mall, serves among the most delicious of breakfasts: flaky buns stuffed with sweet, simmered turnips, steamed buns filled with spiced pork or black mushrooms, crusty fried pies stuffed with pungent messes of sautéed leek tops, and small, steamed pork dumplings bursting with juice.

The dynamic of a northern Chinese breakfast is easier than it looks: you order some soy milk (unless you'd rather have a bowl of noodles), and then some stuff to go with the soy milk. It's as simple as bacon and eggs.

Soy milk itself isn't much, really, a white fluid served either cold or hot, salted or sweetened, in bowls big enough to feed eight or nine people at least, but designed to be eaten by one. (If you consume enough of the stuff, recent studies hint, the cholesterol in your system may just melt away.) Neither as luxurious in texture as the Cantonese *doufu fa* nor luscious as the hot, fresh bean curd served in Korean specialty restaurants, the sugared soy milk at Yung Ho—and at most other northern-style Chinese restaurants—is a resolutely nonexotic substance, with a thin consistency that feels a little like nonfat milk in the mouth, and a chalky, vegetable blandness that is just like supermarket tofu, only sweeter.

Paired with the dumplings, though, the soy milk's flavor opens up, becomes less monotonous, tempers the richness of simmered stuffings and the greasiness of fried ones, marrying with the food the way cow's milk does with brownies. I can't say that most people would ever bother drinking soy milk on its own, but it is hard to imagine a Yung Ho breakfast without a bowl of the stuff.

The traditional accompaniment to soy milk is a long twisted cruller, and Yung Ho does crullers very well, crisp and slightly chewy on the outside, fragrant with the smell of hot oil, giving way to an interior that is about 90 percent air.

For another buck or so, you can have the cruller smeared with a salty paste of pounded meat and wrapped inside a cylinder of sticky rice, which sounds kind of weird but has the kind of textural contrast you might expect from a great sushi roll. You may have tasted Taiwanese cold-case appetizers in places like Mandarin Deli and Dumpling Master—cheeselike pressed bean curd, shredded tripe, tiny dried anchovies seasoned with chile, simmered pig's ear.

But there are new flavors here, even for the jaded. Sticky rice, stuffed with stewed pork, steamed in a bamboo-leaf capsule, and stingingly flavored with cinnamon, is not sweet but otherwise has the mouth-searing effect of an Atomic Fireball jawbreaker. In the beef-noodle soup, a raw-vinegar sensation opens out into a subtle rush of chile heat and then the rich, shimmering pungency of what I imagine are long-simmered organ meats, a sequence of tastes that is almost biological in intensity.

Yung Ho has a small sideline in something they call egg cakes, thin wheat flapjacks with scrambled eggs cooked into them, made stretchy with taro, flecked with green herbs and fried. Oyster pancake is an egg cake stuffed with mollusks, like a tenderer version of the classic Chiu Chow oyster omelet, sauced with kind of a sweetened catsup. Which leads us to *hubei doupi* (I like to imagine that the dish rhymes with "scooby dooby," although it probably doesn't), which is a catsup-smeared egg cake wrapped around a mound of rice that in turn conceals a mound of fried pork. *Hubei doupi* may be sort of trailer-park Taiwanese cooking, but the stuff is as tasty as chicken-fried steak.

YUU

2101 SAWTELLE BLVD.; (310) 478-7450. MON.–SAT., 6P.M.–2A.M.

For a long time, the most intimidating menus in Los Angeles were those found at the publike Japanese restaurants known as *izaka-ya:* long, untranslated lists of custards, vinegared sea creatures, and variations on spiced cod roe. *Izaka-ya* portions are tiny; regulars seem to order as many courses as they might at a dim-sum breakfast. Offerings are intensely seasonal. I've been to about a dozen local *izaka-ya,* and had spectacular individual dishes, but after most of the meals I felt as if I had sat through a lengthy subtitled film that I didn't really comprehend.

Yuu, an *izaka-ya* tucked into the corner of a Westwood strip mall, is sort of an elegant place with blond wood, exposed beams, and tablecloths whose lime-green color suggests less a leisure suit than the hue of freshly grated wasabi. Half the people seem to cluster around the long sushi bar in one corner, nibbling on the usual slivers of red clam and yellowtail, pouring rounds for one another from big bottles of Asahi beer. Groups of business-suited Japanese, ties loosened halfway to their belts, sit around tables and toast one another with thumb-size vials of cold sake. There are always a few hairy music-industry guys, which is a predictable indicator of great Japanese food in this town, and a table or two of elegantly dressed women, and a wide-eyed college student who is facing down raw fish for the first time.

At Yuu, the "secret" of *izaka-ya* cuisine reveals itself: you order sake, and then some snacks to go with it. Then you order some more sake (or beer), and repeat the process as often as you can afford. (Individual dishes are relatively inexpensive, but the bill adds up fast.) Yuu has about a dozen different sakes to try, including Onigoroshi, which smells like fresh-cut melons—try it cold—and Harushika, which is better hot.

You might start with the tart seaweed salad *mozuko;* grilled Japanese eggplant, *nasu dengaku,* smeared with a dark bean paste nearly as pungent as hoisin; fried soft-shell crab; a grilled tofu steak in spicy sauce; a vegetable casserole, *yasai no takiwase,* in which poached slices of carrot, snow pea, lotus root, and Japanese pumpkin are arranged carefully as they would be in a painting by Chardin. A shiitake-clam consommé, of clear, smoky flavor, is served in a teapot and poured into a tiny, flat cup. A piece of whitefish is wrapped with seaweed into a sort of sushi-roll configuration with a chunk of avocado and a strip of salmon, then deep-fried and served with a tart dipping sauce. Bits of shrimp and vegetables are mixed into a batter and fried into delicious little balls: *ebi shinzo.* Yuu's repertoire seems endless.

The menu here is divided into three parts: the regular menu, a photocopied Japanese-language list of daily specials, and a shorter seasonal menu, which appears both as a Japanese-only sheet taped to the back of the main menu and in English translation tucked into a thin folder.

On the seasonal translated menu, you may find tender, salty abalone sautéed with asparagus tips, or juicy salt-grilled mackerel, or the sweetest possible shrimp tempura. A whole flounder is served two ways, like the double-pleasure flounder at Monterey Park Chinese seafood joints: fried fillets that melt from crispness into nothingness on your tongue; a fried fish frame that is about 95 percent crunch. On the regular menu there is wonderful grilled cod that has been marinated in sake lees, good enough to make you realize why half the fancy restaurants in Seattle have that dish on their menus; diced conch, cooked in broth and served simmering in its own shell, which has a small flame lit beneath it; cold tofu with soy and writhing *bonito* shavings.

If you are lucky, the waiter will not become too testy when you ask him to translate from the list of specials, and you might end up with rich, expertly cut *toro* sashimi, or the shiitake consommé, or a crisply fried roll of sweet shrimp and pumpkin. But the tragedy of Yuu is this: you will never figure out how to order your favorite dishes again.

ZABUMBA

10717 VENICE BLVD., CULVER CITY; (310) 841-6525. SUN.-WED., 5P.M.-11P.M.; THURS.-SAT., 5P.M.-MIDNIGHT.

The Brazilian restaurant Zabumba is as soccer-mad as any three British pubs, with a welter of video screens tuned to the games, World Cup schedules handed out with the check, and at least one waitress who wears a uniform consisting of short-shorts and a Brazilian-flag halter top, which may be sort of a southern hemisphere analog to Daisy Duke. Brazil's 1994 victory is commemorated on the side of the restaurant in block letters so high you suspect they can be seen from space. And on game days the restaurant opens at 8:30 A.M.—dawn for the party-mad Brazilians who hang out here.

Zabumba is the center of expatriate Brazilian life in Los Angeles; headquarters of the local samba club; a hive of Brazilian karaoke; and a steady venue for all forms of Brazilian entertainment this side of Xuxa lookalike competitions. When a game is not on, taped arena concerts churn from the restaurant's several video screens, and occasionally you can see a waitress dancing by herself behind the long bar, blissfully unaware of the customers semaphoring wildly for their checks. (Brazilian dental-floss bikinis are actually listed for sale on the menu.)

Zabumba is by no means the best Brazilian restaurant in Los Angeles; in fact, the grill cuisine at the converted hamburger stand Café Brasil, just a block away, is more consistent. Zabumba is less a center of *ximxim* and jungle-fish stews than a place to gulp a shrimp pizza and a glass of passion-fruit juice between band sets.

Zabumba's appealing, if dumbed-down, version of the Bahian stew *moqueca*, shrimp or chicken cooked with coconut cream, palm oil, and a mash of sautéed vegetables, is significantly less intense than the *moquecas* a few miles north at Itana Bahia. Something called Max Jr. involves a chicken breast marinated with garlic, mustard, and a little oil, then grilled to a sort of leatheriness. The *milanesa* is less the crisp, pounded thing you find by that name all over Latin America than a regular steak, lightly breaded and cooked to a bare medium-rare.

Zabumba, you will not be surprised to hear, has an extensive pizzeria menu, and there seems to be an appreciative audience here for pizzas topped with things like bananas and cinnamon, chicken and corn, or chicken and hearts of palm. Toasted sandwiches, on discs of the sort of flying saucer–shaped pizza bread you find at Angeli, are mostly glued together with melted white cheese and plumped out with things like ham and Portuguese sausage or fried bananas and cheese, which tastes like something Elvis might have liked if he'd come from Minas Gerais instead of Tupelo.

"This sandwich is really good," exclaimed a six-year-old of my acquaintance. "How come we haven't been to this restaurant before?"

ZACATECAS RASPADOS

422 N. FORD ST., EAST L.A.; (323) 264-7651. DAILY, 10A.M.–9P.M.

Los Angeles is a wonderland of exotic ice desserts, the purple yam-garnished Filipino ice parfaits called *halo halo*, the oozing majesty of Taiwanese slush, blended Indonesian ice slurpies with coffee and avocado, squishy Vietnamese mung-bean sorbets, Hawaiian shaved ice, and ethereal Japanese green-tea ices. A visit to an Asian supermarket will probably reveal fruit-stuffed balls of sticky rice, red-bean popsicles, and durian ice cream that smells bad enough to offend people in the next state. Near downtown, it's easier to find fresh-mango *paletas* than it is to find Creamsicles.

But the longest-lived of ice desserts in Los Angeles may be the East L.A. tradition called *raspados*—Mexican snow cones—which are basically handfuls of pebbly ice mounded into paper cups and drenched with syrup. In some Eastside neighborhoods, you can buy *raspados* from the *raspados* man, who pushes a small cartful of ice and syrups through streets and parks, ringing a little bell and crooning *"ras-PAAA-dos"* like an extra from a production of *Porgy and Bess*. In other neighborhoods, you find *raspados* at the local grocery store, or at one of the handful of *taquerías* with a sideline in *raspados*. *Raspados* are pretty good in most of their incarnations, though not terribly different from the snow cones you may have eaten as a child in, say, Iowa—even the stands that advertise "natural" flavors tend to have gallon jugs of commercial syrup under their counters. People just don't expect that much from a snow cone . . . until they happen across Zacatecas Raspados.

Zacatecas Raspados is a shiny snow cone palace in one of the oldest parts of East Los Angeles, down the street from the old *chorizo* factory and right next door to La Fama, which many people (including me) consider the best Mexican bakery on the entire Eastside. Before Caltrans and the county decided that the Belvedere neighborhood would be better off bulldozed to the ground, this was the epicenter of small-town Mexican-American life in Los Angeles, as close as you could get to the Sonoran countryside without crossing the border. (My wife's great-grandfather owned the local blacksmith's shop up until the war, and bucolic 1930s Belvedere has assumed the mythic place in the family legend that Jaffa orange groves have in the stories of third-generation Palestinian refugees.) Now Belvedere is mostly taken up with freeway interchanges and sprawling parks, and except for a *carnicería* here and there, a few decrepit taverns and this block of Ford Street, you would hardly know it exists. But still—there are *raspados*.

Zacatecas Raspados's snow cones, while refined, are less the smooth, shaved stuff you find in the Asian places than crunchy, super-cold crystals. There are layers to these *raspados*; first loose ice scooped into the plastic cup, then syrup, a packed-down dome of ice on top, with a conical hole poked through the center, then syrup again. The two densities of ice lend the *raspados* the sort of textural complexity you usually don't find in a snow cone; the packed ice also melts much more slowly than the loose ice, which means that it stays crunchy for a fairly long time, even on hot afternoons.

The syrups are homemade from pineapples, mangoes, papayas, boiled down to their essence, still a little bit pulpy—especially the strawberry and excellent guava—and not too sweet. There is *rompope*, eggnog traditionally made by nuns; a delicious syrup made with shredded coconut; an intense, runny Mexican boiled-milk caramel, *cajeta,* that oozes down between the fissures in the cracked ice like butter into hot toast. A syrup made from walnuts steeped in milk brings out the bitter, winy flavor of the nut in a way you may not have experienced outside the context of an expensive French-pastry shop: spectacular. These are only snow cones, mind you—this is not the place to come when you're looking for something with the subtlety of Berthillon's blackberry ice or even Campanile's blood-orange sorbet—but they can be powerfully good.

Zacatecas Raspados is also known for its freshly fried *churros rellenos,* which are the familiar dowel-shaped Mexican doughnuts reamed out with a metal device and filled with a sticky, drippy caramel sauce that will adhere to your floorboards and gum your shoelaces together for week.

ZANKOU CHICKEN

5065 SUNSET BLVD., HOLLYWOOD; (323) 665-7842. DAILY 10A.M.–
MIDNIGHT. 1415 E. COLORADO ST., GLENDALE; (818) 244-2237. DAILY.

Nothing on heaven or on Earth may be as severe as the Armenian garlic sauce served at Zankou Chicken, a fierce, blinding-white paste the texture of puréed horseradish that scents your car, sears the back of your throat, and whose powerful aroma can stay in your head—and your car—for days. A couple of drops is enough to flavor a hunk of bread; a modest schmear will do for an entire *shwarma* sandwich. Go ahead, Ultra Brite; go ahead, Lavoris; go ahead, CarFreshener: My money's on the sauce. It's also good with chicken.

Everybody knows about Zankou, which started as a small, tiled takeout stand in a grimy Hollywood Boulevard mini-mall on Armenian Restaurant Row and spread into a mini-empire of half a dozen restaurants. Zankou is famous for its barbecued chicken sandwich, which is rolled in a pita with tomatoes and enough of the sauce to make a lasting impression on the next few dozen people you meet.

This is what you eat at Zankou: barbecued-chicken sandwiches, excellent falafel, *shawarma* carved off the rotating spit and served warm, with superbly caramelized edges and sweetly gamy as only properly overcooked lamb can be. There is wonderful *mutabal,* a smooth, creamy roasted-eggplant dip, with a sesame top note and a powerful smoky flavor, served with a dusting of spice and a slick of good olive oil. The hummus is fine and grainy, and the spit-roasted chickens are superb: golden, crisp-skinned, and juicy, with developed chicken flavor, the kind of bird that makes you want to scour the carcass for stray bits of carbonized skin and delicious scraps of flesh, or hoard your favorite bites . . . that rich chunk of dark meat right where the leg joins the thigh, or that tender strip running along the top. Such chicken really needs no embellishment—but a little bit of garlic sauce couldn't hurt.

•

INDEX

Made in the USA
Las Vegas, NV
06 March 2022

45126267R00203